PEACE OPERATIONS SEEN FROM BELOW

The CERI series in Comparative Politics and International Studies

Series editor CHRISTOPHE JAFFRELOT

This series consists of translations of noteworthy publications in the social sciences emanating from the foremost French research centre in international studies, the Paris-based Centre d'Etudes et de Recherches Internationales (CERI), part of Sciences Po and associated with the CNRS (Centre National de la Recherche Scientifique).

The focus of the series is the transformation of politics and society by international and domestic factors—globalisation, migration and the post-bipolar balance of power on the one hand, and societal dynamics, ethnicity and religion on the other. States are more permeable to external influence than ever before and this phenomenon is accelerating processes of social and political change the world over. In seeking to understand and interpret these transformations, this series give priority to social trends from below as much as the interventions of state and non-state actors.

Founded in 1952, CERI has fifty full-time fellows drawn from different disciplines conducting research on comparative political analysis, international relations, regionalism, transnational flows, political sociology, political economy and on individual states.

BÉATRICE POULIGNY

Peace Operations Seen from Below

UN Missions and Local People

Kumarian
Press, Inc.

Published in 2006 in the United States of America by
Kumarian Press, Inc., 1294 Blue Hills Avenue,
Bloomfield, CT 06002 USA

Published in 2006 in the United Kingdom by
C. Hurst & Co. Publishers,
41 Great Russell Street, London, WC1B 3PL

Printed in India.

Library of Congress Cataloging-in-Publication Data

Pouligny, Béatrice.
    [Ils nous avaient promis la paix. English]
    Peace operations seen from below: UN missions and local people/
Béatrice Pouligny.
        p. cm.
    Includes bibliographical references and index.
    ISBN-13: 978-1-56549-224-0 (pbk: alk. paper)
    ISBN-10: 1-56549-224-2 (pbk: alk. paper)
    1. United Nations—Peacekeeping forces. 2. Peacekeeping forces
—Moral and ethical aspects. 3. Humanitarian assistance. I. Title.
JZ6374.P6813 2006
341.5'84—dc22

2006005799

CONTENTS

Contents

MAPS AND GRAPHS

PREFACE

Pel preuk hat prane
Rô seirl boeuk lane
Lô ngeik chol bar

(In the morning we do exercise
In the afternoon we go out in the car
In the evening we go back to the bar)

Phnom Penh, November 1995. This couplet was still being chanted by the children of Phnom Penh whenever UNTAC (the United Nations Transitional Authority in Cambodia), which had left the country two years earlier, was mentioned. Their parents had plenty of anecdotes to recall those UNTACs[1] with their 'bizarre' behaviour, whose 'real' reason for coming to the country was still not understood. Their accounts bore a strange resemblance to those I had collected a few weeks earlier in El Salvador, where people nicknamed the United Nations mission *Vacaciones Unidas* ('united holidays'): a play on words in Spanish (the UN being *Naciones Unidas*) that came from a far-right daily newspaper hostile to the United Nations presence, but was widely adopted on the street. In this game of derision the peoples of countries where UN peace operations are carried out compete in imagination to think of names to call the 'Blue Helmets'. In their time the Bosnians had their '*schtroumfs*'. Everywhere, the 'oddness of whites' (the Haitians' refrain of '*Blan yo dwòl*') arouses the same questioning, the same attitude of distance associated with similar reasoning. Most subject to mockery is the view of UN soldiers going out jogging or for their night occupations. This banter often hides many frustrations, as was made plain when, on 31 January 2001, inhabitants of Freetown in Sierra Leone denounced, over a local radio station, the arrogant blue helmeted soldiers, driving too fast and spending their time on the beach, for acting as if they were on holiday. In other places the more or less spectacular landing of UN forces was what undoubtedly captured youth's memories the most. They swear that they have witnessed

---

[1] Cambodians called the mission, and its members, by the acronym.

a scene worthy of a Hollywood blockbuster; an impression that I often shared myself. At Port-au-Prince, the launching of Operation Restore Democracy in September 1994, and at Mogadishu in December 1992 (Operation Restore Hope), the deployment of the American-United Nations machine, in front of television cameras and journalists gathered to cover the event, left unusual memories that were recalled with hilarity.

But these images and descriptions describe an encounter for which a full historical account has not yet been produced. Indeed, in reading about peace operations in the abundant literature published on the subject in the last few years, one is surprised by the small amount of attention generally paid, apart from the sensational and anecdotal, to the way in which those missions have been experienced by the different elements of the societies concerned.[2] It is in fact quite revealing that, when questioned, political and social actors in countries where those missions have, in recent years, been deployed, they mention that this is the first time that their opinion has been asked. This book aims to contribute to filling this gap, by suggesting a local interpretation of the recent history of peace operations.

This project grew out of my experience as an actor and as a witness in several UN peace operations launched during the 1990s. On the ground I, like many observers, was often struck by the apparent scale of such interventions, their frequently superficial nature, but also the multiple ways through which their history was written on a daily basis, often far from the current affairs projectors. In fact the nature of those operations has radically changed, moving away from the classical form of peacekeeping.[3] Present-day missions—described as 'multidimensional' or 'multifunctional'—imply much further intervention in restructuring domestic political and social orders. By their nature, their mandates affect crucial aspects of the organization of the societies concerned as well as the values on which they are founded. The organisation of electoral processes and the promotion of human rights and civil society are examples of the tasks entrusted to these missions, while others take over entire sections of the administration of the countries. Despite the fact that the reaction to such interventions may vary greatly, one may predict that they potentially affect large components of these societies, precisely at a time when crucial elements of the relation between political and social order are renegotiated. In addition, these missions are deployed more widely throughout the countries, no longer just at the borders or front lines. This also increases

---

[2] This omission is equally striking in the report of the high-level panel on peace operations set up by the UN Secretary General, called the 'Brahimi Report' (A/55/305—S/2000/809, 17 August 2000).

[3] For this reason I adopt the generic term 'peace operations'.

the number and type of actors who interact directly (no longer only peripherically or indirectly) with the missions. Now, most of these actors are civilians. True, even when they are part of armed groups, they only partially correspond to classical patterns of regular armed forces. Finally, UN missions are deployed in fragmented societies; the usual structures of mediation between the different segments of the societies are generally weak, increasing the influence of dominated actors. As Steven R. Ratner rightly points out, "the new peacekeeping is a fluid phenomenon"[4] and requires better consideration of local processes within which it operates.

This means distancing oneself from the classical approaches which continue to dominate international security studies, and which tend to make the intervener a sort of sole actor confronting human, natural or environmental 'obstacles' in the accomplishment of his mission. The interaction between UN missions and local societies continues, in the existing literature, to be widely approached through global, homogeneous, static categories. But on the ground, divisions of the friends/enemies, civilians/military type do not always make much sense. Military personnel engaged in peace operations sometimes search in vain for constituted armies, a hierarchy, officers to discuss with. Even when they find some sign of these structures, part of their logic refers to other categories. A not insignificant number of fighters have little in common with the image of the soldier, or even that of the guerrilla. As for the civilian population that humanitarian logic would like to reduce to the status of passive or neutral 'victims', they assert themselves, to some extent at least, as authentic actors, capable of rethinking their situation and commenting on it, continuing to make political choices, indicate preferences and even make commitments.

So far the few studies that have attempted to take account of those local dimensions have tended to confine social groups within fixed patterns of behaviour. Frequent reference to the 'degree of immediate acceptance or rejection by the local population',[5] and soldiers' fear of ending up being

---

[4] Steven R. Ratner, *The New UN Peacekeeping: Building Peace in Lands of Conflict after the Cold War*, New York: St Martin's Press, 1995, p. 24.

[5] The criterion of the only investigation of this sort on a classical mission, in the Gaza Strip: John Galtung and Ingrid Eide, 'Some Factors Affecting Local Acceptance of a UN Force: a Pilot Project Report from Gaza', pp. 240–63 in John Galtung, *War and Defence: Essays in Peace Research*, Copenhagen, Col. 2, 1976. The 'degree of immediate acceptance or rejection by the local population' is frequently mentioned as a key to the success or failure of a mission, and it appears as a central preoccupation of Western governments when they contribute troops. Source: documents of the US Foreign Policy Studies Program, the UK Foreign Office, and the Foreign Affairs and Defence ministries in France, consulted on a confidential basis.

perceived as occupation forces, are revealing examples of this approach, as is the focusing on the 'spoiler' or the 'warlord'.[6] But practical experience on the ground encourages us to think of the variety and plurality of social logics that coexist, at the same time, with their own rhythms and references. It obliges us to think of the interaction between members of UN missions and local peoples in plural and dynamic terms.

Intervening in a country through a peace operation means getting involved, in one way or another, in a tangle of actions and reactions that needs to be understood and managed as best as possible. This implies understanding the logics and representations peculiar to different groups of actors. To do so, my approach resolutely follows in the line of comprehensive sociology, seeking to get as near as possible to the viewpoint of local actors. My aim was not to retrace *exactly* what was happening or had happened—if only because such an exercise was impossible—but *to take seriously how individuals and groups that I met understood and explained, subjectively and empirically, their interaction with the United Nations missions.* Comprehensive sociology proposes entering the other's subjectivity, in an attempt to decentre oneself in order, as we are invited to do by the philosopher Paul Ricoeur, to try to 'understand the other'. So I have paid special attention to the daily life of the people as of the UN peace missions. For such an exploration a detour is necessary through the imaginary and the institutional and social processes that shape the worlds in which the people and the missions live, and which can help in understanding their behaviour.

This analysis is based on original empirical material gathered during in-depth research in El Salvador, Cambodia and Haiti, and less concentrated investigations relating to the missions in Somalia, Mozambique and Bosnia-Herzegovina.[7] Reference is also made to more recent UN experiences in Guatemala, Kosovo, East Timor, Sierra Leone, the Democratic Republic of Congo and Afghanistan. The abundant and diverse sources used include more than four hundred interviews, from villages and shanty towns to centres of national and international power, and thousands of pages of archives and documents of a wide variety, collected in the

---

[6] See Stephen John Stedman, 'Spoiler Problems in Peace Process', *International Security*, vol. 22, no. 2, fall 1997, pp. 5–53; William Shawcross, *Deliver us from Evil: Warlords and Peacekeepers in a World of Endless Conflict*, London: Bloomsbury, 2000.

[7] The missions concerned were the United Nations Observer Mission in El Salvador (ONUSAL), the United Nations Transitional Authority in Cambodia (UNTAC), the United Nations Mission in Haiti (UNMIH), followed by three other missions in Haiti (the United Nations Support Mission in Haiti, the United Nations Transition Mission in Haiti, and the United Nations Police Mission in Haiti, the United Nations Operation in Somalia (UNOSOM), the United Nations Operation in Mozambique (ONUMOZ), and the United Nations Protection Force in Bosnia-Herzegovina (UNPROFOR).

different fields.[8] All the individual interviews were carried out in a semi-directive form, while group interviews were carried out in a non-directive form, receiving specific treatment. In addition, in several countries I attended debates on the United Nations presence, organised in student circles, by human rights organisations, or by district or peasant associations. I also took many opportunities for informal discussions, in a non-directive form, so as to check certain aspects of the investigation (concerning, particularly, the representations of UN missions in collective memory). I am convinced that those contacts—made in the street, in markets, in buses and passenger lorries, along roads, during evenings in their company sometimes told me as much as the more formal interviews, especially as I was brought a bit closer to the subjectivity of the people I met. In some cases those contacts were my only possibility to meet, under cover of informality and anonymity, some actors such as former soldiers or members of armed groups, village chiefs, mediums, traditional healers and others. With some rare exceptions (where my knowledge of the local languages was insufficient), I carried out the interviews without any intermediary. Specific work was done with linguist and anthropologist colleagues, specialists in the countries concerned, so as to discern the different levels of language used by the people I spoke with, possible references to concepts external to the language, and their greater or lesser integration into the local language. I then made systematic checks through non-directive interviews, especially with groups.

As part of this approach I also had to resort to alternative tools and bring into the analysis different forms of cultural expression, regularly used outside the political sphere, which had a specific political meaning in certain circumstances, due to their symbolic importance. These included mural paintings and refrains composed for the Carnival in Haiti, music and poetry composed during the war in El Salvador, plays on words and reinterpretations of prophesies in Cambodia, and oral poetry as a traditional tool for spreading of information and mobilisation in Somalia. On the basis of what could be exploited on the ground, I selected the most significant modes of expression in each society, checked the use made of them at the time of UN interventions, and, where necessary, tried to understand the collective representations (even non explicit) and the practices that were thus revealed.[9]

[8] Files on the various missions and a complete list of sources (including a list of interviews) can be consulted at this internet address: http://www.ceri-sciences-po.org/cherlist/pouligny/indexen.htm

[9] For this part of my research, I benefited from the experience and the precious advice of Denis-Constant Martin, who for many years has been working on and promoting a 'cultural' approach to the political. See Denis-Constant Martin (ed.), *Sur la piste des OPNI* [*Objets politiques non identifiés*], Paris: Karthala, 2002.

There is an additional difficulty that analysts share with practitioners when they work in conflict or post-conflict situations: much of the key information about the conflict is either difficult to obtain or has been manipulated. Statistics concerning refugee flows, for example, are the object of various dealings and interpretations, even manipulations, among local authorities, belligerents, humanitarian organisations, Western governments and other involved groups. The very way in which the conflict is defined and presented at the international level has more to do with diplomatic battles (for example, in debates within and surrounding the United Nations Security Council) than with the conflict itself. On the ground, explanations and visions of the conflict are generally as numerous as the people you meet. Hence the researcher's role is to facilitate understanding of those various representations: how and to what extent they are articulated and respond to each other, how and to what extent they may influence and sometimes constrain actors' behaviour, and how they shape reality and are reshaped themselves. In other words, the scholars must accept that the work of reconstituting events has more to do with objectification than objectivity, which in these environments is impossible. Then, any researcher must guard against various reactions. As may happen to a humanitarian worker or a journalist, he may be tempted to "rewrite" the history, to impose his own 'authentic' version of events or simply to construct his own narrative. As well, he may be propelled to 'simplifying' situations that are too complex to understand, explain, or deal with. Saying that we know the answers when, in reality, we have everything to learn, or thinking that the other person's reality can be reduced to what we can comprehend of it are temptations that we must all be on our guard against. In fact practitioners, and those who have had to prepare the way for decision making, know how simplification is rarely good counsel.

Trying to 'understand' rather than 'explain' also means emphasising the limits of all theorisation and categorisation where there are often only partial, ambiguous and provisional answers for processes that are reconstituted *a posteriori* by the analysis. This assumes a permanent labour of self-criticism, which is not something to be taken for granted in situations that shake up all our fixed assumptions. Where the mind wants to be reassured, the researcher must think of situations in all their complexity, far from well drawn images that are perhaps comforting for his 'good conscience' but are of little help in advancing knowledge and reflection. This is never acquired once and for all; in every investigation and at every 'site', the mind goes through different phases. I have sometimes had to put myself in precarious positions and 'take risks', often less physical than mental: risking a severe jolt to what makes me human, gives me faith in humanity and keeps me going. I find that this is complicated by the customary operational and validation methods of research. There is in fact always a strong temptation to look for details in the field that will corroborate theories and neat typologies (not that these are my forte!) and any other intellectual constructs that are fostered by my working environment, leaving aside (albeit unconsciously) anything that would contradict them. If reality does not fit our image of it, it is highly likely that reality is ultimately wrong.

The difficulties are no less great at the analytical stage. They raise, *inter alia*, the question of the status of the other person's words. All those who have conducted investigations by interview will have encountered the same scruples in striking a balance between respect for individual stories that are revealed in this way—this respect being reinforced in contexts of violence by the fact that such stories are generally tragic—and the distance which is essential for an analyst seeking to clarify the facts and understand them, including things left unsaid, half-truths, falsehoods and misrepresentations, made in good faith or otherwise. The position of those being interviewed is obviously different depending on whether the present is being interpreted or the past reinterpreted in the light of what has ensued, a form of 'reviewing' of their story. Besides suppression and distortion due to the passage of time, there can be conscious lying. The use of different techniques and information sources can help to cross-check, compare and verify data. The position of the researcher differs too, according to the observation period. Almost by definition, he or she intervenes 'in the aftermath'. As Clifford Geertz wisely recalls in his memoirs, the change is not like a street parade that we might watch passing by. A little like the American cavalry, we always arrive too late, unavoidably after the event.[10] Even though I may be at the scene, I will only ever see a very small facet of what has happened.

Personally I always find the analysis and writing phase much more painful than the actual 'field-work' phase. One cannot constantly encounter the ambivalences present across our world and not feel somewhat unsteady when putting forward an interpretation of them that a tiny detail can sometimes overturn. There is always a risk of underestimation or error in the comprehension of what is happening in other registers of reality that cannot be captured at the same moment. It is necessary to accept this. Not to claim that my interpretation is 'better' than the others or totally invalidates them, but rather to suggest a possible complement. To give my readers as many clues as possible so that they will know 'where I am

[10] Clifford Geertz, *After the Fact: Two Countries, Four Decades, One Anthropologist*, Cambridge, MA: Harvard University Press, 1995.

coming from' and how I worked with the subject. To accept that some avenues of investigation have not proved as fruitful as I would have wished and that some questions remain unanswered. That is the approach suggested in these pages. That entails constant questioning and the acceptance of non-discoveries (more frequent than one would like) or of unexpected and startling discoveries of facts which defy analysis and then allow the analytical process to develop, including in directions one had not envisaged. As the psychiatrist Boris Cyrulnik suggested in one of his books, dead-ends, question marks and 'blank walls', even if they are difficult to cope with at the time, are also what provides backing.[11] I never stop doubting.

Some simple intuitions guided this work. The first is that UN missions are in interaction, locally, with a great variety of political and social actors, spreading far beyond the categories traditionally studied, which consist essentially of dominant political actors. Such studies underestimate not only the large number of modalities used for expression of the political in each context, but also the variety of contacts that members of UN missions have in practice with local peoples. So I have tried to understand which actors embarked on interaction with peace operations, which positions—sometimes moving ones—they occupied in the interaction, and to which inter-relation networks they belonged. This exploration led bit by bit to comprehension of what was being forged in the in-between zone, with many points of linkage—or non-linkage—between 'micro' and 'macro' levels, between the daily work of a mission and the political level of its global strategy, between what happens in a remote village or in the shanty-town of a capital and what is played out in the plush calm of UN missions or negotiating rooms. Chapter 2 reports on this exploration while Chapter 1 explains the circumstances in which peace operations have intervened in the countries studied.

When one meets those who have embarked on local interaction with United Nations missions, it is very quickly understood that they have not remained inactive. The situations in which they appear in analysis indicate the adoption of many-sided strategies, which in some cases may belong first and foremost to the category of 'anecdotal, individual and isolated resourcefulness'[12] but very often go beyond that category by their recurrence, the collective character they bear, and especially their linkage to other levels of action. I have tried to understand the mainsprings of these strategies through analysis of observable behaviour, of the facts, but

[11] Boris Cyrulnik, *Sous le signe du lien*, Paris: Hachette, Pluriel series, 1998, p. 310.
[12] See Jean-François Bayart, 'L'énonciation du politique', *Revue Française de Science Politique* 3, June 1985, p. 359.

also from within, trying to understand the interaction as the actors themselves perceived and tested it. This operation was based on some simple questions. What were the main objectives pursued by politicians, soldiers or militiamen in arms, peasants, or shanty-town dwellers when they started interacting with a member of a United Nations mission? What means were at their disposal to achieve those aims, and how did they exploit them? What factors (arising from the situation and from basic structures) appear to have determined their choice? How did they understand the Blue Helmets' mission? How did they experience that 'interference' in their society? By induction and successive comparisons, Chapters 3, 4 and 5 propose to bring out the numerous rationalities at work and to understand the relations between observed facts, collective representations and codes of communication. The way in which local people look at peace operations leads to the redefinition of most notions and patterns governing the action of the 'international community' in this area. It also recalls the extreme diversity, especially human diversity that runs through those UN operations.

Seen in this way, the United Nations teams appear to be diverted by the local socio-political game to its own use, as well as affecting it. The war-peace transition that they are supposed to accompany is not played out on battlefields or along front lines, but at the very heart of the state-society linkage, in the triple crisis of political links (relations with the state), social links (with the community and the most immediate environment such as the district) and domestic links (family and inter-generational) that characterise most contemporary conflicts. In fact the tasks now assigned to peace operations are evidence of this; with very few exceptions, they are entrusted with 'restoring law and order'. That amounts to nothing more nor less than intervening in a social contract, in the relationship between society, the individuals that compose it, and the state. This involves particularly the effective exercise of a security function whose nature remains problematic, especially in the linkage between its military and police components. The building of peace in a given society also involves complex and often paradoxical social, political and economic processes. For this reason the peace engineering promoted by the UN missions suffers from a number of ambiguities and deficiencies. Chapter 6 sets out to analyse these complexes.

Nobody today can give a ready-made answer to the challenges of peace building. But one can try to think of the current dead-ends in the process and the conditions for attempting to get round them. The analysis proposed in these pages suggests some avenues of thought on this, posing questions in their military, political, social and economic dimensions, but also, above all, in their human ones.

Acknowledgements

This book records the main findings of research undertaken for my dissertation in political science. In addition, it is the fruit of about 15 years' field experience in countries torn apart by violence and war in all their forms. I have met many people during the journey and they all accompany the few reflections I have tried to transcribe into these pages. To start with, there are those who gave me hospitality, helped me get to know their countries, and shared a bit of their history—all those with whom exchanges very often went beyond words. In meditation in churches, temples or pagodas, in long hours spent in crowded buses and lorries, on muddy and collapsed roads, in mountains and plains, in districts where people had earnestly urged me not to go, in the maze-like corridors of shantytowns, through joyful or sad evening gatherings. In discussions at markets, or around the fire, learning from other women the tricks of their daily life, like a family member at mealtimes. In exchanges lasting for hours on those voting days which never ended, in places at the far end of the world. In waiting... I have often learned to listen to other silences, other looks, other gestures. And I still feel the pain—unabated—of the loss of so many friends and the horror of all those anonymous, violent, absurd deaths. This puzzle of images has constantly inspired me throughout the writing of these pages, just as I have constantly held in mind the faces, the attitudes, often the very tone of voice of everyone who gave me 'interviews', including those with whom the exercise was particularly difficult (and there were some!). If their number is too great for me to name them all, they know that, well beyond this book, I owe them a great deal. I do not forget all the witnesses and actors of United Nations missions who, while often wishing to remain anonymous, shared their experiences with me and, in some cases, placed personal documents and archives at my disposal. I thank them all sincerely for these gestures. Beyond the doubts, difficulties and frustrations, their words were evidence of the fundamental human dimension of those missions, in their achievements as in their failures.

I enjoyed many rich and varied exchanges with researchers interested in the United Nations and peace operations: Mats Berdal, Barbara E. Harrell-Bond, Chip Carey, Simon Chesterman, Christopher Coleman, Elizabeth Cousens, Donald C. F. Daniel, Michael W. Doyle, Tom Farer, Jeffrey Herbst, Mark Hoffman, David Holiday, Ian Johnstone, David Malone, Craig Murphy, Michael Pugh, Oliver Richmond, Benjamin Rivlin, Adam Roberts, Robert Rubinstein, Nicholas Sims, Andy Smith, Jack Spence, Bill Stanley, Thomas G. Weiss, Sandra Whitworth, Marie-Joëlle Zahar, and various colleagues of the Academic Council for the United Nations System (ACUNS).

In particular, I must mention the historians, sociologists, anthropologists, economists, linguists and specialists in various countries, who gave me the benefit of their knowledge and their passionate attachment to their 'field'. Besides the way they placed themselves at my disposal, I am grateful for the trust they showed me. My thanks go to Natalija Basic, Xavier Bougarel, Michel Cahen, Soizic Crochet, Hector Dada, Alain Daniel, Marcel Djama, Maurice Eisenbruch, the late Christian Geffray, Rafael Guidos Véjar, Raoul Marc Jennar, Christian Lechervy, Fabienne Luco, Roland Marchal, Marie-Alexandrine Martin, Christine Messiant, Véronique Nahoum-Grappe, Gérard Prunier, Alain Rouquié, Roberto Turcios, Lionel Vairon, Knut Walter. My thanks also to the numerous people who, having acquired knowledge in varied capacities of the countries on which this research has concentrated, gave me the benefit of their experience and their contacts. I am also grateful to those who helped me cross the bridge to other disciplines, especially Roberto Beneduce, Bernard Doray, Boris Cyrulnik, Max Pagès and Françoise Sironi for their reflections as psychologists and psychiatrists. Thanks also to the interdisciplinary research group on peace building after mass crimes, which I inspired jointly with Jacques Sémelin at the Center for International Studies and Research (of the National Foundation of Political Science) in Paris in 2001–2.

I thank Patrice Mitrano and Roberto Gimeno of the cartography workshop of the Paris Institut d'Etudes Politiques, who helped me produce the maps appearing in this book; and Dana Mason, Luke Patey and Gregory Cales for their help in creating the website attached to this book.

Investigations in the field, and those conducted in the United States and Great Britain, could not have been made without the support of the National Foundation of Political Science, the Fondation pour les Etudes de Défense, the Direction de la Coopération Scientifique et Technique of the French ministry of Foreign Affairs, and the Fondation Charles Léopold Mayer pour le Progrès de l'Homme. My thanks to all those who placed their confidence in me.

Colleagues who followed this project from its beginnings have also been a great support, starting with my thesis supervisor, Bertrand Badie, and my supervisors at CERI, Christophe Jaffrelot and Christian Lequesne. My thanks also, for their comments and encouragements at various stages of the research, to François Constantin, Yves Daudet, Jean-Luc Domenach, Pierre Hassner, Jean Leca, Denis-Constant Martin, Javier Santiso, Marie-Claude Smouts. And my thanks to the senior officials of the Centre d'Analyse et de Prévision (CAP) of the ministry of Foreign Affairs and the Délégation aux Affaires Stratégiques of the ministry of Defence who, calling on my expertise on peace operations, enabled me to translate my research findings in operational terms. In particular, I must mention David Malone and his colleagues of the International Peace Academy for regularly inviting me to discuss these questions with representatives of the UN Secretariat and member states in New York; thanks also for their hospitality and availability.

I do not forget the students with whom I worked at the Institut d'Etudes Politiques in Paris and Lille, and in various foreign universities, as well as senior NGO staff, senior civil servants, diplomats and military officials of different countries for whom I arranged training sessions. They enabled me to pursue the dialogue started in various theatres in a different way, and finally convinced me, if it were still necessary, of the imperative need to think of the diversity and complexity of our world.

Finally, all of those who, even at a distance, were by my side through the years, especially in the most painful moments. They know what I owe them. Christophe Almy and Olivier Nief, Marie-Cécile and Vanguelis Bricas, Anne-Sophie Boisgallais, Carol Guy-James, Geneviève Hergott, Anne Lacour, Anne and Philippe Lavigne-Delville, David Morgant, Florence Meunier, Daniel Urrutia Balutansky, Brother Antoine. Thanks for being there.

I have had plenty of company throughout this long research. However, I am still solely responsible for what I have tried, not without difficulty, to record from it.

Paris, March 2006   B. P.

ACRONYMS

ACABQ	Advisory Committee on Administrative and Budgetary Questions (The United Nations, General Assembly)
ADEFAES	Association of Demobilized Members of the Armed Forces of El Salvador
ADHOC	Cambodia Human Rights & Development Association
AMODEG	Association of Mozambican Demobilized from the War
ANKI	National Army of Independent Kampuchea
ARENA	Nationalist Republican Alliance (El Salvador)
ASEAN	Association of Southeast Asian Nations
CNS	Supreme National Council of Cambodia
COPAZ	National Commission for the Consolidation of Peace (El Salvador)
DPA	Department of Political Affairs (UN Secretariat)
DPI	Department of Public Information (UN Secretariat)
DPKO	Department of Peace-Keeping Operations (UN Secretariat)
ECOMOG	Economic Community of West African States Monitoring Group (ECOWAS)
ECOSOC	Economic and Social Council (UN)
ERP	The People's Revolution Army (El Salvador)
FADH	Haitian Armed Forces
FAES	El Salvador Armed Forces
FANLPK	Armed Forces for National Liberation of Khmer People (Cambodia)
FMLN	Farabundo Martí Front for National Liberation (El Salvador)
FNCD	National Front for Change and Democracy (Haiti)
FNLPK	National Front of Liberation of Khmer People (Cambodia)
FPL	Popular Liberation Forces (El Salvador)
FRAPH	Front for Advancement and Progress of Haiti
FUNCINPEC	United Front for an Independent, Neutral, Peaceful, and Cooperative Cambodia
FUNDAPAZ	Foundation for Peace (El Salvador)
HDZ	Croatian Democratic Union
HVO	Croatian Defence Council
ICITAP	International Criminal Investigation Training and Assistance Program (Department of Justice; United States)
ICRC	International Committee of the Red Cross
IFOR	Implementation Force (Bosnia-Herzegovina)

Acronyms

IMF	International Monetary Fund
INGO	International non-governmental organisation
IOM	International Organisation for Migration
KFOR	Kosovo Force
KID	Conference for Democratic Unity (Haiti)
KID	Khmer Institute of Democracy (Cambodia)
KONAKOM	Congress of Democratic Movements (Haiti)
LICADHO	League for Promotion and Defence of Human Rights (Cambodia)
MBO	Muslim-Bosniac Organization
MICIVIH	International Civilian Mission in Haiti (UN/OAS)
MIPONUH	United Nations Civilian Police Mission in Haiti
MNF	Multinational Force (Haiti)
NATO	North Atlantic Treaty Organisation
NGO	Non-governmental organisation
OAS	Organisation of American States
OCI	Organisation of Islamic Conference
ONUC	United Nations Operation in Congo
ONUCA	United Nations Observer Group in Central America
ONUMOZ	United Nations Operation in Mozambique
ONUV	United Nations Verification Office in El Salvador
ONUVEH	United Nations Observer Group for the Verification of the Elections in Haiti
OPL	Organisation of the People in Struggle (Haiti)/Lavalas Political Organization (until 1997)
OSCE	Organisation for Security and Co-operation in Europe
OUA	Organisation of African Unity
PANPRA	National Progressive Revolutionary Party (Haiti)
PBLD	Buddhist Liberal Democratic Party (created by the ex-FNLPK, Cambodia)
PDL	Democratic Liberal Party (created by the ex-FANLPK, Cambodia)
PKD	Party of Democratic Kampuchea (formerly PCK, Khmer rouges, Cambodia)
PLB	Open Gate Party (Haiti)
PNC	National Civil Police (El Salvador)
PPC	People's Party of Cambodia
RENAMO	Mozambican National Resistance
SDA	Party of Democratic Action (Bosnia-Herzegovina)
SDS	Serbian Democratic Party
SFOR	Stabilisation Force (Bosnia-Herzegovina)
SNA	Somali National Alliance
SNF	Somali National Front
SNM	Somali National Movement
TKL	Little Church Community (basic community movements in Haiti)

UN	United Nations
UNAMIC	United Nations Advance Mission in Cambodia
UNBRO	United Nations Border Relief Operation (Refugee camps on the frontier between Cambodia and Thailand)
UNCIVPOL	United Nations Civilian Police
UNESCO	United Nations, Educational, Scientific and Cultural Organization
UNFICYP	United Nations Force in Cyprus
UNHCR	United Nations High Commissioner for Refugees
UNICEF	United Nations Children's Fund
UNIFIL	United Nations Interim Force in Lebanon
UNITAF	United Task Force (Somalia)
UNMIBH	United Nations Mission in Bosnia and Herzegovina
UNMIH	United Nations Mission in Haiti
UNMIK	United Nations Interim Administration in Kosovo
UNOSOM I	United Nations Operation in Somalia I
UNOSOM II	United Nations Operation in Somalia II
UNPREDEP	United Nations Preventive Deployment Force (Yugoslav Republic of Macedonia)
UNPROFOR	United Nations Protection Force (ex-Yugoslavia)
UNSMIH	United Nations Support Mission in Haiti
UNTAC	United Nations Transitional Authority in Cambodia
UNTAG	United Nations Transition Assistance Group (Namibia)
UNV	United Nations Volunteers
USC	United Somali Congress

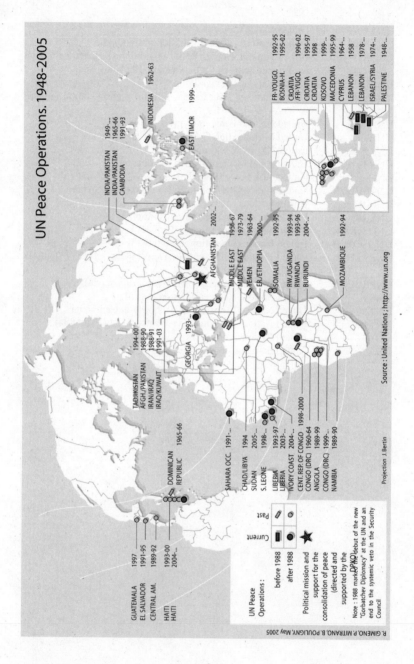

UN Peace Operations. 1948-2005

Source : United Nations ; http://www.un.org

Projection J.Bertin

R.GIMENO, P.MITRANO, B.POULIGNY, May 2005

UN Peace Operations :

	Current	Past
before 1988		
after 1988		

★ Political mission and support for the consolidation of peace (directed and supported by the

Note : 1988 marked the debut of the new "Gorbatchev Diplomacy" at the UN and an end to the systemic veto in the Security Council

GUATEMALA 1997
EL SALVADOR 1991-95
CENTRAL AM. 1989-92
HAITI 1993-00
HAITI 2004-...

DOMINICAN REPUBLIC 1965-66

SAHARA OCC. 1991-...
CHAD/LIBYA 1994
SUDAN 2005-...
S.LEONE 1998-...
LIBERIA 1993-97
LIBERIA 2003-...
IVORY COAST 2004-...
CENT.REP.OF CONGO 1998-2000
CONGO (DRC) 1960-64
ANGOLA 1989-99
CONGO (DRC) 1999-...
NAMIBIA 1989-90

INDIA/PAKISTAN 1949-...
INDIA/PAKISTAN 1965-66
CAMBODIA 1991-93
INDONESIA 1962-63
EAST TIMOR 1999-...

TADJIKISTAN 1994-00
AFGH./PAKISTAN 1988-90
IRAN/IRAQ 1988-91
IRAQ/KUWAIT 1991-03
AFGHANISTAN 2002-...

MIDDLE EAST 1956-67
MIDDLE EAST 1973-79
YEMEN 1963-64
ER./ETHIOPIA 2000-...
SOMALIA 1992-95
RW./UGANDA 1993-94
RWANDA 1993-96
BURUNDI 2004-...
MOZAMBIQUE 1992-94

GEORGIA 1993-...

FR-YOUGO. 1992-95
BOSNIA-H. 1995-02
CROATIA /FR-YUGO. 1996-02
CROATIA 1995-97
CROATIA 1998
KOSOVO 1999-...
MACEDONIA 1995-99
CYPRUS 1964-...
LEBANON 1958
LEBANON 1978-...
ISRAEL/SYRIA 1974-...
PALESTINE 1948-...

xxiv

Total Troop Deployment in UN Peace Operations

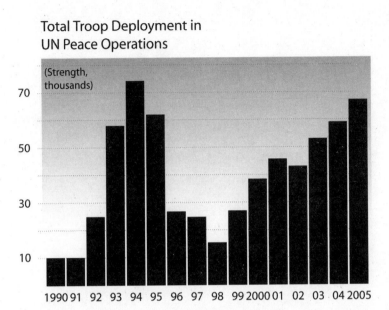

(Strength, thousands)

UN Peace Operations Budget and UN Regular Budget

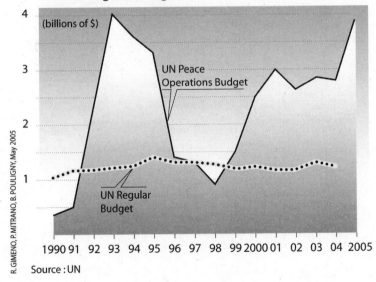

(billions of $)

UN Peace Operations Budget

UN Regular Budget

R. GIMENO, P. MITRANO, B. POULIGNY, May 2005

Source : UN

1

INTRODUCTION

THE UNITED NATIONS BETWEEN WAR
AND PEACE

A peace operation is largely conceived in the antechambers of international negotiations. Its implementation is mainly discussed and decided in the corridors of the United Nations Secretariat and the Security Council. That is where the 'crisis' to which the operation is supposed to respond is analysed and qualified according to parameters that often have very little to do with the local and regional context. Yet what is played out in New York is not totally unrelated to the changing situation in Port-au-Prince, San Salvador, Phnom Penh, Mogadishu, Maputo or Sarajevo: the main actors in the conflicts bring those parameters into their own strategies, in particular trying both to anticipate international reactions, and to influence them, just as they are trying to impose their own moving representations of the situation. It is in this muddy situation that a United Nations peace operation lands in a country and begins to deploy over its territory. Its progress then depends on the parallel games being played out at the international, regional and local level, and the consequences that may accordingly follow the modes of intervention that are decided on.

THE NEW FORMS OF PEACE OPERATIONS

The operations analysed in these pages do not have much in common with the classical peacekeeping operations, following the scheme imagined on an *ad hoc* basis during the Suez Crisis in 1956.[1] Those operations predominantly deployed in cases of inter-state conflicts, even though some of them had an intra-state dimension. Some missions were even deployed on the territory of one state only: the United Nations Force in Cyprus

---

[1] The first UN peacekeeping mission was established in January 1949, to watch over the borders between India and Pakistan (UNMOGIP is still deployed today). But it was with Suez that the bases of the peacekeeping doctrine were really laid down.

(UNFICYP), the United Nations Interim Force in Lebanon (UNIFIL). But they were interposition forces whose actions took on a routine from one case to the next: supervising the observation of a cease-fire, surveillance of front lines or buffer zones or even demilitarised strips, exchanges of prisoners and, possibly, monitoring disarmament operations. This routine came to an end with the operation in Namibia (the United Nations Transitional Assistance Group, UNTAG) in 1989–90, both the most complicated and the largest since the operation in the former Belgian Congo in 1960–64.[2] The UN Secretariat turned it into a sort of laboratory, and the model was rapidly transferred to other situations which, for their part, went beyond the still classical framework of decolonisation: El Salvador, Angola, Cambodia, Mozambique, Rwanda, Haiti.[3] The operations in Somalia and the former Yugoslavia marked a further stage with the authorisation to resort to force to protect humanitarian aid; however, the ultimate objective was still held to be the restoration of peace and the support to rebuild state infrastructures. This approach was applied more recently in Sierra Leone, the Democratic Republic of Congo or Ivory Coast, but also in Kosovo and East Timor, marking a new departure with 'transitional administrations'. In all these cases, the objective was no longer to interpose between two states or even two armies, but to assist the installation of the foundations necessary for the restoration of law and order in a given society. Peacekeeping in the classical sense has become subsidiary (in El Salvador, Cambodia, Haiti, Mozambique, etc.) or has been subordinated to other aims (such as the distribution of humanitarian aid in the cases of Somalia and Bosnia) in operations that have become definitively more complex than in the past. Three major elements may help understand the conditions of such developments and also distinguish the different operations: the nature of their mandate; the dating of

---

[2] At the time, the Security Council decided to intervene in an internal conflict without any major impact beyond the borders of the country concerned. It did so by sending in an observation force under the heading of peacekeeping, which was later transformed into an interposition force. In addition, this mission was the first to involve a fairly broad civilian and police component, with a mandate including maintenance of order; that mandate was modified subsequently to include guaranteeing the territorial integrity and political independence of the Congo. The crisis that followed this episode was especially serious, paralysing the United Nations Security Council in particular. For thirty years, the United Nations Operation in the (ex-Belgian) Congo (UNOC) remained the exception. To a lesser extent, since the UN came to take over the tasks of administration of the country, the operation in West (ex-Dutch) New Guinea in 1962–3 strayed broadly outside the 'classical' framework of peacekeeping, at least in the UNTEA (United Nations Temporary Executive Authority) component linked with the UNSF (United Nations Security Force).

[3] More limited missions, following the same model, were also deployed in South Africa and Guatemala. For a general overview of missions deployed since 1948, refer to the map on page xxiv.

each mission in relation to the end of hostilities and the resort or non-resort to force to impose international will; and, lastly, the role given to the UN in the whole process.

Over-ambitious mandates

The United Nations Observer Mission in El Salvador (ONUSAL) was the first whose objectives were above all geared towards the construction and consolidation of peace, a theme close to the heart of Boutros Boutros-Ghali, Secretary General at the time. It was one of his major proposals of his *Agenda for Peace*.[4] ONUSAL appeared to be original in two ways: firstly, in El Salvador the UN sought not only to stop a conflict but also to attack the roots causes of the civil war—hence a multi-dimensional operation, described as an integrated one; secondly, for the first time in United Nations history, a mission aimed at institution-building in an independent state. From July 1991 onwards, a team of about a hundred observers entrusted with verifying the implementation of the San José Agreement on Human Rights was gradually deployed in the country. When the cease-fire came into effect on 1 February 1992, ONUSAL was turned into a mechanism geared basically towards verifying the implementation of the peace agreements in their various components: the cease-fire and the measures relating to it, the reform and downsizing of the armed forces, the creation of a new police force, the reform of the electoral and judicial systems, and a host of economic, political and social issues considered indispensable for peace building (including land tenure and human rights issues).[5] In May 1993, at the request of the government, backed by the Frente Farabundo Marti de Liberación Nacional (FMLN), Security Council Resolution 832 added to the mandate the supervision of general elections held in March 1994. Thus ONUSAL's mandate covered a very wide range of issues. Similarly, the four aspects of the United Nations Operation in Mozambique (ONUMOZ)—political, military, electoral and humanitarian—to which extra tasks in police matters were added, followed the same model.[6] In that mission the UN also tried to draw lessons from the failure of the operation in Angola.

[4] *Agenda for Peace*, New York: United Nations, DPI/1247, June 1992.
[5] The peace agreement that ended the Salvadorian conflict was signed on January 16, 1992 at Chapultepec in Mexico. It followed the Act of New York signed on December 31, 1991, setting down the agreement of the two parties on a cease-fire, which came into effect on February 1, 1992, and it consolidated six groups of agreements whose aims, as fixed in the Geneva framework agreement, were to end the armed conflict by political means, promote democratisation of the country, guarantee respect for human rights, and reunify Salvadorian society.
[6] The United Nations Security Council's adoption on October 13, 1992 of Resolution 782, under which ONUMOZ was created, followed the signing of a general Peace Agreement

In Cambodia, the global and integrated character of the UN action was strengthened. After a preparatory phase,[7] the United Nations Transitional Authority in Cambodia (UNTAC) had six main tasks assigned to distinct components: coordinating the return of refugees and displaced persons (with the High Commission for Refugees as the leading agency); supervising and verifying the cease-fire, the withdrawal of foreign troops and the demobilisation of at least 70 per cent of the parties' armed forces; organising and coordinating free and fair elections; encouraging respect for human rights (this task being assumed by the Human Rights and Civilian Police Components); supervising or controlling existing administrative structures; and coordinating a vast support programme for the rehabilitation and rebuilding of Cambodia. A seventh component was created to fulfil the task of information and education, initially depending on the office of the Secretary General's Special Representative. UNTAC was a particularly clear illustration of the multiplicity and complexity of the tasks now assigned to UN peace operations. But some elements made it a unique case; besides UNTAC's specific position as a 'transitional authority', the ambition to rebuild a state—indeed, a nation—was in this case clearly affirmed, backed by a clear international mobilisation and the attribution of unprecedented resources (about 22,000 military and civilian personnel and more than $1.6 billion).

Behind the declared objective of 'restoring democracy', this political engineering was also applied in Haiti, though in a more restrained and ambiguous way. On 31 March 1995 the United Nations Mission in Haiti (UNMIH), following the restoration of the constitutional government, took over from the Multinational Force led by the United States under Operation Restore Democracy. At the time, the mission aimed at maintaining the secure and stable environment created by the Multinational Force, in particular to ensure that legislative elections in June and presidential elections in December could take place in good conditions; providing technical assistance for the organisation of the polls; and assisting

by the Mozambique government and Resistência Nacional Moçambicana (RENAMO) on October 4, 1992.

[7] On October 16, 1991 (that is, a few days before the Paris Conference and the signing of the peace agreements), the Security Council decided to create a preparatory mission (Resolution 717, creating the United Nations Advance Mission in Cambodia, UNAMIC). Its deployment was authorised by Resolution 718 of October 31, 1991, which ratified the signing of the agreements. UNAMIC was assigned three principle tasks: facilitating communication between factions by dialogue and persuasion, and trying in that way to secure respect for the cease-fire; preparing an anti-mines preventive campaign to protect the population; and preparing for the arrival of UNTAC (set up by Resolution 745 of February 28, 1992).

in the professionalisation of the armed forces and the new Haitian police.[8] The first objective, defined in extremely vague terms, immediately gave rise to divergent interpretations, varying over time.[9] As for the profession-alisation of the armed forces, it was rendered obsolete by their dissolution by President Aristide on his return from exile. Consequently, the training of the new police force took on added importance. The main task of UNMIH, and the missions that followed, was the monitoring of the new police force, with some elements of on the job training.[10] As in El Salva-dor, the initial and principal training of the police was in the hands of the International Criminal Investigative Training Assistance Program (ICI-TAP), a body under the US Department of Justice and financed by the US administration.[11] In fact, in view of the inadequacies and limitations of this initial training, UN civpols were called to play a role largely above the one initially forecast. The position of civpols is even more ambiguous when, as in Cambodia and Mozambique, local polices do not receive any additional specific training programme.

In Somalia, in 1993, member states also assigned extremely ambitious objectives for the UN: to re-establish the country's institutional structures, to achieve national reconciliation, to contribute to the Somalian state-build-ing (with ambitious programmes regarding the police and the adminis-tration of justice), to create conditions for participation by civil society in the democratisation process, to continue the demining programme and help the repatriation of refugees.[12] However, as in Bosnia, the peace func-tion assigned to the first phase of UN operation in Somalia (UNOSOM I) was subordinated to a humanitarian objective: supervising the cease-fire in Mogadishu, ensuring the protection and security of UN staff and equip-

---

[8] Security Council Resolutions 940 and 975, which in this way revised the initial mandate provided for in 1993, backing the Governors Island agreements between General Cédras—the head of the threeman junta then in power in Haiti—and deposed President Aristide. At the time the mission was supposed to help the modernisation of the armed forces and the establishment of a new police force.

[9] For example, the Secretary General's report of January 17, 1995 (S/1995/46) added the protection of international staff and essential installations. In this way, the idea of a deterrent and rapid reaction force was crystallised, an idea that was to become the essential expression of that vague formulation. However, the conditions for employment of that force were never to be clarified.

[10] The United Nations civilian police progressively came to play a wider accompanying role; the final phase of the UN presence was, moreover, entirely oriented in that direction with MIPONUH (the United Nations Civilian Police Mission in Haiti), created by Reso-lution 1141 of November 28, 1997.

[11] Outside these missions, ICITAP has intervened in more than a hundred countries around the world, notably complementing the Antiterrorism Assistance (ATA) programme, which for its part comes under the US State Department.

[12] Resolution 814 of March 26, 1993, which set up UNOSOM II.

ment and supplies from the harbour and the airport, escorting humanitarian aid convoys in the city and its immediate surrounding area.

In the former Yugoslavia, the United Nations Protection Force (UNPROFOR) was initially set up in Croatia as an interim arrangement to create the conditions of peace and security required for negotiations of an overall settlement of the Yugoslav crisis. Its mandate was extended to Bosnia, in June 1992, to ensure the security and functioning of Sarajevo airport and the delivery of humanitarian aid to the city and its environs. In September 1992, the mandate was extended to cover the whole of Bosnia-Herzegovina, but remained humanitarian in nature. This was also the case for decisions concerning the air exclusion zones and the establishment of 'safe havens' for the population. UNPROFOR was a clear illustration of a humanitarian approach adopted in parallel with, or as a substitute for, political action—an ambivalence characteristic of the 'international community's' action over the past decade, oscillating between typically short-term humanitarian responses and an ambition to reshape domestic political orders.

Peace operations in wartime

The Bosnia and Somalia cases also illustrate an inversion of roles. In both countries peace forces were sent to intervene in wartime, as state members were not able (and did not want) to enforce peace. Therefore, UNPROFOR's mandate was extended to Bosnia in June 1992, two months after the outbreak of open conflict in that country. A proper combatant force was sent only after peace was signed in December 1995 (the Dayton Agreements). Then, the peace force handed over to a fighting force, IFOR (then followed by SFOR) under the command of the North Atlantic Treaty Organisation (NATO), to manage the military aspects of the international operation in Bosnia.[13] In other instances, peace forces are usually sent in situations of neither war nor peace which may also be very ambiguous and fragile. In El Salvador and Cambodia, as in Mozambique, missions intervened in accordance with an agreement among the parties in conflict— hence, in theory, in peace time. But in El Salvador, when the first observer team was deployed in July 1991 (essentially consisting of civilians accompanied by police officers and some military liaison officers), to verify the implementation of the San José agreement on human rights,[14] negoti-

---

[13] The handover was made official by a Security Council Resolution of December 15, 1995 (S/RES/1031). The decision to establish the United Nations Mission in Bosnia-Herzegovina (UNMIBH) was taken on December 21, 1995 (S/RES/1035); it was comprised of a civilian office and an international police force (the UN International Police Task Force).

[14] Agreement signed on July 26, 1990.

ations had not yet ended and, in the absence of a cease-fire, fighting was still going on. In reality, that situation was much less atypical than it seemed to be. An armed conflict never ends on a fixed date, whether by a truce or a peace agreement.

This blurring of boundaries goes far in illustrating how the traditional dichotomy between operations under Chapter VI and those under Chapter VII of the Charter now seem less and less explanatory. The convenient reference to Chapter VI is a reminder that the peace operations conducted for nearly fifty years were not foreseen in the Charter. Those operations—caught between Chapter VI, devoted to diplomatic measures, and Chapter VII, providing for resort to coercion, especially military coercion—were based on three principles: the consent of the parties in conflict to the deployment of 'Blue Helmets' (the UN does not impose its presence, it is invited to intervene); the impartiality of the troops; and resort to force only in cases of self-defence. Somalia was the first country where a United Nations peace operation was given the mandate to resort to force in pursuing its mission. At that time there were only four precedents for member states being authorised to undertake military action under that chapter: in response to the attacks on the Republic of Korea, in 1950;[15] to authorise interception of tankers transporting oil for Southern Rhodesia, in 1966; and twice in the Iraq-Kuwait conflict, in 1990 and 1991. However, in Somalia, for the first time in United Nations history, a coalition of member states was authorised to use force, in the name of the Organisation, to intervene in an internal conflict, for humanitarian purposes. Certainly there was an attempt to maintain the fiction of local authorities' agreement; at the beginning of 1992 the interim President, Ali Mahdi, gave his agreement to the deployment of the United Nations, but he had virtually no authority in the country. The same fiction was adopted in Haiti. Formally, it was the deposed but internationally recognised government that in 1993 approached the Security Council to ask that the trade embargo against Haiti recommended by the Organisation of American States, following the coup d'état against the first democratically elected president of the country, should be made universal and binding.[16] Two days before the adoption of Resolution 940 of 31 July 1994, the President of Haiti addressed a letter to the President of the Security Council calling for 'prompt and decisive action'. One decade later, a letter signed by the President of Haitian Supreme Court (who provisionally assumed the

---

[15] However, in this case authorisation for the use of force was finally given, exceptionally, by the General Assembly and not by the Security Council, then paralysed by the Cold War.

[16] Letter of June 7, 1993 to the President of the Security Council by the Permanent Representative of Haiti to the UN (S/25958—June 16, 1993).

presidency of the country after Aristide's forced exile) "authorized" the deployment of international forces.[17] However, in Somalia as in Haiti, beyond respect for certain forms, it was in fact Chapter VII that was invoked, relegating sovereignty rhetoric to second place. Without armed forces of its own, the UN therefore had to resort to delegation. Operation Restore Hope in Somalia and Operation Restore Democracy in Haiti (as the interim force deployed at the end of 2004, under the US leadership) were undertaken by multinational coalitions headed by the United States, acting under a United Nations resolution, not under the Organisation's leadership. These operations were followed by a United Nations phase very similar to other peace operations conducted under Chapter VI of the Charter: UNOSOM II in Somalia, UNMIH, and then the interim force in Haiti. In recent years this repartition of roles has been adopted many times: NATO operations in Bosnia and Kosovo, Operation Alba led by Italy in Albania, INTERFET in East Timor led by Australia, Artemis led by France in Ituri (East Congo) etc.

In recent years, this mixture of types of intervention has provoked stormy debates in United Nations circles. This has regularly led observers to predict the end of major international humanitarian operations. In fact it is not so much the realities of war and peace as the pusillanimity of diplomats that dictates the rhythm of decisions about peace operations.

Short-term agendas and exit strategies

In Bosnia, the 'Blue Helmets' action was marked as much by the failure of four successive peace plans, a succession of conferences and meetings of the 'Contact Group' and, even more, fluctuations in positions within the Security Council, as by changes in the balance of forces among the belligerents on the ground. In Haiti, the multinational coalition claimed to be restoring not peace, but democracy. Yet the return of the constitutionally elected president to the country was considered less important by the US administration than the date fixed for the passing of the baton between the multinational coalition and UNMIH, March 15, 1995. Now, this deadline did not define in what way Haiti enjoyed a 'secure and stable environment' (the same vague wording was use in 2004).[18] Whereas the achievement of such a goal was supposed to mark the transition from the multinational to the UN force, the only criteria were those of the American administration and the need to end, as soon as possible, an operation that was somewhat risky for President Clinton on the domestic political scene.

---

[17] S/2003/163, February 29, 2004.
[18] S/RES/2004/164, February 29, 2004

In theory, things are less hazy in operations following a peace accord. An agreement usually includes a timetable for various provisions coming into action (cease-fire, activities of demobilisation, disarmament and re-integration, elections, and so on). The deadlines for these proceedings are generally the object of minute negotiations. They serve as beacons on the road from war to peace. But even in such cases the parameters external to the conflict often seem the most decisive. When the extension of an operation is under negotiation in the Security Council, an opportunity arises to re-open other negotiations, including on the nature of the man-date. In cases where there are no clear landmarks and calendars for lack of peace agreements, as in Haiti, Somalia and Bosnia, the extensions of mandates are key moments in the life of the operation. In Haiti, after an initial period of one year, the United Nations mission was extended various times for very short periods and under different acronyms.[19] A fairly similar scenario took place in Somalia: while UNOSOM I and UNITAF lasted only a few months,[20] the duration of UNOSOM II was extended six times, while its mandate and size were reduced along the way. In Bosnia, after its first twelve-month, UNPROFOR's mandate was never extended for more than six months at a time. In addition, each extension gave rise to adjustments to the mandate, corresponding most often to the addition of new objectives, superimposed on earlier ones or even contradicting them, without a real effort at coherence on the part of Security Council members. Humanitarian action, peacekeeping, military enforcement and political action were never brought together in an overall plan. Security Council debates and resolutions reveal the ceaseless attempt to compromise among divergent aims. For example, the dispatch of a force with a rather limited humanitarian mandate contrasted with the very tough language of preceding declarations and resolutions. In the absence of agreement defining an objective for the intervention in Bosnia, it was a solution following the principle of the 'lowest common denominator' that was finally adopted.

It is quite easy to understand that more or less serious uncertainties related to particular situations on the ground are reflected in the timetable

[19] UNMIH was extended on February 29, 1996 'for a final period of four months' and with reduced numbers involved. This was the only concession that the government of China—irritated by the success of Taiwan's diplomacy with small countries like Haiti—agreed to make; it agreed to a decision for the successively renamed subsequent missions. There was a similar very jerky progress in the mixed UN/OAS civil mission (MICIVIH) that was deployed in parallel with the UN mission.

[20] The first UNOSOM I observers arrived in Somalia in July 1992, but the coalition headed by the United States intervened in December of the same year, before giving way to UNOSOM II on May 4, 1993.

of UN missions. An extension for some months, some weeks, or even some days makes it possible for the UN to not commit straight away. But this short-term management method is most often related to considerations wholly removed from the situations themselves. Among these, financial questions have in recent years tended to occupy an increasing place in all decisions taken at the UN. The need to balance budgetary needs within an overall decreasing peacekeeping budget generally leads to very short-term management.[21] In any case a mandate of a few months is easier to get accepted in negotiations. On the ground, that means that teams work to very close deadlines and must be prepared to pack at any time—a prospect that diverts a good deal of time and energy from the work that they are supposed to be doing in a country. The concern of political and military decision makers' to arrange exit strategies for themselves undoubtedly had an impact on peace operations in the 1990s. Outside Europe (Westerners have accepted the fact that in the Balkans their interventions are long-term), the date for the end of an operation must be known from the time it is launched. Cambodia has been a very good illustration of this scenario. In Cambodia, the mission's deadline was fixed from the beginning: Security Council Resolution 745 of 28 February 1992, which established UNTAC, scheduled the holding of elections for May 1993. In fact, the mission ended with the promulgation of the Constitution and oath swearing ceremony by the King, who appointed the two co-prime ministers on 24 September 1993. In that model the electoral processes tend to be a major landmark for the UN Secretariat. As we shall see, this can have serious consequences on the ground.

In contrast to classical missions, some of which have been deployed for nearly forty years, the timing of contemporary, multidimensional peace operations seem to be ephemeral, contrasting both with the ambitions of the mandates and with the timing of social and political changes that they seek to influence. In Cambodia, UNTAC was the most ambitious, most expensive, but also the most short-lived operation. Its mandate started officially on 15 March 1992. By 2 August 1993 UN Forces began to withdraw, while the Repatriation Component and most of the election personnel had already left the country. The Military Component of UNTAC completed its withdrawal in mid-November 1993, even though the Secur-

---

[21] The treatment of the financial dimension is complicated here by the fact that there is a duplication of decision making levels; the missions' budgets are examined and approved not by the Security Council which authorises the creation of the missions and all subsequent provisions, but by specialised committee of the General Assembly (the Fifth Committee and ACABQ), under Article 17 of the Charter. The financial question was important, notably, in the decision not to risk extension of a mission like UNTAC, which cost nearly $100 million per month.

ity Council decided on November 4 to extend the period of withdrawal of some components until December 31, 1993.[22] The essential part of the operation thus lasted 18 months, with full deployment for about six.

UN roles in the peace process

Between one country to another, UN peace missions occupy a very different position in the overall arrangements that usually accompany the settlement of an armed conflict. A good example of a classical case is UNOSAL in El Salvador. The peace agreements gave the UN a key role in supervising the process. As in Cambodia, the UN was not competing with any other international organisation on the ground. But its role was still limited to that of verifying the implementation of the agreements, while the Salvadoran government continued to carry out its normal duties. During that period, the UN also continued to play its role of good offices, as the negotiations went on throughout the application of the peace agreements (with a major task of *recalendarización*). However, this role was carried out by ad hoc missions of the UN Secretariat and by representatives of 'friend countries' while the UNOSAL team on the ground was concentrating more on its role of supervision. As we shall see, this repartition of the roles has had important consequences on the perception that the various Salvadoran actors had of the UN mission in their country.

The position of UNOMOZ in Mozambique was very similar: no direct international competitor on the ground, supervisor of the implementation of peace agreements. Nonetheless, the negotiating position of the Special Representative of the UN Secretary General appeared to be stronger than the 'friend countries'.

In Haiti, as in Somalia, the UN operation took over from a multinational coalition headed by the United States. In both cases, the UN was not dominant on the ground, and even ran the risk of being confused with US lead operations, even when they succeeded each other in time (MNF and UNMIH in Haiti, UNITAF and UNOSOM I and II in Somalia). In Bosnia, the UN intervened in parallel with several other international bodies. Its involvement in the crisis marked the failure of the diplomacy developed through the Conference on Security and Cooperation in Europe (CSCE) and the European Union. Throughout the conflict, key European countries played on this plurality of institutions. With the decision to resort to air strikes, NATO also came to scene, complicating the picture yet again. Finally, the United States played a decisive independent role with the

---

[22] S/RES/880 of November 4, 1993. The last administrative staff left the country at the end of May 1994.

appointment of a mediator, Richard Holbrooke, in July 1995. In such cases, the UN appears to be even more dependent on the way Western diplomacies play on the different international arenas.

The position of the UN mission in Cambodia illustrates a third configuration. As a transitional authority, entrusted with administration of Cambodia throughout the transitional period preceding general elections,[23] the UN was in a position close to that of a true trusteeship authority, such as had been experimented with in Namibia—a precedent that served as a reference for various aspects of the Cambodian mission. The UN exercised control over the existing administration and was fully in charge of the organisation of the electoral process. The country remained under UN authority until the installation of a national government following the elections of September 24, 1993. However, the case of Cambodia did not take place within the framework of decolonisation; the matter of placing the country under the UN legal trusteeship during the transitional period went unquestioned. Hence the idea of duplication of functions with a Supreme National Council (SNC), holder of national sovereignty, delegating power to UNTAC during the transitional period, the Cambodian seat at the UN remaining vacant.[24] While the principle of delegation was accepted in February 1990, during a meeting of the various Cambodian parties in Jakarta, discussions on the exact role of the UN never came to a conclusion. The extent of UNTAC's authority and hence its position in the resolution of the conflict, with respect both to the SNC and to the government of the Cambodian state—which controlled most of the Cambodian territory and the administration of the country—remained the object of continuous debate. In many respects the situation of the UN operation in Cambodia was repeated in East Timor and Kosovo. These real trusteeship operations could be considered 'hard' versions of UNTAC—but, in the interim phase, with a bicephalous power arrangement comparable to that attempted in Cambodia.

In these peace operations the provisional substitution of the state authority represented an unprecedented degree of UN involvement, though the UN was not in the position of an occupying force as has clearly been

---

[23] These arrangements, originally proposed by the government of Australia, made it possible to get around the problem of forming a transitional government. A solution to the question of power sharing came up against two key obstacles, arising from the Phnom Penh regime's refusal of a four-party government on the one hand and, on the other, the problem of the status of the Khmers Rouges and recognition of the genocide.

[24] Until then the Cambodian seat at the UN had been occupied (in the name of 'Democratic Kampuchea') by the coalition formed in 1982 by the three groups opposing the government established in Phnom Penh, under the name of the 'Coalition Government of Kampuchea' and at that time, the 'National Government of Kampuchea'.

the case with the American authority in Iraq, But, on the ground, local actors did not perceive the different UN missions very differently from other cases. Questions such as 'Who is in charge?'; 'Who is legitimate?'; 'What about our sovereignty as people?' receive moving answers. They refer to processes that are not at all linear, and demonstrate a subtle dialectic of 'them' and 'us'. In other words, for local people, the question of getting the UN as an 'authority' or not is not so crucial. Indeed, in observing what is going on, on a daily basis, it is easy to understand the limits of control that can in practice be exercised by UN missions over a reality that to a great extent eludes them. Moreover, being a transitional authority or not, UN missions largely apply the same political engineering to the different countries. This is partly due to the rotation of staff from one mission to another, but also reflects the development of a specific approach to security issues for the last decade. To that extent, UN peace operations, whatever their model, are very revealing of the dominant contemporary images of war and peace.

INTERNATIONAL VISIONS OF WAR AND PEACE

The end of the bipolar order raised hopes for the building of a more peaceful world. But the euphoria surrounding the idea of a 'new international order' that would enable the implementation of 'global security'—with all the false pretence that went with this new discourse—did not last long. The late 1980s did however alter noticeably the inter-state context in which security questions were debated, in particular within the United Nations. For instance, it made possible a noticeable revival of the Security Council, which for the first time in four decades was not systematically paralysed by the East-West rivalry and the use of the veto.[25] For a few short years this encouraged the idea of a 'rebirth of the United Nations' marked by Boutros Boutros-Ghali's *Agenda for Peace*. But the years that followed revealed that this new start was a lure. The changes in working methods and the role of the Security Council were obvious. But, more than anything else, a close observation of UNSC practices shows the consequences of the disruptions in the perceptions of international security issues, which probably created more uncertainty than what was expected at first.

---

[25] The United States and the USSR had been able to reach an understanding during that time on putting decolonisation on the agenda of the General Assembly; but subsequently, there was a fairly strong consensus, among the great powers and the newly independent states, on respect for the principle of non-interference. The cases of apartheid and Southern Rhodesia were the two exceptions to this rule.

Consequences of the end of the bipolar order

The end of East-West rivalry contributed to the resolution of a number of conflicts, such as in El Salvador. After twelve years, the end of the conflict was due to a great extent to the exhaustion of Salvadorian society as a whole and the impossibility for either of the two sides to win the war. However, the end of the international and regional support that both had received was crucial in bringing about an end to the war, as was the direct involvement of the United States and the Soviet Union (and then the Russian Federation) in negotiations. The calendar of events in fact revealed the decisive role played by the international context. The UN General Assembly had the El Salvador case before it since the early 1980s, but only began to play a role—at first a modest one—in the negotiations between the Salvadorian government and the guerrilla resistance (represented by the Frente Farabundo Marti de Liberación Nacional, FMLN) in 1989. Following a joint letter from the American and Soviet Foreign ministers at the time, the Secretary General was given a mandate by the Security Council to make his good offices available.[26] His representative took part in the meeting between the two parties at San José in Costa Rica in October 1989. This followed the Mexico City agreement signed on September 15, 1989, in which the two parties declared that they would continue the process of dialogue in an effort to reach an understanding through political agreements that would put an end to the armed conflict by political means and invited the Secretary General to send a representative as a 'witness'. In December 1989 the two sides separately requested the Secretary General to play a more active role in the negotiations. The agreement signed in Geneva on April 4, 1990 marked the real start of the process of negotiation between the Salvadorian government and the FMLN; it set out the framework for negotiations. A month later, at Caracas, an agenda was agreed for the negotiations, whose first phase opened at San José in June 1990. Again, and on several occasions, American and Soviet diplomacy intervened directly. Following a meeting between George Bush and Mikhail Gorbachev, at the end of July 1991, a communiqué was published urging the Secretary General to 'participate directly' in the negotiations. On August 1, 1991, in a joint letter, the American Secretary of State, James Baker, and the Soviet Foreign minister, Alexander Bessmertnykh, asked the Secretary General to intervene to secure progress in the talks, deadlocked at the time; they called on him to take personal leadership of the negotiating process and press both sides to reach rapid agreement on remaining political issues.[27] The process was

[26] S/RES/637, July 27, 1989.
[27] Document S/22947 of August 15, 1991.

then considered to have been bogged down, and on the ground fighting never stopped. On December 3, a joint American-Soviet statement called on the government and the guerrilla resistance (which, under the auspices of the United Nations, had resumed peace negotiations with each other, on November 25, in Mexico) to conclude a cease-fire urgently 'in order to consolidate progress already made and put a definitive end to the conflict'.

At the time the two great world powers wanted to implement a new approach to regional conflicts, as was shown also in the Cambodian case. In 1979 the Security Council was called upon to examine the country's situation for the first time, following Vietnam's military intervention in Cambodia in December 1978. However, the lack of unanimity among the five permanent members of the Security Council prevented the adoption of any resolution. In 1979 the Cambodian question was examined in the United Nations General Assembly during its regular session. The Assembly requested the Secretary General follow the situation closely and use his good offices to contribute to a peaceful solution of the problem. From July 13 to 17, 1981, an international conference on Kampuchea was convened by the General Assembly in New York. The Special Representative of the Secretary General for Humanitarian Affairs in South-East Asia went to the region several times, as did the Secretary General in 1985. In the same year, in a report to the General Assembly, he put forward the main elements of an overall political settlement in Cambodia. In 1987 dialogue was started, in France, between Prince Norodom Sihanouk and the Cambodian Prime Minister Hun Sen, who had held the post for the past two years. But it was not until 1989 that the situation actually began to change, thanks mainly to the new relations established between the United States and the USSR and some peripheral elements in the transformation of the international scene.[28] The first Paris conference, in July-August 1989, was unsuccessful because of Sino-Soviet dissensions; the main stumbling blocks revolved around the formation of a transitional government before the holding of general elections and the problem of a cease-fire. On January 15 and 16, 1990 the five permanent members of the Security Council debated an Australian motion and put forward a 16-point plan. During the year, several meetings followed without making significant progress. On August 27, 1990 the Five put forward a framework for a comprehensive political settlement of the conflict, in five chapters, which was approved by the Security Council on September 20, 1990.[29] In 1990 and 1991, in conjunction with informal meetings held in

---

[28] The beginning of the thaw in Sino-Soviet relations, Vietnam's resolve to put an end to a conflict that was undermining its economy, initiatives by Thailand, etc.

[29] S/RES/668 (1990): the plan was also approved by the General Assembly on October 15, 1990 (Resolution A/RES/45/3).

Jakarta between the parties, permanent Security Council members met for consultations, alternately in Paris and New York, until the peace agreement was signed in Paris on October 23, 1991 at a conference that brought together representatives of 18 states, the four Cambodian factions and the UN Secretary General. In this sense, Cambodia was a good illustration of the central role now played by the Security Council—and, within it, by the Permanent Five—in conflict resolution.

As well as being instrumental in Cambodia, this new international context undeniably played a role in the settlement of the Mozambique conflict. A number of analysts have shown how deep the RENAMO guerrilla movement had its roots in local conflict dynamics;[30] it was far from being solely a puppet group manipulated by outside, primarily South Africa, powers. All however agree on the importance of external factors in the outbreak of the conflict, its duration, and the decision of the protagonists to turn to negotiation. In a scenario quite close to the one in El Salvador, the absence of a decisive outcome to the war was joined with the effects of changes in the international environment and their repercussions in the more immediate regional environment. The political changes occurring in South Africa were, very clearly, a fundamental regional influence. The country's government played an important role throughout the negotiations, alongside other neighbours of Mozambique such as Botswana, Malawi and Zimbabwe. The government of Italy, due to the mediation initiated by the Catholic Community of Sant'Egidio, played a highly specific role in the opening of negotiations in November 1990. The former colonial power, the government of Portugal, and the two main protagonists in the Cold War were also present: the Russian Federation—the Soviet Union having played an important role in the region—and the United States, which was to play a particularly active role, especially with respect to RENAMO, a group it had backed for a long time.

Thus, changes in the international context made it possible for the Security Council to invest efforts in the resolution of conflicts that had strong domestic components but had been fashioned by the logic of the Cold War. The same is also true of the Somalia case. The rivalry between the United States and the USSR had given Somalian authorities a lever for obtaining substantial economic and military assistance, first from the

---

[30] I am thinking particularly of Christian Geffray's pioneering study, but also of the works of Michel Cahen, Jean-Claude Legrand, Otto Roesh and Ken Wilson. Reference can be made to the comprehensive synthesis made by Alex Vines, *RENAMO: From Terrorism to Democracy in Mozambique?*, revised edn, York: University of York Centre for Southern African Studies/Amsterdam: Eduardo Mondlane Foundation/London: James Currey, 1996.

Soviet Union and then from the United States. One of the consequences was the acquisition of large quantities of arms. Hence, in the mid-1970s, Somalia had the best equipped armed forces in sub-Saharan Africa. The availability of arms in large quantity in a Somalia collapsing into anarchy, after the fall of President Siyad Barre in 1991, was a legacy of that rivalry. But the Somali case illustrates another peculiar feature of the post-Cold War period: a broadening of the UNSC agenda. At the time when the Secretary General became involved in the Somalia problem, the internal situation had already deteriorated. However, it did not really encroach beyond the Somalian borders, the refugee flows were still very small compared with what was happening in other parts of Africa. In addition, a distinguishing feature of the Somali crisis was the absence of any clear geopolitical, economic or ideological issues at stake. Certainly there are oil deposits in Somalia and the penetration of Islamist movements in the region was viewed askance by some security services of the US administration. However, in contrast to other theatres of operations, the 'international community's' intervention in Somalia could not be only explained by the involvement of interests in the classic sense of power politics.

The UN Secretary General became involved in the resolution of the crisis from the beginning of 1992, trying to broker a cease-fire. The deterioration of the security situation in which humanitarian agencies had to operate and the worsening of the famine (whose victims were then estimated to number 300,000) led to an increase of public awareness of the situation. In the Security Council resolution that authorised an humanitarian operation,[31] the situation was described as constituting a threat to international peace and security. A new leap, both conceptual and qualitative, was made with Security Council Resolution 794: for the first time in history approval was given under United Nations cover for intervention by a military force in a sovereign state for humanitarian purposes.[32] The case of Bosnia provides the second example, illustrating the place of humanitarian considerations in United Nations responses to conflict situations. UNPROFOR in Bosnia-Herzegovina was never considered as a classical mission in which the United Nations deployed forces to separate the two parties and then tried to forge a peaceful resolution of the conflict.[33] It was the humanitarian situation that, from the early summer of 1992, stirred the members of the Security Council into action, whereas,

[31] S/RES/767 of July 27, 1992.
[32] S/RES/794 of December 3, 1992.
[33] It was only because of the Washington Agreement of March 1, 1994 that UNPROFOR assumed a role of interposition between Bosnian Muslims and Croats, creating a separation zone to be demilitarised and disarmed.

only a few months earlier, the intensity of the conflict had led them, on the advice of the Secretary General, to reject the idea of an interposition force.[34]

Among other peculiarities, UNPROFOR was the first United Nations operation of this sort in Europe. During the Cold War, the European continent was a taboo area of intervention for the UN (the United Nations Force in Cyprus being a limited exception in this respect). Thus, the operation in Bosnia illustrated the changes which had occurred with the end of the bipolar world order; but it also showed the limits of those changes. The appearance of 'consensus' among members of the Security Council, seen in a certain number of other cases, was not present in the Bosnian case. No common position was ever adopted on either the nature of the crisis or the ultimate objective to be assigned to the UN action in Bosnia-Herzegovina. The Westerners, themselves divided by contradictory considerations, had to convince the other Security Council members, foremost amongst them Russia[35] and China (and, to a lesser extent, members of the Non-Aligned group of states). Therefore, throughout the Bosnian crisis the Security Council played an essentially reactive role. Concern to resolve the conflict and put an end to the atrocities was far from being the primary consideration, and it brought about varying analyses of the situation, making several governments very reticent about seeing the UN intervene even on the strictly humanitarian level.

Here, the Somalia case presented a major difference from that of Bosnia: it was clearly presented as a situation where the state had collapsed, leaving the field free to those who were described as 'bandits and looters, respecting neither law nor religion'. The use of force against such activities was comparable to an international police action, much more than to a military intervention. Somalia, presented as an exception, was not supposed to cause panic among countries holding fast to the sacrosanct principle of sovereignty; the Chinese government, which abstained on the Iraq question and showed reserves over Bosnia, was able to back the resolutions on Somalia without too many reservations. The aim in Somalia was supposed to be to preserve the international order. An obvious parallel exists here with the case of Haiti. In Haiti, the state was presented as having 'collapsed', but the idea of an 'international crisis'

---

[34] Reports of the United Nations Secretary General, May and June 1992 (S/23900, S/23400, S/24100).

[35] It was over Bosnia that Russia used its veto for the second time since the end of the Cold War, on 2 December 1994, to oppose a draft resolution concerning transport of products between the Federal Republic of Yugoslavia and Bosnia. The preceding Russian veto had occurred on May 11, 1993, over a minor question of financing of the United Nations Force in Cyprus; it had then been interpreted as a warning. From 1945 to 1988 the USSR had used its veto 114 times.

underwent an unprecedented extension: there was no civil war, and it was a long way from being equivalent to the humanitarian situations that lay behind the Council's decisions on Somalia and Bosnia. The opposition that arose due to the broadening of the Security Council's security agenda was very visible. Therefore, the decisions over Haiti were the result of lowest common denominator compromises. In particular, the United States, the party most concerned, on several occasions had to perform a real balancing act to avoid a Chinese veto.

To understand this situation it is useful to recall the debates that had already taken place on Haiti before the 1991 coup d'état, at the time when, in the previous year, the first democratic elections in the country were being organised. In June 1990, the provisional President of Haiti, Ertha Pascale Trouillot (appointed after the departure of General Avril), sent the Secretary General an official request for help with the electoral process. The request was first submitted to the Security Council, but under pressure from China and the Non-Aligned states, the question was referred to the General Assembly without the Council holding a meeting on the subject. It was the Assembly that gave the Secretary General a mandate to respond favourably to the Haitian government's request, though not without a heated debate before the adoption of the resolution.[36] After the first round of elections, on December 16, 1990 the majority of the ONU-VEH civil and military teams left. Their withdrawal continued despite the warning shot, an attempted coup d'état by Roger Lafontant on January 7, 1991. On February 7, 1991 (the day when the newly elected President took office) the last UN civilians left Haitian soil. For most member states the concern was, first of all, that there should not be too much or too prolonged "interference" in affairs which were still considered to be domestic.[37] It was only after the coup d'état of September 30, 1991 that for the first time the Haiti question was formally put on the agenda of the Security Council. However, for reasons closely related to those that had prevailed in 1990, it was once again passed on to the General Assembly. For two years, it mostly confined itself to backing the action of the Organisation of American States. Various resolutions adopted between 1991 and 1993 on human rights remained symbolic. The only concrete contribution was made with Resolution A/RES/47/20/B, adopted on April 20, 1993, which authorised the UN's participation in MICIVIH (the International

---

[36] A/RES/45/2 of October 10, 1990, creating ONUVEH (United Nations Observer Group for the Verification of the Elections in Haiti).

[37] In the 'Blue Book' on Haiti, the Secretary General's office admitted publicly, in 1996: 'Avec le recul, on peut regretter ce départ immédiat. Le maintien d'une présence internationale, même réduite, aurait peut-être calmé le jeu et changé le cours des choses.' cf. Nations Unies, *Les Nations Unies et Haïti: 1990–1996*, Série Livres Bleus des Nations Unies, vol. XI, New York, UNDPI, 1996, p. 18.

Civilian Mission in Haiti) alongside the OAS. Otherwise, the two years period preceding the take over of the Haiti file by the Security Council was one of little activity on the UN's side.[38]

It was not until the summer of 1993 that the Security Council really took charge of the Haiti case, adopting coercive measures of an economic nature, in view of the 'unique and exceptional conditions' of the Haitian situation and the threat that it accordingly represented for international peace and security.[39] The continuation of the prevailing situation in Haiti was presented as constituting a menace for the region, most notably, because of the flood of refugees towards neighbouring states (the same argument justified the UNSC resolution to deploy an international force after Aristide's forced exile at the end of February 2004).[40] The criteria for describing the Haitian question in terms of a threat, were debatable, to say the least; the only element backing that description—the possible 'risks' linked to the flood of 'boat people' from Haiti reaching the coasts of the United States—had largely been dealt with from the moment the American intervention began. At that point Washington had decided that even if their applications for political asylum were accepted, Haitian refugees would no longer be admitted to American soil, but would be temporarily placed in 'security zones'. This argument later disappeared from American official discourse, replaced by defence of democratic values and human rights; as was demonstrated by President Clinton's Speech to the Nation on the eve of the American intervention in Haiti. These contradictions did not fail to be mentioned during numerous debates at the UN on the Haitian question. The description of the crisis and the Security Council's competence in the case were regularly contested, especially by members of the Latin America and Caribbean group of countries. This clearly reveals the confusion of perceptions that now prevail among international decision makers regarding world security problems.

Cloudy perceptions of conflicts

The interpretations that decision makers and analysts make today on security questions differ fundamentally from the image formed during the

[38] Certainly the Secretary General participated more or less actively in the political resolution of the Haitian crisis. First he sent two of his senior officials to take part in the high-level mission sent by the OAS to Haiti from August 18 to 21, 1992; later, following General Assembly Resolution 47/20 of November 24, 1992, he appointed Dante Caputo of Argentina on December 11, 1992 to be a Special Envoy to Haiti, who in January 1993, in addition, became Special Envoy of the OAS Secretary General, replacing the Colombian Ramirez Ocampo.
[39] First resolution adopted on June 16, 1993: S/RES/841 (1993).
[40] S/RES/2004/164, February 29, 2004.

classical wars and decades of bipolar order. The traditional distinctions between intra-state and inter-state, between civil war and international war, often seem of little use now that the internal and external dimensions of conflicts are increasingly entwined. This contributes to their spread and to the overlapping of spaces across which they are structured. Thus, conflicts can be simultaneously local, regional and sometimes even international. The current situation in the Great Lakes region of Africa is a particularly clear illustration. The conflict in Bosnia-Herzegovina, started after the end of the Cold War, had confirmed the obsolescence of our classical interpretations. While analysts disagreed from the outset about its nature, it is probable that—to use the terms in which the question has been most usually put—the Bosnian conflict has been at the same time both a 'civil war' and a 'war of aggression', as the two aspects have been so closely interlocked. The Bosnian case is perhaps the one where the very definition of the conflict—a civil war or an international war?—was the most important issue at stake, both for outsiders and for the protagonists.

Conflicts during the Cold War had already foreshadowed this scenario; they emphasised, *a posteriori*, how much the international context may have distorted our interpretation of conflict dynamics at that time. This was proven by the wars that for decades tore apart countries such as El Salvador, Mozambique and Cambodia. The whole history of Cambodia portrays a continuous overlapping of national, regional and international factors (the latter consisting of repeated invasions). After the end of the French Protectorate, in 1953, the country fell victim again to the effects of neighbouring conflicts, starting with the Vietnam war.[41] The war that ravaged Mozambique from its independence also directly involved neighbouring countries: the former Rhodesia and then South Africa, which backed the guerrilla resistance; Botswana, Malawi and Zimbabwe, which were involved militarily on the ground to protect road and energy links on which they depended for supplies (especially the Beira, Nacala and Limpopo corridors).[42] These wars also led to a considerable flows of both

[41] King Sihanouk, to whom the French handed over power, drew close to China and supported North Vietnam against the United States. This was the political alignment behind the coup d'état of March 18, 1970 by General Lon Nol (backed by South Vietnam and the United States) in the struggle against the Communists. With the aid of the Vietnamese Communists, the Khmers Rouges launched an offensive against Lon Nol, leading to massive intervention by the American air force in May–June 1970. American raids on Cambodia continued until August 1, 1973. In 1975 a Communist offensive drove Lon Nol out and the Khmers Rouges seized power. A pro-Vietnam opposition movement was rapidly established. In 1979 the Vietnamese army invaded Cambodia following repeated incidents in the frontier zones; it withdrew ten years later.

[42] Thus the government of Zimbabwe, from the end of 1982, sent contingents of soldiers, with the agreement of the Mozambican government, to protect those corridors. They

population and arms and to criminal trafficking in their immediate regional environment, as was illustrated by the conflict in El Salvador.

However, in none of these countries can the war be reduced to its East-West or regional dimension. Those dimensions were in fact superimposed on deeper-seated conflicts relating to local political, social and economic issues. In each case, though in varying contexts and forms, the stakes at issue related at the same time to the process of state construction and formation,[43] to relations of the state with society, and to the resulting changes in power relations and distribution of wealth among different social groups. These conflicts are most often articulated around an urban/rural divide on which recurring land disputes are superimposed. Wars are fuelled notably by struggles for control of land and homes (including in urban areas) and natural resources (including water, which is crucial in some countries and as precious as some other goods such as diamonds, gold and oil). These clashes are often exacerbated during the peace process, because of the massive population displacements as well as demographic, economic and social changes induced by the conflicts. This encourages linkage between highly localised conflicts and the more national issues that peace missions have to confront. Such a configuration can be seen in contexts as varied as El Salvador, Cambodia, Somalia and, more recently, Ivory Coast, Liberia, Sierra Leone or the Democratic Republic of Congo.

It is often difficult to imagine the impact of armed conflicts on the structures of societies and their relations with the state. War indeed destroys a country, but still more, it transforms it profoundly, including its social and cultural values. Where massacres on a large scale have taken place, as in Cambodia, Guatemala, Bosnia-Herzegovina, Rwanda and the Democratic Republic of Congo, such crimes and the atrocities that accompanied them (mutilation, rape, destruction of homes or indeed of whole neighbourhoods, etc.) bear enormous individual and collective consequences. As do the long years of 'exile' within the country or in camps on the borders. Studies by anthropologists and psychiatrists have given a glimpse of the unspeakable feeling that any visitor can discern in

---

were steadily drawn into the logic of the conflict, while RENAMO attacks became more dangerous. As for Malawi, its troops took part from 1990 onwards in the protection of the Nacala Corridor.

[43] Jean-François Bayart has borrowed from Bruce Berman and John Lonsdale the heuristic distinction between 'state-building', as a conscious effort at creating an apparatus of control, and 'state-formation' as a historical process whose outcome is a largely unconscious and contradictory process of conflicts, negotiations, and compromises between diverse groups. See Jean-François Bayart, 'L'historicité de l'Etat importé', *Les cahiers du CERI* 15, 1996; Bruce Berman and John Lonsdale, *Unhappy Valley: Conflict in Kenya and Africa*, vol. II: *Violence and Ethnicity*, London: James Currey, Nairobi: Heinemann, Athens: Ohio University Press, 1992.

discussions with local people—the feeling of having been robbed of oneself, thrust out of this world, out of time, out of all humanity. But they have also shown how these societies constantly tried to re-create systems of reference, on the margins of those individuals and institutions which, even in the refugee camps, tried to impose a mode of organisation over them.[44]

With the operations in Somalia (1992–5) and Haiti (1994–2000), the question of the state was posed by outsiders in terms of 'failed states' and 'collapsed states', and there was an interesting reversal of perspective vis-à-vis traditional approaches to security questions: war (or, in the case of Haiti, a 'threat to regional and international peace and security') arose no longer from the strength of states but from their weakness. The situations in Haiti and Somalia presented two complementary facets of the reality embraced by this link between conflict and weakness of the state, and in doing so it emphasised the limitations of analysis conducted in only those terms.[45] In the case of Haiti such analysis fails to see the importance of changes in relations between society and the state. In the case of Somalia—often bracketed together, too hastily to say the least, with Haiti—it also skims over, with amazing speed, the history of a state structure, which at best was only barely sketched out. This means that there is a risk of forgetting that in Somalia, too, 'there was a mis-match between a society whose traditional mode of political practice was, according to Lewis, "democratic to the point of anarchy", and the highly centralized, authoritarian, militarized and violent post-colonial state ruled by a tiny, westernized elite class.'[46] This mis-match is the essence of Somali conflict, and explains why the conflict relates both to rebuilding of the political order and to leadership within that order. The twenty years of Siyad Barre's dictatorial regime tended to exacerbate those tensions. Thus, the conflict was based on different dynamics which fed on each other: the decay of a wholly privatised state apparatus, aggravated manipulation of

---

[44] I refer to the work that I co-edited with Simon Chesterman and Albrecht Schnabel, *After Mass Crime: The Challenges of Rebuilding States and Communities Following Mass Violence*, Tokyo/New York: United Nations University Press, forthcoming.

[45] To recall William Zartman's suggested definition of the collapse of a state: 'It refers to a situation where the structure, authority (legitimate power), law, and political order have fallen apart and must be reconstituted in some form, old or new.' An example of uses of this analytical approach can be found in Jean-German Gros, 'Towards a Taxonomy of Failed States in the New World Order: Decaying Somalia, Liberia, Rwanda and Haiti', *Third World Quarterly* 17, September 3, 1996, pp. 455–71.

[46] See M. Doornbos and J. Markakis, 'Society and State in Crisis: What went Wrong in Somalia?', p. 16 in M. A. Mohamed Ali and L. K. Wohlgemut (eds), *Crisis Management and the Politics of Reconciliation in Somalia*, Uppsala: Nordiska Afrikainstitutet, 1994.

clan solidarity, increased opposition between urban and rural dwellers and the struggle for control of land.

Although this approach to understanding the conflict has tended to be minimised in favour of interpretation in 'ethnic' terms, it also applies in part to the outbreak of war in Bosnia-Herzegovina. That war, in fact, belongs in a context of transformation of reality and state legitimacy in the Yugoslav space. It turned out that 'it was in Bosnia-Herzegovina that the chaos of rival state building occurred with the most violence'.[47] The worsening of the economic and social crisis, at a time when the Communist regime was exhausted, played a central role in the break-up of the country and the outbreak of the conflict. Economic, political and social frustrations came to be 'converted' in the 1980s into grievances of an identity-based nature, in which religious allegiance was given new importance. This 'nationalist conversion' of frustrations of another nature followed a line of continuity from the Communists' own relations—ambiguous ones, to say the least—with community sentiment, and from certain common political practices in Socialist Yugoslavia. The absence of political choice was partially compensated by the possibility of choosing one's nationality in censuses, which also had an impact, because it acted as a way of denouncing the inequalities between old and new elites, among regions and between rural and urban zones. Indeed many disparities were aggravated by the modernising project of the League of Yugoslav Communists.

All those frustrations were to be used by the nationalist parties in an effort to destroy systematically everything in the fabric of society that could counterbalance community-based logic. The identity-based register—at the heart of a conflict whose violence was related first and foremost to 'ethnic cleansing'[48]—was used by politico-military entrepreneurs for these precise purposes. They exacerbated pre-existing identifications, promoting a logic of separation and fear that the organised massacres and the brutalities that accompanied them were aimed at reinforcing. There have been numerous conflicts, especially in Asia and Africa, where such a strategy has been applied by political actors. The various sorts of manipulation involved in exacerbating communities' fears of each other for political purposes may be fraught with consequences. They contribute to

---

[47] Cf. Xavier Bougarel, 'Bosnie-Herzégovine: disparition or recomposition?' p. 49 in Jacques Rupnik (ed.), *Les Balkans. Paysage après la bataille*, Brussels: Complexe, 1996. See also Susan L. Woodward, *Balkan Tragedy: Chaos and Dissolution after the Cold War*, Washington, DC: Brookings Institution Press, 1995, pp. 21–145.

[48] The detailed figures for the victims, and the reports published particularly by UN experts (including those by Tadeusz Mazowiecki and Cherif Bassiouni) indicate clearly that the primary aim was the forced displacement of the people in order to ensure the ethnic homogeneity of the territory under the control of each group.

redefinition of lines of partition between 'us' and 'them'. The identity of the 'Other', and one's own, may then be reconstructed on the basis of any religious, 'ethnic', clan, geographical, linguistic or other criteria, denying the plural and dynamic character of registers of belonging that every individual normally experiments. Exercises in rewriting of history or genealogical charts have almost no limits.[49] However, situations as varied as Cambodia, Bosnia-Herzegovina and Rwanda have shown that even in such circumstances, it is not simply the inter-ethnic (or inter-communal) tie that is in question in the dynamics of conflict. Relations between generations, between sexes, between social groups, between urban and rural dwellers, between farmers and nomads are also in question.

Therefore, the issues at stake in contemporary conflicts are no longer so well defined and clear as classical analyses suggested. The military and territorial aspects are still present, but they can be secondary. The development of situations on the ground depend more on complex and changing political configurations among and within the 'camps' involved. The search for international recognition, while it tales various forms, tends to become a central concern in this context: the wars became wars of legitimacy as well. The belligerents, divided among the origins of the conflict, seek to impose on the outside world an interpretation of the conflict that would favour their position and—they think—lead intervening forces to adopt a certain attitude. Whether it is a matter of defining the conflict or the political, social and economic issues at stake, or of building one's own status or even one's own identity in war and peace, local actors try to play on several registers at the same time.

The naming game: how the 'international community' qualifies a crisis

Logics of internal implosion have been increasingly considered to constitute new risks for 'regional and international peace and security'. The principle of state sovereignty can be bypassed when a collapsed state no longer plays its role towards its people. However, the resistance provoked by this broadening of the Security Council's agenda is very noticeable. This has been very clear in the cases of East Timor and Kosovo, while the observer can easily think of many situations where, although the local authority was at the least failing in its duty to defend its people, nothing was done to put an end to massive, systematic violations of human rights. The new international security equation is far from being applied uni-

[49] See Denis-Constant Martin (ed.), *Cartes d'identité. Comment dit-on 'nous' en politique* , Paris: Presses de la FNSP, 1994.

formly. This explains why putting the crises on the agenda and defining their character became major international issues, as has been illustrated by UN Security Council debates.

The permanent members play a decisive role in this process. In fact the Council—to which the UN Charter assigns the main responsibility in maintaining international peace and security—has a twofold discretionary power: first of all, in qualifying the situations referred to it, that is, determining whether they constitute 'any threat to the peace, breach of the peace, or act of aggression', as mentioned in Article 39 of the Charter; and then deciding what action to take. The examination of crises since the late 1980s has brought out the extent of this power as well as the *de facto* broadening of the Council's agenda. In practice, any crisis is declared a threat to international or regional peace if the Security Council calls it so, for reasons relating more to the interests of member states than to an actual analysis of the nature of the situation itself. Certainly debates are regularly confused by the presence of moral discourse and references. Questions relating to human rights, for example, or more recently protection against international terrorism, are mixed with much more classical issues of power. In addition, Cold War era practices often remain highly topical (especially when one considers the importance still attached to the idea of a sphere of influence). Criteria are in practice employed, even if not admitted, to decide where humanitarian empathy will or will not be applied. Such practice is barely related directly to the seriousness of the crisis concerned and the magnitude of the human tragedies. And that is indeed where the illusion lies. While a universalistic discourse proclaims worldwide security, international commitment appears very selective, governed by criteria that are often not admitted. Furthermore, the debates in the Council, far from showing the existence of common values, bring out not only profound contradictions among states but also great volatility in positions adopted between one crisis and another. Moreover, as was illustrated by the multiple Security Council resolutions on Bosnia-Herzegovina, these contradictions exist even between one stage in a crisis and another. Agreements, for lack of consensus, are often reached on the basis of a lowest common denominator. Lastly, what is at stake in most of the debates is much less the type of response that needs to be made to a concrete situation, as the sharing of power among member states: within the Security Council and between that body and the General Assembly—at whose expense the Council has extended its field of competence *de facto*[50]—

[50] The issues at stake in such discussions can be better understood when one recalls that any reform of the Council (which could lead, in particular, to its enlargement) has been blocked for many years. But it goes beyond a conflict between the Security Council and

and also, increasingly, between the UN and other bodies, especially regional ones.

All this shapes the vision peacekeepers have of a given situation on arrival in a country. Their vision can turn out to be fairly far removed from the structures of situations and conflicts which in fact they will have to deal with on a daily basis, and the behaviour of the parties they have contact with. However, the disconnection is not absolute; there are echoes, often distant but real, because war entrepreneurs themselves often play on what they perceive to be differences in position between one foreign policy and another, between one negotiating partner and another. Understanding this intermingling is generally complicated by the fact that the analysts themselves are often giving divergent definitions of a conflict. This difficulty is rarely admitted, and yet it is revealing in more ways than one. It recalls not only the limitations of our work as analysts but also, and above all, that the conflicts under consideration have many facets. It is rarely possible to confine them within uni-dimensional definitions or categories. The differing accounts of the conflicts given by protagonists, diplomats and analysts, are permanently subjected to new, and sometimes contradictory, changing representations and imaginaries.[51] A member of a peace mission does not have to choose among these representations but rather understand how they are articulated. This effort at moving out of one's self, for which peacekeepers are entirely unprepared, is none the less indispensable if there is a wish to understand how, in the host society, the people with whom they will be in contact, are likely to behave towards them, and why. In the initial phase this depends on the way peacekeepers move into the space where the war-peace transition is to be played out.

LOCAL GEOGRAPHY OF UN PEACE OPERATIONS

The geography of peace operations carried out by the UN today no longer has anything in common with the patterns of classical missions. Where they exist, front lines no longer have much meaning. As in peace, war is played out in the heart of the socio-political space, physically and symbolically: in seats of power as in the narrow streets of a shantytown or on roads in the middle of nowhere. Hence, the number of staff deployed, their geographical distribution and the modalities of their deployment, to some

---

the General Assembly, as has been shown by debates e.g. within the UN Commission and Sub-Commission on Human Rights.

[51] See Jan Nederveen Pieterse, 'Sociology of Humanitarian Intervention', *International Political Science Review* 18, January 1, 1977, p. 77.

extent influence what takes place in the interaction between peace operations and local people.

To understand the influence of deployment it must be noted that the
actual numbers employed by operations (all categories included) vary
considerably. These variations occur not only in the course of missions,
but also from one mission to another: 20–30,000 people for the most
extensive, at the height of their deployment (as in Cambodia, Somalia and
Bosnia-Herzegovina), 6–7,000 for medium-scale operations (as in Haiti
or Mozambique). These figures need to be considered alongside additional information regarding, in particular, the physical and human geography of the countries concerned. With comparable numbers of staff, the
UN mission in Mozambique had to cover a territory thirty times greater
than in Haiti, and a much larger population. In addition, depending on
whether staff members are deployed over the whole of a territory or not,
harmoniously or not, specifically along communication routes or in key
regions, they will have more or less numerous opportunities for interaction, with varying categories of local actors.[52]

Very partial deployments

Most often deployment is very partial, but reinforced by patrolling teams
in the provinces. In Cambodia, UNTAC teams responsible for supervision
over the country's civil administration were based in Phnom Penh and in
the provincial capitals. A mobile team was put in place during the mission, but as they were not able to be everywhere at once, surprise operations could only be carried out with difficulty. Most often, the drawers
had been cleaned out before the unit arrived. Only relatively late in the
course of the mission was it possible to mount 'lightning raid' operations.
In Haiti, at the time of the March 1995 handover by the United States-led
Multinational Force to UNMIH, the two main places of deployment of the
United Nations military contingents were Port-au-Prince, the capital, and
Cap-Haïtien, the main city in the north. A smaller contingent was deployed in two other cities (Gonaïves in the west-central part of the country
and Jacmel in the south). This was based on the Multilateral Force's
arrangements to concentrate almost exclusively on Port-au-Prince and
Cap-Haitien; only Special Forces were present in the rest of the country,
with patrols and dispatch of reinforcements by helicopter at hand when
needed. UNMIH reformed its deployment to achieve better distribution
across the country. In particular, police teams established offices in every
regional capital, with military contingents joining them. Essentially, the

[52] See the maps on which these various modalities of deployment are represented.

role of military contingents consisted of patrols to mark the UN presence; this was the traditional policy of 'showing the flag'. But a shortage of numbers meant that patrolling would be limited to vehicles passing along only the major roads. At the beginning of the operation, more than a third of the staff members were concentrated in the capital and its metropolitan area; that proportion increased sharply later on. In the spring of 1996, all the military personnel were based in Port-au-Prince, where they composed a rapid reaction force.

Some missions have been deployed predominantly along certain access routes and in frontier districts, according to a pattern very similar to classical missions. In Mozambique, infantry battalions were deployed, from September 1992 onwards, at three points—Maputo, Beira and Nampula—and along the four transport corridors that cross the country and link it to its neighbours. The absolute priority then was security for those axes, to permit the rapid departure of foreign troops from the country in accordance with the peace accords.[53] This form of deployment continued to characterise the UN operation. Only from the spring of 1994 onwards was the military presence extended, especially in Zambezia Province, the most populous in the country but one not traversed by any of the main transport corridors.[54] The failure to 'show the flag' in that province had been criticised by a number of observers. As the elections approached, the question of the 'visibility' of ONUMOZ' presence and of a wider deployment was raised by the Security Council, but the end of the operation was already drawing near.[55]

The material conditions prevailing in a country must also be taken into consideration. A country covering just a small area can have a highly degraded infrastructure, especially away from the main roads. For example, from the outside one might consider that in countries as small as Haiti and El Salvador, 'even from the most remote parts of the country, people can catch a bus and come to the capital to see the people of the mission',[56] but one needs to experience this first hand to understand what a real expedition this is. In fact, it is not usually one bus but several buses followed by a lorry, before finally finishing the voyage on foot. The case was parti-

---

[53] They were troops from Zimbabwe and Malawi, deployed with the agreement of the Mozambique government to ensure the security of those communication routes vital for these countries, and gradually drawn into the conflict.

[54] A Bangladeshi company was deployed at Quelimane, followed by a Brazilian company at Mocuba.

[55] Cf. Report of the Security Council mission to Mozambique from 7 to 12 August 1994, para. 60 (S/1994/1009, August 29, 1994) and Statement by the President of the Council on September 7, 1994 (S/PRST/1994/51).

[56] Interviews at the UN Secretariat General and with senior officials of international NGOs (New York, January 1995).

cularly difficult in El Salvador, where some departments had no permanent office or team but were covered by another provincial office.[57]

Travel conditions can be just as difficult for the international staff. It is possible for a team in one region to travel, by day, to a neighbouring local government area. But in doing so the team simply 'passes' by adjacent areas. The difference between 'passing by' and 'staying' is much more than a difference of words, especially when one is in an unfamiliar environment. In many countries, however small they may be, the majority of the population has not had any direct experience with the peace operation. At best they may have seen soldiers or a car passing by once or twice, or more rarely, actually stopping. There is no lack of testimony about entire zones where inhabitants have said they 'have never seen' peacekeepers or indeed think they have left the country well before the actual date of withdrawal. Even in a country like Cambodia where the deployment was massive and more harmonious than in most of the other cases, it was sometimes means of transport or security conditions that considerably limited movement by teams within the regions. At best, most Cambodians had two contacts with UNTAC: at the time of registering to vote, and when voting. So opportunities for encounters have often been very limited.

Variations according to categories of staff

In addition, opportunities for interaction with local populations varies according to whether deployed staff are military personnel, civpols or civilians. Even outside of the duties that go along with their positions staff members have varying degrees of contact with people in the country. Military and police personnel are the most 'identifiable', though not always easily discernible, for the general population. They are in uniform, and wear a blue beret or helmet. The civilians, on the other hand, except when elections take place, generally do not wear any distinctive sign apart from an identification card that not all of them wear visibly. When away from their white vehicles with the more or less recognisable painted-on name of their mission, they can very easily pass for members of NGOs or any other organisation. In addition, the civilians generally move around in much smaller groups, most often in pairs. Lastly, the civilians, who make up a minority in UN peace missions, are also those who are most likely to have the least contact with local actors. They can be divided into three groups: the first covers the immediate entourage of the heads of missions,

[57] In addition, a public opinion survey carried out by a Salvadorian institute, at the end of 1991, indicated that 77.1 per cent of the people questioned did not know where the nearest ONUSAL office was. See IUDOP public opinion survey carried out from October 12 to November 2, 1991: results published in *Proceso* 498, December 11, 1991.

the second (also small in numbers) the officials deployed on the ground for civilian tasks, the third (the great majority) the staff posted to offices of the mission in the capital. Among the international civilian staff, there is an average ratio of one professional to 2.5 general service or field service staff. For most of those employees, the main places and opportunities for interaction come from their journeys between their residences and the mission office, the hotels, restaurants and shops that they frequent, and from the fact that they recruit local staff, particularly for their domestic needs.

There are also differences between military and police personnel. An initial distinction must be made among the military: between military contingents and the military observers (milobs) armed with one side arm for 'self-defence'. The milobs (who are not present in all operations) are found notably in military cantonment zones where some of the belligerent forces are disarmed and then demobilised. These represent the main occasions for interaction with local actors, but are one-time occasions. From their side the military contingents are generally the most numerous and the most visible. They are the ones people see 'passing by' in convoys. Their main function is generally to ensure a visible deterrent presence. Occasions for contact can be nil or, in contrast, very numerous according to the context, to the places they are deployed (such as in safe areas or along humanitarian corridors, as in Bosnia), and to the additional activities that they may develop (small-scale quick impact projects). However, in daily life the military contingents can also be those most cut off from the people as they stay in camps established outside the cities and live off their own food rations. It is also known for commanders of contingents to forbid their men to 'frequent with the people'. For their part, civpols live in the town, either in hotels or private houses that they rent close to their offices. As well, they go shopping in stores and go to restaurants, and so on. However, their presence is very small in comparison to other mission staff, and in most cases much more discreet. While soldiers may go on foot patrols, police, who are not armed, rarely do so. For the local actors likely to make contact with them this distinction is important. Therefore, occasions for interaction are conditioned by highly diverse parameters relating both to the functions and to the daily lives of members of peace operations.

Finally, there are simple realities that sometimes need to be recalled. Possibilities of contact and possibilities of communication are two distinct matters. In Cambodia, the average was one interpreter per district (two at the most if twofold translation into French and English was necessary). Therefore, even if they could move around more readily, teams were often left without any available interpreter and therefore could not always communicate with the population. Which means that, for local people, they were only 'passers-by'.[58] Within UNTAC, the situation of the United Nations Volunteers (UNV) is often cited in analyses as a unique case insofar as they were the only ones to have taken lessons in the Khmer language and culture before their posting to the provinces. But the real effectiveness of that experience has rarely been evaluated.[59] The diagnosis made by former volunteers questioned during research was categorical: 'We did not learn much and we were unable to manage without interpreters.'[60] The same diagnosis was made by former members of MICIVIH who took lessons in Creole before their deployment to the Haitian provinces. However, the experiment was not extended to the UNMIH military and civpols, the majority of who, in 1995, did not speak French, much less Creole. Moreover in Haiti few interpreters were employed by the UN, at least by comparison with the multilateral force, which in addition included Creole speaking American soldiers of Haitian origin. Even though definite progress has been made by most peacekeepers in mastery of English, the principal if not the only working language within the missions, the operations' budgets are generally already insufficient to pay for the interpreters needed for communication among the mission members themselves. The problems are particularly acute for civpols, who are supposed to be with the local police for training, on the ground.

Some methods of deployment may reinforce divisions

Consequently, the ways in which physical space is occupied are not neutral. Some options, without sufficient analysis, may even reinforce local logics of conflict. The town/country division which has appeared very strong in almost all the operations often exacerbates a central imbalance in the very dynamic of the conflict, as in the Sierra Leonean conflict and, to a smaller extent, in Ivory Coast and Haiti. This was seen very clearly in Somalia. In the latter country the struggle for control of immediate economic resources—humanitarian aid—from the end of 1992 was superimposed on a twofold battle between commercial elites and for

[58] Interviews with former UNTAC members including former United Nations Volunteers (Phnom Penh, November-December 1995).

[59] Except, notably, by the programme itself, which considered that the results achieved by that organisation were very meagre. See Giles Whitcomb and Kanni Wignajara, *Collaboration between UNTAC and United Nations Volunteers: Evaluation*, Geneva: UNV/ UNDP, 1994, pp. 7, 13, 22.

[60] This statement, made by Vijah Singh, former District Electoral Officer, in Preah Vihear Province, was very close to those made by all his former colleagues I met (Phnom Penh, November 28, 1995).

the control of land. Now, the deployment of troops being largely centred on the towns—in particular Mogadishu, which itself was divided in two—was not neutral in respect to these divisions. Moreover the military deployment remained limited to about a third of Somalia's territory, excluding Somaliland altogether, and was carried out in ways varying considerably from one phase to another.

In the majority of peace operations, the fact that the suburban zones are almost entirely free from any international presence similarly has many consequences. It is particularly striking in the capital cities where the missions' attention is essentially centred on discussions at the level of the political and military elites. As the inhabitants of the popular districts put it, 'They stay in the higher spheres', 'They do not lower themselves to visit us or even receive us.' In addition, the division of labour between the team at the mission headquarters and the 'regional' team in charge of the capital zone is often uncertain so, at the end of the day, nobody takes care of entering into contact with this component of the local society. Moreover, the suburban districts where the majority of the inhabitants of the cities live, and where they are more or less organised on a community basis varying according to country, are often an enigma for members of peace operations who, albeit with some exceptions, refuse to venture there. When they do so, they remain in the main streets, while the real life of those districts begins in the side streets and alleyways where one has to venture forth on foot and do work closely resembling that of community police or any social worker. As a result the inhabitants of poor districts and shanty towns often see peacekeepers only when they are called in to carry out punitive operations against local gangs. These are clearly unpropitious occasions for a first encounter. Because of all these different factors, too little interest is shown in the community actors produced by the urban environment. In some countries—as in East Timor and in Afghanistan where the UN mission, strictly limited in scope, is also geographically restricted—whole regions, and hence wide segments of the population, have been increasingly marginalised. Such situations are generally exploited immediately by local warlords and may affect adversely the capacity of the future state to govern itself.

In other contexts, as in Sudan and Bosnia-Herzegovina, the definition of safe areas and 'humanitarian corridors' helps to produce not only a new geography of humanitarian action but also new dynamics of conflict. When aid is distributed from the capital, generally a substantial portion of it is grabbed, worsening the imbalance in relation to the rest of the country and possibly creating consequences for the dynamics of the conflict itself. When the UNPROFOR mandate was extended to Bosnia-Herzegovina in June 1992, the operation was concentrated around Sarajevo airport and the access routes for humanitarian aid. In 1994, redeployment was made around the Bosnian capital, opening up 'blue routes' between Sarajevo and central Bosnia. The definition of 'safe areas' may also play a similar role to that of the refugee camps in other crises. In Bosnia again, from May 1993 on, while humanitarian aid was being sent on a massive scale, the creation of six 'safe areas' (Sarajevo, Tuzla, Bihac, Gorazde, Srebrenica and Zepa) probably had a more substantial influence on the dynamics of the war than on the protection of the civilian population.[61] Some observers have argued that the deployment of UNPROFOR—responsible for protecting distribution of aid—and the creation of an air exclusion zone in fact halted Serb military superiority and made it possible for the Muslim community to survive the first two years of war and isolation in enclaves. In addition, even beyond the logics of diversion (such looting estimated between 30 and 50 per cent, varying at different points in the conflict) and the infiltration of humanitarian convoys to provide supplies of food, clothing and even weapons for the troops, the blockades and sieges of towns and villages became sources of large profits for some actors. The mere establishment of transport corridors for delivery of aid, and humanitarian corridors for movement of people from one place to another, plays an equally important role in the dynamics of a conflict. In regions where winters are severe or rainy seasons formidable, considerable means are required for the laying and maintenance of roads, which provide for the delivery of humanitarian aid but are also used by belligerents, sometimes making it possible for opening new fronts.

While these parameters alone do not entirely determine what happens in the interaction between peacekeepers and local peoples, they still play an important role. In particular, they contribute to the expectations of the various actors concerned and their perceptions of a peace operation, its ultimate aims, and the issues at stake. The missions' objectives, often very broad and vague ones, are in practice related to numerous representations concerned with re-establishment of the international and local order and the rebuilding of a country, even of a state. But these varying elements differ, sometimes considerably, on the part of both the outsiders and the local people they are in contact with. Merely recognising this should lead the UN officials to analyse more deeply the circumstances in which they are to operate as well as the different misunderstandings to which their mere presence may give rise. In practice it also means that more attention should be paid to the mechanisms used when a UN mission moves into the socio-political terrain of a country. It is possible to design very simple and

---

[61] See especially the analysis by Xavier Bougarel, *Bosnie. L'anatomie d'un conflit*, Paris: La Découverte, 1996, pp. 18–19.

concrete tools in order to monitor this deployment on a daily basis, and adjust it according to the main goals assigned to it. In many instances UN missions seem to lack both access to basic interactive electronic tools developed for such basic tasks as mapping, and the basic human knowledge and good direction which would avoid gross errors in their daily interaction with local people. There is no inevitability in the way some missions seem to fall apart very quickly and some societies seem to 'reject' or 'not like' outsiders. At any time there is a possibility to influence the course of events to ensure better conditions for interaction, or at least to manage them. From that point of view the UN peace operations really need more voluntarist and sensible management. The shortcomings observed since the beginning of the 1990s relfect how far thinking about problems of international security too often remains detached from the social, political, economic and fundamental human realities on the ground.

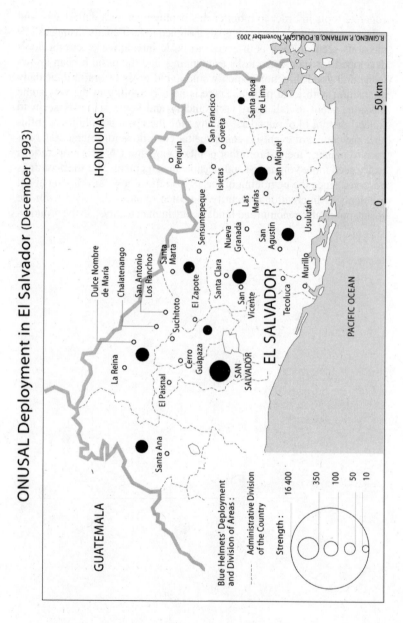

ONUSAL Deployment in El Salvador (December 1993)

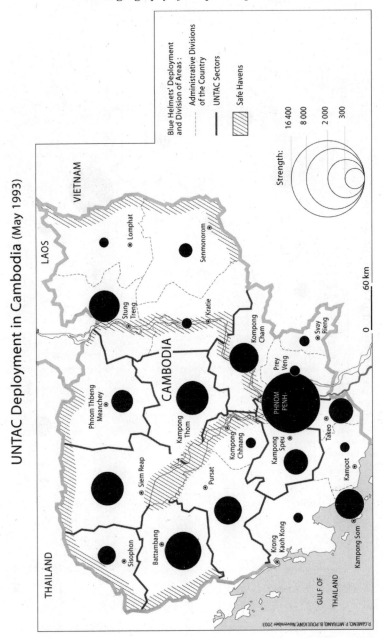

UNTAC Deployment in Cambodia (May 1993)

Blue Helmets' Deployment and Division of Areas :

Administrative Divisions of the Country

UNTAC Sectors

Safe Havens

Strength:
16 400
8 000
2 000
300

VIETNAM

LAOS

THAILAND

CAMBODIA

Lomphat

Senmonorom

Stung Treng

Kratie

Kompong Cham

Svay Rieng

Prey Veng

PHNOM PENH

Phnom Thbeng Meanchey

Kampong Thom

Kompong Chhnang

Kampong Speu

Takeo

Siem Reap

Pursat

Kampot

Sisophon

Battambang

Krong Kaoh Kong

Kampong Som

GULF OF THAILAND

0   60 km

R.GIMENO, P. MITRANO, B. POULIGNY, November 2003

Maps

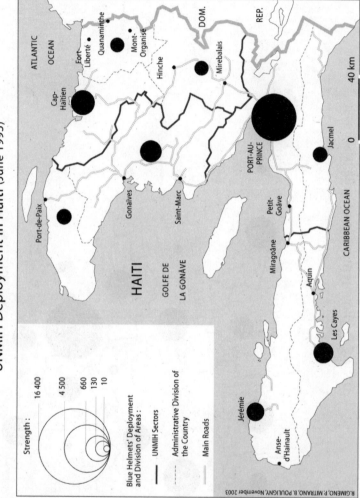

UNMIH Deployment in Haiti (June 1995)

ONUSOM II Deployment in Somalia
(November 1993)

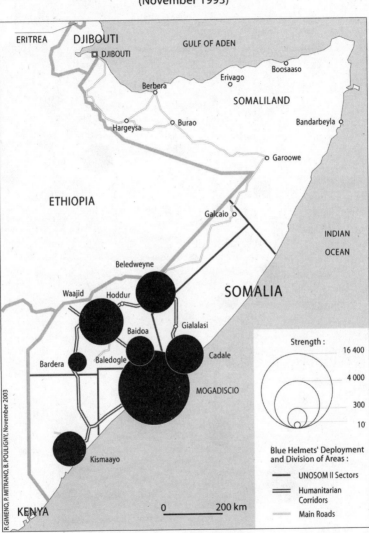

Maps

ONUMOZ Deployment in Mozambique
(October 1994)

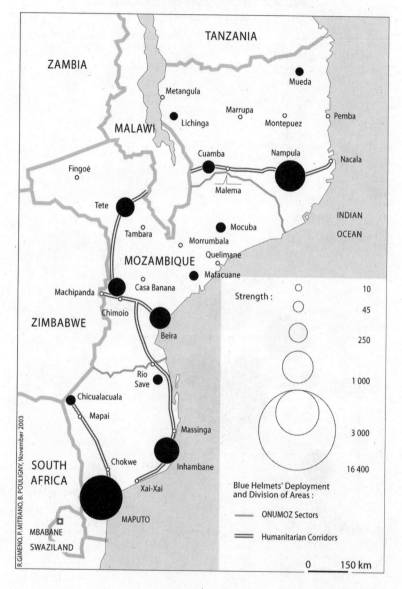

UNPROFOR Deployment in Bosnia-Herzegovina
(March 1995)

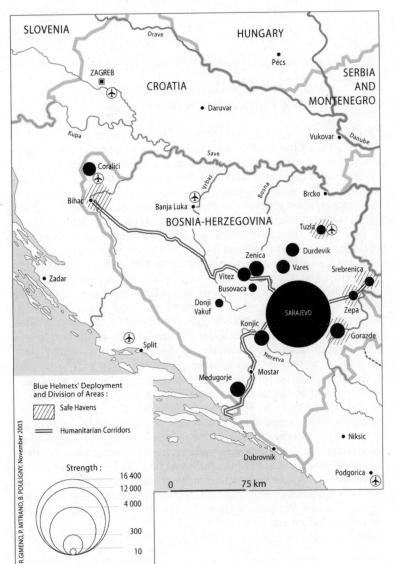

2

THE VARIOUS FACES OF
LOCAL POPULATIONS

April 1995, a rural area of the Balan *commune* in the north of Haiti. UNMIH has just taken over from the multinational force headed by the United States. To compensate for the way previous deployment was confined to the main cities, patrols have been organised in rural areas. The troops must 'show the flag', as the expression goes. Four vehicles and a light armoured car arrive: machine-guns are set up on the bonnets of two of them. There is panic in the village. Some soldiers get down from their vehicles, weapons in hand, and take up position in what they think is the centre of Balan, this conclusion based on the fact a tree of imposing size and a chapel are in the immediate vicinity. Four of them enter the small house adjoining the church, thinking it must be the presbytery, they return shortly after. The man who seems to be the head of the detachment summons a group of villagers who have stayed near the tree to observe the operation. However, as he speaks only broken English and the people he is addressing speak Haitian Creole his requests are made to no avail. Finally, the soldiers get back on their vehicles and leave.

On that day the patrol stopped in several villages. Each time, the lieutenant-colonel at the head of the group tried to find a priest, without success. His instructions were to locate members of the clergy, thought to represent 'base communities'. They were connected to the church and acted as a point of organisation for the rural and urban poor, which in turn were thought to be the only organisations present in rural areas and to be favourable to President Aristide. Failing to find clergy, the group did not speak to anyone, and reported no incident when they returned to their headquarters in the evening. The mission had been accomplished: to 're-assure' Haitians by showing them that UNMIH was there and had the means to protect them.

On their side, the inhabitants of Balan gave their account:

There was a movement of panic at first. Cars and tanks arrived at high speed...and then the soldiers stayed there, without talking to anyone... People were under

42

pressure because when Haitian soldiers stopped here, they acted like that. We were afraid. Then the group entered the presbytery, still without saying anything. We were afraid they had come to look for Father Marcel. And then they left. That was the only contact we had with "those people"... The white Americans who were there before [that was how the inhabitants described the soldiers of the Multinational Force who carried out Operation Restore Democracy], they came here once; but they came with an interpreter. They wore khakis, had no helmets and did not carry heavy weapons like "those people". They came to explain to us what they had come to do and to ask what we needed. And then they left. People were not afraid then... But "those people", what do they want? And all those weapons? If they think they can make the men of FRAPH [a paramilitary group formed after the coup d'état against President Aristide, responsible for considerable violence around the country] afraid with that... Well, if they are not against them, are they against us?[1]

Such a scene could be witnessed in any of the countries where a UN peace operation had been deployed. For the majority of the population the presence of the 'blue helmets' is often no more than big Toyota Land Cruisers and other all-terrain vehicles in white colours, with armoured cars possibly added, waving a blue flag, seen passing along the main roads and, more rarely, stopping. For the members of missions themselves, there is a great temptation to consider that apart from the 'factions' fighting for power, society is in a state of total anomie, filled with fear, 'debased by destitution', 'predisposed to submission', 'incapable of planning and without leaders', as some of them have stated during my investigations. This feeling is perhaps stronger when they venture into the poorer districts of towns. In these huge shanty towns, simple passage of UN men through the area, in San Salvador, Port-au-Prince or Mogadishu, is followed or even taken in charge by people of the community network structuring those areas.

When missions try to identify 'civil society' against a 'failed' state, to play NGOs, intellectuals, women, religious groups or 'elders' against 'warlords', to play 'low politics' against 'high politics', their task is not necessarily easier. At Kismayo, in the south of Somalia, humanitarian organisations and UNOSOM learned, at their expense, that local actors did not develop in entirely separate worlds, that they were linked by many changing ties of solidarity. Similarly, some of the people they had contact with changed hats as individuals, assuming alternately the roles of faction representative, traditional elder and intellectual. Even among politicians, the heads of missions have sometimes had difficulty in finding their way. Though obvious, the divisions brought out by conflicts between government and guerrillas in El Salvador and Mozambique, between 'democrats'

---

[1] Individual and group interviews, Balan (northern Haiti), May 2, 1995 (extracts, translated from Haitian Creole).

and 'putschists' in Haiti, between 'pro-Vietnamese' and 'anti-Vietnamese' in Cambodia, etc.—seem to be constantly called into question, and seemingly 'unnatural' alliances are formed and switched. During the war in Bosnia-Herzegovina changes in the political and social configurations of the conflict, between communities and within communities, were often more critical than the changes in the strict military balance of forces. This was a reality that, on the ground, did not help the 'Blue Helmets' to understand a war in which they appeared to be no more than helpless bystanders. Similarly, negotiations at the centre were not enough when local commanders, at one roadblock after another, claimed to follow orders from nobody but themselves.

If former members of peace missions are asked who were the people they dealt with in the host country some reply that they met 'everyone, from the President to the road-sweeper', others that they had practically no contact with the locals. Both these answers are partly true. In fact, a very broad range of actors are likely to enter into contact with members of peace missions, although in different places, at different moments and in different ways. If one understands the different situations in microsociological terms it makes it possible to distinguish politico-military and economic entrepreneurs from social and community actors. Through this sort of analysis it is possible to discern variations both in the nature of the ties uniting members of the societies in question, in the places and objects of interaction with UN missions, and in the ultimate aims they pursue. Discerning this requires distancing oneself from the many preconceptions made of local societies. The situations in which peace missions are called upon to intervene are generally characterised by a very high degree of fluidity, defying the traditional criteria used to define the status of political and social actors, this status being permanently altered following a large number of logics and issues. From each society there emerge 'worlds' that never seem to come in contact and yet are linked by a multitude of symbolic and material ties. Hence, both analysts and practitioners must understand what separates the various networks and what links them together. Specific attention must also be paid to people employed by the missions locally since they may play a crucial role as intermediaries. Not only are they sometimes the only 'locals' with whom UN staff are in contact, but they are also a concrete interface between them and local people.

THE SPHERE OF POLITICAL, MILITARY AND ECONOMIC ENTREPRENEURS

In traditional peace operations, the blue-helmets were generally confronted with two major 'parties' to a conflict, each having its own political and military branch. Contacts with the political actors were for the civilian negotiators, contacts with members of the opposing armed forces for the military. This division of labour remains partially valid today, but the situation has become considerably blurred. By their very nature—essentially taking place within states—present-day conflicts bring out heightened confusion among military and political actors, as well as economic entrepreneurs. The strategies of all these actors tend to be towards the same objective: securing political and economic profits, or indeed the seat of central power. Where a constituted national army still exists, it has the appearance not of a protector of the nation's territory against external aggression, but of one of the protagonists in an internal war. These situations bring out new difficulties in comparison with the 'classical' interpretation that had formerly been made of conflicts. Now analytical patterns need to be cut across, points of separation moved, angles of observation multiplied, in order to go beyond appearances and understand who the political negotiating partners of UN missions are, and how they are positioned in the local political arena.

A variety of political interpretations

The signing of a peace agreement does not necessarily give peace missions a pacified environment for intervention. It does however create the advantage of immediately identifying the principal partners with whom the UN will negotiate. From this viewpoint, the task seems to be simplified. In the absence of such an agreement, the struggle to impose oneself as 'the main UN interlocutor' becomes more intense, extending down to the most local level. Somalia is a good illustration. On January 27, 1991, as Siyad Barre fled, the race to pick up the pieces of power was started immediately. Two days later, the United Somali Congress (USC), one of the main armed opposition movements against the dictatorship, announced in the name of the Manifesto group—named after the manifesto in which various groups of opponents of the regime called for the dictator's departure in May 1990—the formation of a provisional government with Ali Mahdi Mohammed, of the Abgaal sub-clan of the Hawiye, as President and Omar Arteh Ghalib, of the Isaaq clan, as Prime Minister. As an 'interim government', it tried to establish itself straight away as the United Nations' sole negotiating partner. For opposition groups that had not been consulted, this unilateral announcement was a real betrayal; it precipitated the break-up of the fragile coalition that had fought to overthrow the regime. Two conferences organised in Djibouti in June and July 1991 tried to overcome the crisis, without success. Mohamed Farah Aydid (of the Habir Gedir sub-clan of the Hawiye) formed his own faction within the USC and, in September 1991, established a rival government in the southern part of the capital. Coalitions were formed around the two men who instantly imposed their competing leadership. In the Mogadishu zone, each group based itself on a clan and began to arm; fighting for control of the city began in September 1991. Control of some cities in the south also changed hands successively, while the supporters of Siyad Barre continued to launch attacks. The situation deteriorated very quickly with civil war and drought in the centre and south of the country. Talks were organised in New York in February 1992 under the auspices of the UN, the Arab League, the OAU and the Organisation of the Islamic Conference, in order to try to contain the crisis. An agreement on an immediate cessation of hostilities and maintenance of the cease-fire was reached on March 3, 1992 between Ali Mahdi and Mohamed Aydid. It was followed by talks aimed at securing the two parties' consent to allow the deployment of military observers to supervise observance of the cease-fire.[2]

No group ever gained control of the whole country. According to sources there were between twelve and twenty political groups, more or less organised along clan divisions. It was very difficult to measure their strength and representation. Their ideological positions were vague and their objectives, beyond the capture of power in Mogadishu, were not clear. Above all, the alliances and groupings were highly changeable. It was not certain whether senior UNOSOM officials' knowledge of these various elements was as weak as several analyses suggested; the risks involved in too much polarisation of political negotiations around two strong men of the capital seem to have been clearly identified.[3] But in such situations, for anyone confronted with the difficult task of securing and maintaining an agreement among such a large and diverse number of groups, there is a great temptation to stick to a 'simplifying' set-up—in geographical ways, among others, since UNOSOM's deployment reinforced the polarisation of attention on the capital and the relegation of the northern part of the country to a special position. In the northern part, Somaliland, posed a specific dilemma for the UN. Officially, the 'Somaliland Republic'—which has never been recognised internationally—was treated by the UN as 'a part of Somalia', but deployment across the territory presumed some minimal contact with the local authorities who had opted for independence after the fall of the dictatorship.[4] This contra-

---

[2] The two men sent separate letters conveying this agreement to the United Nations Secretary General on March 27 and 28, 1992.

[3] Internal documents consulted, along with interviews conducted at the UN Secretariat.

[4] The Somali National Movement (SNM), formed in 1981 by representatives of the Isaaq of the north of the country, offered the strongest resistance to the Siyad Barre regime from

diction—all the sharper because the region was to be the calmest—was never to be overcome.

To some extent Somalia foreshadowed situations the UN would encounter later on in Afghanistan and, more recently, in the Democratic Republic of Congo. It represented an extreme of what happened in other areas. Indeed, even dual or seemingly, exceptional polarised configurations have a number of deceptive pretences. The general tendency is towards fragmentation of the local political arena, for a number of reasons. There can be major evolutions within each camp during the peace process. Similarly, political actors identified within each group can pursue partially divergent objectives. The situation in El Salvador is a good example. In that country the conflict was highly polarised. The peace agreements were signed between the Salvadoran government, backed mainly by the ARENA (Alianza Republicana Nacionalista), founded in 1981 as a party for struggle against the guerrilla resistance, and the FMLN (Frente Farabundo Martí de Liberación Nacional), created in 1980, a politico-military structure bringing together the five main components of the guerrilla movement—in December 1992, the FMLN was legalised as a political party. In fact, each group went through major changes within its ranks as well as in relations with its allies.

On the right, was President Alfredo Cristiani, a prosperous businessman, and a symbol of a 'new generation' of the elite trained abroad. He headed ARENA from 1985.[5] Elected president in the first round of voting in 1989, he played a major part in the whole peace process. But the peace option was far from being accepted by everyone within the ranks of his party. While a number of young businessmen took up position on his side, Cristiani was overwhelmed to a wide extent by forces on the far right. He was called a 'traitor' because he held talks with the guerrillas and accepted the presence of ONUSAL in the country. He, and the delegation that accompanied him to the talks, was the target of a press campaign orchestrated by groups close to the army, a part of the business sector and the big landowners. These groups were in fact the historical base of the party, and were thought to have the most to lose in a peace process. When the negotiations approached their conclusion, extremist organisations such as the Cruzada Pro Paz y Trabajo, claiming to be inspired by Major Roberto

---

1988 onwards. Instead of continuing the civil war against a new regime, the leader of the SNM, Abdurahman Ahmed Ali, proclaimed the 'Somaliland Republic' on May 18, 1991; he became its president, at the head of an interim government pending elections held in May 1993. A 140-member central committee—a sort of parliament—of the Republic of Somaliland then elected Mohamed Haji Ibrahim Egal as president.

[5] He was put in that position by the founder of the party, Major d'Aubuisson (who died in 1992), then concerned in improving his party's image.

d'Aubuisson, placed large inserts in the Salvadorian press, denouncing the 'secret negotiations' and 'the ARENA-FMLN alliance'. During the implementation phase of the agreements, senior ONUSAL officials had many opportunities to confirm the 'non-monolithic' character of the ARENA party, while a number of small parties emerged in its immediate ambience.

On the left, similarly, there should be no illusions about the 'bloc' constituted by the FMLN. In reality, the five components of the Front formed two blocs, and divergences between them emerged from the beginning of the peace process. On one side there was the ERP (Expresión Renovadora del Pueblo, previously called the Ejército Revolucionario del Pueblo), headed by Major Joaquín Villalobos. This group represented the FMLN's second military force during the war. It gradually drew closer to the Social Democrats; but that development caused divisions in its ranks. In December 1993, 40 per cent of the militants, disagreeing with that political turn, were expelled from the party. The ERP and the RN (Resistencia Nacional), which had emerged from an earlier breakaway of part of the ERP, proposed dissolution of the FMLN and its transformation along social-democratic lines; they saw themselves as being in the centre of the political spectrum. The other bloc, for its part, portrayed itself as the heir to the historic role of the FMLN; its members considered that the others were guilty of betrayal. On that side were the FPL (Fuerzas Populares de Liberación), the Front's largest armed group, the PCS (Partido Comunista Salvadoreño) and, lastly, the PRTC (Partido Revolucionario de los Trabajadores Centroamericanos), originally established all over Central America. In 1993 they were joined by those expelled from the ERP, who formed the Tendencia Democrática. The split between the two blocs was consummated with the refusal of the ERP and RN to take part in the FMLN convention of December 1994. Sanctions were voted against the leaders of the two movements. During the convention, the FMLN was turned into one single political party; with a new leadership elected in December 1995. The movements originated from the first bloc founded by the PSD (Partido Social Demócrata) in March 1995. Led by Joaquín Villalobos, it included former members of the ERP and RN, as well as a group originating from the MNR (Movimiento Nacional Revolucionario), the historic representative of social democracy in El Salvador.[6] The latter group included former members of the FPL political and diplomatic commission during the war. The PSD gradually drew closer to personalities of the so-called 'moderate' right, such as Alfredo Cristiani, and some Christian Democrats. Together they advocated a centre coalition, which was established by a pact signed at the end of 1995, the San Andrés Pact.

[6] The MNR had been founded in 1965; its former leader, Guillermo Ungo, died in 1991.

All the groups derived from the Salvadorian 'left' constituted a coalition for the 1994 elections: the Convergencia Democrática, whose leader, Rubén Zamora, was the coalition's candidate for the presidency.[7] Thus, major change occurred within the cloudy ensembles of Salvadorian political parties during the peace process. Alignments were strong throughout the first phase and the main political leaders tried to maintain this impression for as long as possible, but it was difficult to cover up conflicts of interest that may have explained important discrepancies in the relations with the UN.

In other circumstances the 'democratic-undemocratic' distinction may be just as oversimplified, as was shown by the case of Haiti. The objective of operation Restore Democracy—the initial multinational phase—identified, in theory, two groups between which all efforts at negotiation had failed: on one side a legitimate President with a majority of the population behind him, along with all those supposed members of the 'democratic camp'; on the other, 'putschists' headed by military officers, the people behind them (essentially certain big multi-millionaire families), and traditional political parties. This binary view made it possible, *a priori*, to simplify the understanding of the situation in which the United Nations mission was intervening, and to reduce it to a configuration comparable to classical cases in which there is a peace agreement.[8] However, when UNMIH entered into action in March 1995, the mission's political leadership had one main partner—President Aristide, who with his immediate entourage was pursuing his own agenda—and a number of political actors who, quite apart from the democrats v. putschists divide (not always as obvious a line to draw as it seemed), were continually dividing among themselves. Even the coalition claiming to follow Aristide, the *Bò tab la* platform,[9] which was formed for 1996 legislative and presidential elections, disintegrated very quickly after the proceedings. Within the coalition the major component, the Oganizasyon Politik Lavalas (OPL),[10] itself

---

[7] The Convergencia Democrática was itself originally a coalition, founded in 1987 by three parties.

[8] UNMIH's initial mandate, in July 1993, followed on from the Governors Island agreement signed by President Aristide and General Cédras; the failure to respect that agreement by the military side contributed to the American choice of the military option. Governors Island accords had fair resemblance to a peace agreement, except that it did not aim to end a civil war. It was that mandate that was revised in 1995.

[9] Literally, 'at the edge of the table'.

[10] It followed from an initiative by people close to Aristide, aimed at providing a structure for the 'Lavalas movement' that had brought the President to power. The movement's name came from the main slogan of the campaign for Aristide's election in 1990: *Titid ak nou se lavalas* ('Titid and we are an avalanche'), incarnated in a 67 per cent vote in his favour and, above all, an unprecedented voter turnout.

a non-structured movement led by a small group of intellectuals, was placed in an ambiguous position by Operation Restore Democracy. Indeed, its leaders had progressively based its strategy on President Aristide not returning.[11] In addition, a majority of the parliament members, elected in 1995 under the banner of the party, themselves quickly came to behave as free riders. René Préval (Aristide's Prime Minister at the time of the coup d'état in September 1991) was chosen as candidate for the succession. He very soon distanced himself from the OPL, as was shown by the increasing tensions in his relations with his Prime Minister, Rosny Smarth, who resigned in July 1997. As for his relations with Aristide, they were the subject of varying assessments, both in the political leadership of the UN mission and at UN headquarters. Was Préval a 'new Aristide' or just a 'puppet' of Aristide?[12] In fact Aristide, retiring from public life, went to work quickly to establish a political and economic network whose declared objective was to prepare for his return in 2001. After the Fondation Aristide pour la Démocratie, in March 1996, he launched the Fanmi Lavalas on November 3 of the same year. In January 1997 the movement was formally registered as a political party and began to recruit candidates. The partial election of April 6, 1997,[13] was marked by the rivalry between the two main factions of the Lavalas movement, as most of the traditional political parties boycotted the vote. In the vote, the Fanmi Lavalas candidates returned in greater numbers in comparison to the OPL's. The OPL demanded cancellation of the first round of parliamentary and local elections, declaring that the voting had been spoiled by rigging, and threatened to boycott the second round. The results of the 1997 elections were not recognised; President Préval played a delaying game, while he had no prime minister (and hence no government). This situation continued until the general elections of December 2000, which were held in even more disputed conditions and prolonged a constitutional crisis that finally nearly degenerated into a civil war and led to the forced exile of President Aristide in March 2004.

Thus, the Lavalas movement, which occupied the essential portion of Haitian political space and whose members were the main negotiating partners for successive UN missions, appeared to be a network of

[11] Interviews, Port-au-Prince, March–April 1995, February–March 1996, and party internal documents consulted.

[12] Interviews in Port-au-Prince (February–March 1996) and at the UN Secretariat (New York, November 1997).

[13] That vote was for one-third of Senate seats, the replacement of two vacant deputies' seats, and the election of 133 urban delegates and members of 564 *commune* section assemblies (ASEC)—a crucial stage in the establishment of territorial institutions provided for in the 1987 Constitution.

complex, shifting relations, often among personalities rather than groups. But its division into two major tendencies was accomplished in 1997.[14] Thereafter the OPL was associated with very odd groups. The Espace de Concertation, formed at the end of January 1999, and then the Convergence Démocratique were surprising alliances among political actors whose labelling as 'democrats' was astounding in view of their past record. However, those politicians had some things in common. They considered themselves personal victims of Aristide, who had ruined their dreams of coming to power at one time in their political careers. In addition, not having any electoral base, they were convinced that the 'international community' could help them to get closer to power without having to go through elections. However, the 'international community' neglected them for a long time. The very special conditions in which the American intervention took place, as well as the formulation of its aims (a return to constitutional order, which was taken to mean almost exclusively the return of the elected President) explain why, until the constitutional crisis that started in June 1997, the 'international community' was greatly polarised on the personality of Aristide. This attitude was partly the consequence of a very clear strategy on the part of Aristide himself—as he aimed to maintain his position as someone who could not be bypassed—but considerably complicated judgments about his effective role, his relations with President Préval, and his control over the various power networks that grew up around him. It also obscured ongoing changes in the way in which Aristide was perceived by the majority of the population.

To a large extent Aristide's game, following his own agenda, independent of any political party or clan, is closely comparable to that of Prince Sihanouk during the Cambodia peace process. On paper Sihanouk represented only one of the four parties signatory to the Paris peace agreements: the FUNCINPEC (Front Uni pour un Cambodge Indépendant, Neutre, Paisible et Coopératif) which was allied to the FNLPK (Front Uni pour la Libération du Peuple Khmer) and the PKD (Parti du Kampuchea Démocratique, the Khmers Rouges' party), against the State of Cambodia, headed by the Parti du Peuple Cambodgien (PPC), considered to be pro-Vietnamese. Prince Norodom Sihanouk had been overthrown by a coup d'état in 1970.[15] He always chose to receive the different party leaders separately and not together. Similarly, he never ceased to pursue his own strategy, as illustrated by his bilateral talks with the head of the ruling Cambodian government, Hun Sen, in France in December 1987

[14] It was symbolised by the OPL's change of name to 'Organisation du Peuple en Lutte', the reference to *Lavalas* disappearing.
[15] He regained the title of King in 1993.

and January 1988, against the opinion of other members of the resistance. In addition, Sihanouk did not spare his allies from his habit of sudden changes in mood and was far from enjoying harmonious relations with the leader of the FUNCINPEC party which he had founded: Norodom Ranariddh, his own son, and Sam Rainsy, another FUNCINPEC leader, whom he suspected of seeking vengeance for his father, killed on Siha- nouk's orders. His relations with the Communist government were equally ambiguous and highly unpredictable. Before the other opposition leaders' returned to Cambodia, he announced an alliance between the State of Cambodia and the FUNCINPEC. In an address to the nation two days after his return to his country, he said notably, that the PPC and FUN- CINPEC 'will probably win a majority of seats in the National Assembly' and 'should form a coalition government'.[16] The other parties to the Paris agreements, which had not been notified beforehand, cried foul. They would soon have many other occasions to complain. The Prince's strategy was clear enough: he was seeking to strengthen the position of a gov- ernment which had publicly shown its intention to back his return to the centre of political life, and had organised his triumphal return to Phnom Penh. Five days later, the PPC published a declaration recognising Siha- nonk as 'head of state since 1960' and declaring Lon Nol's coup d'état in 1970 'illegal'. Caught off guard by this, the other parties had no choice but to follow suit. Barely a week later, Sihanouk's office published an additional statement announcing that Sihanouk had been head of state without a break since 1960. However, the State of Cambodia government was also to feel the effects of Sihanouk's successive changes of front.

Prince Sihanouk constantly played an independent card in his relations with UNTAC. Upon naming himself 'Father of the Nation', *Samdech Ov* ('My Lord Papa'), he was obliged, in order to maintain his position, to remain to some extent above the fray. Thus he did not vote in the general elections of 1993, and let this be clearly known. Similarly, and for various purposes, he used his repeated journeys away from the country as a way of distancing himself from the political game. The fact that the presidency of the Supreme National Council (Conseil National Suprême, CNS) was conferred on him gave blessing to this special position. It should be recalled that the CNS was endowed 'throughout the transitional period, the independence, national sovereignty and unity of Cambodia'.[17] In addition to UNTAC, represented at the highest level, and the ambassadors of the 'Extended P-5' who attended as observers, the CNS comprised

---

[16] Text of speech by Norodom Sihanouk (*Summary of World Broadcasts*, November 19, 1991, FE/1233, B/2–5).
[17] Article 3 of the Paris Agreements.

representatives of the four parties to the peace agreements. As president of the Council, Sihanouk had a *de facto* power of veto. He was also to play on the unclear division of labour between that body and UNTAC.[18]

When there exist continued armed clashes, even on a limited scale, the actors who count and who appear to be the most evident interlocutors for the 'international community' are those who have nuisance power or, to put it plainly, those who have arms and use them to achieve their ends. Political actors who do not simultaneously play on the military stage are most often marginalized in practice, as happened to some political actors in Somalia and some 'citizen' parties in Bosnia-Herzegovina. At the time when the latter country's independence was proclaimed on March 3, 1992, it was led by a collegiate presidency headed by Alija Izetbegovic, appointed after the elections of November 1990. But the Bosnian government was essentially based on the two nationalist parties, Muslim and Croat: the Democratic Action Party (SDA) and the Croat Democratic Union (HDZ), which shared power temporarily during the year 1992.[19] The Serb Democratic Party (SDS), the third ranked party in the 1990 elections, had already withdrawn from the joint government; on April 7, 1992, the Serb Republic of Bosnia-Herzegovina was self-proclaimed. The leaders of these three parties were to be the main political negotiating partners for the various international envoys, as for senior UNPROFOR officials. In the following months, they rapidly established control over the entire political space, even eliminating the moderates from their own camps. With the outbreak of the conflict, there was practically no opportunity open for an alternative route, such as that of the so-called 'citizen' parties committed to Bosnia's territorial integrity and its multi-ethnic character. These alternative parties were close to the intellectual movements that organised a peace demonstration in front of the Bosnian parliament building on April 5, 1992 while fighting was starting in the suburbs of Sarajevo: They were recruited from the ranks of ex-Communists and their strength was that of a political machine. But they were to have little space to express themselves and exist in their own form, with a few exceptions, as in Tuzla where the policy of the municipal authority and citizen organisations was able to preserve a relative independence from the Sarajevo government. Even so, few parties succeeded in maintaining their own existence, and none managed to gain real acceptance as a political negotiating partner with the outside world.

---

[18] Sihanouk let it be understood very early on that he would be playing on that situation and on the reality of the control by the United Nations (cf. the address he gave two days after his return to Cambodia).

[19] A parallel alliance was concluded between the Bosnian army and the HVO (Croat Defence Council).

The monopolising of political space by one actor has even greater impact when, as in Kosovo and East Timor, the UN intervenes in territory controlled by a political apparatus that had clandestinely functioned for years. Officers of the Kosovo Liberation Army (UCK) had already taken control of municipal government areas when NATO troops arrived in Pristina. Similarly, in East Timor, the National Council of Timorese Resistance (CNRT), a federation of all the underground networks that had kept the resistance going, rapidly took control of the territory once calm had returned. In both those countries, but in a particularly striking way in East Timor, UN representatives based their support to a great extent on the dominant political forces to exercise authority which, in reality, they themselves possessed only very superficially.[20] In many other situations the way in which peace negotiations are conducted and pursued, once agreements have been signed, most often plays into the hands of dominant actors who seek to monopolise the political space, to the exclusion of all others.

In El Salvador, the peace agreements provided for establishment of a National Commission for the Consolidation of Peace (COPAZ). The COPAZ was to allow 'civil society' to take part in the 'process of change resulting from the negotiations'.[21] In reality the COPAZ that was installed on October 11, 1991 in San Salvador, comprised representatives of the two parties signatory to the agreements—the government and the FMLN— but also the other political parties then represented in the National Assembly, as well as two observers (the Catholic Church, represented by the archdiocese of San Salvador, and ONUSAL). The peace agreements gave it substantial functions of supervision and preparation of the draft legislation proposed in the agreements.[22] However, in practice, discussions proceeded essentially within the restricted confines of a triad of ONUSAL, the government and the FMLN, and COPAZ was confined to a formal and very limited role. The Coadjutor Archbishop of San Salvador confirmed: 'COPAZ was there to discuss the problems, but everything was settled under the table…COPAZ was elbowed aside.'[23] Former senior ONUSAL officials admitted that they did not think 'that everything had been done to allow COPAZ to play its part.'[24] This was even more striking in Mozambique, where there was a government forces-guerrillas configu-

[20] I am grateful to Raphaël Pouyé for on the spot information on those two countries.
[21] New York agreement of September 25, 1991, article 1 (1).
[22] For example, for the establishment of a new police force or the creation of the *Procuraduría para los Derechos Humanos* (local ombudsman)
[23] Interview with Mgr Gregorio Roza Chavez, Coadjutor Archbishop of San Salvador, 1 September 1995.
[24] Interviews in San Salvador, September 14, 1995.

ration very similar to the Salvadorian situation. None of the structures provided for in the peace agreements, or established later, were open to any Mozambican participants other than the two parties.[25] None, for example, involved the sixteen other political parties officially registered at the time of the elections, forming what was sometimes called the 'unarmed opposition'. Neither the two main parties to the conflict—strongly dominated by the personalities of their respective leaders who dealt personally with most decisions, Joaquin Chissano for FRELIMO and Afonso Dhlakama for RENAMO—nor ONUMOZ allowed them the smallest of space.

Even when they try to 'simplify' the task of identifying their negotiating partners, the UN officials are often forced to face certain realities. In practice the local political configurations often present an additional difficulty: apparent divisions are not enough to understand the local situation, or else, are mixed up with other factors. These can be generation-based factors, as those that affected the PPC, the ruling party in Cambodia, and even such a seemingly monolithic group as the Parti du Kampuchea Démocratique (PKD—the Khmers Rouges' party). Specialists studying that movement in particular do not agree about the nature and the exact lines the main divisions ran through.[26] All agree, however, both on the existence of those divergences and on the reality of the pressures reported to be exerted by the 'hard liners' camp during the peace process. This put in a delicate position the two Khmers Rouges representatives on the Supreme National Council: Khieu Samphan[27] and Son Sen—the military leader, relieved of his responsibilities after he (like Ieng Sary) declared himself against the withdrawal of the movement from the peace process. After the definitive decision of the PKD leadership not to take part in the peace process, Khieu Samphan's position in relation to the movement's leadership in Pailin was uncertain. Such was the case even if he remained the principal (if not the sole) representative in dealings with UNTAC and

---

[25] The entire process was placed under the control of an international Supervision and Control Commission (CSC), under the chairmanship of the Special Representative of the Secretary General and comprising of, besides the ambassadors of France, Britain, Portugal, Italy and Germany, representatives of the Mozambican government (the Frente de Libertação de Moçambique) (FRELIMO) and RENAMO (Resistência Nacional Moçambicana). That commission was itself at the head of a series of commissions responsible for implementation of the various aspects of the peace agreement, essentially on military matters.

[26] Interviews with Steve Heder and Christophe Peschoux, and UNTAC analysis unit confidential notes consulted.

[27] A former minister under Sihanouk, considered the most 'presentable', he was the main representative in dealings with UNTAC (it was he, in particular, who signed all correspondence addressed to Yasushi Akashi) and the King.

the King.[28] On several occasions he let it be understood by his negotiating partners that he could not make a commitment on his own and would not necessarily be followed by the leadership. Internal UNTAC documents show very clearly the game Khieu Samphan constantly played with that prospect of a split, and the difficulties on the UN mission's side in assessing what it really amounted to.

In Cambodia, at the time of the peace process, another pattern of analysis had to be recognised: the one distinguishing 'interior Cambodians' from 'expatriate Cambodians', the self given name of those returning from exile. The division did not correspond entirely to the one between PPC members and the resistance. The discrepancy was proven by the solid links between royalists and Communists, who had never left the country, and who could demonstrate such relations to be stronger than their strict political allegiance. That sort of division also proved very significant in East Timor and in Iraq, showing the limits of voluntarist policies for favouring the return of members of the diaspora from exile. Finally, and most importantly, the interpretation of political divisions according to 'factions' needs to be overlaid by another interpretation, according to networks (especially family networks), that best fits with the traditional mode of management of the political sphere in Cambodia. The family order is indeed the archetypal reference of the social and political order. 'Family ties impose obligations... In any case, parties follow the lines of family ties. They are made up of a "patronage network", and people belong to them more because of contacts than out of political conviction.'[29] These networks can also have a territorial base, on the assumption that a person is symbolically related to someone from the same area. Political labels, in these conditions, have a definite relative importance, and changes of alliances can cause surprise if such other references are not borne in mind. In many countries this interpretation in terms of networks—family or lineage networks—in reality often fits the traditional mode of management of the political sphere better, as is also illustrated by the cases of Somalia and Afghanistan, where the social and political spheres are organised according to a highly fluid clan system, clan loyalty being a very elastic resource that can be used and manipulated by skilful political entrepreneurs.

This intermingling of allegiances and loyalties is often difficult to grasp for ordinary civilian or military staff involved in peace operations. It is all

[28] According to various sources of information, it would seem that this decision was taken at the end of May 1992, during a meeting held near the Thailand border.
[29] See François Ponchaud, 'Elections et société khmère', p. 148 in Christian Lechervy and Richard Petris (eds), *Les Cambodgiens face à eux-mêmes? Contributions à la construction de la paix au Cambodge*, Paris: Fondation pour le Progrès de l'Homme, 1993.

the more crucial for them to have some minimal knowledge of these matters because they are in contact with local agents of the political system whose actions will have meaning at the intersection of those various logics. They may be administrative officials of the state (or of what is left of the state structure), elected representatives, or people representing political parties or more or less circumscribed politico-military groups. The UN missions have contacts with certain administrative agents of the state or of parallel para-structures for implementation of precise parts of their mandates; this is particularly the case where missions specifically deal with aspects of human rights and the administration of justice. Teams handling these questions regularly have to deal with judges and prosecutors, as well as officials of the prison administration (with institutional connections varying according to country). Those men and women may have, at their level—often a much localised level (zone, region, department, commune, etc.)—a relative high degree of autonomy, and may play a partly autonomous game. They will, above all, assume positions with regard to their various allegiances between which they will have to choose. Former members of UN missions, who were questioned concerning such matters, testified that the political affiliation of the people concerned was usually not a decisive element for understanding or predicting their behaviour.

Shifting alliances between political and military actors

It is not much easier to pin down military negotiating partners and their relations with political groups. The transition from war to peace leads, almost by definition, to profound changes in interactions between these two groups. To be fully understood these evolutions should be examined with at least some historical knowledge. This is particularly crucial where, as in El Salvador and Mozambique, history has linked the army intimately with the exercise of politics. In El Salvador, the peace negotiations depicted a break from the past. Over fifty years of military rule (1930-79), the army not only acquired a good deal of property (agricultural land, buildings) but also established, especially in the rural areas, a vast system of social control which gave it a substantial rural patronage network. This network was strengthened by the very strong militarization which society underwent during the civil war.[30] Until the 1980s, the Salvadorian Armed

[30] It was at the end of 1931 that the Salvadorian army entered the political scene, in a coup d'état following the first free presidential elections in the country's history. In 1932 peasant revolts were suppressed in a bloody manner; the oligarchy threw itself into the hands of the army. A government party called the Partido Pro Patria was created; it was to dominate the country's politics until the 1980s and mark the predominance of the army

Forces (FAES) posed as the guarantors of the political, economic and social system. From the 1982 elections onwards, under the pressure of their American allies, they left power formally to civilians and concentrated on fighting the war. In 1988–9 the idea began to gain ground that the war could be continued indefinitely. It was no longer advantageous to the oligarchy which controlled the essential portion of national wealth, since it halted any real business development in the country. In November 1989, the murder of six Jesuits by members of an elite battalion led to the abandonment of the army by the US administration, which could no longer defend such methods. The signing of the agreements, in part against the will of the military, was a true 'collective trauma' for the FAES. Once the war was over, it no longer had an 'enemy within' to fight; as for external threats to the country's security, they seemed limited and had much more to do with the American boss.[31] In addition, a number of military personnel, accused of gross human rights violations, felt they had been 'thrown overboard' by the ARENA. During the peace operation, members of the general staff of the FAES were involved in communication with mainly the heads of the military component of ONUSAL. They were very reticent about any dialogue with civilians and felt reassured by being able to deal with military personnel of other countries, especially Latin America.[32]

An altogether similar situation occurred in Mozambique. The relations between the army and the political authority were based on the permanence of the old elites that had led the struggle for independency, and on a sharing of the 'national cake', which to some extent was built into the very history of the FRELIMO party-state: the Makonde elites reigned over military matters, since their community had provided the essential portion of the fighters during the liberation war; the South provided the political cadres and the civil service. Since the regime had emerged from a

---

over political authority. The Partido Revolucionario de Unificación Democrática (PRUD), an attempt at a party-state on the Mexican model, and then the Partido de Conciliación Nacional (PCN), succeeded it in 1949 and 1961; however, neither was ever to succeed in turning into a mass party.

[31] Interviews with Mariano Castro Moran, former military officer, head of the revolutionary junta of 1961; David Escobar Galindo, member of the governing council of the military academy; Knut Walter, academic; and members of the general staff (San Salvador, August–September 1995). Cf. also Philip J. Williams and Knut Walter, *Militarization and Demilitarization in El Salvador's Transition to Democracy*, University of Pittsburgh Press, 1997; Knut Walter, *Las Fuerzas Armadas y el Acuerdo de Paz. La transformación necesaria del ejército salavdoreño*, San Salvador: Fundación Friedrich Ebert, 1997.

[32] Interviews with David Escobar Galindo, members of the general staff and senior United Nations officials (San Salvador, August–September 1995).

war of independence and had always lived in a state of war, the army did not occupy the 'classic' position of an instrument in the hands of the civil power; its weight in the running of the country was great. In addition, the general staff and the officer corps were still dominated by the old guard of armed nationalist liberators or freedom fighters. Therefore, for the Mozambican army, the transition to peace also meant a historic break from the past, a break for which its chiefs were not ready, or about which they argued fiercely at least. This was evident from the firm stance maintained constantly by Alberto Chipando, minister of Defence since 1975, leader of the hard-line faction within the FRELIMO party and considered the guarantor of the institution's interest. His conduct during the peace process indicated that the interests of FRELIMO's military and political leaders partly diverged during this period.

Another effect of peace processes is to sharpen the divergence of interests between leaders and their base. Most of the questions linked to the transformation of the military and the disposal of its members (especially the fate reserved for those responsible for violations of human rights during the war) are still unresolved at the moment when a peace operation is deployed in a country. Consequently, the majority of men under arms think they have much to lose in the process. The case of El Salvador is typical of that situation. During the peace negotiations, the Salvadorian army never really acted as a bloc. This not only forced its representatives to manoeuvre as best they could, but also reinforced the division between its negotiators, senior officers who had received assurances from the US administration, and the others.[33]

For a peace mission, what is essential is generally to ensure a necessary minimum amount of cooperation on the part of the military leaders whose power of obstruction is most serious. But in day-to-day matters the rank and file can present just as many problems to blue helmets, especially in the demobilisation phase and afterwards. In El Salvador as in Mozambique, former guerrilla leaders swapped their military uniforms for civilian clothing and established themselves in the capital where they became 'respected' partners for the UN. By proceeding to transform the guerrilla movement into a political party, they hastened its break-up. But within both the FMLN and RENAMO, middle-ranking officers knew that their political reconversion was not assured. Thus, their preoccupations in the war-peace transition phase were closer to their men's than to their superiors'. In Mozambique, in the regroupment camps, demobilised soldiers did not conceal from UN observers their feeling of having been 'abandoned' by their superiors.[34] Some of them formed an association of

[33] Interviews in San Salvador (September 1995).
[34] Interviews with ONUMOZ milobs (Beira, November 1994).

demobilised soldiers, AMODEG (Associação Moçambicana dos Desmo-
bilizados de Guerra), which also contained a significant amount of majors
and captains from different units.[35] They were behind uprisings and hos-
tage-taking carried out to put pressure on the United Nations mission. In
October 1994, on the eve of the elections, they threatened to disrupt the
democratic process if the UN did not take their future more seriously. The
Association also included demobilised members of the guerrilla force
(RENAMO). As in El Salvador, it was the camp commandants who most
directly felt both their loss of status in relation to the men who had been
under their orders, and the discrepancy between their fate and that of the
better trained high officers, who either left for the capital (to become
members of various commissions, or prepare for the elections) or were
integrated into the new army and sent abroad for training.

Demobilised regular soldiers were not the only ones to try to apply
pressure in this sort of transition, as was shown by the associations of the
demobilised set up in El Salvador.[36] In fact they consisted essentially of
some thousands of former members of the armed forces who were
declared ineligible for reintegration programmes, especially when they
had left the ranks of the FAES before the agreements or had belonged to
local or civil defence patrols not covered by the agreements. From 1994
onwards those associations embarked on violent acts, involving ONU-
SAL on several occasions, although the UN tried to keep its distance. In
Mozambique, the 'irregulars' tried, sometimes by force, to obtain some
economic advantages from the UN, while 'regular' soldiers for their part
were receiving a lump sum on demobilisation. The figure recorded for
implementation of their disarmament—50,000—was probably far below
the real one. In fact 50 per cent of the armed opposition consisted of 'wan-
dering bands' (the *mudjibas*) who lived by war and were not under the
control of RENAMO.[37]

It is generally all the more difficult to evaluate the degree of control by
leaders over the 'margins' of their movements because they may play
readily with that argument, like the RENAMO leaders in Mozambique,
the Khmers Rouges leaders in Cambodia, General Aydid in Somalia or
the Serb and Croat leaders during the war in Bosnia-Herzegovina. This

[35] Originally, the association was set up by men who had belonged to the Presidential
Guard, who revolted on October 3, 1992 on the eve of the signing of the Rome
agreements. The Association grouped demobilised soldiers of the Mozambican Armed
Forces and RENAMO alike. It was estimated to have numbered up to 60,000 members
out of a total of 95,000 soldiers demobilised.
[36] The Asociación de Desmovilizados de la Fuerza Armada (ADAFAES) and the AEGES,
formed shortly afterwards.
[37] See especially Michael Cahen, *Mozambique. La révolution implosée*, Paris: Harmattan,
1987, p. 81.

breaking up of military groups contributes greatly to the instability that characterises the period of transition from war to peace. The large quantity of small arms in circulation increases the nuisance power of militias of all sorts, combining military and economic objectives, while former members of 'regular' armies may turn to banditry, continuing activities pursued during the war.

In the theatre of war itself, increasingly, there is a thin distinction between constituted armies and politico-mafioso militias, arising from organised crime or from more localised logics. In Bosnia-Herzegovina, in 1992, some sources counted seventeen local militias; subsequently some factions disappeared or were incorporated by one of the dominant groups.[38] Fluidity of relations among groups seems to have remained great throughout the conflict. For example, some armed formations were able to associate themselves with either the Bosnian or the Croat army, according to circumstances. Similarly, switching of alliances (especially between Bosnians and Croats) was most often a function of highly localised conditions, as were the rivalries and splits within each of the camps. In fact, although the belligerents pursued diverging political objectives, the pursuit of these could depend, locally, on fluctuating alliances. Apart from the games leaders played on this theme, most analysts consider that there was not complete assurance as to the control of the armies of various paramilitary groups (especially in the case of the Bosnian Serbs), even if the armies had generated them, notably to make up for the effect of desertions. What caused this situation to develop was the characteristics of a two-tier 'generalised military system' in the Yugoslav Republic (the Yugoslav army on the one hand, territorial forces and the police on the other) and, at the same time, the collapse of the system altogether. The assumption of autonomy by the various militias was generally linked to the fact that there was very little resemblance of a front line in the Bosnia-Herzegovina war.[39]

In some countries groups of 'part-time bandits' are made up, especially, of young boys and girls for whom armed struggle has become a means of social ascent, as well as survival. In a number of contemporary wars, they form a whole social group on their own, which needs to be analysed as such. The Mooryan of Mogadishu and the SNM's 'auxiliaries' in northern Somalia[40] were in the image of adolescents in many contemporary con-

---

[38] See Barbara Ekwall-Ubebelhart and Andrei Rakevsy, *Managing Arms in Peace Processes: Croatia and Bosnia-Herzegovina*, Geneva: UNIDIR, Disarmament and Conflict Resolution project, 1996, p. 10.

[39] I am grateful to Natalija Basic, Xavier Bougarel and Véronique Nahoum-Grappe for their precise explanations on this point.

[40] See Gérard Prunier, 'L'anarchie pastorale', *Revue Nouvelle* 85/11, November 1992, p. 18; I. M. Lewis, *Making History in Somalia: Humanitarian Intervention in a Stateless*

flicts: heavy drug takers, sometimes described as robbing and killing as a way of life. From one country to another, it is difficult to assess the degree of control exercised over these groups of young fighters, often cut off from family solidarity, who can 'sell' their services to armed groups according to the circumstances. Their profiles, behaviour and modes of organisation are not far removed from those of the 'child soldiers' in Liberia, Sierra Leone, the DRC and Angola, or even from the gangs organised in the poorer districts of some capital cities, like San Salvador and Port-au-Prince. In such contexts the creation of village or district militias, true self-defence movements, can be a response, initially, to violence from 'below' faced within a state that has constantly marginalized the people. But with more or less forced allegiance and manipulation, networks rapidly become mixed up. While it continues, violence can become an opportunity itself. It creates new values, makes it possible to attain new sorts of status and overturns hierarchies, while more or less controlled disorder can be a cover for some to pursue their own economic interests.

All this has very direct consequences for the blue helmets on the ground. For instance, negotiating with the military leaders may be insufficient when passage for humanitarian convoys needs to be organised. A local commander may authorise passage, but at the next roadblock another commander, though belonging to the same army, may adopt a contrary position. Similarly, negotiating a cease-fire with the main parties to a conflict can be doomed to failure, as happened in Bihac in Bosnia-Herzegovina in the summer of 1994.[41] Allegiances are often essentially individual in nature, and all the more difficult to assess because they can change many times during the conflict.

When, as in Haiti, it is an entire military and paramilitary apparatus that turns to banditry, the situation creates an even greater dilemma for the UN Forces. In fact, in that country, the military and paramilitary personnel were not demobilised and did not return to barracks either; they 'disap-

---

Society, London: LSE/Centre for the Study of Global Governance, 1995, p. 8; Roland Marchal, 'Un espace urbain en guerre. Les *mooryaan* de Mogadiscio', *Cahiers d'études africaines* 33/2, no. 130, 1993, pp. 295–320.

[41] The Croat and Muslim forces of Bosnia had reached agreement on an American proposal to form a federation with confederal links with Zagreb. But it did not take account of the strong man of the zone, Fikret Abdic. When forces of the Bosnian army retook control of the zone, in the summer of 1994, after violent fighting, Abdic called for help from the Serbs of Krajina and decimated Izetbegovic's forces. A rich businessman of the town of Velika Kladusa, Abdic headed *Agrokomer*, the business which was the region's lifeline, and was a typical example of a local leader with a very extensive network of support through patronage.

peared'. On his return to his country on October 15, 1994, President Aristide took a series of measures that resulted in the *de facto* dissolution of the military institution, so that its members were dispersed; it included the former paramilitary corps' members. This elimination of the army by stages was made official by a highly symbolic presidential decision: the offices of the general staff of the armed forces were handed over, on January 25, 1995, to a new ministry, the Secretariat for Women's Affairs. The remaining military personnel—all 'other ranks'—were in part assigned to an interim police force set up on January 6, 1995. The Haitian Senate had approved the separation of the police and the army on November 29, 1994.[42] Thus, one of the main actors that the Multinational Force, headed by the United States, had started to interact with at the time of its deployment disappeared *de facto* soon afterwards.[43] The members of the Force no longer had any counterpart, except for the interim police force which was ill-trained, unarmed, deprived of all means of action, poorly motivated and very mixed in composition. Besides former members of the Armed Forces of Haiti (FADH), who were given summary recycling courses by American and Canadian instructors, the interim police force comprised of former Guantánamo refugees selected by the US, as well as some Haitians trained in Canada. Each group operated with different uniforms, which added to the confusion. That was the situation that UNMIH inherited when it took over. It did not have a very clear vision of who were the 'interim' police, the main counterpart of UN-MIH's civpols. Those police did not want to take risks because they were poorly paid and knew that their future was uncertain.[44] Among President Aristide's entourage people did not want to hear anything about them.[45] After passing tests, a minority of them could receive training and join the new police force; the rest were supposed to be demobilised, but no pro-

[42] That separation had been written into the 1987 Constitution but no law making it effective had followed.

[43] The American administration had chosen to negotiate with the military leaders; that was the mission of the negotiating team headed by ex-President Jimmy Carter, with Senator Sam Nunn and General Colin Powell, which on September 18, 1994 signed an agreement allowing the intervention of US troops to proceed peacefully, with the collaboration of the Haitian military. But the 'collaboration' in practice seemed very variable, and came to a halt very quickly. Haitian soldiers were arrested, their weapons confiscated. The situation began to break down in the senior command of the FADH also. On October 3, 1994, Colonel Michel François fled to the Dominican Republic. The two other leaders of the Troika left in their turn on October 13, into exile organised by the US administration in Panama.

[44] In January and February 1995 the UN was already taking responsibility for seeing that every police officer was well paid.

[45] Interview with Nicole Lannegrace, Political Adviser to Lakhdar Brahimi, Special Representative of the UN Secretary General in Haiti, and private interviews with advisers of President Aristide (Port-au-Prince, April 1995).

visions were made for this. A year had to go by before the first group of new police officers trained by ICITAP assumed duty; they were the ones UN civpols were responsible for guiding and training on the ground. On December 6, 1995 the interim police force was wound up.

For the military component of the mission, the situation was still more difficult. Originally, Security Council Resolution 940 provided for a contribution by UNMIH to the 'professionalising of the army'. But the army vanished from circulation; soldiers and paramilitaries quietly 'evaporated' into thin air. As for the ex-officers of the former FADH who remained in the country or went to the Dominican Republic, they started private security companies and went on with similar business conducted during the coup d'état, especially in league with the drug traffic for which Haiti was a transit point. All this happened while no disarmament programme was carried out. The irony of the recent history in Haiti is that these lines could be applied identically to the circumstances in which a new multilateral force, subsequently headed by the U.S., deployed again in the country after Aristide's forced exile, in early March 2004, almost a decade later.

Economic entrepreneurs

Local situations must also be analysed in terms of political economy. Whether it is for immediate purposes (finding resources, especially for war) or longer-term ones (negotiating reorganisation of a country's economic structures), economic entrepreneurs, when they are not the political and military actors, seem most often to be in a position of alliance or renegotiation with them. Three major types of motivation explain their interaction with peace operations.

First of all, some actors have direct interest in the economic dimension of UN missions' mandates. When the missions follow a peace agreement, they may also take measures to help the economy of the countries where they are intervening, or to contribute to the reconstruction phase. Here, essentially, the peacekeepers appear in an indirect role. The most important resources likely to be diverted—resources coming under humanitarian aid or assistance for a country's reconstruction—belong to the traditional channels of bilateral and multilateral aid. In addition, aid donors often feel little inclination to embark rapidly on programmes that are not part of an emergency phase; unfortunately, when money for reconstruction comes, it often comes much later on. This economic function is more central when a peace operation acts as a transitional administration, as in Kosovo, East Timor or Cambodia. In the latter country UNTAC was to ensure that the country's macroeconomic situation did not deteriorate too quickly and, above all, that state property was not squandered. Thus measures were taken to regulate sales of state property, to avoid drastic increases in the prices of essential products, and to stop the depreciation of the riel, the national currency.[46] While some of these actions directly affected the existing state structures and the PPC, those concerning the distribution of basic foodstuffs such as rice, or even the currency, more directly affected the people who controlled the essential part of trade in Cambodia, namely, members of the Sino-Khmer Diaspora. Linked by close alliances usually sealed by marriages, those traders controlled the essential portion of trade as well as the construction and service sectors, the three major pillars of the non-agricultural economy of the country. But there must be no illusions about the separation of tasks between the political and economic spheres. In fact, in the Khmer socio-political system, economic actors serve as bridges between different clans, thanks to vast networks of patronage that operated as mechanisms of exchange: one group gives the protection, the other the money. In a period of reshaping of the socio-political landscape (the 'peace process' being such a period) it was this system of bridges that was redefined; that explains, on the PPC side and the FUNCINPEC side as well, how divergent economic interests contributed to continual fragmentation of the movements.

In addition, the transition from war to peace brings in a train of economic changes. In El Salvador war had been a lucrative business for some economic actors, with the creation, in particular, of true monopolies. But the conflict also contributed to a change in the country's economic structure. The emergence of a new class of 'modern' entrepreneurs, and above all the privatisation of the banking system, led to a transformation of the economic landscape, and broke the monopoly of the big landowners over all the key sections of the economy, especially credit. The war also encouraged an economic logic in which very quick profits became more attractive than simply growing coffee beans. It was no coincidence that the peace agreement was signed by a President who was also a representative of the new generation of business men. The army explicitly asked the employers' organisations not to take part in the peace negotiations; they took advantage of this later, claiming not to be bound by certain aspects of the agreements, but they knew that the army would no longer defend their interests.[47] These various issues lay behind the talks between ONUSAL

[46] For example, in February and March 1993 UNTAC put rice on the market, with then help of the World Food Programme (WFP), so as to discourage hoarding and bring prices down.

[47] Interviews with Roberto Murray, businessman close to ARENA, founder of the FIS and FUSADES (Fundación Salvadoreña para el Desarrollo Económico y Social); Juan Hector Vidal, Executive Director of ANEP (Asociación Nacional de la Empresa Privada), spearhead of the traditional employers; Ricardo F. Simán, Chairman of the

and the Banco de las Tierras on land transfers. In addition, the peace talks provided for the creation of a Foro de Concertación Económico y Social in which representatives of the private sector would sit alongside trade union representatives. An ONUSAL representative took part in the meetings. After refusing for a long time to take part in the Forum, the employers' organisations did everything to block the discussion of the most sensitive aspects of the reorganisation of the country's economic and social life.[48] It is rare for peace agreements to assign such importance to the economic and social dimensions of a conflict. But the war-peace transition, like the transformation of a political regime (Haiti being an example), always coincides with major rearrangements among the political, economic and military spheres.

This category of actors is also the first to be affected by the economic consequences caused by missions' presence. In practice, immediate spending from expatriates has an economic impact. This first aspect affects private individuals who have houses to rent, restaurants, hotels or car rental agencies. Most often the more privileged sections of the population are those who can take advantage of such assets; they generally control other sectors of the economy as well. At this level, interaction with members of the missions can be fairly limited—it is not uncommon for members of the missions never to have any contact with the owners themselves—and follow an essentially commercial logic. Nevertheless, some economic operators may be very proactive in seeking to divert this flow of money in their direction by any means possible. Such practices are amplified where politico-military entrepreneurs control certain networks of supply indispensable for missions, fuel supply for example. In Bosnia, trafficking in petrol was essentially divided among the various armed groups, according to highly classical logics of rent sharing. The military leaders of the various armed forces occupied key positions within those networks, in terms very similar to what happened in Cambodia (members of the Cambodian state army and the Khmers Rouges being the most concerned in this case). In East Timor, at Dili, petrol supplies were controlled by the former underground branch of the CNRT, the FALINTIL, which creamed off about a third of them for its own profit, while former military personnel allied to the Indonesian army had switched over to cross-border trade from West Timor and sold petrol to the New Zealand battalion based at Cova Lima (Suai).

Cámara de Comercio e Industria de El Salvador, and Pablo Tesak, First Vice-Chairman of the ASI (Asociación Salvadoreña de las Industrias), who played a major role within the Forum (San Salvador, September 1995).
[48] Interviews, and Forum documents consulted.

However, where the structures of the economy have taken more time to adapt to the context of war, politico-military actors who control major economic interests can initially see the arrival of foreign troops as a seriously disturbing event. This was what happened in Somalia in 1992-93, and in Bosnia-Herzegovina during the war. In Mozambique the army was a central economic actor, controlling some trading (especially in petrol) and smuggling networks linked with South Africa. It could sometimes be more as traders than as soldiers that some senior Mozambican military officers reacted badly to the peace operation.

Therefore, United Nations staff must expect to encounter, on the ground, directly or indirectly, a very wide range of actors linked by many variable ties, with multiple meanings. It is important to understand these ties for what they are. When key actors in a conflict or a peace process belong to many networks at the same time, their behaviour needs to be understood in their capacity to move from one network to another, maintaining—sometimes deliberately—confusion as to their real status and, still more, their intentions. These games contribute to the moving of frontiers of the political sphere over time; this makes it necessary to think of every socio-political organisation as something not closed, and to reconsider what the intervening forces habitually consider as the political 'centre'. The call by political anthropology for broader understanding, taking account of all social practices and daily power relations, is particularly relevant here; it calls for a little more broadening of the view taken of societies where peace missions are deployed, as well as taking an interest in 'ordinary citizens'.

INDIGENOUS 'CIVIL SOCIETIES'

The citizens of countries where peace operations are deployed have varying opportunities for interaction with the UN military and civilian staff. In many cases those contacts, on a daily basis, are more or less fortuitous and individual. However, they can also be based on collective logics, particularly important when the individuals concerned carry out a certain number of functions in their home communities. Identifying these negotiating partners is not easy. Members of UN missions need to separate themselves from the frequent errors committed in attempting to understand conflict and post-conflict situations.

First, the lines of analysis followed by intervention are mostly based on the figure of the victim—the civilian—passive, and seen as an undifferentiated mass. But on the ground, the peacekeepers need to be able to think of the people they encounter as persons capable of being other than victims, of asserting themselves—to some extent at least—as genuine actors, rethinking their situation and expressing something about it. In practice groups pass at precise moments from a passive position, indeed a position of being simply excluded from the socio-political game, to a very active position, becoming full-scale actors, even if only for a time.

Secondly, in non-Western contexts UN members—as most outsiders— tend generally to look for structures representative of a 'civil society', that is, organisations corresponding in reality to the forms they have taken in modern western societies—NGOs, trade unions, etc. Either they do not find any, or they find groups that claim this label, mirroring Western societies. But these groups are far from covering the range of different modalities of collective organization, and may have difficulty in establishing links with other forms of existing arrangements, especially at the community level. In actuality, the idea of 'civil society' refers to a variety of different realities, and has been weighed down by an excessive load of meanings assigned to it since its origin. Historically, this idea has derived sustenance from philosophical trends that do not wholly cross-check with each other.[49] 'Civil society' in Locke, the Scots thinker of the eighteenth century, or Hegel—to name only three decisive stages in development of thought on the subject—has to do with greatly differing representations of social reality. But contemporary discourse on 'civil society' seems to have forgotten this historical variety. Nevertheless, it should help us remember the importance of considering the behaviour of actors thought to be representative of local 'civil society' in both the diversity of their repertoire of actions and the frequent ambivalence of their relations with the population as a whole and the politico-military entrepreneurs.

The distinction suggested by Ferdinand Tönnies, between social ties and community ties, can help to break away from essentialist and rigid categories, so as to approach the diversity of networks that organise the life of local societies.[50] Social ties are essentially governed by utility and reason, while organisations based on community ties are motivated by affection and the interiorising of common values. Of course, in reality, the limits between both modalities of organization are not fixed. Moreover, they relate to social categories that vary greatly from one context to another. Nevertheless, this distinction appears relevant in different contexts and particularly useful to understand the variety of forms of organisation existing from one society to another, distinguishing between

---

[49] See the genealogical analysis put forward by Sunil Khilnani, 'La "société civile", une résurgence', *Critique Internationale* 10, January 2001, pp. 38–50.

[50] See F. Tönnies, *Communauté et société. Catégories fondamentales de la Sociologie pure*, Paris: Retz, 1977.

community based groups and those in a median position between the political sphere (in its professional, and even institutional sense) and the community sphere.

Formal social organisations

In view of the nature of peace operations' mandates, human rights associations are among the main social actors with which the missions interact. They can also be the first beneficiaries of programmes to promote 'civil society'. Upon its arrival, in mid-March 1992, the human rights component of UNTAC assumed that 'Cambodia lacked almost all the normal resources necessary for a functioning civil society'.[51] Therefore, it directly motivated the creation of Cambodian human rights associations. With UNTAC's direct assistance three organisations were created during the period: the Ligue Cambodgienne pour la Promotion et la Défense des Droits de l'Homme (LICADHO), Human Rights Vigilance of Cambodia, and Outreach. These organisations were founded by Cambodians of the Diaspora, from whom their organisers essentially came, and who benefited from the help of foreign advisers financed by Western NGOs. The case was similar with a fourth organisation created, initially under the impulse of UNTAC, by two former Cambodian members of UNTAC: the Institut Cambodgien des Droits de l'Homme.[52] Two other organisations working close to human rights issues were also to receive UNTAC aid: the Cambodian Defenders Association and the Khmer Institute of Democracy.[53] This configuration of a UN mission set up as the promoter, indeed the direct founder of local NGOs, recurred in several countries, including situations where, as in Somalia, the developments on the ground limited considerably the reconstruction work carried out by the UN. The case of Cambodia was however exceptional in its extent, which explains certain biases in the way organisations existing before UNTAC's arrival were perceived.

'There is a widespread perception, generated in part by UNTAC itself, that UNTAC created the first human rights NGOs in Cambodia. But the first such NGO, the Association des Droits de l'Homme du Cambodge

---

[51] To quote the exact words used by the former director of the UNTAC Human Rights Component. Cf. Dennis McNamara, *UN Peacekeeping and Human Rights in Cambodia: A Critical Evaluation*, The Aspen Institute, Meeting on Human Rights and UN Peacekeeping, Geneva, August 1994, 1 (mimeo).

[52] Meng Ho Leang and Kassie Neou had been international interpreters with UNTAC. Interviews in Phnom Penh (November–December 1995).

[53] Under the impulse of the Office of the United Nations Centre for Human Rights in Cambodia, the number of NGOs has been multiplied since the end of UNTAC.

(ADHOC), was in fact created in December 1991 by fifteen academics and civil servants in Phnom Penh, two of them former political prisoners released on the eve of the signing of the Paris accords. UNTAC's direct involvement with local NGOs only began in earnest in about June 1992.'[54] This clarification comes from one of the founders of that organisation and is important. It explains the difference between that organisation's situation and the others: its members were not from the Diaspora, and their approach, initiated in the late 1980s, was part of an effort to promote an alternative position vis-à-vis the political sphere. This history also led to a very different relationship with UNTAC, which deliberately fuelled confusion about its role in the origins of Cambodian NGOs. The strong criticisms of UNTAC by the leaders of ADHOC, their request to be treated as 'partners', the difficulties encountered with the Human Rights Component of UNTAC were identical to those encountered by the missions in El Salvador and Haiti, where there were local human rights NGOs already in existence before the arrival of UN missions, and also in more recent operations, as in the Democratic Republic of Congo.[55]

For all these organisations, the presence of a UN mission has resulted in an unequal, one-way relationship. In El Salvador, apart from 'very formal contacts', there were 'declarations of good intentions on the part of ONUSAL, but they were never put into concrete form, except in terms of transmitting information of human rights violations for organisations making that type of investigation; but it was always one-way traffic, with no reciprocity.'[56] It was only during the period preceding the closure of the division that the heads of NGOs noted 'intensified relations'. The San José Agreement on Human Rights provided for close collaboration with the local associations and institutional support but it was only in the final stage that work was started.[57] Although reasons for interaction were numerous, relations were often distant and strained.[58] The same words were used by the leaders of Haitian organisations, to relate a 'one-way' rela-

---

[54] See Clodagh O'Brien, Dinah Pokempner and Thun Saray, *The United Nations in Cambodia: An NGO Perspective*, Aspen Institute, Meeting on Human Rights and UN Peacekeeping, September 1994 (mimeo), p. 16, and interview with Thun Saray, Founder and Chairman of ADHOC (Phnom Penh, December 29, 1995).

[55] Investigation in Ituri and North Kivu, July–August 2003.

[56] Recollection by Francisco Díaz Rodríguez, Director of the Centro para la Aplicación del Derecho (San Salvador, September 1, 1995).

[57] Interviews with Celia Medrano, spokeswoman of the Comisión de Derechos Humanos de El Salvador, and Francisco Díaz Rodríguez (San Salvador, August 24 and September 1 1995).

[58] The only moment when contacts were developed on a regular basis was the election period; several of these NGOs were involved in following up the process of voter registration, in which many problems arose.

tionship.[59] From the end of 1994, the date of MICIVIH's return to Haiti, contacts were very distant, with very few formal meetings with Haitian organisations.[60] On his arrival to the country the Special Representative of the Secretary General made a first contact, but there was no follow-up, and the human rights NGOs themselves did not want any: 'The UNMIH people are there with their forces and they do not need anything or anybody.'[61] The only exceptions were due to individual initiatives by members of the UN missions who thought that some information would be more useful in the hands of local organisations than in the missions' desk drawers. Similarly, some heads of organisations spent time paying court to members of the missions, because they thought they could get some individual advantage from them. The local organisations' reluctance towards UN staff is often echoed by the international staff's feeling that the people they are dealing with are 'very difficult'. Therefore, there is a strong temptation to create, or instigate the creation of, 'home-grown' NGOs, more malleable and capable of forming a true patronage network.

Two aspects merit special emphasis regarding human rights organisations. The first concerns relations with international NGOs which also intervene in countries, most often in the form of short-term missions: Amnesty International, Human Rights Watch, Africa Watch, Lawyers Committee for Human Rights, as well as organisations with a more general remit such as the International Crisis Group. All the heads of such organisations, who were interviewed, in their main offices and in the field, testified that despite the short time spent in a country they estimated having had more contact and better co-operation with UN missions than the missions had had with local organisations.[62]

---

[59] Interviews in Port-au-Prince, April 1995. However, the report of the experts sent to prepare for the UN component of MICIVIH recommended that the mission should work 'in close cooperation with the existing human rights organisations and structures in Haiti' (UN/Doc. A/47/908 par. 29). Similarly, the Manual given out to members of MICIVIH laid down: 'The Mission...shall seek...to promote and develop partnership with Haitian institutions and organisations, or others included in the reality of Haiti'; the NGOs are 'called upon to be privileged partners' (Manuel de la MICIVIH, *Orientations et directives pour les observateurs de la Mission civile internationale OEA/ONU en Haiti*, revised and amended 2nd edition, Port-au-Prince, August 1993, pp. 18, 69.

[60] It reached the point where the Executive Secretary of the Platform of Haitian Human Rights Organisations declared, with a touch of malice, 'We don't even know if they are still in the country' (Yolette Jeanty, Port-au-Prince, April 24, 1995).

[61] Statements by Necker Dessables and Chenet Jean-Baptiste, National Justice and Peace Secretariat (Port-au-Prince, February 22, 1996). Cf. interviews with Yolette Jeanty (April 1995, February 1996).

[62] Interviews conducted in New York, Washington and various countries where peace operations were deployed, between 1995 and 2001.

This obviously did not stop those NGOs from being very critical of UN work as illustrated by the numerous reports published by such groups on the subject.[63] None the less, this closeness is a reminder of something seen on many other occasions: the fact that the culture of INGOs, perceived as emanating from the 'North', is much closer to that of inter-state organisations than to 'Southern' NGOs. Representatives of local NGOs clearly denounce that which they call the collusion, at their expense, between large Northern NGOs and the United Nations. Therefore, INGOs are not perceived to be mediators between local NGOs and the UN. Moreover, although in various UN operations several members of missions' human rights divisions came from INGOs that had previously been in contact with local NGOs, it did not improve relations.

There is another element worthy of consideration in understanding the situation of local human rights NGOs: the frequently observable ambivalence of their relationship with the political sphere, beyond the specificities linked to each particular situation. While the notion 'non-government organisation' suggests autonomy from government organisations, NGOs are often intimately connected with their home governments in relationships that are ambivalent and dynamic, sometimes cooperative, sometimes contentious, sometimes both simultaneously. This is particularly unsurprising when considering the very nature of the subject considered. Outsiders should put aside this image of associations as part of a segment of society that would be separate from politics and even 'depoliticised'; this is simply not the case as human rights issues directly refer to the way a society is organised and the power exercised. The common under-estimation of the close ties existing between political actors and members of 'civil society' is related to the idea of a dichotomy between what is supposed to be or not to be political. This notion is omnipresent in the political engineering promoted in various regions of the world, especially in the setting of peace operations. Obviously, even in Western contexts, this distinction is far from being so clear-cut; but it tends to be considered in an even more rigid way in places where 'civil society' is presented as an alternative to a dysfunctional or even 'failed' state. Circumstances on the ground show the limitations of such an approach, especially in conflict or post-conflict situations. The configuration of political forces may explain the limited space for organising interests autonomous of the parties to the conflict. In El Salvador, indigenous NGOs were established during the war period and had mainly campaigned against governmental human rights violations. They were *de facto* close to the FMLN. This is easily

---

[63] See the general Bibliography and the bibliography by countries on the Internet site on the book: www.ceri-sciences-po.org/cherlist/pouligny/index.htm.

understandable in terms of the polarised nature of Salvadorian society during that time. The case was the same with Haitian organisations, whose leaders had even more ambiguous relations with the political sphere. In addition, several of them hold political posts at the same time, in the parties of the Lavalas tendency. The deepening divergences among them largely echoed the atomisation of the political landscape within the so-called 'democratic' camp, and the differences among their leaders' agendas. In Haiti, leaders of NGOs intervening in other sectors, while exercising political functions in parallel also used their 'NGO' hats to make contact with senior UN officials.

Thus, registers for action can be confused, because individuals can pass from one network to another and introduce themselves to members of missions under different standings. It often happens that heads of NGOs who interact as individuals with UN mission members are close to political parties, or even exercise more than one function at a time and play on the resulting ambiguity in their contacts with the missions. In El Salvador, the peace agreement provided for a formal process of participation by organised social actors with the Foro de Concertación Económico y Social in which eight trade union organisations, some of them federations, participated alongside the employers' organisations. The Salvadorian trade union movement then appeared highly fragmented; its capacity for mobilisation, at the end of the war, seemed to be almost nil; and, above all, it had very little autonomy in relation to the political parties, and not really its own agenda. 'The trade union leaders present at the forum were at the same time political leaders, and accordingly were not interested in trade union autonomy and relationships as trade unions', a local observer noted, citing the example of Francisco Martinez, who was at the same time member of the political commission of the PRTC (a component of the FMLN), general secretary of a trade union organisation, and coordinator of the workers' commission within the FMLN. 'For him, what mattered was what he could gain as a political actor, as an FMLN man; he was not interested in the Forum and may even have feared that it would be counter-productive.'[64] While only two of the trade union organisations concerned had organic links with the FMLN, the others did not succeed in finding an autonomous space, as they were unable to mobilise their bases. Similarly, many Salvadorian NGOs were not only created in the context of the war but rose out of political parties, with which they remained closely identified. Having lost part of their identity and being plunged into a universe of harsher rivalry, they went through a crisis of conscience, all the more severe because their representative character was called into

[64] Interview with Hector Dada, sociologist, FLASCO (San Salvador, September 7, 1995).

question by the communities with which they worked. Thus, it was a very fragmented sector, without any real representativity or legitimacy, and concerned above all for its own survival.

The space for organising interests outside the parties to the conflict is even more limited when a UN operation starts while a war is still going on. However, outsiders are tempted to look within the 'civil society' for an alternative to 'warlords'. In Somalia, one part of the United Nations approach was to distinguish precisely between faction leaders' and 'civil society actors' (groups of women, lawyers, intellectuals, religious people, etc.) who were invited to take part in reconciliation meetings and on whom the creation of district committees was supposed to be based.[65] In reality, such groups were directly connected to the so-called 'factions'; in this case, to Ali Mahdi. Similar contacts have been developed with women and with groups of intellectuals, in view of promoting an alternative to the power of 'warlords'. But, considering what most Somalia specialists explain about the solidarities inside the clans, this strategy appears dubious. Daniel Compagnon, a French specialist on Somalia, indicates: 'The "intellectuals" [did] not constitute an autonomous group, but they [were] implicated in politico-military factions and [were] often the first to articulate a clan-based discourse.'[66] Furthermore, while they were considered as alternative negotiating partners for the peacekeepers, locally some of them (including representatives of women's organisations, whose role in the conflict in Somalia is often underestimated) played an important function in the various mobilisations against the presence of the foreigners.[67] The expression of sentiments of this nature is often seen as 'taboo' because it is perceived as a way of discrediting the individuals concerned. However, a minimal analysis of this type is essential to understand the various dynamics at work in the local societies. It is even more crucial to analyse attentively the links maintained by local humanitarian organisations (through which aid distribution passes) with the various parties to the conflict. In fact, the volumes of humanitarian aid that are at stake are generally very large. The many forms of trafficking

---

[65] This work was facilitated, notably, by the Life and Peace Institute, a Swedish NGO which organised meetings, financed by bilateral aid, in collaboration with the UN.

[66] Daniel Compagnon, 'Fausses pistes', *Politique Africaine* 50, June 1993, p. 131. Antonio Torrenzano, for his part, emphasises the difficulty which they always had to find their situation, especially in relation to their clans, and their inability to suggest an alternative: *L'imbroglio somalien: historique d'une crise de succession*, Paris: L'Harmattan, 1995, pp. 105 ff.

[67] See especially Daniel Compagnon, 'Somalie. Les limites de l'ingérence humanitaire. L'échec politique de l'ONU', *Afrique Politique*, 1995, p. 196; African Rights, *Somalia: Operation Restore Hope: A Preliminary Assessment*, London, May 1993, p. 32.

established on this basis fuel, to a great extent, the military-mafioso networks.

These various elements are a reminder of how the nature of state-society relations and the changes in them need to be considered in a way both open and interactive, in concrete historical trajectories. As some analysts have pointed out, one must guard against the tendency to 'romanticise' the 'civil society' sector. In practice some sectors of society can be just as discredited as the state.[68] Lastly, the people who head these organisations belong essentially to the elite, like the political entrepreneurs, and however important it is, that group constitutes one side—and not necessarily the most important one—of a much larger story.

Community actors

In rural zones as in the poorer districts of the cities, peacekeepers have contacts with actors who are mainly organised on a community basis. The frequency of these contacts has been highly variable. While the presence of the UN missions seems massive in the capital, and possibly in some provincial cities or where safe areas are established, it is much more discreet in rural areas where, at best, people have on occasion seen white vehicles with a blue flag passing along the road. Community actors are more directly affected than elites by some points in the missions' mandates—for example, assistance for the return of refugees, reintegration of former fighters, de-mining operations, land problems.

In El Salvador, the reintegration programmes concerned, in addition to the former fighters, the civilian population living in zones under guerrilla control during the conflict, and members of families of dead fighters.[69] Of the various routes proposed for reintegration, the one dealing with settlement in rural areas, through the land transfer programme, was by far the most important. Representing 64 per cent of the total aid programme, it came directly under the ONUSAL mandate, at least for the first phase. The people concerned were organised on a community basis, conforming to the model developed by the refugees from Honduras returning to El Salvador, after 1984, in zones often controlled by the guerrillas. Those *repoblaciones* were generally organised on the basis of strong ties of soli-

[68] See René Lemarchand, 'Uncivil States and Civil Societies: How Illusion Became Reality', *Journal of Modern African Studies* 30/2, 1992, p. 187.

[69] The reintegration programme, piloted by the UNDP in particular, was, according to that body, meant to deal with 60,000 internally displaced people and 26,000 repatriated people, as well as around 1.5 million inhabitants of some 115 *communes* considered particularly affected by the war.

darity created among families in the camps.[70] During the ONUSAL period many communities (present in more than half of the regions) besides returning refugees, included internally displaced people. They were generally headed by a management committee (*junta directiva*) that was elected; it was this committee that dealt directly with the land problems. In addition, regional confederations were also created gradually in the various districts where communities were established.[71] The Coordinadoras de Comunidades y Repoblaciones (later called Coordinadoras de Comunidades para la Reconstrucción) were responsible for the coordination of activities among communities. Their executive committee was made up of members elected by their respective communities. It was often these delegates who, in their zones, were at the frontline for potential contacts with the ONUSAL teams, especially on human rights and land issues. Meanwhile, meetings have also been organized for a harmonization of the strategies to follow the discussions with ONUSAL. Coordination has been partly ensured at the national level through the Movimiento Comunal Salvadoreño, which was closely linked historically with the FMLN, but sought to become autonomous after the peace agreements.[72] The Coordination Council of the Movimiento Comunal Salvadoreño—oscillating between its community roots (members of the council came from affiliated communities) and a classical 'middleman' logic, on the lines of existing NGOs—regularly gave advice to members who had complaints to make to ONUSAL. Also, in this capacity it met members of the UN mission in San Salvador. The general weakness of the social movements at the end of the war was contrasted with the extraordinary vitality in the community movement, which organised itself in a very concrete way to interact with the peacekeepers.

In Haiti the community-based groups cover a vast range of organizations in neighbourhoods, small farmers (organized around problems of land and water), of urban workers (craft unions, workers in sub-contracting factories in the Port-au-Prince industrial zone, the transport operators' union of the metropolitan zone to which the drivers of collective taxis or *tap-tap* belong, etc.); women and youth, but also religious organisations, linked with the Catholic base communities and the *vodou* structures. For example, the new generation of peasant associations set up in

---

[70] A community could number between 50 and 1,000 families. The functioning of those communities was originally often based on a strong egalitarian ideology.

[71] The departments of Chalatenango, San Vicente, La Paz, San Miguel and Morazán.

[72] The Movement did not concern only the *repoblaciones*, and it was essentially established in zones formerly controlled by the guerrillas. In 1995 it grouped together 253 communities.

the 1980s, during the last period of the Duvalliers' dictatorship, partially followed the basis of *vodou* community work organisations, called *konbit*. By 1994, at the time of Operation Restore Democracy, that network had been greatly weakened by the repression—which had been specifically directed against it—following the coup d'état of September 1991, and it kept its distance from the *Blan*, staying in a position of observation. At the same time the fact that UNMIH did not have any mandates on socio-economic issues meant that its interest in establishing contact with the population was limited. As a young member of a peasant association at Bocozelle (Bas Artibonite) said, 'If you want to see them other than in their cars, you have to pay.'[73] But, that did not stop peasant groups, for example, from trying to involve members of the mission in certain landed property or security problems. It was also with this sort of partner that the so-called 'Quick Impact Projects'—started by the military contingents, most often with bilateral funding—sought to have dealings. These projects are present in all missions but are of different magnitude. In Haiti they aimed to provide symbolic compensation for the lack of any economic and social programme in the mission's mandate.

Contacts usually occur in quite different ways in urban areas, but they confirm the importance of looking more closely at how collective life is organised at the grassroots level: the interactions with outsiders often take place by design rather than by pure chance. For example, in the few cases when ONUSAL civpols or milobs visited suburban neighbourhoods in San Salvador, members of the district associations[74] surpervised their presence, even if only for a few minutes. Most often those visits would not have led to any direct contact. 'They did not talk to anybody and nobody talked to them' was the reaction recorded most often. In the few cases where one of the ONUSAL members asked questions, relating to an incident of human rights violation, those who had informed them were people who had been appointed in advance, for that purpose, by the district organisation. Similarly, the attitude towards foreigners had always been discussed in advance. A very similar scenario was to be found in the suburban neighbourhoods of Haiti during the MNF and succeeding UN missions. In Port-au-Prince, the capital, the suburban districts had exploded under population pressure. District committees, workers' groups and

---

[73] This was an allusion to the fact that they had to pay to travel to the town (in this case Saint-Marc) where the nearest office of the UN mission was established. Interview in Gonaïves, May 3, 1995.

[74] Often called a 'community', with frequent links both to the religious communities and to the mafioso networks maintained by drug dealers and gangs of youths (the notorious *maras* who modelled themselves on the Los Angeles gangs).

women's organisations belonged to an increasingly fragmented social fabric of organisations that, until shortly before, had provided a structure for these *peyi andeyó*,[75] in the very heart of the cities. As such, none of these structures had any direct interaction with members of the United Nations mission. However, it was through them that orders were passed on—in a way very close to what happened in San Salvador—about the attitude that was best to follow if the mission members left their cars and ventured into the narrow streets in the heart of the shantytowns (which happened very rarely), or if they asked questions. In 1996–97 the situation became more complicated in many districts of Port-au-Prince, with the proliferation of so-called 'people's' organisations closely linked to armed gangs, newly created, in a mix of petty crimes, drug trafficking and political discourse. However, by this time the UN had taken a clear decision to stay well in the background and leave the Haitian police in the front line. Thus, for the organisations present, in the poorer districts of the cities, especially in Port-au-Prince, the mission had definitely 'disappeared' over the horizon.

From one situation to another the idea of 'community' can relate to highly variable forms of organisation and mediation. In the countries' recent history, the modalities of organisation and projection in the public space have often undergone profound transformation. The change stems from various factors: contacts with national and international NGOs intervening in the area of humanitarian aid or development, according to a project-oriented approach that implies the existence of a certain type of 'organised' partner on the ground; effects of repression and war, leading in particular to major displacements of people to refugee and displaced person camps or to cities, which hastens the break of former community ties according to the imperatives of survival; effects of violence within the group, especially when this violence has been used by political entrepreneurs; transformation of identities and frameworks of reference, etc. To grasp this, an accurate and dynamic analysis of each social fabric is requested, one which assumes, that outsiders overcome the impression of disorganisation, or even anomie, often given of societies at war or just emerging from conflict. In fact, war transforms social and political foun-

---

[75] An expression which generally described rural dwellers, considered as separate to the extent that from 1945 onwards the word *abitan* (meaning 'peasant') was put on birth certificates for inhabitants or rural areas who came under the Rural Code and not the Civil Code like other citizens. Not until May 15, 1995, was this discrimination ended by presidential decree. I deliberately extend this idea of 'outsiders' to the suburban space and to the shanty-towns sometimes wedged within the better-off residential districts of Port-au-Prince.

dations profoundly, at least as much as it destroys. From this perspective, the community-oriented analytical approach should help to understand how collective life continues to organise itself, even amid many difficulties.

In Cambodia, more so than in most countries, especially in the rural areas, the population was generally seen by UNTAC members as 'unorganised'. Certainly the various traumatic episodes in its recent history, and most especially the four years of the Khmers Rouges regime, forced people to withdraw into themselves, in a desperate effort to survive. All accounts speak of the omnipresent fear and suspicion, even in the heart of the family which the Khmers Rouges' Angkar (Organisation) had explicitly set out to destroy, as well as all other social structures. But from 1979 onwards, in the refugee camps and in the country controlled by the Vietnamese, the profoundly rural Cambodian society reorganised itself. When the peace process began, it looked like a complex network of groups of people and family loyalties, social organisations, traditional institutions and modern administrative structures. In particular, it was family ties and good neighbourly relations that structured the *phum*,[76] the basic population unit. Several mutual aid systems expressed and gave force to this form of solidarity.[77] Essentially interaction with members of UNTAC passed through the *phum* chief, in particular for all activity linked to the electoral process and, in some cases, to request aid or pass on complaints to the mission.[78] It was the *phum* chief who assembled the inhabitants for voter registration and polling day. As he held administrative authority conferred on him by the government, the *phum* chief was an agent of the administration, but he was also often the head of a family network, chosen by cooptation among the 'village wise men' (the elders). The latter were generally also members (*achar vat*) of the pagoda committees (*kanakamaka vat*), the main 'collective' structure in rural areas, which generally comprised of several *phums*.[79] This connection is interesting to note as the pagodas were very often used during the UNTAC period as meeting places for transmitting information on electoral process and on human-rights. The pagoda, a true centre of life with various

---

[76] This word is almost untranslatable; it denotes the 'inhabited place', and is generally translated 'village', but is in fact of varying size.

[77] Interviews with the anthropologists Fabienne Luco, Soizie Crochet and Walter Aschmoneit (Paris, Siem Reap and Kompong Thom, November–December 1995).

[78] Interviews with former UNTAC interpreters, former UNV district electoral officers and several chiefs of *phums*.

[79] The ties uniting the inhabitants of one or several *phums* with a pagoda are symbolised by the fact that the ancestors' ashes are laid in the pagoda. People go to the pagoda for the feast for the dead and the celebrations of the third and the hundredth day after the death. In addition, the pagoda is a place for socialising for the aged and for people on the margin (widows and orphans).

buildings and a community meeting place (the *sala*), was the only place where a Cambodian rural community could meet; most often a pagoda covered several *phums*, up to eight or ten. The pagoda committees (*kana-kamaka vat*) and pagoda support groups (*vein*) constituted, until recently, what was probably the nearest Cambodian equivalent of 'civil society'. That network was also central to the way in which the problem of refugees and internally displaced persons was managed—an important aspect of the peace operation.

Thus rural Cambodia appeared as a complex network of actors and loyalties at the time of UNTAC's presence, profoundly disturbed by the violent events that had shaken the country during the preceding decades. However, it was far from the 'disorder' or 'anomie' depicted by many outsiders. As Cambodians often told me: 'our culture did not die with Pol Pot or the regime that followed'. The role of Cambodian 'wise men' was very similar to the role played in Mozambique by the 'traditional authorities', the *regulos* mobilised by the parties to inform the local people of elections, but also by ONUMOZ, for which they were often the sole point of contact in rural areas.[80] They also played an often decisive role in operations for resettlement of refugees and displaced persons.[81] Even in areas of utter desolation, such as Bunia in eastern Congo in the spring and summer of 2003, and still more in refugee camps, social life is very quickly reorganised, structures of control included in this process.

But it would be wrong to make a too hasty dichotomy between reconstruction 'from the top down' and 'from the bottom up'. The case of Somalia is a reminder of how reality is often more complex than this simple alternative would suggest. With the formation of district councils, UNOSOM's strategy involved not only diversifying their interlocutors, but also laying the foundations for a reconstruction of the country that would be out of the hands of the 'warlords'.[82] Within this framework the mission's main negotiating partners were the elders, male family heads who, in the traditional set-up, met in assemblies (*shir*) and took decisions

---

[80] A bit like the *phum* chiefs in Cambodia, those *regulos* were recognised or imposed as chiefs during the Portuguese colonial period. It could happen that they were mere puppets or, in contrast, legitimate chiefs re-invested with state tasks by the colonial administration. During the war they were used alternately by FRELIMO and RENAMO, while the village structure was thrown into confusion by the fighting. So their role also underwent changes over time.

[81] Private interviews in Mozambique in October–November 1994 and direct observation, at the time of the elections, in the Beira region.

[82] In September 1993 UNOSOM helped establish 40 district councils out of the 77 districts of Somalia (not including Somaliland), as well as three regional councils at Garowe, Bakool and Baidoa, created in mid-October 1993.

by consensus.[83] Thus they occupied a central position in the organisation of Somali society. While analysts disagree on the exact social status of the elders, they generally agree on the fact that there are many who claim that status, which makes leadership difficult to maintain for a very long time, as are relations between elders, factional politicians and militia leaders, competing and cooperating, according to the circumstances. So elders could neither be simply considered as 'marginalized' nor simple puppets in the hands of the 'warlords'.[84] They belonged to complex and moving networks of solidarity, often playing the role of mediator, but also an essential role in the recruiting of fighters. A part of UNOSOM's strategy consisted of playing off the elders against the 'warlords', while they were largely out for their own mutual advantages. Some of them, as individuals, wore several hats, assuming several roles alternately.

Questions about the degree of linkage among these various networks of actors are central if one is to understand what is changing in the societies concerned. It has direct implications for interpretation of the potential for collective mobilization, but also for the possibility of finding alternatives for interlocutors considered to be uncooperative. The issue is generally less to choose between 'the top' and 'the bottom'—if one can in fact distinguish them—but to understand what happens in between. In a conflict or post-conflict phase, linkages between the different networks that structure the socio-political fabric are in the midst of deep transformation, sometimes by violent means. In a case such as Bosnia-Herzegovina, the changes in the political and social configurations of the conflict, between communities and within communities, have probably turned out to be more decisive than the changes in the strict balance of military forces.[85]

Religious actors: a specific case

In this connection religious actors occupy a special position. To understand the role that they are likely to play, it is crucial to approach them in all their variety—of many sorts. There is variety in all religion, in its forms, interpretations, practices, authorities; also in the existing religions

---

[83] Ioan Myrddin Lewis has devoted a number of works to the description of this system, including *A Pastoral Democracy*, considered by many as the reference book on the subject (London: Oxford University Press, 1961).

[84] Like the analysis made, for example, by Andrew S. Natsios, 'Humanitarian Relief Intervention in Somalia: The Economics of Chaos', p. 86 in Walter Clarke and Jeffrey Herbst (eds), *Learning from Somalia: The Lessons of Armed Humanitarian Intervention*, Boulder, CO: Westview Press, 1997.

[85] On this subject see the analysis by Xavier Bougarel, *Bosnie, anatomie d'un conflit*, Paris: La Découverte, 1996, p. 77.

in each country (which generally include both institutionalised churches and traditional religious actors who, even if not visible, may play a crucial role of mediation and interpretation). In fact, it is often in a connection between two religious registers that the role of those actors should be understood. There is also variety in the modes of intervention of religion into politics, and in the functions it is able to carry out: a function of mobilisation (in a conflict, but also against the presence of foreign troops, where necessary); a function of socialisation (especially at the level of the elites, but also in the integration of those excluded); and a function of substitution for partisan bodies or trade union-type organisations that are outlawed in times of closure of the political space. This last function is often allied to a role of popular forum. It is in these various capacities that religious actors may try to make contact with peacekeepers, which in return see them as possible facilitators of their popular acceptance, as peace activists, and more broadly as members of the 'civil society' which has to be encountered—or, on the contrary, as dangerous fanatics, especially if they are of the Islamic faith.

In El Salvador, while 90 per cent of the inhabitants are Catholic, a part of the Catholic Church filled a dual popular orator and substitution function from the mid-1980s, when the archdiocese of San Salvador intervened in the dialogue between the government and the FMLN. In the preceding years Mgr Romero, Archbishop of San Salvador, who was murdered while celebrating Mass on March 24, 1980, appeared to many to be 'the sole voice that could be raised to say what was going on' and to propose an alternative to the conflict. But Romero, like his successors— Mgr Rivera y Damas and his coadjutor, Mgr Rosa Chávez—was isolated in a bishops' conference that was in its great majority conservative. However, from his mediation attempt the archbishop of San Salvador retained a unique position in the peace process: he was present at the peace signing ceremony in New York and also took part in the work of the COPAZ (where he was usually represented by his coadjutor), as an observer alongside ONUSAL. In that capacity he met senior officials of the UN mission as well as parties to the conflict on a very regular basis. Throughout the process he also continued to act as a people's tribune, notably through his Sunday sermons in which he always devoted at least fifteen minutes of commentary to the events of the week. ONUSAL, obviously, received its due share of his evaluation and criticism, which, it was known, were not always to the taste of those concerned.[86] Senior

---

[86] Interviews with former senior officials of the mission. The newspapers the next day systematically echoed the archbishop's sermon. That practice was also followed by Mgr Rosa Chávez while he kept in his post.

ONUSAL officials also had contacts with other religious actors, especially the Jesuits, members of the governing committee of the José Simeón Cañas Central American University (UCA). Through their journals they played a sustained critical role, throughout the UN presence.[87] The UCA was unanimously regarded as a 'major political force in the country', and former high ONUSAL officials said they were 'leaders of opinion with a considerable role'.[88] Their editorials, as well as statements by the UCA governing committee, were awaited expectantly. The Jesuits had their own networks and had been very active in contact with the UN negotiating team during the phase preceding the peace agreement.[89] Historically, the UCA had also been closely linked with the networks of Church basic ecclesial communities created under a movement that started in El Salvador in 1969, partly at the UCA's instigation, in the spirit of the theology of liberation. But the strength of that link was uncertain at the time of the peace process, except for some individual cases. In addition, the Church base communities were then faced with direct rivalry from the neo-Protestant Pentecostal and Charismatic movements, which were highly financially supported and offered an alternative to the strong ideological polarisation of the war. However, when a charismatic priest was present in the region or the district he often came to be accepted in practice as the 'natural' interlocutor for members of the UN mission.

In Haiti the substitution role played by the Catholic Church, in the last years of the Duvalier dictatorship, closely resembled what happened in El Salvador. In the 1980s, under the influence of Liberation Theology from Latin America, a progressive trend shook the Catholic hierarchy as Jean-Claude Duvalier's regime began to totter; it encouraged the development of base communities (*Ti Kominote Legliz*, TKL) as well as various development and education movements. Deriving support from a considerable network of social works and schools, the Church gave widespread backing to the mobilisation movement that led to the dictator's departure in 1986.[90] That network also contributed to the training and socialisation of a number of men and women who still hold key political posts today, some of whom remain close to influential members of the clergy. During the

---

[87] Those publications echoed in particular the reports of the Institute of Human Rights of the University (IDHUCA); a synthesis of its criticisms of ONUSAL was published in a report by IDHUCA, 'La misión de observadores de las Naciones Unidas en El Salvador', *Radiografía de un proceso de paz: ¿borrón y cuenta neuva?*, San Salvador, August 1995.

[88] Recollection by Philippe Texier, former Director of the ONUSAL Human Rights Division, Paris, March 7, 1995.

[89] Interviews in San Salvador and New York, January–September 1995.

[90] The famous phrase uttered by Pope John Paul II on a visit to Haiti in 1983, 'Something has to change here', was widely taken up for political mobilisation. The Church networks were also very active in 1986–7, during discussions on the new draft Constitution.

years of transition that followed, the progressive branch of the Church played an increasing political role, symbolised by the election of a priest to the presidency in December 1990. Historically, however, the Catholic Church had always played the role of legitimising the established authority. This switch provoked unendurable internal contradictions. The Catholic hierarchy hardened its stance and, after the September 1991 coup d'état, took up a position clearly on the side of the putschists. Fiercely opposed to the embargo and then to the military intervention, it adopted a low profile vis-à-vis those whom it called the 'occupying forces'. Members of UN missions generally only paid 'courtesy visits' to the local bishop. However, they regularly received the attention of priests who claimed the progressive branch of the Catholic Church or indeed the base communities movement—a claim that was supposed to give them legitimacy in the eyes of outsiders. For those foreigners it was not always easy to discern the real place of those actors either in the political game— the individuals concerned were generally present at political meetings and held leading positions in the parties—or in relation to the Church base movements, whose real impact they often found difficult to assess. The task was obviously not made easier for them by some of the people they were dealing with, who presented themselves falsely as representatives of such movements[91]—such claims being angrily denounced by leading figures in the TKL, who readily claimed to be helpless when their name was used by political parties claiming to be rooted in their bases, or when priests 'go to international meetings or meet Brahimi in the name of the TKL when we have no contact with them.'[92] Similarly, the contacts with the Civilian Mission in charge of human rights (MICIVIH) took place on a highly individual level, most often with non-Haitian priests (and, rarely, nuns). Among the international staff there was often a strong temptation to go to those 'who resemble [them]'.[93] Among the Haitian political actors Aristide, as a former priest, was the one who most used these connections; some priests remained very close to him while others went over to the opposition. On April 23, 1995 he organised a meeting at the presidential palace between the Special Representative of the Secretary General and members of the progressive clergy, who he had obviously chosen himself.

In Cambodia as well, clergy—Buddhist in this case—have always had ambiguous relations with the political sphere. They consequently show

[91] Interview with Nicole Lannegrace, Political Adviser to Lakhdar Brahimi, Special Representative of the Secretary General in Haiti (Port-au-Prince, April 22, 1995).

[92] Interviews in the shantytowns of Port-au-Prince and in the provinces, and with the Secretary General for Coordination of the TKLs of Port-au-Prince (February–March 1996).

[93] Interviews with MICIVIH members in Paris, Port-au-Prince and Gonaïves, 1995–6.

great concern to maintain a specific status—which explains why the main Buddhist leaders called on people not to go to vote in 1993.[94] By keeping their distance in this way, they maintained the best guarantee of a diffused political influence and a prominent social role, through education in par-ticular. The Khmers Rouges period was a cut-off point for Buddhism as it was for all Cambodian society, as the Pol Pot regime set out to destroy all social structures that did not seem immediately useful for the advancement of its ideological project. Pagodas were destroyed and a part of the clergy decimated. After the defeat of the Khmers Rouges, the Vietnamese authorities who controlled the country sent bonzes to Vietnam for training and rapidly saw that it was in their interest to get the support of the clergy for rebuilding the country. In the refugee camps on the borders, the bonzes were similarly used by the parties, essentially as a means of social control. It was in this context that there emerged in exile true leaders who advocated a bigger role for the bonzes and built up considerable political and financial support networks in Europe and the United States, most often connected with Cambodian political networks. They mobilised in favour of peace and were present at all the peace talks. On returning to Cambodia, they set up as key interlocutors for UNTAC. Three individuals emerge as playing particularly central roles: Maha Ghosananda, Yos Hut Khemacoro and Heng Monichenda. All three had, in the years preceding the peace agreements, continuous contacts with United Nations organizations (some having worked for them as consultants), particularly in the refugee camps on the border. They had assets—especially financial—that were not negligible. They took up positions as partners of UNTAC according to a twofold register. On the one hand, they emphasised the social role traditionally played by the pagoda, whose central place they wanted restored; some actively advocated for UNTAC to use the pagoda as such, especially for its civic education campaign preceding the elections. On the other hand, they presented Buddhism as a possible bridge between the Western idea of human rights and Khmer values. There was rivalry in some cases between their initiatives.[95] To some extent there was also

[94] Interview with the Venerable Bhikkhu Yos Hut Khemacoro, co-founder of the Coalition for Peace and Reconciliation and Pouleu Khmer ('the enlightened Khmer'), a coordinating body for Cambodian individuals and organisations created after the 1993 elections; founder of the 'Mission for Peace in Cambodia'; President of the Fondation Bouddhique Khmère (Phnom Penh, Wat Langka Pagoda, November 19, 1995).

[95] Interviews with Samdech Preah Maha Ghosananda, Yos Hut Khemacoro, Heng Monichenda; Ou Bun Long, of the Khmer Buddhist Society; Liz Bernstein, co-founder of the Coalition for Peace and Reconciliation; and Father François Ponchaud, missionary priest (in Cambodia until 1975, then in the camps in Thailand; back in Cambodia in 1993): Paris, Phnom Penh, Battambang, March, November and December 1995. Plus consultation of personal archives of former UNTAC members.

rivalry with the human rights NGOs, some of whose senior figures did not conceal their distrust of 'these bonzes who exploit Buddhism as a political and financial springboard, because they themselves are not practicing Buddhists'.[96]

In wartime, religious actors mainly appear in a mobilising capacity, as allies of political entrepreneurs. In Bosnia-Herzegovina, religion served essentially as a resource for mobilisation for political actors, preaching differentiation from the infidel 'others' and the legitimacy of a 'just war'.[97] The central role of religious structures in nationalist mobilisation emerged very clearly in the case of the Muslim community, as Xavier Bougarel's research has shown.[98] Political manipulation was not absent vis-à-vis the other religions, and this went so far that the conflict gained a religious dimension, on which the main politico-military actors played.

When it comes to making peace, the intervening forces have often been tempted to think only of the positive aspect of the role of religious actors, except if, as in Somalia or Iraq, fear of the 'Islamist menace' is stronger than liberal discourse in favour of 'civil society'. However, there can be no getting round this ambivalence of religious actors. The case of traditional healers and mediums illustrates the point. While they may be part of the problem, because they have made alliances with or were manipulated by war entrepreneurs, they are also a local resource which must be taken into account all the more because—as we shall see in contexts as varied as Cambodia, Mozambique and Haiti—they have played an 'invisible' but essential role in the way local people have tried to understand and manage their contacts with the peacekeepers.

It is these complex networks of interaction that outsiders should be able to decipher in a minimal fashion at least. The status and position of the people they deal with—as individuals or groups—can vary considerably during their stay, as well as their capacity for action and mobilisation. That explains the importance of getting away from perspectives that would tend to see local societies as a shapeless, homogeneous, static whole, or to suppose that overall, local people are 'indifferent' to the peace process, as one very often hears said. Although it is a tricky subject, understanding of the way people view the UN's action in their country is important. Their perceptions of the peacekeepers and their strategies may be very different

---

[96] Interviews in Phnom Penh, December 1995.

[97] Srdjan Vrcan, 'The War in Former Yugoslavia and Religion', *Religion, State and Society* 22/4, 1994, pp. 377, 373.

[98] See especially Xavier Bougarel, 'Un courant panislamiste en Bosnie-Herzégovine', pp. 275–99 in Gilles Kepel (ed.), *Exils et royaumes: les appartenances au monde arabo-musulman aujourd'hui*, Paris: FNSP, 1994; 'Discours d'un ramadan de guerre civile', *L'Autre Europe* (Lausanne) 26–7, 1993, pp. 171–97, and discussions with the author.

from those of the political, economic and social elites. They may be just as decisive for the daily work of a UN mission. That should impel yet a closer look at all those individuals or groups who may be in median positions, as may very well be the case with the local staff employed by the missions.

'LOCAL' EMPLOYEES OF UN OPERATIONS

December 11, 1992, 9 a.m.: Chongola, on the edge of the Cambodian forest, in a zone controlled by the Khmers Rouges. A United Nations Volunteer (UNV) electoral supervisor for the district, arrives to carry out voter registration of the inhabitants of the *phum*. He is accompanied by blue helmets carrying sacks of rice, and Cambodian employees of UNTAC, including two interpreters. The Khmers Rouges leader in the zone, Dk Thorn, opposes these operations. Talks start between him and the two Cambodian interpreters, who are originated from the area. One of them knows Dk Thorn personally; the other is a retired schoolteacher, respected for his advanced age, a 'wise man'. The three men go to the side to argue. The Khmers Rouges leader agrees that the rice should be distributed to the inhabitants and the bonzes, but he does not want to hear anything about voter registration. For him, 'UNTAC is an agent of the Vietnamese'. The negotiations drag on; UN international staff gets impatient. Finally, at about 4 o'clock in the afternoon, a compromise is reached. A group of men and women will be registered by the Cambodian election staff.[99]

Similar scenes occurred in other parts of Cambodia. Even when operations proceeded normally, it was the local staff who made the first contacts in the *phums* and explained how the registration must be carried out. A former UNV who had been a district electoral officer recorded: 'In my district, I never ventured to make a speech to the inhabitants; in view of the translation problems, it would have served no purpose. It was much more effective to explain to the interpreter what one wanted, and he then went to explain to the people. Later it was the local election staff that we had employed who made contact with the people in the villages, and chose people with whom we should negotiate. We knew nothing of the country, we could not speak the language, we had no choice.'[100] In countries where UN missions are deployed, local employees of international organisations (the UN, the OSCE, the UNHCR, the EU, etc.) and military contingents have a very special function. In some cases they are the only contacts that

---

[99] Interviews in Phnom Penh and Kompong Thom, December 1995, and UNTAC staff's reports consulted.
[100] Interview at Phnom Penh, November 28, 1995.

members of the missions are really going to have with 'the locals'. Generally, they are at the direct interface between the local population and the outsiders while continuing to be involved in local socio-political life.

The idea of a 'broker', developed in a number of works of political anthropology, reveals very well the different dimensions that such an intermediary position can assume. To understand them, a distinction must be made according to the posts held by such staff. From one mission to another, three categories of employees are found: the administrative and support staff, interpreters and guides, and local professionals. This is a very simple classification, taking account both of the higher or lower degree of responsibility linked to tasks carried out and the position occupied in interaction (greater or less visibility at the interface with the local population). The staff assigned to logistic and administrative support work in offices, possibly in and around military camps, and carry out subordinate tasks: secretarial work, reception, repairs, maintenance, etc. The essential part of the local staff of UN peace missions falls into this category, and is based in the capital. It has limited visibility, especially in the eyes of the local people who, with some exceptions, have no access either to the missions' offices or to the military camps. Unless someone knows personally an employee of the United Nations mission, most only have a very limited glimpse at what that specific category of staff represents. That category can also include domestic servants, recruited directly by the missions' international personnel; with some exceptions,[101] those servants are not directly employed by the missions. They can bring the numbers of people employed locally by UN mission members up to several thousands. At the time of elections, additional local staff members are also employed, for a short time, to help the international electoral observers.

Interpreters and guides are the most 'visible' and they are often at the direct interface between the United Nations intervention forces and the local actors. Hundreds of them worked in Cambodia where in practice, outside some circles in the capital, knowledge of Khmer was indispensable for any communication, however limited. In other missions they are generally fewer in number, for three reasons. First, as happened in El Salvador and Haiti, the international language used locally (in those cases, Spanish and French) is supposed to be known by the mission's staff, especially the civpols for whom it is supposed to be a condition of employment. In practice, this has been far from happening. Similarly, the

[101] Security staff, for example—particularly numerous in cases like Somalia and Iraq—or staff attached to the Special Representative of the Secretary General can be paid directly by the United Nations mission.

missions presume that the locally used international language is under-stood by the majority of the population (like French in Haiti and the RDC, or Portuguese in Mozambique and East Timor), which is obviously far from being the case. Lastly, at least in past UN missions, the essential part of the (limited) budget provided for interpreting services has been used to meet the needs for interpreting within the missions, whose members, without a common language, sometimes have difficulty communicating. Where interpreters are lacking, drivers often fulfil this role as best as they can. In practice, the importance of the interpreters' role, as well their access to information, varies considerably from one person to another, within the same mission.

A limited number of local employees recruited by offices responsible for public information, and offices of the spokesmen, also fall into that category. Similarly, in countries where peace operations carry out tempo-rary administrative functions (Namibia, Cambodia, Kosovo, East Timor), local staff are employed on direct tasks of administration of the country. This can also occur where the UN aims to contribute directly to the re-building of local institutions. In Mogadishu and several southern regions of Somalia, eight thousand Somali police were directly recruited, equip-ped, trained and paid by UNOSOM II. Elsewhere, judges, customs officials and thousands of future civil servants may be directly employed by a UN mission. The same system is used for the organisation of elec-tions. In Cambodia, 50,000 local employees worked for UNTAC electoral component alongside the international staff. After being trained by the United Nations Volunteers, they handled the essential portion of election activity, from voter registration to the counting of votes.

In El Salvador, Florentín Meléndez, legal adviser to the ONUSAL/MINUSAL mission from 1991 was the only Salvadorean to be employed by the UN as a professional. His position was comparable to that of about ten Cambodians of the Diaspora who were recruited from UN head-quarters with the status of 'professionals': two legal experts within the Civil Administration Component, the head of computer services, mem-bers of UNTAC offices in the provinces. Some of these 'outside Cambo-dians', as they called themselves, acted as interpreters in the main negotiations between the leaders of the mission and Cambodian political leaders, as well as translators of basic texts such as the electoral law.

How to become a UN local employee

The procedures for recruitment of local staff are most often fairly lax, and the task falls on international staff, which usually has neither the sufficient training nor previous knowledge of the local situation. International agencies already present in a country regularly accuse the UN missions of not concerting with them on this matter, and hence of bringing distortion into play. On their side, former international members of missions express serious doubts about both the tests of competence and the 'security checks' that are supposed to be made systematically by the missions. Those who had been put in a position where they had to recruit and manage local staff outside the capital did not conceal their unease with a task that they had to carry out with that much less judgement, because it was assigned to them immediately after their assignments.[102] This was the general experience of the United Nations Volunteers (UNV) deployed across the country, who received no training in recruitment and management of local staff. In Cambodia, those tasks were in fact not even included in the job description, and none had had any previous experience in that area. Yet they had considerable discretionary power and were, in addition, responsible for distribution of pay. This led to numerous conflicts, the extreme case being that of a Japanese UNV who was murdered in Kompong Thom province. In the best circumstances, this left a margin of manoeuvre of some importance to local power networks who tried to control access to positions that could be perceived as potentially useful. In systems with a large element of patronage, access to jobs of this type is rarely possible outside traditional networks, even if the local staff of embassies and other international organisations (including non-governmental ones) also appear to be in a privileged or an intermediary position to give access to a UN job because they have easier access to information.

Having scarcely arrived in a country, members of a UN mission are offered services by a number of 'spontaneous' candidates. In Somalia, recruitment channels varied from one region to another, according to the clans concerned. In Mogadishu the 'clan balance' among local UN employees followed the geography of the control over the capital by the two principal movements. In different countries, according to region, political parties or military groups in a dominant position will in practice try to control positions, even sharing jobs as they share illicit businesses (petrol trafficking during the war in Bosnia, for example). When a mission comes closer to administrative supervision, as in Kosovo and East Timor, local power networks seek to exercise control over recruitment of election staff, police or judges, all the more since the short and medium term issues at stake are so important. In Cambodia, all evidence agrees that all the parties

---

[102] Interviews in the various fields of investigation, in various Western capitals, and during training and debriefing sessions for civilian and military staff taking part in peace operations.

put pressure on local members of electoral registration offices (it was relatively more difficult to get round the international staff at the time of the election itself and the vote count). In Kosova, agents of the Kosovo Liberation Army (UCK) and criminal groups have infiltrated the new Kosovo police service (KPS) and have placed under their control the interpreters who were vital intermediaries for UN civpols in their daily work.

Why does one seek a job in a UN mission?

In practice, the expectations placed on local staff positions are highly variable. This aspect of the analysis is fundamental: it makes it possible to understand how the UN employees are perceived by those around them, and hence the role they are likely to play in interaction. In Cambodia, in retrospect, for former Cambodian employees of the mission and their families, the 'UNTAC' acronym simply meant, 'the people who offered jobs'.[103] In Somalia, in June 1993, a demonstration was organised in Mogadishu to protest against the small number of people recruited by UNOSOM. In Haiti, on April 7, 1995, some days after the transition from the Multinational Force (MNF) to UNMIH, there were demonstrations in Port-au-Prince, in front of the main camp of American troops. During the MNF period the American camp had provided about 700 daily-paid jobs; the demonstrators expected UNMIH to do the same. In Dili in East Timor, at the beginning of 2000, there were successive demonstrations by several thousand people outside the MINUTO offices to call for jobs, leading to some violent incidents. In Baghdad, US forces faced the same kind of demands. Acquiring a job with an international structure means, first of all, securing a regular salary, noticeably higher than the average (although not comparable with the salaries of international staff) in countries where the majority of the population is mainly trying to survive. This motivation is important, but obviously varies according to the local socio-economic situation at the time of deployment of operations, and also to the number of international agencies, also potential employers, present in the country at the same moment. In Cambodia and Bosnia-Herzegovina (at the time of UNPROFOR), the UN was the main international employer in the country. In Haiti and Mozambique, in post-Dayton Bosnia and again in Kosovo, in contrast, the mission had to face stronger competition from the intergovernmental and non-governmental aid structures as a whole.

The importance of this economic motivation has a number of consequences, some being double-edged. First of all, it cannot be forgotten that

---

[103] Interviews in Phnom Penh and the provinces, in November and December 1995. From November 1, 1991, to September 30, 1993, $ 26,285,200 was spent in all on local salaries. Source: Reports by the Secretary General on the financing of UNTAC.

in very depressed socio-economic situations such a position can help restore the social status of the individuals concerned, with the obligations attached to it. Those people generally have to make the people around them profit from their income and, if possible, help some of them get jobs themselves. Thus they play a role of some importance in terms of redistribution of additional economic resources. In practice, in some cases, the sharing out of posts—and hence of the income attached to them—is a stake for the parties to the conflict themselves to play for. In Mogadishu, a city divided in two, the jobs share-out was carried out between the two main politico-military groups. In view of the recruitment channels in operation, the people concerned most often already enjoyed a privileged social status. This is even more clearly the case for jobs requiring specific competence, such as interpreting and translation jobs. Knowledge of a foreign language—even approximate knowledge—is not at the disposal of the average citizen. This can have quite important consequences for the way in which the people concerned are seen by local people involved in dealings with the international staff. In El Salvador and Haiti, for instance, interpreters were very largely recruited among the better-off social class and were perceived as belonging to the most conservative political sector. Local political history explains how in Bosnia-Herzegovina a noticeable proportion of the local United Nations staff (but also of staff employed by other international organisations and, later, by NGOs) consisted of former officials of the former Communist Yugoslavia. In Mozambique, people who served as English-language interpreters (but also as drivers) had generally learned rudiments of that language during time spent in the neighbouring countries as refugees; a number of them returned to Mozambique for this work and left again when the operation ended. In Cambodia, many interpreters were people who had already worked for United Nations agencies in the refugee camps on the border. Former members of UNTAC regularly complained of having had people from the camps (and consequently from the opposing branch) 'imposed' on them (even though the mission tried to maintain a balance in recruitment); this resulted in many problems with the local population.

Intermediaries? Informers? Collaborators?...

Some expectations are particularly linked to the interface position held by local staff of UN missions. However, this depends on the personality of the individual concerned, and, most important, on the perception local actors have on their ability to play an intermediary role, on the one hand and, on the other, the willingness of members of the missions themselves to see them play such a role. All roles at the point of contact between two structures or two groups are not necessarily intermediary roles. If one adopts F. G. Bailey's view that an intermediary is facilitating communication[104], generally it is possible to distinguish two types of situation in which that description fits local employees of United Nations missions: the first, both more common and more difficult to pin down, involves an indirect, sometimes hidden role of informer; the second concerns interpreters and translators who are, in the fullest sense, 'communication facilitators'.

Administrative staff (secretaries, receptionists *et al.*) and drivers, but also, in some cases, domestic servants can have access to a certain amount of information. In fact, it is not impossible that some are used as intelligence agents. The reality of such situations is difficult to assess, apart from isolated examples. When a mission intervenes in a context of continued serious tension, *a fortiori* in time of war, as in Somalia, Bosnia and Iraq, the existence of such agents is well known, but insufficiently taken into account by peacekeepers as a given fact to be managed as such (including to quell rumours that circulate very quickly on that subject). In the majority of UN missions things are much more blurred. The staff based outside the capitals can, if they are on their guard, more easily find out the social relations of local employees outside working hours. Very regularly members of missions have told me that this led them to hide important documents. Others recall this or that example of a local employee who seemed to be making many photocopies. In Cambodia, after the departure of UNTAC, the appointment of former local employees of the UN to posts in the administration was interpreted as a reward for services rendered to those in power. In retrospect, former members of missions expressed above all the conviction that, in day-to-day situations, the local employees 'passed on messages' to them. That often happened in a mild manner; 'They told us, "Hey, I've heard that last night such a thing happened" or "it looks as though..."'.[105] In the other direction, local employees are often approached by the international staff with whom they work, for their knowledge of the local situation. This generally involves requests for immediate information, details about places and people, explanations about such and such an event that they witnessed, etc. The messages transmitted may themselves have limited information value, but they contribute to shaping the vision that international staff may have of the conflict in general or of one situation in particular.

[104] Frederick George Bailey, *Stratagems and Spoils: A Social Anthropology of Politics*, Oxford: Blackwell, 1969, 1970.
[105] Interview in Paris, February 3, 1995.

This influence is noticeably greater in the case of local interpreters and translators. When working with the leaders of the missions and of their various components, the interpreter often has an expanded role. He may try to tone down wording considered too hard. A former interpreter of the UNTAC civilian administration recalled that he held back several times from translating words that the senior United Nations official addressed to the Minister: 'He would never have been able to go and see the Minister again…'[106] A former Cambodian professional staff member of the mission confirmed this: 'The interpreters sometimes had to tone things down, for example when UNTAC men banged their fists on the table and threatened ministers; there are things that are not acceptable in our country… The interpreters could tell people what they wanted about what was happening; I can tell you that many things happened largely above the heads of the international staff…'[107] Though translators of written documents did not work in direct contact, they had a job just as important, especially for intermediary purposes. For those who had to translate documents indicating the position taken by this or that party in negociations, and supposed to be a basis for negotiation or for future laws, the task was particularly delicate, as testified by Meng Ho Leang, member of the UNTAC interpreters/translators team who, notably, translated the electoral law into Khmer. Translations could also be requested by the missions to understand the content of leaflets or documents put out by local movements. It is well known how difficult an art translation is, and how the exact choice of words can prove important in certain conflict situations. At that intermediary level, the missions often chose their interpreters among members of the Diaspora, which is supposed to reduce the risks of partisan bias, but does not avoid it altogether.

In many countries local actors, former members of missions and interpreters themselves acknowledge that many messages were 'lost' or else 'were seriously distorted in translation'. In most cases, distortions or mistranslations were involuntary, occurring simply because the interpreter did not understand what was said in a foreign language or had difficulty in translating it into the local language. That was particularly marked when abstract ideas, which had no equivalent, had to be translated. The coexistence of very different registers most often complicated the task of local interpreters, whose level of training was generally very low. In the various countries of our investigations, the general feeling was that those who had worked as interpreters 'spoke French or English very badly and understood it even less'; this tends to confirm the impression

---

[106] Interview in Phnom Penh, November 29, 1995.
[107] Interview with Klok Buddhi, Phnom Penh, November 20, 1995.

given by contacts that I had with people who in various countries had held interpreting jobs with the UN.

On the ground, when the international personnel have no knowledge or very limited knowledge of the local language, their dependence on the interpreter is almost total, and the possibility of assessing his worth most often limited. 'Sometimes, the sense of what was said was seriously altered. To try to check that the translation was good, we posed other questions, but it was a very long and difficult process, and most often we did not have the time. We knew that at best, the interpretation was approximate.'[108] The international staff usually has no choice, the alternative being not be able to communicate with the local people at all. The interpreter is often the only possible link, and it is often he who in reality chooses the mission's interlocutors. That is particularly important when the mission itself undertakes the organisation of elections and, *a fortiori*, when it works as a transitional authority. Even if international observers are sent specially for polling day, it is the interpreters and the local UN staff whom the voters will approach first.

But it would be an exaggeration to think of them as all-powerful. The position of a local employee of a peace operation is not an easy one. It is also often dangerous. When, as in East Timor, Somalia and Haiti, or more recently in Iraq, international staff members have to be evacuated at one stage of the operation for security reasons, the local staff remain on the spot, generally without any protection. For those who sometimes say they are called 'traitors'[109] it is not uncommon to pay a high price for their compromise. What is both more common and more diffused is the way missions' local employees recall their 'unease' at 'collaborating' with outsiders in positions where they considered themselves 'underemployed', 'ill-treated' or even 'humiliated' because they had to receive instructions from arrogant young volunteers with neither their qualifications nor their experience. The tight security around the missions' buildings is also a frequent source of humiliation for the local staff. In that case, as in every case where security is involved, the people concerned are, first and foremost, not so much UN employees as 'locals'.

---

[108] Interview with Geneviève H. Merceur, former member of the UNTAC 'Civil Administration' component in Siem Reap province, questioned while she was working as Assistant to the Representative of the United Nations Secretary General in Cambodia (Phnom Penh, November 29, 1995).

[109] Even in contexts of relatively less tension, this accusation is a common one, as testified by former Salvadorian employees of ONUSAL (investigations in August–September 1995).

3

PEACEKEEPERS AND LOCAL SOCIETIES: THE ENCOUNTER AND ITS EFFECTS

As a peacekeeper, taking the people you deal with seriously—whether it be a commander, militiaman, political leader, simple peasant or shanty-town dweller—requires understanding how these individuals actually regard you. There are expectations—positive and negative—present before the mission's arrival, and they change during its presence in the country. They are derived notably from the different interpretations that local actors make of the UN mandate. That assessment contributes to defining the outlines of what can reasonably be expected from the UN. Even before its deployment in a country, every mission is thus the object of assessments which will be revised according to the experience local actors have of it. So it is by its nature a dynamic process, and must be understood as such.

DIFFERENT INTERPRETATIONS OF A PEACE OPERATION'S MANDATE

Representations of 'order' and 'peace'

The sort of action needed to be undertaken to re-establish order and peace in a country is related to a large collection of conceptions. 'Peace' is a notion with a wide variety of meanings, while everyone acts as if its content is self-evident. The objectives assigned to a peace mission are similarly defined in relation to a number of representations about the re-establishment of international and local 'order' and the rebuilding of the country or even of the state. It is well known how interpretations of these various elements can differ among UN member states themselves. The same holds true of local actors who can make various interpretations (more or less well informed) of what a peace operation claims to do. Knowledge in local collective history can help peacekeepers better

96

understand the diversity of conceptions of what politics,[1] power, or state is about within a given society. Far from searching for intangible cultural references, outsiders must be prepared to encounter social and political *imaginaires*, with the ambivalence particular to those registers and the permanent reinventions that characterise them. That means that it is better to expect ensembles that, while they do indeed allow actors to think of themselves and of their actions, are neither fixed nor necessarily coherent. The cases of Cambodia and Somalia exemplify, in two very different contexts, the nature of the issues at stake in such a way of comprehending local systems of reference.

In Cambodia politics had little in common with the sphere the United Nations authority implicitly took as its reference. This had to do with relations among family units, and involved systems of alliances and patronage networks. These relations could also have a territorial base, because one is symbolically related to someone from the same area. In these conditions political labels have a very relative importance, possibly involving surprising changes of alliance. Family ties impose obligations. The parties are in any case akin to family ties. They are formed out of a patronage network, "one belongs to them through contacts rather than out of political conviction."[2] As the anthropologist Jacques Népote remarked, 'in Cambodia Westerners found themselves in another galaxy'.[3] The understanding of relationships among the principal political actors was peculiarly disrupted by this. In addition, some of the more or less implicit references on which the peace agreement and the UNTAC mandate were based seemed to be out of place. For example, raising the question of 'national reconciliation' with political entrepreneurs made little sense in a society that structurally lived with rivalry among its elements and permanently redefined its relations among networks. Politics can help harmonise the interplay of family rivalry, but by re-ordering it within one, single 'family'. The language of kinship is substituted for that of the political, especially in expression of matters related to authority. Sihanouk is the *Samdech Or* ('My Lord Father'). Illegality or political rebellion is approached etymologically with reference to disobedience to parents. In these conditions the way in which the elections and, especially, their results were managed in the spring of 1993 under the authority of

---

[1] 'The political' must be understood here in its 'substantial' aspects, its properties, more than in its institutions (the formal aspects). Cf. Georges Balandier, 'Le politique des anthropologues', in Madeleine Grawitz and Jean Leca (eds), *Traité de Science Politique*, Volume 1, chapter V, Paris: PUF, 1991, pp. 309–34.

[2] François Ponchaud, 'Elections et société khmère', p. 148 in Christian Lechervy and Richard Petris (eds), *Les Cambodgiens face à eux-mêmes? Contributions à la construction de la paix au Cambodge*, Paris: Fondation pour le Progrès de l'Homme, 1993.

[3] Private interview.

Sihanouk—disregarding the verdict of the polls, although they had returned a clear majority—is seen in a new light. The 'Father of the Nation' settled the matter 'within the family', outside UNTAC. Similarly, that reference to the family register can explain, among other things, that the state is seen as patrimonial property.[4] In view of this, the idea that the UN would be able to exercise economic control over the public administration was based, at best, on a pious wish. In reality, many members of UNTAC's Civil Administration Component confided that they had the impression that 'many things were going on above their heads' or that they 'did not understand much of what was going on'.[5] To them, the government ministries seemed to be 'empty'; what essentially mattered was probably going on outside their walls.

Similarly, the ideas of 'state' and 'law' do not exist in the Khmer language, still less the idea of the 'rule of law'. The main ties linking family networks, as well as the allegiance to the King—the sole expression of possible 'unity'—have to do with the world of the invisible and the religious register. To denote the ideas of 'state' and 'law' and even 'man',[6] the Khmer language has borrowed terms from Sanskrit or Pali, which makes it possible to play on a dual linguistic register. But all these terms are placed in a separate compartment, understood as being outside Cambodian culture; they are not 'Khmer-ised'. This does not prevent them from being manipulated, which is exactly what happened with the democracy and human rights vocabulary that accompanied the UNTAC mission, although the mission made a specific effort to translate the Universal Declaration of Human Rights and other reference documents into Khmer. This apparent disconnection between the local conception of the political and that brought in by United Nations engineering made it possible, in particular, for political entrepreneurs to play on the large number of different registers in dealing with outsiders. The analysis put forward by Raoul M. Jennar on the use of constitutions by Cambodian political leaders is revealing from this viewpoint: constitutions are not 'a photograph of the regime, at most they made it possible to observe the major preoccupations of the ruling class, including the image of the country that they aimed to offer to foreigners.'[7]

---

[4] The Khmer word for 'governing' (*Som Riep*) literally means 'eating kingship', using the language of eating that is found in many other cultural contexts.

[5] Private interviews in Phnom Penh, Paris and New York.

[6] The idea of 'man', and personal forenames, do not exist in the Khmer language either. Each person is called after his place in the network and the family hierarchy (parents-children, older-younger, nephew-uncle, etc.). The individual has no identity outside the group.

[7] Raoul M. Jennar (ed.), *Les constitutions du Cambodge, 1953–1993*, Paris: La Documentation Française, 1994, p. 10.

The Somali example also illustrates this common ambivalence of registers. Most analysis have emphasised, as Gérard Prunier notes, how the United Nations intervening forces and their Somali opposite numbers 'belonged to two completely different conceptual fields', the former being 'helpless in the face of people who had value systems completely alien compared with their own.'[8] A major difficulty, in a country like Somalia, arises from the fact that interpretations of 'political culture' and its changes are themselves very varied. As a young Somali anthropologist noted, 'Somali anthropology is as divided as the country.'[9] However, all specialists—whether they considered the permanence, transformation or decline of the traditional structure of Somali society in the face of an oppressive state[10]—agreed in the final analysis on the extreme diversity of registers in play, and the flexibility of social and political codes that served as references for Somali political actors. The major Somali politico-military entrepreneurs were able to develop contradictory visions of reconstruction of the Somali state (or of what the 'international community' presented as such). This plural view is in part embedded in variable historical trajectories in different parts of Somali territory, where colonial rule was superimposed on the various 'orders'. In the north (Somaliland), under British rule there was an 'empty colony', with little development; the lack of real interest on the part of the colonial power generally preserved traditional social forms. In declaring secession at the fall of Siyad Barre dictatorship, the Somali National Movement (SNM) played the card of the absence of a state. In the south, the Italian Fascist state sought to impose its rule in an arbitrary and violent fashion (even after the restoration of Italian rule in 1950). Siyad Barre was its true heir, playing on the dual register of 'modernity' and 'tradition'. Afterwards, Ali Mahdi essentially invoked the idea of rebuilding a supposed 'national unity'. This had the double advantage of being intelligible and 'reassuring' for his Western negotiating partners. Moreover, since it involved a centralised state and given the territorial spread of his group, it was advantageous for him to invoke this image. On his side, Mohammed Aydid pursued a regional approach which he initially thought was the way favoured most by the

[8] Statement recorded in Paris, May 10, 1995.
[9] Private correspondence with Marcel Djama, author of 'L'espace, le lieu, les cadres du changement social en pays Nord Somali. La plaine du Hawd (1884–1990)', Social Anthropology doctorate thesis, EHESS, Marseilles, 1995, 2 vols. See also his very interesting film, *Somalie, le prix du sang versé*, La Sept/Arte et Point du Jour, France, 1995.
[10] One gets some idea of what 'use' the dictatorial state serve when taking into account that in 1993, Somalia was not only considered by the UNDP as one of the poorest nations in the world, but also as one of the most militarised, with five dollars spent on the armed forces for every dollar spent on education and health—the second highest ratio in the world (Source: *Human Development Report* 1993).

United States; in view of the changes in the alliances concluded by his group, it would also work in his favour territorially. It is fascinating to observe, in Aydid's case in particular, how the different anthropological interpretations were used in succession.[11]

The trading elites did not all have the same interests in seeing the 'restoration' of a central political authority, which would have meant the return of the former ruling classes who had, for two decades, kept some of them on the margins of economic life. In fact, after the fall of Siyad Barre, regional and transnational networks were profoundly transformed.[12] Beyond clan solidarity, this explains how, under attack from the international forces, some Somali businessmen provided considerable help to someone like Mohamed Aydid.

In Somalia, the way in which the notion of the 'clan' is used is another example of political entrepreneurs' capacity for playing on what are presented as registers that cannot be reduced from one to the other. A clan groups together several *diya* ('blood price') payment groups,[13] linked with each other; it may have a territorial definition, particularly for groups of farmers, but also that of a shared interest, the most significant being those related to economics. This system is considered the most stable one in a social and political reality that is at the same time very fluid.[14] But clan loyalty has always been a highly elastic resource, used and manipulated by political entrepreneurs and military adventurers.[15] When the latter have abundant supplies of money and weapons, their margin for manoeuvre is increased. Therefore in both the state-oriented register and the clan register Somali political actors have played on the flexibility of their socio-political system of belonging. Which explains a good deal of the difficulties their UN negotiating partners found in their ambition to achieve 'national reconciliation' and, still more, 'reconstruction' of the Somali state.

---

[11] Aydid often claimed to believe in the 'pastoral democracy' described by Lewis to show that the state models proposed by outsiders did not correspond. A rationalisation of this set of ideas can be found in his book: Mohamed Farah Aidid and Satya Pal Ruhela, *The Preferred Future Development in Somalia*, New Delhi: Vikas Publishing House, 1993, pp. 149 ff.

[12] See Daniel Compagnon, 'Somalie: les limites de l'ingérence humanitaire. L'échec humanitaire de l'ONU', *Afrique Politique* 1995, pp. 195–6.

[13] The *diya* payment group corresponds to a kinship group (*tol*) defined contractually within the clans and sub-clans grouping families of a close lineage. It acts as a unit for paying and receiving collective reparation for homicide and other damages (the 'blood price'); thus it is the basis for an informal contract (*heer/xeer*), the legal basis of Somali political and social life.

[14] The country has about 100 clans, whose size and power vary considerably. All clans belong to a 'clan family'; that is the highest level of 'potential' political allegiance in Somalia.

[15] See Ioan M. Lewis, *Blood and Bone: The Call of Kinship in Somali Society*, Lawrenceville, NJ: Red Sea Press, 1994.

One has only to think of the operations carried out more recently in Sierra Leone and East Timor, and the extreme malleability of political representations and loyalties in Afghanistan, to understand that this is a central element in most UN peace operations. As much as, if not more than, in the institutional 'appearances', the 'reconstruction' issues are displayed in the very substance of the political sphere and the places where the state is, in practice, being constructed. In this setting, power relations among actors themselves carry vast importance. In particular, this explains how the actors envisaged by the United Nations as possible allies—because they seem to share certain reference ideas such as 'democracy' and 'civil society'—may turn out to be much less cooperative than expected. In practice, what matters in their eyes is the contest waged among themselves for access to power.

The reference ideas mentioned are particularly important among politico-military elites, but find echoes in the conduct of social and community actors, as is shown by the cases of El Salvador and Haiti. In both countries the way in which the political and economic elites, the army and the majority of the population, historically constructed their visions of and relationships with the state is critical. It improves the understanding of how these various groups perceive the action of successive UN missions. In particular, the reference to building of a 'rule of law' has been interpreted in the light of historical experiences in which the interests of the elites and those of the majority of the people were clearly opposed to one another. So, in disturbingly similar ways—extending to the vocabulary used—when dealing with the UN as with the state, the majority of the people in those two countries considered their situation to be that of 'the loser'. Throughout the conflict in El Salvador the state, in the service of a minority, left many of its functions to be assumed by external actors, starting with the American administration. The powerful neighbour's involvement in the civil war was very strong (with the presence of numerous military advisers, massive arms supplies, etc.). As for the elementary services that the state is supposed to provide for its people, they were largely taken in hand by local and international non-governmental organisations (NGOs), which constituted so many 'states within a state'. On the arrival of the United Nations mission, Salvadoreans were expecting to see a 'super-NGO', which in its turn would substitute itself for the state. But ONUSAL did not fill that role. Indeed, 'ONUSAL acted as the state' (that is, 'it behaved as one'); 'it was not different from the state'; it too 'was not for [them]'.[16]

---

[16] Interviews in the suburbs of San Salvador and the regions of Chalatenango and Santa Clara, August–September 1995 (translated from Spanish).

There are striking similarities in the way relations with the state and those with the United Nations mission were expressed during my investigations in Haiti. For the majority of Haitians, the United Nations mission's reference to the building of a 'rule of law' was interpreted in the light of a threefold historical experience. First there was the experience of the divide between legality and daily life, the texts of laws having always been separated by an unbridgeable gap from most of the rules that in practice governed social relations;[17] the legal texts were therefore at best useless, and at worst in the service of the strongest, of injustice; in addition, they tended to freeze that which, in the reality of social relations, had shown a great deal of flexibility. The second significant experience was of control over violence, which, when the state failed to exercise it at the community level, had to take other routes. In the rural areas, a code of relationships was gradually established based on reciprocity and mutual respect; collective control was ensured particularly within the framework of the extended family; every individual was sustained, identified and also positioned. This system of regulation was broadly transplanted to suburban districts, where it managed essentially to master internal violence; violence was coming from the outside, and particularly from the repressive state. This system was toppling at the time when the United Nations mission was deployed, as the repressive apparatus was dispersed but not disarmed. 'Non-political' violence appeared in the poorer districts; theft, especially of livestock, occurred increasingly in rural areas. The very principles of living together, and especially of survival—all the more vital in over-populated areas—were affected by this. It is in this context that the hopes placed initially in the American and then the United Nations military for curbing this harmful trend need to be understood. When their intervention very quickly appeared either ineffective or threatening to social order, people returned to strategies of dodging—the famous *mawonaj* of Haiti. Here entered the third type of experience to which Haitians referred to implicitly when speaking of their experience of the United Nations mission. Throughout history they have learned to size up the people who imposed themselves over them. *Leta*, the *seksyon* chief who embodied authority in daily life,[18] was a *chyen* (a dog) who could eat you (*manje*). The 'eating' register coexisted with a 'vampire' register: the holder of power was also a *pwazon rat*, poison.[19] So, for generations (in fact,

---

[17] This wide gap was particularly striking on questions of landed property, on which the very wording used by men of law and by peasants diverged. It is equally significant for matters relating to family law.

[18] Those army auxiliaries were the basis of the network of repression in rural areas.

[19] This vampire register is related to the witchcraft register, well known to Africanists in particular. As in other countries, it can coexist with a contrary register in which the fact

since Haiti's independence in 1804), *Leta* had been considered as the main enemy, the permanent danger from which you had to protect yourself by avoiding contact as much as possible. If there was no other recourse, one played the idiot. You always had to say yes to anyone representing authority, whether he came from the city—the *boujwa*—or from abroad—the *Blan*.[20] What observers often interpret as resignation has to do, before anything else, with survival and a strong dose of pragmatism. It is striking to note that in interviews with various community organisations, the *Blan*—that is, 'foreigners', both American soldiers and members of the United Nations mission—were described in terms very similar to those used to describe the state. Just as in El Salvador, the same terms were used, where people said the UN 'is acting as the state' (*yo fè Leta*), but in Haiti with the nuance that '*fè Leta*' was also an insult in everyday language.

In practice, relationships with the intervening forces went through two phases. First there was questioning: people sought to explain the attitude of the *Blan*, very much as they traditionally asked questions about the state and the dominant elites, who belonged to a different world: '*Nou pa konprann sa Blan yo ap fè*' ('We don't understand what White people do'), '*Nou pa wè anyen*' ('We see nothing, we understand nothing'), '*Blan yo dwòl, ki sa yo gen nan tèt yo*' ('They are odd, how can they function well?'). Later, especially from the moment intervention was judged to be counter-productive by mission members, far from seeking contact with them, people protected themselves against them. While at the local level this second option did not totally exclude possibilities of friction or, on the contrary, of collaboration, it largely dominated interaction until the withdrawal of the last members of the mission in 2001. Again, the way in which it was expressed was very revealing. '*Si w kite yo, yap manje w*' (literally, 'If you let them, they will eat you'; that is, 'they will get you' like the Haitian state, a *chyen*, could get you). The head of a youth organisation explained: 'In Haiti, we are used to everything political being highly dangerous, even fatal. If you go around without disguise, you can be had without gaining anything. With the Whites, it's the same; it is much more likely for them to have you than the other way round.'[21] In dealing with the

---

of 'eating' is related—as we have seen similarly in connection with Cambodia—to what some have termed the 'politics of the belly'. In Haiti, since the 1996 Carnival, the theme of the 'big eaters' of the presidential palace has been very present in refrains.

[20] Joan Dayan gives some revealing examples of dodging behaviour produced by this relationship with the state: Joan Dayan, *Haiti, History and the Gods*, Berkeley: University of California Press, 1995, pp. 95–7.

[21] Interview with Toto, member of the committee of Chandèl, a youth organisation, Port-au-Prince, 25 April 1995 (translated from Haitian Creole).

UN as with the state, the person who is not even recognised as a citizen is 'always the loser'. So, he is suspicious; he does not rebel, he plays tricks. *'Nou vag yo'* ('We pay no attention to them, we avoid them') was an expression that spread like a *leitmotiv* during the second year of the mission's presence, and was often allied with a certain irony: 'Really, they are still in the country, you think? No, you don't understand, they aren't here any more! Anyway, we can't see them!…'[22]

Sizing up the aims of a United Nations mission

One needs to get right inside this changing intertwined pattern to grasp how local peoples can understand peace operations, and especially an operation's mandate. The more specific assessment of what can reasonably be expected of them assumes that a mandate's objectives are more or less known. From that point of view, the elite and the rest of the population do not have the same level of information. Hence the factors behind their constant assessments of those they have to deal with are not the same either.

For political actors, whether a mission is deployed as part of the implementation of a peace agreement or without such an agreement affects the situation radically. If there is an agreement, it has generally been the object of long negotiations among the parties, just as the mission's mandate has been. That of course does not prevent either divergent interpretations or, obviously, attempts to secure favourable adaptations of what has been conceded on paper. While the broad objectives are laid down, the essential part of the 'how' remains to be defined. In fact, maintaining this element of vagueness is often considered by negotiators a condition for signing of an agreement; if everything was made clear, the parties would never sign. That aspect is emphasised when there is a central diplomatic dimension to agreements, as happened in Cambodia; the practical implementation details mattered less at that time than securing an agreement to take the matter off the international agenda. The various parties potentially have more room to manoeuvre if they know how to take advantage of the uncertainty so created. Even so, the existence of such a framework of reference is at least a point for taking bearings for the various protagonists.

In the absence of such a framework, the situation seems much more uncertain. This state of uncertainty generally has implications for all components of the mission. The main danger then seems to be not so much the raising of 'exaggerated hopes' (a fear often expressed by senior UN offi-

[22] Translated from Haitian Creole.

cials), but absolutely contradictory interpretations. In Somalia the main politico-military actors initially sized up the UN operation's objectives in the light of their struggle for power. The presence of such a mission could appear either favourable or unfavourable to such an aim. Before any military action, the mandate for protection of food distribution clearly threatened an important power resource for those leaders. On other matters, the mission was assessed in accordance with the scenarios expected to favour the redistribution of power. The main point in common between the two main politico-military leaders, Ali Mahdi and Mohamed Aydid, had to do with their concern to be considered the major, if not the sole partners in negotiations.[23] As for the political leaders of the secessionist territory of Somaliland, they desperately needed economic aid but remained highly sceptical towards aid that was often described as 'too little, too late, too slow, and too bureaucratic'.[24] Above all, they continually suspected that the UN had a 'hidden agenda' for reunification of the country. Hence any proposals heading in that direction and, *a fortiori*, any involving deployment of United Nations troops were very regularly rejected.

In Bosnia-Herzegovina, the arrival of United Nations troops gave rise to absolutely contradictory views, visible well before they were deployed. In view of the different roles played by the UN in management of the crisis, as well as the objectives of their mission, it is the expectations of the UN side that must be examined. Each one of the parties had then different reasons for preferring the involvement of the UN rather than that of the European Community.[25] The Serb part—particularly its leader, the President of Yugoslavia[26]—was suspicious of the EC and considered some of its members as hostile. It expected from the UN—where Yugoslavia had enjoyed some support through the Non-Aligned Movement—a 'non-interference' that would guarantee maintenance of a profitable status quo. In addition, the Serbs considered that the concern of a certain number of UN member states to avoid the chaos that would have resulted from a fragmentation of the country could only work in their favour. Probably one should link that specific assessment with the Bosnian Serbs'

---

[23] Private interviews at the UN Secretariat, New York, January 1995.

[24] As stated by the minister of Planning, quoted by P. S. Gilkes, *Two Wasted Years: The Republic of Somaliland (1991–1993)*, Save the Children Fund (UK), August 1993, p. 50.

[25] During this period the UN Secretary General, through the agency of his special envoy Cyrus Vance, took the baton from the European Community whose plan had been rejected.

[26] Yugoslavia's Representative to the UN addressed a letter to the President of the Security Council on November 26, 1991 calling, in the name of his government, for the establishment of a 'peace keeping operation in Yugoslavia' to reach a peaceful solution within the framework of the Hague Conference.

request in the summer of 1992 that United Nations troops should guarantee the cease-fire and establish a protectorate over Sarajevo.[27] The extension of the UNPROFOR mandate to Bosnia,[28] within a limited humanitarian framework, seems to have been interpreted by the Bosnian Serbs as a clear indication that 'the Westerners would never go further'. This would explain also their persistent doubts, later on, about NATO threats of armed intervention. The experience of the European mission in Croatia similarly encouraged the Bosnian Croats to favour playing the United Nations card. The case was the same for the Bosnian Muslims, them too turning towards the UN. Even before the war broke out, President Izetbegovic several times requested a preventive deployment to 'avoid the spread of violence in the Republic'. In March 1992, when the independence of the Republic was proclaimed he made many declarations and appeals for deployment of UN Blue Helmets. On May 12, 1992, he called for intervention to help him 'restore order'. At the UN Secretariat it was thought the conditions for a peacekeeping operation had not been met.[29] These calls revealed mistrust towards the European Community, particularly strong among the Bosnian Muslims. They had just been put under intense pressure to accept the division of Bosnia into 'cantons'.[30] When the extension of the UNPROFOR mandate to Bosnia was limited to humanitarian tasks, this was a serious blow to them. Not only would the Blue Helmets not be an interposing force; their presence would rapidly seem to be an obstacle for the possibility of real military intervention. Then, the Muslims had either to force the UN troops to go beyond their mandate or to convince member states to deploy another mission.

In the absence of a peace agreement a multinational force can be seen alternatively, by one or other of the groups in conflict, as being possibly useful or hostile towards their endeavours. Any matter left unclear will be exploited, especially by political and military entrepreneurs in positions of strength on the ground. This is generally aggravated by the fact that the objectives of such operations, often very vague, are an object of dispute among the various intervening forces themselves, besides varying over time and being not entirely implicit. Obviously, local actors play on this, explaining in part the extreme volatility of such situations.

The uncertainty is often still greater for social and community actors who are generally kept out of political discussions and have limited information at their disposal on what the UN is supposed to do in their

---

[27] See especially Susan L. Woodward, *Balkan Tragedy: Chaos and Dissolution after the Cold War*, Washington, DC: Brookings Institution Press, 1995, pp. 285–9.

[28] Resolution 758 of the Security Council, June 8, 1992.

[29] See Reports S/23836, of April 24, 1992, and S/23900.

[30] According to the 'compromise' proposed in Lisbon on February 23, 1992.

countries. Lacking real indications to go on, their expectations are governed by both the suffering endured during the violence and the immediate needs arising from the conflict. Social organisations (especially human rights organisations) are inclined to see a peace operation as a 'super-NGO', but one that must deal with them on equal terms. Initially, the presence of an international mission opens up a space for them to act more openly and with hope of better protection for their members. But very soon they realize international forces are occupying that space in their place, overshadowing rather than supporting them. Hence their relationship is generally one of rivalry. The backing expected by such organisations does not fit in well with the precautions taken by UN missions to preserve a certain balance, indeed certain 'impartiality'. Local human rights NGOs expect the missions to take their side openly since they defend internationally recognised and protected rights. Indeed, disappointment and mistrust gradually take over from initial expectations, far from being fulfilled. The fact that international NGOs land with the peacekeepers on a massive scale plays a decisive role, since they tend to saturate the space at the expense of the local organisations. An additional factor is that the idea of observing or monitoring attached to some aspects of peace operations (such as those dealing with human rights or, to some extent, with policing) is often very poorly understood by the local organisations, for whom peace building requires voluntarism and explicit action—what is the point of accumulating reports that serve no purpose? The criticism towards UN civpols is usually also very high, particularly in cases where they mentor local police and pretend not to do the job in their place. The usual weakness of judicial systems does not help either as it may lead to situations where, for instance, an offender arrested by the police may soon be released by a corrupt or simply inefficient judge. The UN is also often denounced for practising a type of 'self-censorship' in its reports, not understood by local NGOs.

The expectations of community actors are more difficult to discern. Obviously one cannot claim to be able to assess the way a people as a whole understand the objectives of UN missions, even in cases such as El Salvador where opinion surveys were available.[31] The observer always runs a big risk in projecting his own ideas. My own approach, more limited and targeted, aimed at understanding the popular assessment from a representative sample of community actors in each country. Where I was able to carry out in-depth investigations on that point, one idea recurred,

[31] In El Salvador, an opinion survey by the IUDOP, carried out from October 12 to November 2, 1991, showed that 52.3 per cent of the people questioned did not know what ONUSAL's task was (results published in *Proceso*, no. 498, December 11, 1991).

with some allowances for translation: with the arrival of the Blue Helmets, 'We hoped we could breathe'. A moderate hope, fairly well summed up in the words of a Haitian peasant: 'What can we expect, really? We don't know. We say to ourselves, "What are they going to bring us here?" and we hope... without really hoping.'[32] One element that seems crucial in defining the way in which peace missions are perceived upon their arrival lies in the scale of deployment. There is plenty of testimony recalling in particular the white all-terrain vehicles that invade the streets, and the hotels taken over and occupied by people moving around hither and thither. But there is an important reservation: 'We don't see what they are doing'. And during investigations, the resulting incomprehension was expressed in exactly the same terms: they are seen 'running around everywhere in their big white cars' or 'travelling around', but basically 'They solve nothing', 'They do nothing', 'They just look around'. Quite often impatience also appears: 'If it's to find out about the situation, we don't need them. There exist thousands of findings and reports. Everybody knows what's wrong in this country. Why spend more money for that?'[33] This perception is prevalent throughout the countries under intervention, but it is particularly marked in the capital cities, where the strong concentration of resources and the decrepit state of the social and economic environments in which missions' intervention generally takes place. In these conditions, the subtle points of what comes under, or does not come under, the UN mandate is not easy for the average person to understand. For them, on one side there is their own infinite and immediate needs, and on the other, a mission with plentiful logistic resources that could meet those needs. This is illustrated by an anecdote recorded by community organisations at Morasán in El Salvador. In 1992 they were preparing to celebrate the patron saint's feast; for eight years it had not been possible to organise the celebrations in normal conditions due to a lack of security but also electricity and water. A delegation went to the local ONUSAL office to request generators and containers of water. The idea that the mission's mandate did not cover this had not entered their minds. The mission had come for the sake of peace, and the first symbol of the return of peace for the region was organising the patron saint's feast. If the mission, which had its cars and all its logistical assets, was not useful for that, of what use was it?[34]

This gap between the means at their disposal and what they are able to offer under their mandate is clearly resented by many members of the

[32] Words recorded in northern Haiti, May 2, 1995 (translated from Haitian Creole).
[33] Words recorded at Port-au-Prince, April 25, 1995 (translated from Haitian Creole).
[34] Interviews in San Salvador, September 1995 (translated from Spanish).

missions. However, the community actors and 'ordinary' citizens of the countries where they intervene generally show a high degree of pragmatism. Not having been informed about what a mission is supposed to do, they naturally 'judge by results'. Furthermore, as the operation proceeds, with small gains secured and refusals experienced, the assessment of what can reasonably be expected of both the mission in general and this or that person in particular, matures. People's accounts clearly reveal this process of observation that is directed at the way requests are examined, at what is done with information passed on to the mission, and on the follow-up of visits during which the people are asked what they 'want', etc. In El Salvador, members of grassroot organisations have explained to me how, gradually, they understood 'that nothing could be expected from them', 'that meetings never led to anything, that everything was very formal.'[35] And then there was this observation: 'We are used to nothing being done for us; in reality, it is the contrary which would have been surprising.'[36] Disappointment did not stop people from trying their luck, 'because after all, it costs very little to ask.'[37] An attitude which is considered to be quite fair by the missions' members.

The disappointment is managed with greater or less fatalism from one country to another. In Cambodia, while the population of the cities tried to get some immediate advantages, in the rural areas as a whole people seem to have absorbed much more quickly the fact that, 'Nothing should be expected from that mission'. A former United Nations Volunteer recalls: 'Many of them showed openly that they did not feel concerned by "our problems", as the interpreters told us.'[38] Even where security issues were acute, people were able to show a philosophical attitude, like one *phum* chief put it: 'We quickly understood. When a shot was fired, the United Nations soldiers left. This meant that it was not the real force that had come to bring peace. We understood it was necessary to go on waiting.'[39] The head of a community development organisation declared, 'UNTAC may have made some efforts in terms of education in human rights, but people still saw violence and murder, and saw that UNTAC did nothing.

[35] Interviews with members of the Consejo Coordinador del Movimiento Comunal Salvadoreño (San Salvador, August 28, 1995), with delegates of base communities in the lower-class district of La Chacra (in the south-eastern suburbs of San Salvador; September 13, 1995), and with *repoblaciones* communities (Santa Clara and Chalatenango Regions, September 1995); translated from Spanish.

[36] Words spoken during the General Assembly of the Guarjila community, in northern Chalatenango, September 16, 1995 (translated from Spanish).

[37] Translated from Spanish.

[38] Recollection by Béatrice Trouville, former UNV (Electoral Component), based in Batheay district, Kompong Cham province (Phnom Penh, December 18, 1995).

[39] Words recorded in Kompong Thom region, December 16, 1995.

If there were problems in the street, most of the time they did not even stop.'[40] A district chief recalled: 'The UNTAC people never went further than here [the district headquarters]; they never went into the district itself, where you went. There was a company here but they stayed in the centre of the district, they did not move around. UNTAC was afraid of the Khmers Rouges. They were afraid of people who had weapons...When they agreed to move around, it was well after everything had become calm again. Many soldiers told me that they thought about their country a lot, they did not want to die in Cambodia, their family was waiting for them at home. I don't know if their commanders sent them to protect the peasants; I only know what I saw—which was not doing that. We had to go on getting by in other ways. That is what I said to the *phum* chiefs and peasant delegations who came to see me: "You should expect nothing from those people; they will do nothing to protect you."'[41]

In Haiti, when problems of insecurity developed in a troublesome way, 'UNMIH does not do anything'; 'If we call them, they say it is not their job—but what is their job?'[42] Worse still, 'The United Nations people, whenever they hear shots from somewhere, they leave; 'If there is a problem, they take to their heels, they do not want to put their security at risk';[43] 'When we call them, either we never see them or we see them arriving at least an hour later, when they are sure it is all over';[44] 'The United Nations are like our firemen, you know, they always arrive too late', said a women's organisation leader.[45] The situation was particularly delicate to manage at that time, in a country where the army had been

---

[40] Recollection by Meas Nee, head of the Khmer community development organisation Krom Apwehap Phum (Battambang, December 7, 1995).

[41] Recollection by Huy Chiet, district chief of Maung Russey under UNTAC (Maung Russey, Battambang province, December 7, 1995).

[42] That image was also partly inherited from the Multinational Force preceding the United Nations mission, as is shown by the cartoon published on the front page of January 1, 1995 issue of the daily *Le Nouvelliste*, summarising the past year's events. On one side some people suffering from acts of repression, and others shouting '*SOS volè*', are shown; on the other side are American soldiers, sheltering behind their barbed wire, armed and helmeted, looking on without moving. A commentary says, 'This is not our job!' (*Le Nouvelliste* no. 34,882, December 30, 1994–January 2, 1995).

[43] '*Gade mesye sa yo, yap veye kò yo*' was a phrase often heard in the street in April–May 1995 (literal meaning 'See how they look after their own skin'). Similarly, the representatives of operational organisations of the UN system who were present in the country did not conceal their incomprehension and strong disapproval of this inaction (private interviews in Port-au-Prince, April 1995).

[44] Comment by a district organisation leader, Bel Air, Port-au-Prince, May 24, 1995 (translated from Haitian Creole).

[45] Comment by Evelyne Larieu of Solidarite Famn Aysyen, Port-au-Prince, April 24, 1995 (translated from Haitian Creole).

dissolved and there was not yet a police force capable of taking its place. The commanders of detachments of 'Civpols' (the UNMIH civilian police) did not conceal their helplessness: 'We have to explain that we are here to support the interim police force, not to replace it. But that force is non-existent, it does not have the means to operate and its members know that they are going to be laid-off when the new police force is formed. Besides, people have no confidence in them.'[46] As for the United Nations military personnel (much more numerous), their presence was only supposed to provide a deterrent.[47] A member of the Civilian Mission (MICIVIH) confirmed this: 'When there is a problem, at best we go to the spot and the military go by in their cars. It is simply a ritual, nothing else. But this in itself is not going to ensure people's security. In fact, most of the time, we are of no use at all.'[48]

When a battle broke out between two rival gangs, in a lower-class area of Cap Haïtien (Cité Lescot/Pont Neuf) in the north of the country, the blue-helmeted troops 'had a few rocks thrown at them, so they left. In reality they did not know how to control the situation.'[49] For the senior officials of the mission the reaction was in accordance with instructions: both soldiers and police were supposed to avoid getting involved in that sort of event; they must simply watch to see that things did not get worse, and for that reason they generally returned to the scene after the event. For the inhabitants of the district, it was a sign of ill will and incompetence. This impression was reinforced a year after the mission's deployment by persistent rumours suggesting that UNMIH was itself experiencing cases of assault and robbery (especially of weapons) against its members. The chief of staff confirmed that there were incidents, which he said were 'isolated'.[50] This was a powerful symbol: 'They can't even protect themselves, how can they protect us?' This was the question asked by most people I interviewed at that time.[51]

---

[46] Comment by Commander Sharif A. Salem, Commanding the North department (Cap Haïtien, May 2, 1995); interviews at Les Gonaïves and Les Cayes.

[47] This gap between reality and a mission's mandate, in which neither soldiers nor civpols were supposed to ensure order themselves, has also been emphasised by the Special Representative of the Secretary General, in Lakhdar Brahimi, 'La Mission des Nations Unies en Haïti. Mode d'emploi pour une mission de maintien de la paix', p. 59 in Yves Daudet (ed.), *La crise d'Haïti (1991–1996)*, CEDIN-Paris I, Cahiers Internationaux, Paris: Ed. Montchrestien, 1996.

[48] Words recorded at Gonaïves (confidential interview), May 4, 1995.

[49] Words recorded during a meeting with a group of building workers, members of the Solidarite Travayè Ayisyen-SOLTRA organisation (Cap Haïtien, May 1, 1995).

[50] Interview with Colonel William Fulton (Port-au-Prince, February 24, 1996).

[51] Interviews in Port-au-Prince (February–March 1996).

Thus, generally, community actors learn quite quickly to size up UN peacekeepers. The process of learning also extends to the results obtained from interventions of outsiders, especially when those are judged harmful to social order. This appeared very clearly in my investigations in rural areas in El Salvador and Cambodia. In both countries, the problems of concern for local people essentially involved robbery and road accidents. In Haiti, the way in which United Nations military or police personnel handled cases of theft rapidly exasperated the inhabitants. 'They treat people as one and the same, whereas some are victims and others culprits. They say that people steal because they have problems and they share the loot; that means that the thief has the right to steal, and the *zenglendo*[52] have now found people to intervene on their behalf.'[53] In rural areas it was theft of goats and pigs, sometimes of cattle that occurred most often, while in urban areas theft was more diversified.[54] More than anything else, it was the treatment of arrested thieves that led to recriminations: either 'they escape' or 'they are released by the UNMIH people who say they are unfortunate characters.'[55] In actual fact, as a leader in the Justice and Peace Commission observed, 'With some exceptions, it is not the mission itself that releases the thieves; generally, they are handed over to judges and it is the justice system that does not take its course. This is how thieves are released. But in people's minds it is the mission that is responsible, since the prisoners were handed over to them in the first place.'[56] Two reports, on April 25, 1995, over one of the most popular radio stations in the capital, Radio Quisqueya, were highly revealing. One recounted an incident the previous evening in the barracks of Pétionville (a residential district on the hillsides of Port-au-Prince): 'Eleven prisoners placed under UNMIH's direct control have escaped. What does that mean? What security is being brought to us?' In fact the escape took place right before the eyes of the Haitian interim police force. The second report described the arrest in Mariani (a *commune* near the capital) 'by the interim police and Canadian observers' of six armed masked persons: 'The six bandits were later released by the Canadians', said the journalist in conclusion.

There remains a very widely shared perception that 'not only do these people fail to provide us with security, but they in fact endanger

---

[52] The word *zenglendo* (literally 'broken glass') generally means a delinquent.

[53] Interview with Moïse Jean-Charles, spokesman for the Mouvman Peyizan Milo, Milot, Nord department, May 1, 1995 (translated from Haitian Creole).

[54] Interviews in four departments of the country. Livestock are the real moneybox of the Haitian peasant, who often has only one or two animals at best.

[55] Interviews in various regions of the country. Cf. the final declaration of the Kongrè Espesyal MPNKP (Papaye, March 17–20, 1995).

[56] Words quoted from Daniel Roussière, head of the Justice and Peace Commission of Les Gonaïves-JILAPDIGO (Gonaïves, Artibonite department, May 3, 1995).

security.'[57] A suggestion backing those heard from community actors in El Salvador and Cambodia. To understand it one must realise what the revival of delinquency of that type meant for the daily life of the people in districts with extreme overcrowding. In Haiti, members of a peasant organisation were worried, saying, 'We know well what will happen; people will have no other choice but to protect themselves. And how can one blame them? For the small peasant, his animal is the only wealth he has.'[58] In fact cases of mob justice multiplied and, ironically, quickly became a major preoccupation for UNMIH because they disturbed public order...

For senior United Nations officials, this form of insecurity, that develops in practically all the situations where the UN intervened, during an interim period filled with uncertainty, is considered a 'normal' development 'not to be compared with the previous situation'.[59] In private, however, some recognise the severe limitations to this approach: 'It is serious because insecurity is a psychological question. Every incident is magnified. Insecurity is related first of all to everything a person fears. Today, people have the impression that just anything can happen to them. This cannot be corrected by saying "that is not our mandate".'[60]

Signals sent during operations by peace missions

In this process of assessment, the signals sent by members of UN missions themselves play a decisive role. In fact, the arrival of peacekeepers is accompanied, or preceded, by a certain amount of information aimed particularly at making their acceptance by the population easier. The more the intervening forces are concerned about the welcome that may be waiting for them, the more they tend to play on the effect of an announcement and the greater the risk is of distorting the message.

In Haiti, even before the arrival of the first elements of Operation Restore Democracy, in 1994, leaflets were distributed and low-flying helicopters spread messages through loudspeakers saying that the Multinational Force was coming to restore democracy in the country. The particular content of the programme included: the restoration of electricity, building of bridges, road repairs, checks on corruption, etc. The

---

[57] Interview with members of the Akolad Pwilbowo, affiliated to the Tèt Kole movement, Pwilbowo, Nord department, May 3, 1995 (translated from Haitian Creole).

[58] Interview with Michel Renard and Renel Lonirès, members of the coordinating committee of the Pandiassou Group, Plateau Central, May 9, 1995 (translated from Haitian Creole).

[59] Interviews with several Special Representatives of the Secretary General.

[60] Confidential interview, April 1995.

spokesman of the American embassy made numerous declarations in that sense, and informational meetings were organised across the country. Social and community organisations were invited to 'submit plans and talk about needs'. 'The Americans seemed to take an interest in all that was going on, and asked what they could do to help.'[61] In rural areas as in the poorer districts of the towns, public meetings were organised and programmes announced: 'They said we would have water, electricity, all that… They also distributed supplies for the school.'[62] In the Cité Soleil shanty-town in Port-au-Prince, 'the Whites said technicians would come to repair the roads, that from now on we would have no more problems with water and electricity.'[63] Even if 'the Americans never had the intention to do anything at all'—as senior officials of multilateral aid bodies put it bitterly[64]—hopes were truly aroused, at the highest level, as was explained by the head of UNMIH who admitted that this had 'been a preparation for disappointment': 'When Clinton made flights of lyrical oratory here about democracy which would make possible the building of roads and schools and the planting of trees, people understood that it was a commitment by Clinton himself. So how can one be surprised when later they asked, "What has this mission brought us?"'[65] Despite having been broadly announced, fabulous plans to 'put the country back on its feet' were quickly put aside. The confusion dogged the United Nations mission, especially because as the handover from the MNF to UNMIH approached, in February and March 1995, the American ambassador to Haiti, William Schrader, publicly announced the planned content of the United Nations mission's future mandate. The proclamation far exceeded the bounds of the real mandate (vague as that was), both on economic and social matters, and regarding disarmament.[66] This was a way of letting people believe that what had been promised would be carried out in the United Nations phase of the operation. The inhabitants of Mogadishu,

---

[61] Interview with Frantz Guillite, deputy mayor of Les Cayes, former spokesman of the MUPAK (the main people's organisation in the region), former secretary general of the Les Cayes teachers' association (Les Cayes, Sud department, May 12, 1995).

[62] Interview with members of the central committee of the Rasanbleman Oganizasyon Peyizan Limonad, Limonade, Nord department, May 2, 1995 (translated from Haitian Creole).

[63] Meeting with members of the Mouvman Fanm Vayan an Ayiti and the Oganizasyon Rezistans Fanm, Port-au-Prince, Cité Soleil, May 14, 1995 (translated from Haitian Creole).

[64] Interviews in Port-au-Prince, 1995–8.

[65] Words quoted from Lakhdar Brahimi, Special Representative of the Secretary General, head of UNMIH (Port-au-Prince, March 5, 1996).

[66] Interviews with the top UNMIH and MICIVIH officials (Port-au-Prince, April 1995), and reading of the local press.

Kabul and Baghdad would have plenty in common with Port-au-Prince on this subject.

The United Nations' message is generally more modest, but it too tends to 'arouse plenty of false hopes', as heads of missions readily admit. In El Salvador, 'to be seen in a good light by the Salvadorian NGOs, initially [the mission] promised them many things in terms of support…but followed up on nothing.'[67] In that case, this gap between words and deeds was worsened by the fact that, after the first months during which many contacts were made by the mission, relations were much more occasional, 'as the NGOs did not enjoy any priority'.[68] Many of the requests ruled to be 'inappropriate' by senior ONUSAL officials were, in reality, based on literal interpretation of the initial promises. The heads of organisations that I interviewed did not conceal their feeling of having been 'tricked'.[69] What they felt to be a volte-face by ONUSAL led to verbal confrontation and public denunciations of the mission's inconsistency.

The consequences of spreading messages of that sort are all the more serious because there are generally other signals sent out at the same time. In Haiti, the arrival of the troops of the Multinational Force was not only accompanied by promises of a better life, but also by highly symbolic gestures. Electricity and water supplies were restored in many poorer districts of the capital and the main provincial towns. The American army repaired electricity generators and provided massive supplies of fuel. On the evening of September 29, 1994, in Port-au-Prince, a great shout greeted the return of electric light, which some districts had not had for three years. In the towns teams began to clean the streets and regularly collected household rubbish. When people were no longer plunged into darkness at sunset it helped restore a feeling of security in places where the night was seen as a time where violence and death could strike at any moment. In a country where unloading garbage in front of houses was a technique of repression used by the local military, finding a district clean once again was more than a symbol. But the calm was short-lived. On January 15, 1995 the American administration suspended its fuel subsidy and power cuts resumed. When the Multinational Force left, the country plunged back into darkness. '*Anpil Blan, anpil limiyè; ti kal Blan, ti kal limiyè; pa gen Blan, pa gen limiyè*' ['Many Whites, plenty of light; few Whites, little light; no Whites, no light'] was a saying invented for the occasion.

[67] Words quoted from Florentín Melendez, legal adviser to the ONUSAL/MINUSAL mission from the preparatory phase, San Salvador, September 7, 1995 (translated from Spanish).

[68] Ibid.

[69] Interviews in San Salvador (August–September 1995).

The arrival of large numbers of soldiers is also often accompanied by plenty of heavy machinery to the total astonishment of the local people: heavy vehicles, bulldozers, cranes, brand new lorries, lined up in their hundreds on spaces specially prepared around the capitals and airports. As the Special Representative of the Secretary General in Haiti said, 'Incomprehension and perplexity existed in the weeks following the American landing: all those vehicles…were surely going to be put to use, and not only to build military camps!'[70] Just as in Bunia in the eastern Congo the impressive deployment is made in zones that resemble no man's land rather than towns, the shock produced by the encounter is surreal, even to a visitor used to such situations. To counterbalance this impression, UN contingents occasionally take part in road and bridge repair, projects which are also necessary for their movements, or even in improvements to a sports ground, repairs of a local water supply system, roof repairs for a hospital or school, or purification of a well, etc. Larger-scale projects remain exceptional. In many cases, far from the mission being thanked for its efforts to go beyond the limits of its mandate, the initiative is interpreted by local actors as proving that 'they could have done more'. In some countries, as in Haiti or Cambodia, these programs are part of the mission as a whole. But in most cases, the better-off governments allocate funds to their national contingents in UN forces to finance occasional small projects (so-called 'Quick Impact' projects). They aim at making it easier for the local people to accept foreign troops. This most often involves social works (especially access to military hospitals). Activities of this sort arouse very ambivalent reactions on the part of the people. Quite logically, they arouse envy and rivalry. Community groups and leaders, and political actors too, compete to turn aid in their direction, with hopes that are often out of proportion to what can really be offered to them. In fact, more often than not those small projects do not go beyond superficial repairs to a road or the roof of a school or dispensary. These efforts are paltry in relation to both the needs and the means deployed at the same time for the missions themselves. Frequently such aid is also resented as an insulting penny in the hat, and as proof that much more could be done. In several provinces of Cambodia governors reached agreements for UNTAC to repair roads and bridges that they chose. They did not fail to draw maximum political advantage from the operation. But they still considered that it was proof that UNTAC could have done much more for the rebuilding of Cambodia and that they had only been given 'crumbs'.[71] This indicates the ambiguities surrounding action aimed at

[70] Lakhdar Brahimi (note 47), p. 63.
[71] Interviews at Kompong Thom and Battambang.

'securing the support of the local people', action that several analysts have suggested should be developed 'to win hearts and minds'. From one country to another, rather than giving the peacekeepers credit for such efforts, people readily stressed that 'if they had wanted, they could have done much more'. I had many opportunities to observe how that reaction was ill received by Western decision makers, still more by military officers for whom the development of 'civilian-military' activities was an important breakthrough in doctrine. But it fits in with the findings of an investigation by Johan Galtung and Ingrid Eide in the Gaza Strip nearly 30 years ago. When dealing with the 'good works' and other humanitarian activities carried out by UN forces, they noted that they were initially well regarded because they went beyond what the soldiers themselves were supposed to do. However, from the moment these tasks were considered an integral part of a soldier's task, the soldier was judged above all on the basis of what he had not done, which could have been good for the local population.[72]

The military are not the only ones faced with this dilemma. Generally speaking, the responses to requests made from the people for aid—even intermittent aid—are interpreted as a *de facto* recognition of their inclusion in a mission's mandate. Members of missions have often explained to me their difficulty in finding the right attitude to adopt in the face of the numerous demands made on them. In El Salvador, most of them testified that they 'tried to do what they could,'[73] from transporting of wounded or sick to little steps to boost the economy. One explained, 'We solved problems individually. I think it is part of the relationship of trust that can be established with the people at a given moment to say, "It is true that this is not part of our mandate, but if we can do a service at a particular moment, we do it." Now, interpretations at any moment of what is or is not part of the mandate vary considerably. However, it is clear that this sort of attitude encourages many more requests! So you are obliged to say you can't do it, and people resent it much more than they would have if you had stood firm the first time.'[74]

The consequences are altogether more serious when double-talk touches on particularly sensitive subjects such as disarmament. In Somalia,

---

[72] Johan Galtung and Ingrid Eide, 'Some Factors Affecting Local Acceptance of a UN Force: a Pilot Project Report from Gaza', pp. 240–63 in J. Galtung (ed.), *Peace, War and Defence*, Copenhagen: Ejlers, 1976 (Essays in Peace Research, vol. 2).

[73] Interviews with former members of ONUSAL (New York, January 1995) and with the Special representative of the UN Secretary General in El Salvador, head of the ONUSAL/MINUSAL mission (San Salvador, September 6, 1995).

[74] Words quoted from Philippe Texier, Director of the ONUSAL Human Rights Division from July 1991 to July 1992 (Paris, March 7, 1995).

in 1992, initially the American forces announced publicly that there was no general disarmament plan; the main groups were simply requested to store their heavy weapons outside the cities. But this position was to go through many U-turns. On December 29, 1992, 48 hours before a visit by President Bush, aircraft of the US Air Force scattered over the Somali capital 100,000 leaflets in Somali stating that bearing arms would no longer be tolerated in the streets. In the wake of this announcement a vast police operation was launched which lasted over the US President's visit. It resulted in no inclination towards disarmament. The United Nations mission that followed—UNOSOM II—had no mandate on this matter.[75] But, from June 1993 onwards, while the mission's conflict with General Aydid had entered an overt phase, disarmament operations were carried out very selectively in Mogadishu, with very relative success. After November 1993, disarmament became a 'voluntary' operation once again. The whole episode gave a strong impression of lack of seriousness, incoherence and bias at the same time. Two years later the scenario was repeated in Haiti. UNMIH constantly proclaimed that its mandate (which did not come under Chapter VII) did not allow it to carry out disarmament thoroughly. Yet at the same time information was put out about continuation of an 'arms buy-up' programme started by the Multinational Force, and the mission encouraged the people to report possible arms caches. In the minds of the top UNMIH officials this was a matter of showing good will, within the limits of the mission's mandate, in the face of Haitians' expectations in that area. The local interpretation was quite different: 'They are playing a strange game', said the leaders of Haitian human rights defence organisations. 'Sometimes they tell us that it is not part of their mandate to disarm. Sometimes they tell us that they are trying but it is very complicated. Other times again, they shout out everywhere that they have recovered 18,000 or 20,000 weapons. In all this, what really is their mandate?'[76] In many regions of the country, disarmament operations were started and then 'suddenly put to a halt without people understanding why.'[77]

'They themselves do not know what their mandate is'

The signals are also confused because of variations in the interpretations that members of the missions themselves make of their mandates. These

[75] This was in fact the subject of violent polemics between the American administration and the United Nations Secretary General.

[76] Words quoted from Necker Dessables and Chenet Jean-Baptiste, National Justice and Peace Secretariat (Port-au-Prince, February 22, 1996).

[77] Interviews in Port-au-Prince (April 1995 and March 1996) and in the provinces (April–May 1995).

are often inapplicable in the way they have been negotiated in the UN Security Council resolution, and suffer from not always being translated into more precise—above all, operational—real terms at the implementation stage. In the absence of clear directives and uniform methodology and criteria for action, there are often as many interpretations of a mandate as there are members of a mission. This difficulty is not new, as is shown by the results of an investigation through questionnaires carried out by Johan Galtung and Helge Hveem among Norwegian military personnel who took part in UNEF in Gaza and UNOC in the Congo. The authors in that case emphasised the impact of such confusion on relations with the local population.[78] Former members of all missions testify that on their arrival they only received at best very limited information on what their task would involve. There are many who, in response to the question, 'What was your mandate?' would openly answer, 'That's a good question; really, I never knew' or 'Nobody, at any time during the mission, ever told me what I was supposed to do.'[79]

In El Salvador members of ONUSAL often recalled an impression of dashing blindly ahead: they never had any fundamental discussion among themselves about the contents of the mandate or how it should be interpreted. Within each component, their interpretations diverged. In this respect it is symptomatic that some high ranked United Nations officials acknowledged the fact that 'everything was improvised in that mission'. In that case the argument often put forward is absence of any precedent, but this does not entirely explain, nor excuse, the improvisation that prevailed throughout the operation. With a lack of even the briefest job description, 'everyone made his own little mishmash' as best he could; 'Everyone was his own little boss.' Reaction to the same situation could vary radically from one team to the next, from one person to another. This had very obvious consequences in the responses of various requests made by local actors, but also for the work of some components, such as the Police Division. The former adviser of police affairs at ONUSAL headquarters in San Salvador testified: 'No guidelines were drawn out by the heads of the police component for this crucial phase. Everyone did what he liked on the ground. There was complete ignorance about what training programme had been received by the young police officers at the academy. There were huge differences from one team to another.'[80] Even in negotiations with the country's main political leaders, the degree of

---

[78] Johan Galtung and Helge Hveem, 'Participants in Peacekeeping Forces', p. 275 in J. Galtung (ed.) (note 72).
[79] Interviews in Paris and San Salvador (1995).
[80] Interview in Paris, August 10, 1995.

insistence on application of this or that point in the agreements 'depended rather on personalities'.[81] Among the Salvadorian actors this aroused a variety of reactions—often confusion and distrust, but also inclination to exploit these weaknesses. Some political actors admitted that their United Nations negotiating partners 'sometimes made their task easier'—'As there was no follow-up between one discussion and the next, it was often very easy to respond.'[82]

Similarly, in Cambodia, UNTAC staff tried to translate into concrete terms a plan concocted by others, with often clashing interpretations, especially on the most obscure parts of the mandate. Control over the administration was one of these issues.[83] There were particularly divergent interpretations between the heads of the mission component and the top officials of the mission.[84] Within the component itself, opposing visions clashed, as is shown by internal documents and interviews with the individuals concerned.[85] While the director of that component opted for a hard line, his deputy—who arrived a few weeks before him—immediately favoured, out of concern for realism, a 'negotiated' and 'conciliatory' approach to control. At an information meeting organised with officers of the ministry of Defence of the State of Cambodia, on September 3, 1992, he explained: 'There is no question for us of administering in your place. Nor even of intervening in your daily administration, except for getting information…I would like to explain that we do not have any intention of using without discernment all the exorbitant powers given by the Agreements to UNTAC to achieve direct control. Those powers exist, but my preference is for dialogue…' A little further on, he concluded, 'UNTAC is not here to dismantle your administrative structure, but it must simply control the way it functions with regard to the elections.'[86] The head of the Civil Administration Component made his different opinion clear: 'For my part, I did not envisage my work of control as dialogue nor

[81] Interview with a senior official of the mission (San Salvador, September 7, 1995).

[82] Interview with Rodolfo Parker, adviser to President Cristiani during the negotiations and former head of the Unidad de Coordinación de la Aplicación de los Acuerdos de Paz, San Salvador, August 29, 1995 (translated from Spanish).

[83] The largest difficulties encountered in translating that aspect of the mandate into concrete terms is summarised in an internal document drawn up at the end of the mission: 'Réflexions sur le contrôle direct exercé par l'administration civile de l'APRONUC', Phnom Penh, June 18, 1993 (mimeo).

[84] Interview with Gérard Porcell, former Director of the Civil Administration Component of UNTAC (Phnom Penh, December 13, 1995).

[85] Interviews with, in particular, Gérard Porcell and Dominique-Pierre Guéret, former Deputy Director of the same component, head of the Defence department (Phnom Penh, December 13, 1995; Paris, October 23, 1995).

[86] Source: minutes of the meeting, pp. 8 and 9.

negotiation at all.'[87] In fact, he secured adoption of targeted sanctions against certain individuals. As for the special control teams sent out occasionally on the spot, they 'created their own methods for themselves, according to the circumstances, and often made inconsistent responses to similar situations.'[88] Lastly, UNTAC regional directors generally favoured an interpretation of the mandate that made it possible for them to avoid cutting them from the Cambodian officers they had to deal with on the ground—in other words, a toned-down and very flexible interpretation of the idea of 'control'.

The police components of UN missions are often very much affected by this process, as was shown in Haiti. Senior military members of the mission, without hiding their views, repudiated the way the mandate had been translated into operational terms concerning police matters. This undoubtedly added to the difficulties members of the police component faced in dealing with security questions, which were complex, as no programme of demobilisation and systematic disarmament had been started. The vagueness of direction also put the police officers in an awkward position in regard to their military colleagues on the one hand and civilian members of MICIVIH on the other. The latter themselves often had a warped idea of what the civpols were supposed to do, and in the process openly backed the idea that the police 'were not doing their job', confirming an impression largely spread among local people.[89] From this local actors generally deduced that 'the United Nations people [had] many problems themselves', that 'they were mixed up in endless contradictions' and 'they [did] not always know what they [were] supposed to do'.[90] When missions face serious security difficulties, the consequences can be fatal, as has been emphasized by the report of the commission of inquiry set up by the Security Council on the dramatic events in Somalia in 1994. The absence of guidelines and terms of reference at all levels of the mission were particularly stressed.[91] In Bosnia-Herzegovina, the military com-

---

[87] Private interview in Phnom Penh, December 13, 1995.

[88] Interview with Lieut.-Col. Calleja, former member of an inspection team of the Defence department of the UNTAC civil administration (Paris, 23 October 1995), and internal reports consulted.

[89] Interviews, especially in the provinces (investigation visits in 1995 and 1996).

[90] Interviews with political and social actors during the two investigation visits.

[91] Report S/1994/653, New York, February 24, 1994, p. 47. See also the testimony of military personnel who took part in the operation in Somalia, especially that of Colonel Michel Touron (in charge of preparatory operations for the arrival of the French UN contingent in Somalia in 1993) and that of a Major-General of the US Army: Michel Touron, 'Esprit humaniste et aide humanitaire', p. 347 in Académie Universelle des Cultures, *Intervenir? Droits de la Personne et Raisons d'Etat*, Forum International sur l'Intervention, December 16–17, 1993, Paris: Grasset, 1994; S. L. Arnold, 'Somalia: An Operation Other Than War', *Military Review*, December 1993, pp. 26–35.

manders who held various posts of responsibility in UNPROFOR experienced the same confusion: in the absence of a clear objective, everyone groped around as best they could and tried to sort things out in their own individual way. There is abundant testimony of this line.[92]

This lack of coherence, but also of continuity, in UN missions is usually reinforced by a high rate of staff turnover (an average of less than six months spent on a post). Teams who do not have much institutional memory (it is striking, for example, that members of missions usually leave with their archives) can not count on human memory either. Their local interlocutors show much more stability, despite obvious changes in the configuration of forces. This makes it possible for them to reopen some points already negotiated.

The problem of competence of the staff, reported in all the missions, adds to these difficulties. It is a vast subject in itself. The UN Secretariat is far from mastering all the parameters relating to recruitment of staff. In particular, it is almost wholly dependent on member states for supply of military and police personnel, and has almost no control over their level of training. Noticeable efforts at permanent training of staff likely to be sent on missions of this type have been made in recent years, especially among military and police personnel.[93] But the fact remains that 'incompetence', 'inexperience', 'lack of professionalism', 'lack of seriousness' and 'superficiality', even 'laziness' among mission members are recurrent accusations made by local actors of all sorts, and are not denied by members of missions themselves. While it holds no statistical value, it is not totally insignificant to note that 80 per cent of former members of missions whom I interviewed considered that they were not competent for the work expected of them. None had received specific training for the tasks assigned to them. This is even more serious when, between the time of recruitment of staff and their arrival on the scene, the nature of the mission has changed drastically which is the rule rather than the exception in peace operations. Whether one considers the reproaches made by local actors on this point are made in good faith or not, they reveal the low level

---

[92] Among published testimony, see especially John A. MacInnis, 'Peacekeeping and Postmodern Conflict: A Soldier's View', *Mediterranean Quarterly* 6/2, spring 1995, pp. 29–45; Fondation pour les Etudes de Défense, *Opérations des Nations Unies: Leçons de terrain*, chapter on former Yugoslavia, Paris: La Documentation Française, Perspectives Stratégiques series, 1995.

[93] In particular, a training unit was set up within the Department of Peace Keeping Operations (DPKO) of the Secretariat (United Nations Training Assistance Teams now Training and Evaluation Service). Textbooks were prepared and training seminars organised regularly. The team is also able to give help to missions themselves for their specific training needs. See UNDPKO documents and General Assembly resolutions 46/48, 48/42 and 49/37. Several peacekeeping training centres have also been created in various countries.

of credit from which UN staff usually benefit. When their competence is found lacking, they clearly appear in a position of weakness. This is aggravated when—as seems to have happened several times in El Salvador and Cambodia for instance—people exercising responsibility within the missions complain openly to their local negotiating partners about the bad quality of their teams. The difficulties encountered by members of missions in the management of these aspects of the relationship illustrate their narrow margin of manoeuvre. But this is not inevitable. If the way in which local actors assess their negotiating partners is analysed in precise cases, it becomes clear that even if it means overcoming some *a priori* assumptions, they are based on the concrete observation of the behaviour of mission members and a highly pragmatic assessment of their capacities for action. In other words, there is plenty of room left for chance.

MISSIONS' (IN)CAPACITY TO CARRY OUT THEIR MANDATES

The weight of the word: how the UN is hindered by its member states

The biggest source of vulnerability for peacekeepers relates to the imprecision and incoherence contained in the mandates at the time of their adoption (as illustrated by Security Council Resolution 1244 of June 10, 1999, which established the United Nations Mission in Kosovo and contained serious contradictions in its text), or else arising from successive Security Council resolutions superimposed on each other (the example of Bosnia is a textbook case from this point of view). Whatever progress is made later to obtain 'clear, realistic and applicable' mandates (a recommendation included in all reports and analyses that have appeared on UN operations), it must not be forgotten that peace agreements, where they exist, always include an uncertain element which is inherent in its very nature. Mandates adopted by the Security Council, because they are the result of diplomatic compromises, are a mass of imperfections and contradictions. Recourse to Chapter VII, which is increasingly frequent, indicates that there is agreement on taking action but not on the exact nature of the action, and even less on the diagnosis of the crisis under consideration. In many cases the decision to intervene militarily even arises from a refusal to assume a true policy.

Generally local actors, especially political entrepreneurs, become aware quite quickly of these limitations and of the frequent gap between the means at the missions' disposal and the ambitions expressed in the mandates. In Cambodia, UNTAC had to exercise its authority provisionally over a country 90 per cent controlled by one of the parties. The former chief of staff of the armed branch of FUNCINPEC (the ANKI) commented: 'In theory, one could reproach UNTAC for not having asserted control over the administration, and we did; it was in fair fight. But honestly, everyone knew it was quite unfeasible. We, of FUNCINPEC had nothing here. The PPC was the established power. How do you control an established power? It was difficult and they had very little time.'[94] Furthermore, the UN mission's component responsible for control of Civil Administration was by far the most composite as to the origins of its members, which meant just as many experiences (not to say 'cultures'), varying greatly on administrative matters. Above all, it had very limited numbers.[95] As a consequence, in the ministry of Foreign Affairs, for example, during a good deal of the process, only two UN officers were based at the ministry building, with an office on the ground floor isolated from the rest. The former UNTAC director of civil administration in the Siem Reap province said, 'Even if we have had more staff and means, how can one take possession of a country where an administration is already in place? And how could we imagine controlling anything when we did not speak a word of Khmer? It was a farce, and they quickly understood that they did not have much to fear from us.'[96] What that control would involve was itself not clearly laid down, and some omissions handicapped the mission from the start. For example, the mandate provided for control over the various ministries but not over the prime minister himself. In addition, it did not take account of the control exercised by the single party over the apparatus of state. Cambodian political actors, who themselves had conflicting interpretations of that objective of the mission, did not fail to exploit those deficiencies. Ministers regularly sheltered behind the authority of the Party, which for its part escaped control.[97] As for the state officials, they were able to play on the appearances of a power that in reality was exercised largely through other channels. In addition, over the months they put UNTAC's capacity to the test. A former French interpreter in that component testified: 'In the

[94] Words quoted from General Toan Chay (Siem Reap, December 5, 1993).

[95] At the peak of its deployment, on July 15, 1993, the Civil Administration Component had 95 international staff members in Phnom Penh and 123 in the country's 22 provinces. It was drawn from 42 different nationalities. In Phnom Penh (an administrative unit covering a population of one million), for several months control of the municipal government was in the hands of four people; there were 18 at the end.

[96] Interview with Benny Widyono (Phnom Penh, November 29, 1995).

[97] The component's final report is very explicit on those various limitations: UNTAC, 'Final Report of the Civil Administration Component', Phnom Penh, September 16, 1993 (unpublished), pp. 16–17.

beginning, the Cambodian state authorities were afraid of UNTAC because they did not know what its strength was. We felt clearly that they were paying attention. But when they saw that the UNTAC people were satisfied with one meeting per week with the minister to ask for inventories, and that things were beginning to drag on from one week to another, they relaxed.[98] I felt, as time went on, that they took things less and less seriously; they had understood that UNTAC did not have the means to do things itself, that it would always be at the mercy of what they chose to tell it.'[99] A member of a control team in the provinces confirmed this: 'In the beginning, they had some apprehension that UNTAC was coming to replace them and govern in their place; but very quickly they realised that we were not dangerous and, above all, that we were not very numerous.' Some years later, the 'authorities' installed in Kosovo and East Timor came up against similar limitations; although very centralised in their operations, both MINUK and ATNUTO scarcely governed beyond the capitals and real order escaped them.

Although it apparently had more power than in other cases, in reality the provisional 'Authority' of the United Nations in Cambodia did not have any capacity for coercion; its mandate did not come under Chapter VII of UN Charter. Nor did the Paris Agreements provide for sanctions against parties that failed to respect the agreements signed, such as the Khmers Rouges movement. Several times during the first months of the mission the Special Representative of the Secretary General announced that UNTAC was going to penetrate 'in the near future', by agreement or by force, into the zones controlled by the Khmers Rouges. But carrying out this threat encountered serious obstacles; those zones could only be reached by roads that were mined, and the various countries contributing troops applied pressure to avoid loss of human life; in addition, several heads of Western governments clearly stated that they would not resort to force. It was not without cause that the head of UNTAC stated later that he was unable to force the Khmers Rouges to accept deployment of UN forces in zones under their control: 'I did not have either the mandate or the necessary troops.'[100] Several times Norodom Sihanouk mocked UNTAC's weakness. In an interview in July 1992 he declared, 'The Khmer Rouge sees that the gentlemen of UNTAC are very kind. If there is a fight somewhere UNTAC doesn't intervene. On the contrary, it withdraws.'[101] From that point of view the famous 'bamboo barrier' incident in

---

[98] This refers to the inventories intended to check on sales of state land and property.

[99] Words quoted from Sau Phân, former interpreter in the UNTAC Civil Administration Component (Phnom Penh, November 29, 1995).

[100] Statement by Yasushi Akashi, reported in an AFP dispatch of September 13, 1993.

[101] Interview with *Far Eastern Economic Review*, July 30, 1992.

the Pailin region on May 30, 1992 was revealing. On that day, the Special Representative of the Secretary General and the Australian general commanding UNTAC made an about-turn before a Khmer Rouge sentry posted behind a bamboo, barring their passage. The Khmers Rouges, like others, very quickly took measure of the actual UN force.

In Bosnia-Herzegovina, the 'growing gulf between the Security Council resolutions and the means [at UNPOFOR's disposal] for implementing them',[102] publicly criticised by leading officials, undoubtedly lowered the mission's credibility in the eyes of local actors. This weakness was worsened by the piling up of UN mission mandates, following successive Security Council resolutions, without any real attempt at coherence on the part of member states' representatives, who were concerned above all with finding an uneasy compromise.[103] Humanitarian action, peacekeeping, military coercion, and political action, were superimposed without being brought together in an overall scheme. The gap between diplomatic rhetoric and the will to take action was perhaps never as glaring as in Bosnia. In truth the texts of resolutions reflected much less the developing reality on the ground than the need to find compromises between the often diverging positions in Washington, Moscow, Paris and London. Successive military officers at the head of UNPROFOR continually complained of being neither informed nor consulted about the ongoing political negotiations in New York and Geneva. More than a third of the Security Council resolutions decided an extension of the mandate (with additional tasks sometimes contradicting the previous UNPROFOR mandate), without new means being provided and often without any relation to the changes in the situation on the ground. For example, the establishment of border control arrangements by the United Nations, approved by Resolution 787 of November 16, 1992, required deployment of observers on the borders of Bosnia, but the resolution could never be implemented due to a lack of resources.[104] Similarly, the establishment of safe havens drew a bit more on UNPROFOR's resources without any concern for the conditions in which members of the mission could, in parallel, pursue what

---

[102] Public statement by General Francis de Briquemont (BBC *Summary of World Broadcasts*, UNPROFOR, EE/1904 C/4, January 25, 1994).

[103] In addition member states' representatives seemed themselves at pains to follow through with their resolutions. In this respect the debates on the proposal for establishment of a rapid reaction force, put forward by France, the United Kingdom and the Netherlands, are very revealing. They bring out plenty of confusion about the mandates of the new force and of UNPROFOR itself (extending to past events) and radically differing visions. See the debates on Resolution 998 (S/PV3543 of June 16, 1995).

[104] Cf. especially the Secretary General's report to the Security Council, fixing certain conditions for the application of that mandate: S/25000 of December 21, 1992.

was still formally their main objective: security for humanitarian aid supplies across Bosnia. Resolution 844 of June 18, 1993 authorised the deployment of 7,600 extra men, the minimum requested by the Secretary General (while the Force Commander had estimated that, for real deterrence, 34,000 men needed to be deployed). In February 1994, only 3,500 men had been deployed; at Zepa, only a first group of ten soldiers were in place. These limitations did not pass unnoticed by the protagonists in the conflict, especially as they were widely commented upon by the military leaders of the mission and even the Secretary General himself. Lieutenant-General Francis de Briquemont, UNPROFOR commander in Bosnia, when announcing his intention to quit his post, declared, 'I no longer read the Security Council resolutions because they don't help me.'[105] On May 31, 1994 the Secretary General presented to the Security Council a report in which he recommended withdrawal from positions that could not be properly defended, including the enclaves located in the east of the country. In other words, he publicly indicated that those 'safe havens' could not be protected in case of attack. To many observers this seems to have been a major element in the Serbs' decision to attack the Zepa and Bihac enclaves and then to invade Srebrenica before a 'rapid reaction force' (announced then) was eventually deployed. The Serbs also learned what to make of the threats of NATO air strikes.

In Somalia, it is significant in retrospect that the United Nations Secretary General judged the various UN mandates in the country to have been in some respects 'self-contradictory, imprecise and open to varying interpretations, resulting in disagreements over major issues, for example over whether disarming the factions was necessary to establish a "secure environment".'[106] For instance, the resolution authorising the intervention of the multilateral force was sufficiently ambiguous for everyone to make his own interpretation. In practice the various contingents adopted diverging attitudes on the question of disarmament, with the North American contingent, comprising the great majority, receiving very restrictive instructions. The main Somalian politico-military entrepreneurs took advantage of this by extending their control as much as they could. Resolution 814, creating UNOSOM II, complicated the situation even more. The objective—a surrealist one, in many respects—of 'helping the Somalis to rebuild a democratic state' was extraordinarily broad and vague, leaving the

---

[105] Quoted in a Reuters dispatch, 'Belgian UN Commander wants to quit', Reuters News Service, January 4, 1994, reproduced in a number of newspapers at various stages in the mission.

[106] *The United Nations and Somalia, 1992–1996*, United Nations Blue Books Series, vol. VIII, New York: UNDPI, 1996, p. 85.

way open for varying interpretations. How far would the UN get involved in redefining the country's political framework? Whom would it favour? Those questions were inevitable, and each of the options chosen could only be interpreted as alignment in favour of one party or the other. Under these conditions the mission soon appeared, in the eyes of the main politico-military entrepreneurs, as an obstacle to their ambitions.

Discords in the 'international community' on the ground

The difficulties encountered by the peacekeepers in the various theatres are reflected notably in their fairly heterogeneous modes of action. This diversity can, as is well known, be accentuated by the existence of many divisions within each operation. These are more or less visible to the local actors. On the whole local people are not fooled either by the deceptive appearances of unity given by the UN acronym or by excessive reference to the 'international community', even if local discourses often play on appearances. Their understanding of the differing rationalities and interests running through operations is however far from perfect. Even so, exploiting rivalry among governments and institutions remains a classic strategy, at which local political actors are particularly experienced. At the same time the existence of such divisions, and the frequent duplication that they cause, have a cost for local entrepreneurs: loss of time and energy which those concerned complain of regularly—time lost in receiving international delegations, in rewriting the same proposals, in re-submitting the same reports in different formats, and so on.

As in Bosnia, matters become even more complicated when the main politico-military actors have the possibility of playing different cards at the same time: UNPROFOR against NATO intervention, different places and levels of negotiation, bilateral against multilateral, etc. Everyone then tries to make use of the loopholes left by international contradictions to advance their own cause. An actor may accept losing temporarily on one side what he expects to gain elsewhere. He can allow negotiations on a peace plan to drag on while talks are held on safe areas, as Slobodan Milosevic did at the time of the talks on the Vance-Owen Plan. The various episodes in those talks are quite revealing in the way in which each party in that country made use of the contradictions among different diplomacies, consequently defeating the overall process. In practice the proliferation of institutional structures involved in resolution of a conflict highly increases the loci in which intergovernmental logics can be deployed, complicating the diplomatic game, increasing the risks of contradiction and, afterwards, the local entrepreneurs' capacity to take advantage of them. In Bosnia, taking Blue Helmets as hostages was one particularly significant episode of this, illustrating the use that politico-military entrepreneurs made of divisions between member states favouring air strikes and those having troops on the ground. These divergences of interests were directly echoed on the ground. UNPROFOR generals (Generals Briquemont and Hayes) publicly declared their hostility towards those air strikes and doubts about their efficiency; Madeleine Albright, then United States representative to the UN, protested officially at their statements.[107]

One particular expression of these intergovernmental logics is the existence, within UN missions' military components, of parallel hierarchies that intensify the effect of juxtaposition of contingents of different nationalities. Local actors are particularly inclined to exploit such a state of affairs in dangerous operations like those in Bosnia-Herzegovina, but also in Cambodia, Somalia and, more recently, Afghanistan. In Cambodia the former UNTAC commander-in-chief and his deputy both considered that 'The Khmer Rouge recognised the importance of these issues and there were definite attempts to break the unity of the force. Very early in the mission, the Khmer Rouge began classifying some units as "good UNTAC" and others as "bad UNTAC". Some elements of UNTAC were acceptable in their areas and others were not.'[108] General Sanderson stressed the problems encountered as some contingents, sure to be the "good UNTAC", kept the Khmer Rouge propaganda going.[109]

In the course of missions, those differences of approach among contingents are illustrated in particular by small-scale negotiations conducted separately, on a daily basis, with one party or another, so as to guarantee security for the contingents. When the situation deteriorates on the ground, this process tends to add to the vulnerability of each group left in ignorance of what the others have negotiated. The case of Somalia was

---

[107] US Ambassador Madeleine K. Albright, president of the Security Council at that time, met on August 17, 2003, with Secretary-General Boutros Boutros-Ghali to complain about the comments. In notes she prepared for the meeting, Albright said the comments undermined the effectiveness of the threat to launch air strikes. "Publicly telling the Serbs that air strikes will never happen, or be ineffective, works against deterrence and makes it more likely that we will be obligated to resort to air strikes", Albright said in the notes. Albright also raised the issue at a private Security Council meeting the next day.

[108] Cf. Lieut.-Col. J. Damien Healy, 'UNTAC: Lessons Learned: the Military Component View', paper tabled at the symposium organised by the Fondation pour les Etudes de Défense, Paris, June 1995, p. 7 (document communicated by the author).

[109] Lieut.-Gen. John M. Sanderson, 'UNTAC: Successes and Failures', pp. 25–6, in Hugh Smith (ed.), *International Peacekeeping. Building on the Cambodian Experience*, Canberra: Australian Defence Studies Centre, 1994.

characteristic in this respect. The consequences can be serious, especially when these divergences on the ground are linked to more substantial diplomatic disagreements between countries contributing troops. In Somalia, the two main politico-military entrepreneurs fighting for control of the capital, Mohammed Aydid and Ali Mahdi, were able to play on those divergences, just as they encouraged the governments of Non-Aligned countries and other African countries, who were providers of troops that were scorned and even rejected by the dominant states, especially the United States, not to 'let them manipulate them'.[110] In addition to these kinds of antagonisms, there was an open conflict, widely publicised, between the American administration and the UN Secretary General. Those who represented both entities on the ground made no mystery of the multiple uses that Somali actors made of the US-UN quarrels, using one against the other, deliberately spreading false information.[111] Similarly, in Somaliland, the local political leaders played on the divergent ideas of the UN Secretariat and the US administration about deployment of troops on their territory.

Politico-military entrepreneurs can play on such divisions even more with the growing resort to 'delegation' of peace operations. Until recently, at the UN, some precautions were taken to avoid, as much as possible, sending troops from countries considered to be too much involved in a conflict. In practice that rule (like the one which originally provided that contingents from the permanent members of the Security Council should not take part in peacekeeping operations) has been increasingly bypassed. Its effects were reduced somewhat by the fact that the list of contributors of troops to UN missions was submitted to the parties to a conflict before being officially submitted to the members of the Security Council. With the trend towards increasing 'decentralisation' to ad hoc coalitions, this approach—as artificial as it often was—is no longer tenable. An idea of the sort of situation that may result from this can be seen in the numerous problems linked to the role—ambiguous to say the least—of countries which, like Nigeria in Liberia and Sierra Leone or Senegal in Guinea-Bissau, have emerged simultaneously as parties to a conflict and 'peace makers'. But is it not the same with NATO in Kosovo, France leading missions in Ituri or Ivory Coast, US ones in Haiti, and, still more, with the forces allied to the United States in Afghanistan and Iraq?

[110] Press statement by the two movements during 1993.

[111] Private interviews in New York (January 1995). See also the testimony of Ambassador Robert B. Oakley in John L. Hirsch and Robert B. Oakley, *Somalia and Operation Restore Hope: Reflections on Peacemaking and Peacekeeping*, Washington, DC: United States Institute of Peace Press, 1995, pp. 50–1.

On the other hand, apart from those extreme cases, investigations have shown that local people assess the various national origins of contingents with much more pragmatism than international staff generally suggest. Yet again, the fact that peacekeepers are judged by their acts explains that pre-existing prejudices can be made relative. Racism is much more noticeable within the missions themselves and in the language of some local political elites than in the language and behaviour of social and community actors. The way in which African contingents in Cambodia were welcomed and accepted among local people contradicted fairly well the racist assumptions that could be heard on the subject.[112] In Haiti, while the political class, whatever their affiliation, resorted to the most well-worn clichés, there was no equivalent among the people. In this country, every foreigner is called '*Blan*', whatever the colour of his skin, without any racist connotation: '*Yo tout se blan*' ('They are all whites'), even if there are some jokes about 'those whites who are black' (*Blan nwa*). The fact that the United States was in charge has even strengthened the determination not to establish any distinction: '*Sè menm yo menm!*'[113] asserted Haitians I encountered, when I tried to emphasise that perhaps a soldier who was from Benin or Bangladesh could not exactly be considered as a GI or even a 'White'… Furthermore, close similarity of colour or even language does not seem to be a strong point in itself; the testimony of Salvadoreans on their relations with *latinos*, or of Haitians on their relations with black soldiers of the Multinational Force tends to suggest this. That distance was sometimes a real shock for the soldiers concerned, as several GIs sent to Somalia and involved in regular incidents with the inhabitants of Mogadishu have testified.

Internal divisions within operations: the micro-sociology of UN missions according to local actors

Local political and social actors also take into account the divisions they can identify among various components of a mission. These embody and amplify the frequent contradictions among the different objectives of the mandate assigned to a peace operation. Thus in El Salvador, even within ONUSAL, senior UN officials themselves thought the 'human rights' mandate contradicted with that of verifying implementation of peace agreements. Dissension was expressed particularly strongly between the Human Rights and Police Divisions: there were double investigations into

[112] Interviews around Cambodia and with anthropologists carrying out investigations at the same time in various regions of the country.
[113] 'It's them! It's the same people!' (translation without direct equivalence).

political murders, with differing methods and results. In many missions, members of the Human Rights Division soon came to view their diplomatic, military or police colleagues as a 'damned nuisance, because they are always criticising things that are not going well.'[114] That mistrust, clearly resented by the senior officers of the armed forces in El Salvador, was of use to them in their strategy in systematically obstructing the work carried out by ONUSAL on human rights. In particular, they gained a considerable delay in investigations into paramilitary groups which directly touched some bases of their power. In fact, the ONUSAL military chief opposed investigation by civilians of the Human Rights Division, arguing that it was 'a job for the military'; as a result, it was only very late in the course of the operation that investigations were started under that chapter, while the UN had already made the mistake of not pushing for its inclusion in the peace agreements.[115]

In Cambodia, among the concrete problems affecting public security, local political leaders pointed out to top UNTAC officials the contradictions between the demands made by various components. The 'public security' department of the Civil Administration Component and the Civilian Police and Human Rights Components had closely similar tasks in that matter. Their heads fought a true 'guerrilla war by letter' to define their respective prerogatives.[116] The former director of the UNTAC Civil Administration component testified: 'The people of the State of Cambodia confronted us with a number of problems that were insoluble, on a daily basis. Very soon petty crime and serious delinquency increased. The Ministry of Public Security people told me: "Help us, because your Human Rights idiots released all the gangsters, and now look what's happening. You're there to help create a satisfactory atmosphere for holding elections, you cannot let them get away with it..." We were really bothered. We had similar problems with squatters and people occupying land. On the one side there was the Cambodian administration, which enjoyed playing the game and telling us, "Tell us what has to be done because you are there to control us", and on the other side were the UN

[114] Interview with Philippe Texier, Director of the Human Rights Division of ONUSAL from July 1991 to July 1992 (Paris, March 7, 1995).

[115] Interviews with former leaders of the Human Rights Division of ONUSAL (Paris, March 7, 1995 and San Salvador, September 14, 1995), with one of the leaders of the mission, and with high-ranking Salvadorian military officers (San Salvador, September 1995).

[116] Interviews conducted on the basis of anonymity with military and civpols and officials involved in UNTAC (Paris, New York and Phnom Penh, 1995–96), and final reports of the Civil Administration and Human Rights Components: UNTAC, 'Final Report of the Civil Administration Component' (note 97), pp. 25, 30, and 'Human Rights Component Final Report', Phnom Penh, September 1993 (mimeo), pp. 72–3.

civpols who floundered around cheerfully. On a third front, there were the Human Rights people who applied pressure and were almost ready to put our own people behind bars. It was an impossible situation...Our position was to say that the country's institutions and judicial system must continue to function. Our own role was to ensure that they functioned as best as possible... For its part the Human Rights Component felt the courts were not functioning well, and anyone who complained to that fact was in the right, without any need to take the case to a court. This couldn't work, and everyone took advantage of it, possible plaintiffs (many of them were swindlers) as well as the PPC administration.'[117]

As in Cambodia, all missions experience permanent tension among their components, with each working on its own. At the central level, it is the head of the mission (the UN Secretary General Special Representative) who is supposed to ensure coordination. In Cambodia, Yasushi Akashi admitted that his power in that regard had serious limitations. He spoke of 'The electoral component, which had been jealous of its autonomy within the UNTAC...'[118] A member of the mission testified: 'For the first six months, there was a meeting every morning with Akashi; then it changed to three times a week; but decisions were rarely taken at that time. Coordination initiatives were rather linked to privileged personal contacts.'[119] On the ground, each of the seven components acted autonomously and reported directly to its hierarchical superior in Phnom Penh. Even for missions that lasted longer than the ephemeral UNTAC, integration of teams appears to be rather difficult and often only occurs very late in the course of the mission. For instance, in El Salvador, real posts of regional coordinators were created only in the last phase of ONUSAL.

More than anything else, it is in the missions' daily work that conflicts reveal obvious differences in 'culture' between civilians, police and soldiers. Those differences are generally exacerbated by personal clashes, often the most decisive in the long run. In this respect a UN peace mission functions like any other social organisation. The infinite variety of training and professional careers, and of cultural origins, the weight of interstate factors, the numerous difficulties of communication among very diverse nationalities (among civilians, not far from a hundred nationalities represented on average in a mission) and some of them not at ease with the internal working language (generally English), are all complicating

---

[117] Statement recorded in Phnom Penh, December 13, 1995.

[118] Yasushi Akashi, 'The Challenge of Peacekeeping in Cambodia', *International Peacekeeping* 1/2, Summer 1994, p. 209.

[119] Interview with Controller General Dominique-Pierre Guéret, former Deputy Director of the UNTAC Civil Administration (Paris, October 23, 1995).

factors. When it comes to communicating with the outside world, those difficulties of mutual comprehension play a significant role, even though efforts have been made in recent years to smooth them over. These clashes, especially in their inter-personal dimension are also regularly explained by former members of missions in relation to the career aims of the individuals concerned, within the UN or even in their countries of origin. In my investigations, this excessive attention on one's 'own agenda' has regularly been brought up by local political actors. From interviews with former members of missions one could almost believe that the missions are in fact like 'a jungle where you have to find your hole to get accepted, where you have to fight every day to conserve the duties assigned to your post', and one also has to not be afraid of 'stepping on someone else's toes'.[120] The testimonies published by some reveal the extent of the clashes and settling of scores that result from them.[121]

These clashes are now often made public outside the mission by the interested parties themselves, speaking either to their local negotiating partners (especially in order to enhance their own credibility in those partners' eyes) or to journalists. From this point of view any observer has to guard against the amplifying effect of the vast media show surrounding UN missions. In theory members of missions require special permission to speak with the press, but few resist the temptation to get on to the stage in a favourable light, especially with the media of their countries of origin. In front of journalists 'Each person pours out information at the expense of his mates... And generally, people in editorial offices are fond of that sort of story.'[122] The local press may also echo 'disagreements displayed in the public arena, without shame', as happened in Cambodia and El Salvador. In the latter country, within the Human Rights Division, opposing 'clans' even developed their own lobbies with Salvadorian NGOs. Some episodes described in detail by their Salvadorian counterparts are staggering.[123]

Local political and military actors observe the 'show', sometimes with contempt and irritation, often with plenty of pragmatism. 'There were all

---

[120] Words recorded during interviews carried out on the basis of anonymity in Paris with French military personnel and officials who took part in UNTAC, at a private meeting at the National Defence General Secretariat.

[121] See Bibliography at the end of the book and on the website.

[122] Interview in Phnom Penh, November 17, 1995.

[123] Interviews with Christian Bouteille, former member of the Human Rights Division; Maria Julia Hernandez, Tutela Legal (Salvadorian Justice and Peace organisation); Celia Medrano, spokeswoman of the Comisión de Derechos Humanos de El Salvador (CDHES); Carlos Mauricio Molina Fonseca, former Prosecutor for the Defence of Human Rights (San Salvador, August and September 1995).

sorts, and hence people who were more realistic or more favourable to us would talk to us and make it possible to glean information...'[124] The 'secrets' told by members of missions make it possible for local political entrepreneurs to add, sometimes mistakenly, to their assessment of the missions' intentions. Hence this redefines their margins of manoeuvre. In some cases, they seek to derive maximum support from components that look most favourable to them, as well as from 'personal contacts' that they maintain. In Cambodia, members of the two main parties (the PPC and FUNCINPEC) did not conceal how they had quite quickly found out the dominant political tendencies within each component, and hence approached those whom they saw as more favourable to them, whatever matter was under consideration. Testimony by FUNCINPEC leaders left no doubt about the support sought from the head of the UNTAC Electoral Component, who was considered 'the one who paid most attention to [the party's] cause', its 'best ally'. The UNTAC spokesman was considered as another major asset by FUNCINPEC because he was said to 'desire to spread systematically important information for [the party's leaders]; he was aware of the need to counterbalance the weight of the PPC.'[125]

Lastly, some divisions recall how far local situations can be reflected among United Nations actors themselves, with sometimes sharp differences of analysis and position between the Secretariat in New York and field operations, but also between the headquarters of missions, based in capital cities, and the teams deployed all over the country. Political and military actors are very inclined to play on these contradictions and go to seek from one side what they have not obtained from the other. In El Salvador the two main parties to the conflict did not fail to play UN headquarters off against the mission (and the other way round). In that case the dichotomy was sharpened by the division of labour established at the outset between the negotiating team directly attached to the Secretary General in New York and the team on the ground, whose work was supposed to be limited to verification. This distinction aimed to solve the problems posed by the dual function of mediation and verification assigned to the UN. But also to reduce the pressure put on ONUSAL in managing the most difficult parts of the peace process at UN's highest level—such as the creation of a new army and the reintegration of the FMLN in society.[126] Except for a few variations under certain circum-

---

[124] Recollection by Im Sethy (Phnom Penh, December 18, 1995).

[125] Recollection by Pok Marina, spokesman of Prince Ranaridh from 1989 and throughout the peace process (Phnom Penh, December 15, 1995).

[126] See the analysis by United Nations chief negotiator, Alvaro de Soto, pp. 146–7, in Joseph S. Tulchin and Gary Bland (eds), *Is There a Transition to Democracy in El Salvador?*, Woodrow Wilson Center, Boulder, CO: Lynne Rienner, 1992.

stances, the FMLN tended to put its money into the headquarters and the El Salvador government on the heads of the mission on the ground. Indeed, the FMLN leaders made no mystery about this strategy, which was illustrated by several visits by their senior figures to the UN Secretary General in New York, exactly at the 'critical' moments of the process. Similarly, they did everything they could to ensure that some delicate subjects continued to be discussed exclusively at this level, when there were visits from the special envoys or during their own journeys to New York. This was the case with issues of disarmament and purging of the army, which they systematically refused to discuss with the leaders of the mission.[127] On the elections issue, the FMLN leaders ostensibly sought to play the headquarters against the mission, which did not pay enough attention to their complaints. Those responsible for following up the process for the Salvadorian government presented a symmetrical interpretation of what happened. The representative of the Salvadorian armed forces considered that the crises leading to frequent visits by headquarters representatives 'were completely fabricated'; they were aimed at 'short-circuiting the mission'. 'The Mission worked in one direction and headquarters in the other.' Some social actors also tried to play on this division, with much less success, like Human Rights NGOs in conflict with the mission, which travelled to New York to complain and meet with the UN Secretary General.

Division between UN headquarters and field missions also played a significant role in what happened in Somalia. In that case it was sharpened by the influence of past contacts between Boutros Boutros Ghali and some of the Somali politicians and the fact that the UNSG had a high level of personal involvement in the Somali crisis. In addition, he initially chose to send as his representative a man he trusted well, a close contact of long standing: Mohamed Sahnoun. So, when a divergence of views, on the way to deal with the Somali situation, appeared between the two men, the crisis took a highly passionate turn, which soon became irreversible. The Special Representative himself displayed a highly personal style, taking on many initiatives, and going so far that he was quickly seen at UN headquarters as a 'too independent player' who did not hesitate to express criticisms in public. In particular, Sahnoun made numerous statements indicating that he refused to 'have dealings with bureaucrats and the headquarters Nomenklatura'. Ismat Kittani, who replaced him, had the 'good taste' to express his criticisms in private, though firmly and persistently.[128] Beyond questions of form, divergences of analysis, between the heads of

[127] Interviews with FMLN representatives in the Dialogue Commission (San Salvador, September 1995).
[128] Private interviews at the United Nations Secretariat (New York, January 1995).

the mission on the ground and the UN Secretariat in New York,[129] related to the philosophy of the operation: should reconstruction be carried out 'from the top', with the factions, or 'from below', starting with civil society? Depending on the answers to that question, UNOSOM's action was liable to favour one group or the other. This led to hold-ups in the adoption of some decisions, and very wide gaps between announcements made in New York and the reality experienced on the ground. An example of hold-ups in the decision making process was seen in the clashes surrounding the programme for reconstruction of the judicial system. Prepared in Mogadishu, it was stalled at headquarters by Kofi Annan (then in charge of peacekeeping), who thought it was necessary to wait for installation of all the districts in Somalia before starting such a scheme. But it appears that members of the mission were not correctly informed about that decision and thought for a long time that matters were taking their course at headquarters, especially concerning the adoption of the financial measures necessary for the launching of the programme.[130] Another example shows even more clearly the difficulties of communication between headquarters and the mission. While the first 500 troops had not yet arrived in Mogadishu (only fifty unarmed military observers had already arrived), an announcement was made in New York of the dispatch to Somalia of more than 3,000 men, without informing ONU-SOM delegation at Mogadiscio or the leaders of neighbouring countries, and above all without consulting with local leaders, just as Sahnoun was negotiating on this point with Mohamed Aydid.[131] A little later, Sahnoun and his team were again put in a delicate position by an incident concerning delivery of money and military equipment to troops backing Ali Mahdi, in the north of Mogadishu, aboard an aircraft painted with the United Nations' initials (in fact a private Russian aircraft that had previously been chartered by a UN agency, the WFP, the United Nations initials had not been removed). They were only informed about the incident at a late stage, and thought they had not received the backing of headquarters for a serious investigation to be made. In his contacts with

---

[129] Divergences that also widened between decisions taken in Washington and the American command of the multinational force on the ground: interview with John L. Hirsch, political adviser to the United Task Force, posted to Somalia from December 1992 to March 1993 (New York, January 11, 1995).

[130] Private interviews at the UN Secretariat and with a former member of the Justice/Human Rights division of UNOSOM (New York, January 1995, November 1997). See also Martin R. Ganzglass, 'The Restoration of the Somali Justice System', pp. 30–1, in Walter Clarke and Jeffrey Herbst (eds), *Learning from Somalia: The Lessons of Armed Humanitarian Intervention*, Boulder, CO: Westview, 1997.

[131] Mohamed Sahnoun, *Somalia: The Missed Opportunity*, Washington, DC: US Institute for Peace Press, 1994, p. 38.

the mission Aydid took advantage of this incident to reopen some points on which he had previously expressed his agreement.[132]

In Bosnia a growing divergence between negotiations and reality on the ground was equally striking. 'The UN' which conducted negotiations in Geneva and made decisions in New York appeared increasingly distant from 'the UN', which was trying to take action in Bosnia. The Blue Helmets had to deal with tensions that were constantly exacerbated by the negotiations and the successive proposed peace plans. On its side the UN Secretariat did not conceal its irritation at the highly personal logics developed by some commanders of the force (General Morillon among them), which committed the Organisation as a whole without previous consultation. Those divergences were public and could have not have escaped the ears of local actors in their assessment of UN initiatives in Bosnia.

Until recently, UN missions' relations with headquarters were also considerably complicated by differences of view within the Secretariat itself and between the different departments dealing with each question. Because of the division of labour among those departments, missions normally had (independent of administrative and financial questions) at least two principal correspondents at headquarters, apart from the Secretary General's own office: the Peacekeeping and Political Affairs departments, with the Office for Coordination of Humanitarian Affairs added in some cases. In practice, members of the departments have spoken of the difficulty of reaching agreement on division of labour, which led sometimes to struggles for influence, if not at the level of the desk officers at least between their hierarchies. The situation has greatly improved since the 'quiet revolution' started by Kofi Annan and the installation of a permanent special watch office, operating 24 hours a day, but much still remains to be done. The Brahimi Report published in 2000 proposed the establishment, at UN headquarters, of integrated task forces to run each mission, but this proposal was rejected by member states.

While allusions to 'headquarters' by heads of missions denote the UN Secretariat in New York, for the majority of mission staff the name more commonly refers to the headquarters of the mission itself, established in the capital of the country where it operates. The distinction is often sharpened by difficulties of communication and the absence of a smooth and organised flow of information that may go 'up' to headquarters, but never goes 'down' to the teams deployed in the regions. Those teams very often testify to having the impression that what they do 'does not interest' the mission's leaders, who 'know nothing about what is happening on the

---

[132] Ibid., p. 39.

ground', and that their reports are of no use. The mistrust felt by staff 'on the ground' towards those at 'headquarters' (who are all the more in the wrong because they generally have much better material working conditions than those in the provinces) is generally reflected in the cool welcome that the latter say they receive when they visit the provinces. In Cambodia, a former member of the special teams established within the Civil Administration Component to make 'surprise' controls, has spoken of the very lively tension that those visits created. The UNTAC teams in the provinces considered that the visits risked upsetting the good relations established, sometimes with difficulty, with the local authorities. This led to acute crises in certain regions, for example at Battambang, where the local UNTAC team was clearly on the side of the 'locals', in every sense, against the 'headquarters' in Phnom Penh.[133]

Simply by travelling in the interior of the countries any observer can understand that in practice missions may look very different according to region. In similar circumstances, faced with an identical problem, two teams can adopt diametrically opposed attitudes. For instance, the work done by the UN civpols can vary drastically from one region to another. Data collected on the same issues (for example, on human rights or security conditions) are most often not based on common criteria and procedures, therefore difficult to compare. Often there are also sharp disparities in the way in which election monitoring is organised, from one region to another. In El Salvador, Haiti, Mozambique and Bosnia-Herzegovina those disparities were striking.[134] In Somalia, there were hard disputes between the Director of the Kismayo zone and the heads of the UNOSOM political division in Mogadishu over the creation of district councils.[135] Ironically, at the same moment the mission heads in Mogadishu were having to fight with the Secretariat in New York on the same subject. In Bosnia, the two military officers, who most strongly criticised the actions of UN headquarters—General de Briquemont, UNPROFOR commander in Bosnia, and General Cot, commander for the entire former Yugoslavia—

---

[133] Interview with Lieut.-Colonel Calleja, former member of the control team of the UNTAC civil administration (Paris, October 23, 1995), and inquiries at Battambang (December 1995).

[134] Personal observations during elections organised in those countries, and confidential interviews with observers deployed in various regions.

[135] For the former, it was preferable not to rush into the establishment of district councils, and to take time over the reconciliation process. In view of the massive population displacements that he observed in the Kismayo region, he considered particularly that a council created prematurely would very soon encounter problems of legitimacy, and did not conceal its doubts about a model that he called 'colonial'. For his colleagues in Mogadishu, establishment of these councils was, on the contrary, the way to counteract the logic of the 'warlords', and that programme had to be pursued at any price.

were on very tense terms with each other.[136] 'Localism' is therefore a chain reaction. It is reinforced when military contingents, often more numerous and more 'visible', are posted across the country on a national basis, in 'zones of responsibility', as happened in Cambodia, Somalia and Bosnia. An attentive observer of the Bosnian situation noted: 'Often UNPROFOR officers had very local strategies that had nothing to do with UNPROFOR's general policy. When matters were under negotiation, on the ground, the local United Nations officer was first and foremost a local actor.'[137]

If they had any doubts before, the inhabitants of countries in which peace missions intervene quickly realise how much the same acronym conceals very different actors, interests and practices. On the ground, inter-governmental and institutional logics that fashion the reality of the United Nations are extended in unusual forms. The daily work of a United Nations mission thus consists of very many facets, like any social organisation—but the characteristics of a multilateral context complicate the situation even more. Community actors and ordinary citizens generally have a more diffuse perception of all of this than the political elites, but they take on board very quickly the diversity that emerges from it. They learn with plenty of pragmatism how to size up their interlocutors, trying, in each case, to identify who is most favourable to them. In El Salvador, for example, although the ONUSAL military personnel as a whole were seen as rather kindly disposed towards the Salvadorian military, members of communities were able to find some who seemed more 'open' towards them, without paying too much attention to their uniform. Several members of a community of *repoblaciones*, in the Chalatenango region, have testified of this: 'Here we have good reasons not to like the military…But whether they are civilians, military or police, it was no longer what mattered most to us. We knew only that some were more favourable to ARENA, that they helped ARENA people, and that others were more favourable to us…Some would say to us, "Beware of so-and-so"…But we had our own eyes to see what was going on. We didn't talk to just anyone. What they wore was not what mattered most for us.'[138] If necessary they travelled several kilometres to go to a ONUSAL office where the team had a better reputation.[139] During my investigations, people I questioned

---

[136] These disputes related particularly to the NATO air strikes, to which General de Briquemont, like his deputy General Hayes, were openly hostile. The increasing tensions between de Briquemont and Cot and their successive public statements led to their premature departure at the beginning of 1994.

[137] Interview with Xavier Bougarel, CNRS researcher (Paris, December 18, 1996).

[138] Words recorded during the General Assembly of the Guarjila community, in the north of Chalatenango, September 16, 1995 (translated from Spanish).

[139] This happened notably in the Morazán region. The ONUSAL regional office at San

were generally able to name exactly the person or persons to whom their contacts were often confined, but they were almost always unaware of the posts they had held and their status (police? civilian? military?). All these elements ought to lead international staff to revise the highly stereotyped visions in circulation on this matter. Here too, categories are often much less fixed and clear than people imagine. A good deal is played out in daily contacts, often at a highly individual level.

PEACEKEEPERS LOST IN COMPLEX ENVIRONMENTS

Defects in intelligence service and analysis capacity

The extent to which UN peace operations are constrained by local social and political realities has very little to do with the position of classic military operations, more limited in their interposition role. Hence their capacity for action is largely fashioned by their ability to understand the contexts in which they are intervening, and to position themselves in interaction with local societies. On that point, as on others, one can find as many analyses to express indignation at the ignorance and tactlessness that peacekeepers can show or, on the contrary, to emphasise the real changes in United Nations practice over a few years. There are plenty of arguments on either side. To judge between them, there appear to me to be two distinct aspects: general knowledge of the context of intervention that is available to the leadership of the missions on the one hand, and the knowledge that their members have through their daily work on the other. In the course of a mission it is the common failure to join up these two dimensions that has the most consequences.

On the first point, investigations show that both in quantity and quality, those who head the missions have an understanding of the socio-political environment in which they operate that is far superior to what most analyses of the subject suggest. This knowledge is based on several years of UN involvement with the issue, sometimes strengthened by continuity ensured over a long period by some headquarters' desk officers, as in the case of Haiti. Despite the weakness of the UN's institutional memory—on which there has been very clear progress in recent years[140]—missions do

---

Miguel came to be considered by local Salvadorian organisations as 'pro-army', and was therefore boycotted. They preferred to go to another regional office, the nearest being the one at Usulután.

[140] I have personally witnessed these improvements during my research. On this point, despite all the limitations I intend to point out, the UN Secretariat's institutional memory seems to be much better today than what I was able to see in the main Western diplomatic services and a number of large international NGOs.

not make interventions completely *ex nihilo*. In addition, UN missions increasingly call on recognised specialists from various social science disciplines. In this respect, the resources of the mission in Cambodia were quite impressive; the Information/Education Division counted on a pluridisciplinary team of specialists, all of them Khmer experts, coming from six different countries. Their role, within an analysis unit, was to give daily information on Cambodia (especially by following local media) and to prepare systematic political reports on the activities of the various parties to the agreements. The volume and quality of analyses produced in this venture are very impressive,[141] even if some studies dealing with the way the mission was perceived by Cambodians appear very superficial— especially because investigations were few and very incomplete. In the case of Somalia, meetings were organised regularly outside the country, with the most recognised specialists on the country. The consultation process was continued with the help of funds from the Swedish government, although some of the invited experts withdrew in the meantime. In Mozambique the head of the mission included a sociologist and an anthropologist in his team.

Consulting missions' confidential archives, one realises that the analyses produced within the missions are often just as good as those put forward at the same time by recognised specialists of the countries concerned. In that case, how to explain the very harsh diagnosis the latter generally make of the missions' incompetence? The frustrations of those who were not included among the happy few consulted, or who think their recommendations were not followed, and the often very strong rivalry among analysts whose diagnoses and proposals may be sharply divergent, partly explain how the aim of being surrounded by the 'best specialists' is not always an easy task and does not solve everything. Besides, supporters of an interactive analysis of conflict resolution processes have for a long time reminded us that the presence of people whose speciality goes beyond the conflict or the region in question can help throw off often preconceived ideas.[142] More decisively, the disconnection between those diagnoses and the decision-making process at the Security Council is a serious obstacle to the effective adaptation of missions to realities on the ground. This is worsened by the absence of effective capacity in the Secretariat for

---

[141] Some members of that team have published a collective work: Steve Heder and Judy Ledgerwood (eds), *Propaganda, Politics and Violence in Cambodia. Democratic Transition under United Nations Peace-Keeping*, New York: M. E. Sharpe, 1995.

[142] Ronald J. Fisher, 'John Burton, Controlled Communication to Analytic Problem Solving', p. 33 in Ronald J. Fisher (ed.), *Interactive Conflict Resolution*, Syracuse/New York: Syracuse University Press, 1997; John W. Burton, *Resolving Deep-rooted Conflict: a Handbook*, Lanham, MD: University Press of America, 1987.

ensuring an analytical connection between that body and the teams in the countries concerned; a deficit which has not yet been remedied, notably because of the repeated refusal of member states to vote for its funding.[143] Lastly, and more profoundly, it is not so much the general knowledge available to the heads of missions (at headquarters or in the field) that is in question so much as that of their members who are, in reality, the true workers in the operation of day-to-day matters.

From one case to another, several elements can explain this situation. The lack of training and information for staff sent on missions is the first recurrent factor. It is not uncommon for members of missions not to receive, on leaving for the field, any written information—even in summary form—on the country. In most cases, the very short time given to recruitment reduces considerably the possibility, for the people concerned, to prepare themselves on their own initiative for their mission and to inform themselves about the country where they are going to work. Even so, as a former member of ONUSAL noted, 'even if you have read something about the country, you don't have day-to-day intimate knowledge of the country, and certainly don't know who the actors on the ground are. There are things that books can't teach you.'[144] Now, on their arrival in the country, it is rare for staff to receive specific training, and it often remains very embryonic, when it is not almost caricatured. Similarly, while efforts are made to recruit, as a priority, people with previous knowledge of the country, applying that criterion in practice often comes up against contradictory requirements. In El Salvador, except for some members of the preparatory team, the mission later made a point of recruiting staff who had no previous experience of the country, so as to reduce as much as possible the risk of identifying with one or other of the parties—an entirely understandable precaution considering the circumstances, but one that had a cost. In contrast, in Cambodia UNTAC was accused of recruiting people who had already been involved at one stage or another in the country's recent history. In the most polarised situations it can turn out to be very difficult to reconcile good knowledge of the setting with 'impartiality'. More decisive still is the *de facto* disconnection between the work done at the level of missions' political direction and the daily work of the operation as experienced by the civilians, civpols and military. A mission's leadership generally has very little knowledge of

---

[143] However, the Brahimi Report made recommendations that, without resolving the problem as a whole, would have made real progress possible with, especially, the creation of a secretariat for strategic information and analysis, caricatured by some representatives of member states as the United Nations' future 'CIA'.

[144] Words recorded in San Salvador, August 23, 1995 (translated from Spanish).

what is going on, on the ground. On its side, the staff has very little information at its disposal to understand how its action is comprised on the whole. However, it is in this daily work that interaction requires the most flexibility, pragmatism, and capacity for adaptation to a changing context. From this point of view, the closer one gets to what constitutes the ordinary work of a mission, the more important understanding the situation becomes. This assumes circulation of information in two directions: from the head offices of the mission to the teams deployed around the country, so as to adjust general directives to the overall political changes and make it possible for each peacekeeper to be informed and aware of what is at stake at each stage of the peace process; but also from the field to the centre, so that the overall management of the mission takes account of the diversity of realities of operations and their changes day by day. UN peace operations do not have that capacity. Information sometimes goes 'up' but 'never down', as their members tirelessly regret. Even in cases where accurate political analysis has been effectively carried out, as in Cambodia, it was almost completely disconnected from the rest of the mission. Expert opinion was rarely based on the reports of teams on the ground, and only exceptionally was it translated into directives or general memos for all the staff. In most countries the work of collecting data is essentially ensured by military intelligence services. Not only are they scarcely in the habit of sharing that information, but the information is most often not adapted to the pluri-disciplinary character of the missions.[145] In June 2002, at the end of five years of investigation, a report on the role of the Dutch Blue Helmets in the massacre of 7,000 Muslims in the Srebrenica 'safe areas' in Bosnia, whom they were supposed to protect, underlined the decisive part played by defective information at all levels of the mission and the disaster caused by rivalry among the military intelligence services of the various countries. Unfortunately, this diagnosis could apply to most current operations.

This failure of analysis, at different levels of a mission, has a number of consequences. First of all, it explains the very normative and, in the meantime, technically-oriented nature of the information produced by missions—when the information does not appear totally disconnected from local reality. Archives retracing the work of teams in the provinces, as well as interviews with members of missions, confirm this very technically-oriented approach—including activities related to human rights or the organisation of elections—and an almost complete lack of linkage with the highly political dimension of the work. At the head of missions,

---

[145] The views expressed by senior officials of missions about the information provided by military intelligence services are generally very harsh.

those deficiencies explain in part the lack of perspective of which all responsible officials complain: unable, effectively, to have a broad picture of what is happening in the country as a whole, to some extent they act blindly. There is also the feeling of being 'completely devoured' by internal problems. All those who have had to hold posts of responsibility within a mission complain of not having been sufficiently available to deal with the problems of the country, even the problems directly linked to the implementation of the mandate. Disagreements with headquarters, operational obstacles,[146] staff security concerns and problems of communication and coordination within the missions take up much of their preoccupations and, naturally, their time. As with any complex organisational structure, the period of establishment of a mission requires considerable energy, which is therefore not directed at the conflict situation itself, though it is at a critical stage. Lastly, 'routine representation' is also a very time-consuming occupation. Everything conspires to encourage a movement of withdrawal towards the interior of a mission, at the expense of the social and political spheres in which the mission's leaders are supposed to be moving.

This is even more pronounced among the missions' staff. For most of them, the lack of knowledge of local reality is reflected in obvious difficulties in finding a place socially in the host country. Often isolated, or with only very partial contact with the societies in which they are moving (having the impression of being 'in a bubble'), the expatriate staff can develop distorted ideas about their interaction with local people, at two opposite extremes.[147] On the one hand, they can have an excessively positive view of the way they are perceived by the local population, notably because of the superficiality of their contacts with it. With some exceptions, the population does not develop an aggressive attitude towards the peacekeepers; in addition, in many societies the practice is never to say no to a stranger, always to put on a good face. This explains why most UN staff members are unable to anticipate the smallest difficulties or changes in the situation, and can project an excessively optimistic view of their work, far removed from what is going on in the 'real' country at the time. Anyone who has been with United Nations missions in the field has been able to get this impression of a world apart, operating in a vacuum. A matter

---

[146] This aspect has seen some improvement over the years, especially with the transfer, at headquarters, of the logistics division (the former Field Operations Division, renamed the Field Administration and Logistics Division) from the administration department to the peace keeping department to which it is now attached.

[147] Obviously, the attitudes that correspond to this can only be described here as a tendency. Just as with what can be noted among local actors, situations within missions are not fixed and behaviour varies much from one individual to another.

that may have been strengthened by the creation in a little more than a decade, especially among civilians, of a group of individuals moving around from one mission to another with an atypical form of life, divorced from all reality (including the reality of their home countries, where the people concerned do not always succeed in resettling professionally). The effects of any expatriate existence are reinforced here by the narrowness of the circles those people move in, their particularly favourable financial conditions, and the many places they stay in, often over a short period of time (difficulties that humanitarian NGOs have also encountered).

At the other extreme, it is not uncommon that the lack of contact with local reality explains why the same individuals place themselves increasingly on the defensive, in an attitude of withdrawal into oneself, even fear causing certain paranoia. This is particularly noticeable in countries where there are animated worries about staff security, as there were in Cambodia as the elections approached, Somalia, Bosnia-Herzegovina, and more recently Sierra Leone, Afghanistan and Iraq. In Bosnia, during the second part of the UNPROFOR mission most of the UN troops were sheltered in their camps or behind their sandbags, in what the soldiers themselves called their 'bunker'. While the war continued, this lack of information helped to feed fear and reinforce the impression that all the 'locals' were becoming potential 'enemies'. Anyone who has been in similar circumstances knows how much an unknown and ill-understood environment can very quickly come to be seen as threatening, while the 'craziest information' goes around. In Somalia, among members of UNOSOM the feeling spread very rapidly that the population was 'entirely hostile' to them. Typically, gatherings of crowds and assemblages are greatly feared in such contexts. In various places where I conducted investigations, social and community actors frequently spoke of their impression that members of missions (*gringos, UNTACs, Blans, Gals* [in Somali], etc. as the case might be) seemed, in fact, 'to be afraid of people'. Language problems and failure to master the local codes of behaviour can also lead to misinterpretation. Incidents between members of missions and local people have regularly arisen from disproportionate reactions by United Nations soldiers to ordinary disputes, harmless gatherings of people or other 'street scenes' that they did not understand. This can lead to mistaken assessments of situations, and errors with sometimes tragic consequences.

The obsession with 'having problems', the concern to 'limit the risks of things getting out of hand', may paradoxically put members of missions in increasingly delicate positions. Fear is a feeling that feeds on itself very easily. Even in the least tense situations, missions are very quickly seen to adopt a 'low profile' (a recurring expression in interviews with former members of missions). That attitude is reinforced by the serious difficulties they encounter in communicating with the various components of the societies in which they intervene.

The failures of missions' information policies to target local societies

Real efforts made by recent operations in this matter have not resolved the main challenge that still confronts them, summed up by the impression given by local actors in all field investigations: the missions do not communicate *with* them, being more concerned to communicate with the international media present in the country than to address local public opinion. Most important in the mission leaders' minds is the image that the international media are going to give of a mission in the outside world, especially in the critical phases of operations. Several actors have an interest in this: the UN Secretariat with regard to member states, the contributing governments to their domestic public opinion, members of the missions themselves, especially in the hope that people will talk about them in their home countries, etc. As former members of missions admit themselves, their senior officials are generally more concerned 'to sell the image of the mission to the outside world than to establish it in the country'.[148] On their side, local social and political actors criticise the missions for being more concerned with their own publicity and the 'showcase' that is presented than in communicating with the country's population.

The gap between the treatment of the local press and of the international press reveals that bias very well. In Cambodia, press statements were most often put out in English, whereas at that time very few Cambodian journalists understood that language; only at the end of the UN mission, under strong pressure from Cambodian journalists, did press statements begin to be published in both English and Khmer. The same problem arose with press conferences. Whatever their political inclinations, Cambodian journalists agree on at least one point: 'What interested the UNTAC people was the foreign journalists, not us.' One of them explained: 'It was virtually impossible for Cambodian journalists to get a card for access to the UNTAC offices, while foreign journalists came and went there as they wished. We had greatest difficulties in performing interviews or attending press conferences.'[149] This discrimination was the

---

[148] This specific phrase comes from Florentín Melendez, the only Salvadorean employed as a local professional in ONUSAL (San Salvador, September 7, 1995).

[149] Interviews with Pen Pheng, editor of *Rasmei Kampuchea*, started some months before the elections, and of *Phnom Penh Weekly* during the first period of UNTAC, head of the

object of public denunciation in the local press. Radio France International's permanent correspondent at the time confirmed that UNTAC's spokesman 'turned exclusively towards the foreign press. It is true, the local press was in a poor condition, especially at that time, but it was not helped by being marginalised. This situation was closely tied up with the personality of Falt [the spokesman], who very much liked being quoted in the international press and being seen on foreign television channels. The local press did not interest him; it did not have enough prestige.'[150]

In Haiti, international press correspondents acknowledged that 'no effort [was] made for [their] Haitian colleagues. Public opinion in Haiti does not exist for them; what matters is international opinion, which must be reassured that all is going well.'[151] In that country the spokesman spoke only in French, while the most popular radio stations broadcast in Haitian Creole. In addition journalists (and others) found it difficult to speak to UNMIH if they did not speak English.[152] In fact, anyone who telephoned to the mission's headquarters or presented himself at its offices had that experience. The political adviser to the Special Representative of the Secretary General acknowledged: 'We have big problems of communication with the country.'[153] The personality of the spokesman can play a crucial role here. He, as much as, if not more than, the Special Representative of the Secretary General, embodies the mission before the public. From this viewpoint the 'extreme arrogance' of some of them, denounced from one country to another, is highly counter-productive.

In addition to this particular relationship with the press, missions produce their own information material as part of education campaigns that are generally centred on three main themes: explanation of the mission, human rights and the election process, and more occasionally disarmament. However, this aspect of their action is not considered to be a priority, and often has limited resources provided for it. Above all, the material published in this process is generally of very poor quality. The commercials broadcast over local radio and television, to announce the presence of the missions, is generally confined to repeating the mission's acronym as a slogan, without giving real information. Even when missions have the

---

League of Cambodian Journalists; and Pin Sam Khon, Chairman of the opposition Khmer Journalists Association (KJA), editor of the *Khmer Ekareach Newspaper* (Phnom Penh, November 21 and December 2, 1995).

[150] Interview with Marc Victor, Phnom Penh, November 17, 1995.

[151] Interviews in Port-au-Prince, April 1995.

[152] Interviews in Port-au-Prince, April–May 1995.

[153] Interview in Port-au-Prince, April 22, 1995. At the time the great majority of UNMIH members—such as the Force Commander himself and most of the police—did not speak a word of French.

means to produce videos, posters, brochures, leaflets, big streamers and hoardings to be put up in public places, they are often 'superficial propaganda' (as the local actors themselves call it) rather than part of a real information campaign. In addition, it is not uncommon for that material to seem completely divorced from the situation under consideration, especially on human rights questions for which the choice of images and messages is crucial. A former adviser to the Civil Mission in Haiti (MICIVIH) summed up fairly well the criticisms often made of missions' education departments: 'They have a very condescending attitude. The "people must be educated". Obviously that will not do, especially for NGOs who say they themselves have the impression of being treated as "savages".'[154] In fact, the public education campaigns were most often distressingly superficial, when they were not quite simply insulting to the people, their culture and their history. In Cambodia, a former United Nations Volunteer in the UNTAC Human Rights Component admitted: 'There was a way of depicting the Cambodians as savages that I could not endure.'[155]

On the other hand, local actors often complained that there was no local distribution of the reports published by the missions. Written first for the attention of the Secretariat and after in their public form for the attention of the Security Council, they are rarely available in the countries themselves, which local political and social actors resent very strongly, considering that the reports are of primary concern to them. The local human rights organisations are among the ones who feel the need most. In El Salvador, for example, the San José Accord, in which the mission's mandate on human rights issues was defined, also foresaw that ONUSAL surveys would be published through the local media;[156] this was never done. Even more regrettable is the fact that very little publicity was made around the 'Truth Commissions' in the countries where they have taken place, keeping the majority of the population unaware of the process. The few copies distributed in the interior of the country were essentially at the initiative of local organisations, with very modest means. In Cambodia the heads of local organisations, frustrated at the way no information in the area concerning them ever got back to the Cambodians, said they had the feeling 'of being robbed of a part of their history'.[157] Some will argue that, for different reasons, it may not always be desirable to diffuse those reports, an argument which may be accepted in some contexts. My

---

[154] Words recorded in New York, January 13th, 1995.
[155] Words recorded in Siem Reap, December 5th, 1995.
[156] San José Agreement, § 14 (j) and 9 (k), in *Path to Peace*, p. 11.156.
[157] Quoted in Clodagh O'Brien, Dinah Pokempner and Thun Saray, *The United Nations in Cambodia: An NGO Perspective*, The Aspen Institute, Meeting on Human Rights and UN Peacekeeping, September 1994, p. 12 (mimeo).

argument regards the fact that a process that remains entirely confidential may create very counter-productive effects in the local society. It does not serve the process of 'reconciliation'; for instance, the victims and families of victims do not have the possibility to hear that their history, what happened to them, is recognised to be true, to have happened and is condemned as such.

Another problem concerns the level of language used. In most languages different repertoires exist; they need to be taken into account in any work of public education. Even when a principal language is widely dominant, it is not uncommon for the language spoken by the majority of the population, especially in rural areas but also in the poorer districts of the towns, to be noticeably different from the written language or the one used by the elite. In Cambodia, the language used in information material and UN radio broadcasts was incomprehensible for the majority of Cambodians. There were many examples of laborious interpretation where 'at best, 5 per cent of the message was more or less transmitted', according to linguists questioned. Father François Ponchaud, who has been working for many years on translation of the Bible into Khmer, has said in particular: 'Take the Human Rights Charter which they distributed; I challenge you to find a Cambodian in the street or, still more difficult, in the rice fields who can understand the Khmer translation they made of it.'[158] In addition, errors of translation, sometimes with damaging consequences, are not uncommon. A former international interpreter with UNTAC has recorded: 'Most of the seminars and training provided by UNTAC were of no use. Many interpretations were unintended distortions of meaning, simply because the interpreter did not understand what the instructor was saying or the instructor was unable to check the translation of his words.'[159] From one mission to another, local actors rival each other with anecdotes about misunderstandings with more or less harmful consequences.

Since Cambodia, the UN Secretariat has made efforts to establish the missions' own radio stations, which notably avoids the missions being totally dependent on local radio stations to spread their messages.[160] The experience of Radio UNTAC however shows that having a radio station is not a panacea. For the essential part of the mission, its broadcasts were limited not only in time[161] but also in their reach, since the station could

---

[158] Words recorded in Paris, March 21, 1995.

[159] Interview with Kassie Neou, Phnom Penh, November 21, 1995.

[160] That assumes, however, that this objective is considered a priority, which is not always the case; for some other missions (in Somalia for example) the establishment of a specific radio station was rejected by the UN General Assembly committee responsible for the budget.

[161] The radio station made its first broadcast on November 9, 1992, from a transmitter installed in Phnom Penh. Until May, the four producers could only produce one thirty-

only be picked up in Phnom Penh, considerably reducing the impact of the distribution of radio sets by UNTAC (an operation that led to a good deal of trafficking and problems in several regions). Relay stations, to broadcast in most of the zones outside Phnom Penh, only became operational in the weeks before the elections. In the meantime the broadcasts were recorded on tapes distributed to the Electoral Component to be played at public meetings, which occurred very rarely. As, very similarly, my investigations showed in other countries, United Nations operations' radio station was appreciated above all for its music programmes, more diverse than those of the local stations. This is one of the reasons why, after having conducted serious in-the-field investigations, I am very cautious about the real impact of these media, which many analysts have been exaggeratedly enthusiastic about.

The difficulties in establishing a real tool for communication with the local people has three main consequences. First, lack of knowledge of the missions' objectives and unrealistic expectations can not be set right. With a lack of a minimum of 'objective' information, people form their own ideas based primarily on what they see of the mission from their own positions. Obviously it would be unrealistic to expect to achieve knowledge of the details of a mission's mandate on the part of a local population as a whole. However, by largely neglecting the information dimension of their work too many missions increase considerably the risks of being misunderstood. Besides, the fact that the outsiders communicate at best through the language of the elite not only has the consequence of seriously limiting the understanding of the message, it may also be an act that, symbolically, is felt very strongly especially in view of the way United Nations missions have tended to be lumped together with the traditional figure of the state scorning the people and, similarly, not speaking their language. This was expressed in interviews by the inhabitants' feeling of being ignored, since they were never spoken to. Lastly, the communication difficulties may deprive UN operations of a tool that can be very useful at some critical stages of their progress, or indeed of a possibility of counteracting hostile propaganda. At the time of its establishment in El Salvador, ONUSAL, when it should have been laying the foundations of its public position, chose to adopt the lowest profile that one could imagine by limiting its information effort to the bare minimum. The senior United Nations officials' preoccupation was to avoid putting at risk the nego-

---

minute programme per week each, and the information broadcast was strictly limited to that given by the UNTAC spokesman himself. Information became more varied and the daily broadcasting time longer as from May 12, 1993, that is, just before the holding of the elections. The station ceased broadcasting on September 22, 1993.

tiation progress to achieve a peace agreement. But at the same time, some political groups, who were the most hostile to the peace process, waged a virulent anti-ONUSAL press campaign. Unable to react, the mission was in effect forced behind its ramparts. This was exactly what the instigators of the campaign wanted. An outcome pursued mostly by Altamirano Madriz, editor of the daily *El Diario de Hoy*, and Lito Rafael Montalvo, columnist and spokesman of the far right, a man who was closely tied to the general staff of the armed forces, who had a regular column on ONUSAL and whose writing was extremely harsh.[162] 'ONUSAL did a big favour to *El Diario de Hoy* and to all those for whom it spoke by leaving the field completely free.'[163] One of the senior officials of the mission has admitted that the UN was 'afraid of the press' and ought to have 'made a bigger effort at communication, adopting a more sophisticated and more complete policy. It was possible without being aggressive to make an objective, sober campaign explaining matters. We should have explained, clarified, repeated incessantly certain points on which that campaign was concentrated...That was not done. The attacks quieted down but we never recovered the lost ground.'[164] In fact the campaign against ONUSAL was very largely based on 'unease' that was already widespread in society as a whole, not having enough information at its disposal on what the mission was supposed to accomplish.

In Haiti, while security problems increasingly preoccupied the population who felt UNMIH '[was] doing nothing' to resolve them, UNMIH's message, through its spokesman, consisted of minimising the problems, emphasising how insecurity was much worse in other countries or even that 'insecurity forms part of democracy'. In the poorer districts, the response was crushing: 'Falt [the spokesman] takes Haitians for idiots.'[165] In addition, the language used by the UNMIH spokesman clashed with the diagnosis made at the same time in the Secretary General's reports to the Security Council. The report dated January 17, 1995 acknowledged that a large number of Haitians did not feel safe and that 'this is a political reality'. It emphasised the 'necessity to reassure the population which has a phobia of seeing paramilitary networks starting a new reign of terror.'[166] On the ground, the UNMIH spokesman admitted that he had 'groped around a lot on the question of insecurity', but he persisted in his view that 'Haitians must get used to this insecurity, it is a normal development.'[167]

[162] Interviews in El Salvador, September 7, 1995.
[163] Interview with Oscar Bonilla, Vice-Chairman of the Partido Demócrata, member of the COPAZ, San Salvador, September 23, 1995 (translated from Spanish).
[164] Private interview (San Salvador, September 6, 1995).
[165] Interviews in Port-au-Prince (April 1995).
[166] S/1995/46, paras. 28 and 29.
[167] Comment by Eric Falt (Port-au-Prince, May 16, 1995).

On November 11, 1995 President Aristide called on the population to take charge of disarmament itself. Violent incidents followed. The head of UNMIH then held a press conference. For the first time, the message was clear: neither the problems of insecurity nor the existence of weapons was called into question, but it was clearly stated that disarmament must be carried out by the police, with the aid of UNMIH which remained ready to back them up. The people were then called upon to report stocks of weapons. On the UNMIH side, it is stressed that such reports were very few and it was never possible to check the information. Yet at the beginning of 1996 the problem remained the number one priority for Haitians, and continued to make the headlines in the local media. The language adopted then by the mission's spokesman raised tension again: 'Falt is explaining that the population is responsible because it is not collaborating with UNMIH. In other words, it's not their fault but the fault of the population if disarmament is not carried out.'[168] When explicitly accused, by the spokesman, of spreading rumours and keeping up a psychosis, the Haitian media vented their fury.

The consequences can be much worse in situations where a conflict is ongoing, as is suggested by the cases of Somalia and Bosnia. In Somalia, the deficiencies in the information put out by UNOSOM gave more space to Mohamed Aydid to deploy his own propaganda and build up for himself, notably, the stature of a hero fighting bravely against the 'imperialists'. The gap in understanding is illustrated by an anecdote: in July 1993 hundreds of supporters of Aydid demonstrated in southern Mogadishu while UNOSOM scattered around 40,000 leaflets calling on Somalis to 'renounce' Aydid. The case of Bosnia-Herzegovina shows even more clearly how much a mission can put itself in a position of weakness if it is not able to counteract disinformation practiced by the various parties against it. Orchestrated according to the objectives of a particular moment, UNPROFOR was the permanent helpless victim of disinformation organised by the various parties and campaigns to destroy its credibility. In a war situation the media, whether directly controlled by the main politico-military entrepreneurs or not, serve the pursuit of politics by other means, in the fullest sense.[169] In Bosnia-Herzegovina even the rare 'independent' press organs linked to groups of intellectuals (particularly in Sarajevo) operated partly 'under control', especially the SDA, which gave them a space of freedom but also used them to criticise international institutions and the UN.

---

[168] Interview with Necker Dessables and Chenet Jean-Baptiste, National Justice and Peace Secretariat (Port-au-Prince, February 22, 1996).
[169] Jasmina Kuzmanovic, 'Media: The Extension of Politics by Other Means', in Sabrina Petra Ramet and Ljubisa S. Adamovich (eds), *Beyond Yugoslavia: Politics, Economics and Cultures in a Shattered Community*, Boulder, CO: Westview, 1995.

At the heart of a conflict, the main politico-military entrepreneurs play increasingly on the rebound effect of international information, not hesitating to resort to the best specialised agencies for that purpose.[170] Foreign journalists, present on a massive scale during major operations, in areas deserted yesterday and just as rapidly abandoned, depend at the same time on the belligerents themselves, the peacekeepers and non-governmental organisations to have access to places and to information. Direct coverage of an operation (especially if it has a strong humanitarian component), or at least the more immediate presence of the international media, complicates management of images and representations, putting UN missions under real pressure that they have not yet comprehended. Information conveyed by foreign journalists has rebound effects in the countries themselves, through being reproduced by the local media and also through becoming known to the elite who have access to the international press and the web and to the people—often a wider section among the population—who tune in to international radio stations broadcasting daily in local languages on short wave (essentially the Voice of America and the BBC, to a lesser extent Radio France International). Often people listen to several radio stations, and information then travels by informal channels. Together with accounts by representatives of NGOs or other international organisations, the combined action of various media, international and local, helps to fashion images and build up representations of what is happening during a peace operation. Understanding how and to what extent these various narratives are, or are not, linked together and, likewise, how and to what extent they influence actors' behaviour, should be a central dimension of a communication policy for a peace operation, as sometimes they shape reality and are reshaped themselves. Unfortunately the senior officials of missions remain, on the whole, more preoccupied with their international image and their internal problems than by local 'public opinion'.

---

[170] On the propaganda made during the UNPROFOR period, see especially the analysis by Marjan Malesic, 'International Peacekeeping: An Object of Propaganda in Former Yugoslavia', *International Peacekeeping* 5/3, Summer 1998, pp. 82–102.

4

'INTERVENTION' AND 'SOVEREIGNTY'
THE VIEW FROM BELOW

Former peacekeepers sometimes say that they do not understand why the populations never 'greeted them with acclamations'. In fact, it is rare for peacekeepers to be seen as 'liberators', even in contexts where flagrant, massive and systematic violations of human rights have been committed. The circumstances of 'peace' are often costly, if not deceptive. The actions of the 'international community' have generally proved ambiguous enough in the past for local people to be wary of its operations. Conversely, many observers have wondered about the processes by which the presence of a UN mission could strengthen group or even 'national' consciousness in a country where there is an intervention. Others have even contemplated how a mission could avoid being perceived as an 'occupying force'. All these modes of representation of collective reactions to peace operations are equally problematic. The idea of 'occupation' first of all: while peace operations formally bring with them a 'project' (the restoration of a 'state based on the rule of law') and 'political engineering', including structures and discourse on values such as democracy and human rights, they do not have all-encompassing intentions. There is no will to structure the entire space, including the physical space, since the missions occupy it in very variable ways. While they clearly show intentions of restoring 'order', and hence to 'organise', at no moment do peace operations adopt the means that would be required by a true enterprise aimed at 'disciplining' societies, as colonisation pretended to do for example.[1] Here, there is no intention of permeating society. In any event, missions take place over too short a time for these broad societal developments to take place. 'Occupation' also suggests the idea of an oppressive force. On that point, as we shall see, the varying perceptions of

---

[1] To use the expression that Achille Mbembe borrowed from both Max Weber and Michel Foucault to describe the colonisation enterprise. Cf. Achille Mbembe, *La naissance du maquis dans le Sud-Cameroun (1920–1960)*, Paris: Karthala, 1996, pp. 29–30.

the behaviour of the United Nations troops, and the more or less flagrant violations of certain local customs, play a definite role. While United Nations interventions, unlike the American operation in Iraq, are not usually perceived as 'occupations',[2] they can become so in certain circumstances. As for the idea of 'nationalism', the uncertainty that usually surrounds it[3] is reinforced by the characteristic ambiguities made in the multiple uses of this concept by local political entrepreneurs throughout history. In addition, building the state is at the core of the conflicts in which United Nations missions intervene; but it raises questions that are expressed collectively in forms that do not always coincide with the usual categories of 'nationalism'. Thus, the themes of 'nationalism' or 'occupation' can be expressed in various forms in the language used by actors regarding the UN. But these forms are generally included in broader registers, where what is at stake relates first of all to the dynamics of collective identification in the various 'change and exchange practices' from which they are derived.[4] It is there, in particular, that the history of relations with the outside world and the associated representations are revisited which contributes to fashioning of shifting local understandings of notions such as 'sovereignty' and 'intervention'.

THE HISTORY OF RELATIONS WITH THE OUTSIDE WORLD

Such a historical examination can help understand what the imaginary figures of the 'international community' are, what purpose the reference, so often made, to that community by the intervening forces themselves, serves, who is described by the term, and how it is used. The existence of a past period of occupation is, in all cases, an important factor to consider, with all the ambiguities of—often contradictory—memories that have been retained of it. In countries as varied as Somalia, Mozambique and Cambodia, reference to the colonial past was regularly made by local political entrepreneurs in their relations with the United Nations operation. The representations that they use may alternately refer back to processes of building up, through history, a heroic status for rebels fighting

---

[2] In Iraq, in 2003, the United Nations found itself in the unprecedented situation of being lumped together with an occupying force. In addition, it should not be forgotten that the UN was especially associated, in that country, with the sanctions imposed from 1990 onwards.

[3] See especially Benedict Anderson, *Imagined Communities: Reflections on the Origins and Spread of Nationalism*, rev. ed. London: Verso, 1991, and Ernest Gellner, *Nations and Nationalism*, London: Weidenfeld & Nicolson, 1997.

[4] See Denis-Constant Martin, *Cartes d'identité. Comment dit-on 'nous' en politique?* Paris: Presses de la FNSP, 1994, p. 35.

against foreign domination, and to comparable processes for 'traitor' figures—something that has been observed in Bosnia-Herzegovina, especially on the part of Croat and Serb political entrepreneurs.[5]

The way in which local actors perceive members of peace missions at the outset is also fashioned by more recent history, especially when it has been marked by a specific bilateral relationship. The case of El Salvador illustrates this type of situation well. During the conflict, the American embassy in San Salvador was often perceived as the place where the most important decisions concerning the country's future were taken. Debates in Congress and decisions from the White House could even be considered 'more important for the future of this small country than manoeuvres by its politicians or mobilisation by its trade unions.'[6] However, El Salvador has never been a 'banana republic'. It was always a local oligarchy that controlled production and marketing of its dominant product, coffee. It was also the same oligarchy that subsequently controlled infant industries and the banking system of the country. This explains why Salvadorian economic entrepreneurs revealed a certain bitterness towards the American *diktat* which they were subjected to during the war in exchange for financing what they could no longer ensure on their own.[7] For the general staff of the Salvadorian armed forces, the American neighbour was certainly the 'boss' for a long period, but it was above all the party that had 'dropped' them, forcing them to negotiate a peace agreement in which they had much to lose. During the last years of war, the presence of foreign military personnel on Salvadorian soil also influenced the perception the Salvadorians had of the military personnel of peace operations. For the people who remained in the country, the presence of American military advisers left a mark on *imaginaires*; this was particularly true for the former guerrillas, for whom every 'white' person was instantly seen as a *gringo*, hence an American. Throughout the years preceding the peace process, members of the guerrilla forces and the people repatriated from Honduras were in contact with the United Nations Observer Group in Central America, ONUCA.[8] In view of the ambiguity of that group's mission, they retained a suspicion of it which they later

[5] Alexa Djilas, *The Contested Country: Yugoslav Unity and Communist Revolution*, Cambridge, MA: Harvard University Press, 1991, p. 9.
[6] See Alain Rouquié, *Les forces politiques en Amérique centrale*, Paris: Karthala, 1991, p. 112.
[7] Interviews in San Salvador with various private sector representatives.
[8] ONUCA was set up by Resolution 644 of the Security Council on November 7, 1989, in the framework of the Esquipulas process following a request from five governments of Central American countries. It was a military observation mission originally established to verify the application of the security provisions of the Central American peace agreement.

transferred to the ONUSAL military personnel. A scepticism fuelled by
the fact that a certain number of military personnel sent to El Salvador
under the ONUSAL peace operation had previously served under
ONUCA. At the other end of the political spectrum, the presence during
the conflict of international brigades and numerous international NGOs,
often *de facto* allies of the guerrillas in the zones where they worked, left a
mark on the *imaginary* of right-wing political leaders and Salvadorian
military personnel. Very often they described ONUSAL members (especially civilian ones) as 'internationalists'.

No matter what country it is deployed in, a peace mission becomes a
part of history. A part well outside the mission's control because members
readily behave as though nothing has happened before their arrival. Yet
that past explains that, for local people, 'foreigners' had already 'intervened' in many ways in their country. In a number of countries this helps
to understand how responsibility for the war, as well as inadequacies in
peace, is readily placed on the outside world by the political elites. When,
as in Cambodia, people have lived almost permanently under the domination of neighbours for centuries, before being 'protected' by France,
'backed' and then bombed by the United States, 'abandoned' by all and
then 'liberated' by Vietnam, the foreigner is readily presented as the cause
of all evils, past and present.

In Haiti the specific nature of the relationship with the North American
neighbour is even more marked than in El Salvador. It is reinforced by the
memory of an occupation (1915–34) whose objectives had an uncanny
similarity to those of Operation Restore Democracy.[9] That period occu-
pies a very important position in the Haitian collective consciousness, and
heroes of the resistance to the occupying power continue to be revered.[10]
Thus, anti-American sentiments (regularly manipulated by the elites) still
carry some weight among all social classes. Here one sees the full importance of the central role of the United States in international management of Haitian affairs, a role that it adopted from 1994 onwards.
Haitian political actors, of all sorts, did not seek to deny the United States
that position of 'boss'; most of them were stuck in the endless contradictions arising from President Aristide's return under the high protection

[9] The double challenge, which the United States tried to meet at that time, was to train a
professional army and pacify the country on the one hand, and to help economic reconstruction on the other. But it withdrew after nineteen years of difficult occupation
without managing to consolidate the structures of the country, which very quickly
plunged back into serious political crises, including the 1957 one which led to François
Duvalier's accession to power.
[10] Such as Charlemagne Péralte, leader of a peasants' revolt who was killed by the American army; his icon can be seen in many *kay*s (houses) of the Haitian countryside.

of the USA. This course of action, which they had, as a whole, strongly denounced, was implicitly approved by the Haitian population, as was shown by the at least initial friendly welcome of GIs. In addition, the resort to a solution that was not only military, but that came from an external actor, showed the inability of Haitian political actors to work out any solution to the crisis internally. Those ambiguities also explain their own confinement within a logic that was more bilateral than multilateral. The transfer of responsibility at the beginning of 1996, in the mission's military command, from an American general to a Canadian (while the US contingents left), changed nothing. Whether it was present on the ground or not, the United States was master of the game, and that made all imaginable differences unnoticeable. Obviously, while the political situation was deadlocked, especially from the spring of 1997 onwards, the multiplicity of high level American missions went far to reinforce this perception. Whereas the political profile of the United Nations successive missions, for their part, declined noticeably.

Apart from that specific relationship, to understand the ambivalent aspects of relations with the 'Other' in Haitian collective memory, it is important to recall the way in which a culture, language and social organisation were gradually recreated from elements that were all 'external'.[11] In fact Haitian society formed its foundation on a Creole culture, a plural culture produced by constant re-compositions, from 'material re-applied in new construction'.[12] Among the elites, this relationship with the outside world involved massive importation of models (including the Code named after Napoleon, whose armies the black slaves defeated!). These were experienced with a mixture of fascination and repulsion, in the name of nationalism, a discourse that was regularly manipulated by those elites and, during the peace operation, centred on the theme of occupation.[13] This ambivalence was reinforced by growing economic dependency and the difficulties that those elites always had in promoting viable autonomous alternatives. It makes it possible to understand how violent rejection of any attempt at interference in the country's affairs frequently goes together—in a way largely independent of political divisions—with expectations of a solution from the outside. The successive outside interventions in recent years have had all these ingredients: the importing of an electoral

---

[11] When the first slaves and settlers arrived at the island, almost the entire native population had already been wiped out.

[12] See André Marcel d'Ans, *Haiti, Paysage et Société*, Paris: Karthala, 1987, pp. 239–42.

[13] On the many ambiguities in nationalist discourse, and the ways it has been used throughout Haiti's political history, there is a preliminary reflection in a special issue of the magazine *Chemins Critiques*, 'Nationalismes', 3/1–2, Port-au-Prince, December 1993.

model in 1990, models of judicial reform, the imposition of economic sanctions whose effects included a considerable increase in the country's dependency, and new models presented for 'restoration' of democracy. Hence the 'international community', incarnated by default by the UN, has been perceived as the body simultaneously imposing the embargo and failing to invoke the necessary and sufficient measures to foil the coup d'état; the one which did not end the oppressive acts of the military despite the presence of a mission on the scene (MICIVIH); the one who imposed socio-economic reforms and then continuously sanctioned measures; the one from which the elites expect everything and, at the meantime, who is made responsible for any failures, and denounced for its interference. These ingredients are found similarly in most areas where the UN has been called upon to intervene. In Iraq, in addition to the fact that its presence could be seen as *de facto* acceptance of the American occupation, the United Nations was seen first of all as the body that had imposed a total embargo from 1990 to 2003, whose victims amounted to about 500,000 dead (essentially children and the aged), according to the lowest estimate by international NGOs. In addition, it must not be forgotten that from 1998 to 2003 the Iraqi population lived through regular bombing by American and British aircraft over flying Iraq's airspace.

The history of the 'aid culture' must also be taken into account. Many of these countries have a long history of development aid or humanitarian assistance (Bosnia-Herzegovina and Kosovo being fairly big exceptions in this regard). Such a history tends to create a certain relationship with anyone who comes from outside to bring 'aid'. This can help in better understanding some facets of local actors' behaviour, especially when they expect material gains from United Nations missions. Somalia is a good example of a country where the weight of the 'aid and extortion culture' seems particularly profound. Two decades of frequent drought and large-scale refugee flows following the Ogaden war led to a massive influx of aid. All this occurring at a time when the East-West polarisation in the region and the successive patronage of the two great powers of the time ensured a certain 'situation rent'. This led not only to a pronounced dependency on the outside world,[14] but also to certain habits in 'management' of aid, to which donors commonly turned a blind eye. With the conflict that broke out after the fall of Siyad Barre's regime, the groups fighting for power resumed redistribution practices fuelled by emergency

---

[14] In 1990, it was estimated that 80 per cent of Somalia's annual budget was funded from foreign sources: Abdi Ahmed Osman, *The Role of NGOs and Somalia's Development Needs in the 1990s*, International Institute for Environment and Development, Dryland Networks Programme, London, September 1990, p. 4 (Issues Paper no. 20).

aid, which was once again pouring into the country. They also rehabil-
itated, with impunity, a culture of looting. 'Many Somalis are convinced
in all good faith that the money from the international community is their
due, that it does not belong to anyone, which means that it belongs to
everyone, and that there must therefore be no limitations to its use.'[15]
Therefore, the disappearance and theft of UNOSOM goods was related to
a habitual way of managing international aid. In the case of Cambodia the
'aid culture', developed in the refugee camps on the border, was accompanied by frequent misappropriation, to which the aid agencies reacted
with great tolerance. This experience, allied to a certain idea of the material benefits that should go with power, explains why the search for gain
could involve massive theft in the last weeks of UNTAC's presence in the
country: what the mission had brought with it to Cambodia should return
to the Cambodians and benefit those who could get hold of it, others usually
getting nothing.

If that history of aid does not always arouse a resort to large-scale misappropriation, beyond doubt it shapes the relationship with the foreigner.
The resulting relationship often includes many suspicions about the foreigner's real intentions, in countries where decades of international aid
have hardly changed the plight of the majority of the people. When people
do not understand what the 'Whites' are doing, they look for explanations.
In Haiti, the 'Whites' had come to loot the Citadel[16] or were carrying off
soil supposed to contain precious substances[17], or else were coming simply
to 'steal the sun and the fine landscapes that they don't have at home',[18] a
reference regularly found in my investigations, in contexts as varied as El
Salvador, Mozambique, Sierra Leone and Cambodia. It is similar with
criticisms of the high salaries of members of the missions, a perception
partly formed by earlier visits to expatriate circles. In San Salvador, the
mere mention of the missions' acronym (ONUSAL) in chance encounters
in the street or in conversations with taxi drivers brought comments returning invariably to the same observation: 'It's always the same thing

[15] See Roland Marchal, 'Somalie: les dégâts d'une improvisation', pp. 78–9, in Marie-
Claude Smouts (ed.), *L'ONU et la guerre*, Brussels: Ed. Complexe, 1994, and interviews
with the author.

[16] A monument erected in the north of the country, by order of King Christophe, as a
symbol of the strength of the Haitian people. Now renovated, it has been classified by
UNESCO as a World Heritage site. Thus the accusation of its looting was full of
symbolic meaning.

[17] In fact, at that same time, a Canadian company had taken over exploitation of the river
sand and gravel in the Limbé zone in the north of the country.

[18] This last interpretation has been widely echoed in newspapers and leaflets of community
organisations, as well as in the Creole weekly *Libète*—see especially no. 191 of May 22,
1996 (translation from Haitian Creole).

with the *gringos*. They come to make money and travel around. It's not serious, when you see the problems that our country has had. It's always like that.'[19] But such an attitude does not stop people from wondering about them and 'observing them with a great deal of curiosity'...

FIGURES OF INTERVENTION

The discourse of political actors on the theme of 'occupation'—which readily goes too far—generally contrasts with a much wider range of experiences to which societies seem to refer, sometimes in contradictory fashion. The sovereignty rhetoric that local authorities often use immoderately is above all for the ears of foreigners, particularly, of UN officials, not for the population who is rarely mobilised by such language. In El Salvador, the double theme of sovereignty and interference in the discourse of a section of the political class and the military, that strongly rejected the UN presence, was principally used for purposes of intimidation. The press campaign orchestrated by the daily *El Diario de Hoy* aimed less at Salvadorian public opinion than at the senior officials of ONUSAL whom it was intended to 'put in their place'.[20] For those officials the campaign's objective was clear: '*Soverano, soverania* were the words coming most often from the mouths of people we had to deal with in the government, the army and the police. They accused us regularly and publicly of acting too much as interventionists. They always verified that we were well aware of what was being said in the press on the subject. They knew that at least among the top people [of ONUSAL], it was a sensitive topic.'[21]

In Mozambique the Special Representative of the Secretary General summed up what he called the 'classic scenario' in these terms: 'Every time one party was not pleased with ONUMOZ's work, it summoned the press and accused ONUMOZ of interfering in the country's affairs; we often faced these accusations and we were highly sensitive to them...'[22] Certainly press campaigns were waged in the country on that theme, especially during the first months of the mission. They fuelled what was supposed to be a 'great national debate' on 'the consequences of the presence of United Nations contingents in the country, especially for national sovereignty'.[23] The Mozambican government then asked for time

[19] Comment by a taxi driver, San Salvador, August 26, 1995 (translated from Spanish).
[20] Interviews with various political leaders in San Salvador and with Enrique Altamirano Madriz, Editor of the daily *El Diario de Hoy* (September 1995).
[21] Private interview with a former senior ONUSAL official (New York, January 5, 1995).
[22] Words quoted from Aldo Ajello (Johannesburg, October 22, 1994).
[23] See, in particular, what was said on this subject in the United Nations Secretary General's report S/25518 of April 2, 1993, para. 4.

to 'address concerns in the National Assembly about the implications for national sovereignty of such a large and comprehensive international operative'. That gave it, notably, a pretext for delaying negotiations on a status of forces agreement for the UN troops.[24]

It only rarely happens that, as in Somalia, regular appeals are launched for people to unite against an 'occupier' seeking to 'impose guardianship over the Somali people'[25]—apart from intimidation operations such as those undertaken by the military regime in Haiti before the American military intervention. Beyond the caricature displayed in demonstrations organised in the Haitian capital in September 1994, the language used called on classic registers of a struggle against a foreign invasion (resistance/collaboration, defence of the homeland, etc.), as well as international references. Some of it was for domestic consumption, and there were symbolic gestures for that purpose. But the way they were staged and publicised left little doubt about the real intended audience. After the military intervention, several people close to the *de facto* regime, in the presence of many foreign journalists arrived in the country to cover the American operation, laid wreaths of yellow flowers in the Champ de Mars at the foot of the monuments to Toussaint Louverture, the Unknown Maroon and Emperor Dessalines—symbols of the struggle for independence. That symbolic gesture was supposed to 'express the rejection of occupation of the country'. During the first months of the United Nations mission, some political actors warned against the risks of a rise of nationalism and an increase in related incidents if the mission was prolonged. While they maintained that line—which had the merit of being consistent—later on, they adopted much less virulent language when trying to return to the political scene. For that purpose, they sought contact 'with the occupying forces', as they called them.[26] But on the whole the population, for its part, kept its distance from this language, being used in political discourse or in chants composed especially for Carnival on *lokipan* ('the occupiers'). Similarly, in daily conversation, American military personnel or members of the United Nations mission were always identified by the adjective *Blan* ('the Whites') or the pronoun *yo* ('them'), and not as *lokipan*. Moreover, when questioned on this point, community actors firmly rejected that wording. Analysis of the transcription of interviews, as well as

---

[24] See the international press of the time, and United Nations, *The United Nations and Mozambique, 1992–1995*, New York: UNDP, 1995, p. 321.

[25] In particular, this was the central slogan of the demonstration organised against Boutros Boutros-Ghali on January 3, 1993, when he made a stopover in Mogadishu on his way to Addis Ababa.

[26] Interviews in Port-au-Prince and in the provinces, April–May 1995.

available relevant written material, suggests that this refusal to refer to an 'occupation' appears to be related above all to a refusal to let the local politicians escape their responsibilities.[27] It condemned their inability to propose a domestic alternative: 'What have they proposed to us? Nothing'; 'We were there dying like rats and who would raised a finger for that?'; 'Where were they, all those fine people? Was it their children, their husbands that were killed like dogs?' Such questioning was summed up by some church base communities, a little over a month before the military intervention: 'What could an intervention bring that would be worse for us than what the army is inflicting on us now?'[28] People also recalled the existence of a Haitian government and it maintaining of its responsibilities, despite the presence of foreign soldiers and strong pressure from the US administration. A second reason often given for the refusal to speak of 'lokipan' had to do with the intervening forces, in reference to the distance they maintained between themselves and the population—'They can't be occupiers and at the same time be doing so little'; 'It's like a foreign body that never enters into Haitian reality'; 'You can't talk about an occupation because they have not entered into our internal affairs. Anyway, they never stop saying that such and such a thing is not of their concern'; 'We do what we like, that can't be denied, it isn't like the other occupation we knew. The problem is rather that they do nothing for us.'

Beyond rejecting use of a particular word, communities also demonstrated refusal of a particular interpretation of collective history and, sometimes, of collective identity. This was illustrated in Haiti in 1995 in the language used by certain youth groups, especially in Cap Haïtien, rejecting President Aristide's manipulation of history and of certain personalities like Toussaint Louverture. In Cambodia, the term 'YUNTAH' (a play on words with UNTAC) launched by the Khmers Rouges and partially used in the former FNLPK's propaganda met a similar fate.[29] That term evoked ancestral fears of 'disappearance' of the country, 'swallowed up' by the YUN (the Vietnamese). But the Cambodian in the street widely rejected it: 'They are the words of the Khmers Rouges, everyone knows that. Not all things should be mixed together.' For many of them UNTAC

---

[27] All the quotations that follow are taken from individual and group interviews in Port-au-Prince and in the provinces in April–May 1995 and February–March 1996 (translations from Haitian Creole).

[28] Press statement on August 9, 1994 by TKLs of Saint Martin and Delmas.

[29] See Penny Edwards, 'Imaging the Other in Cambodian Nationalist Discourse Before and During the UNTAC Period', pp. 50–72 in Steve Heder and Judy Ledgerwood (eds), *Propaganda, Politics, and Violence in Cambodia: Democratic Transition under United Nations Peace-keeping*, New York: M. E. Sharpe, 1996.

was more associated with a comic song that children hummed, describing the 'typical way of passing the time' of a member of the mission. This reflected quite well the way the 'UNTAC' people were regarded: they were 'observed with plenty of curiosity'—though also with some disapproval of their bad habits—but remained 'outsiders'.

The problems raised by the behaviour of United Nations staff figure commonly in accounts and discourse relating to the UN presence in the countries concerned. They contribute very directly to the accounts centring on the theme of 'intervention'. From one operation to another attention is directed at similar problems: bad driving and consequently road accidents, involvement in illicit dealings, influence on prostitution or even on the spread of the HIV virus in the country concerned. Those questions have tended to occupy an increasing place in published analyses of the missions, with two main preoccupations. First, among international human rights NGOs (including Amnesty International and Human Rights Watch) and also the UN Human Rights Commission, the essential concern is for respect by mission members of international norms regarding protection of fundamental human rights. That preoccupation, echoed by many analysts, is often coupled with a second one: the fear that 'breaches of local custom' may provoke rejection of the missions by the local people. These questions have received increasing attention among senior United Nations officials, as is shown by the way in which their treatment has developed from one operation to another.

In the El Salvador mission, the first in the second generation of peace operations, senior United Nations officials tended to minimise the consequences of these problems. With very rare exceptions in extreme cases (such as that of a Mexican civpol arrested for drugs trafficking in April 1993), the behavioural problems of staff did not lead to punishment or even some minimal follow-up by the leaders of the mission. At headquarters, at the time, people tended to consider that such problems were 'inevitable' when such a large number of soldiers were sent in. In Cambodia the problems encountered were of incomparable seriousness and extent, but the reaction of the leaders of the UN mission reveals a fundamental change in the way such issues were treated, in comparison with the El Salvador mission. In September 1992 a report was prepared by the UNTAC Information and Education Division, recalling a certain number of rules of 'good behaviour' in public.[30] It comprised precise recommendations and was widely distributed within the mission. At a general staff meeting in September 1992, the question of soldiers' behaviour was also

---

[30] See UNTAC, Information and Education Division, *Report on Public Perceptions of UNTAC in the City of Phnom Penh*, Phnom Penh, September 1992.

discussed. Soldiers of UNTAC were then requested not to visit places of ill repute in uniform, or to park United Nations vehicles opposite them. Soon after the meeting, members of international NGOs and some women members of UNTAC published an open letter to the Special Representative of the Secretary General, emphasizing in particular the problems of prostitution and AIDS virus infection. The Special Representative decided in October 1992 to open a Community Relations Office. Written instructions were sent to all UNTAC members. An active campaign was also carried out among the staff about road traffic accidents. The Office in fact had to deal with a number of complaints and a fund was established to compensate victims.[31] The UN Secretariat, aware of the risks of infection, had 800,000 condoms sent to Cambodia. In February 1993 the head of the Civilian Police Component started a new campaign among his men.[32] Some repatriations were ordered—the most severe punishment in such cases, any other penalty being a matter for the state placing staff at the UN's disposal. UNTAC's Information/Education Division also tried to follow this question.[33] One could be inclined to feel that all this was too little, too late; even so, for the most part unprecedented efforts were made, likely a product of pressure from international NGOs.

The case of Cambodia was a turning point. In particular, a number of general instructions were drawn up subsequently, for all United Nations missions.[34] In Mozambique, numerous behaviour problems were noted

[31] The final report of the Community Relations Office (a confidential document) says it received 84 complaints a year (essentially concerning road accidents with cars hired privately by United Nations staff). It also highlights the existence of a number of 'rumours' about rape, which were difficult to investigate (a number of internal memoranda consulted indicate that an attempt at least was made to conduct serious investigations on this subject). Moreover, a complaint of sexual harassment was also made. Lastly, the Office had to deal with some problems with upset husbands or women complaining of having been impregnated by UNTAC members. Regarding AIDS problems, the Office said it had found four cases of HIV positive staff members, and considered that 'the affair had been blown up by some international NGOs and the international press.' Source: Final internal confidential report of UNTAC Community Relations Office, pp. 2–8.

[32] Very firm instructions were given (a ban on visits to prostitutes, for example) and penalties were announced which could go as far as repatriation. See especially Memorandum by Brigadier General Klaas C. Roos, head of the Civil Police Component, on code of conduct for police personnel (February 18, 1993).

[33] See UNTAC Information and Education Division, *Perceptions of UNTAC (from Cambodians in Phnom Penh and Battambang). Some Final Comments*, Phnom Penh, July 12, 1993.

[34] 'Guidelines for the Conduct of United Nations Peace-Keepers' (DPKO); 'Code of Conduct for Soldiers and Military Observers' (document sent to contributing states to be included in training programmes for military personnel). A 'code of conduct' was also drawn up by the Peacekeeping department's training team (UNTAT). A pocket version and a slightly longer one (entitled *We are United Nations Peacekeepers*) were published in 1997.

among ONUMOZ members. There were accusations concerning involvement of Blue Helmets in child prostitution. An investigation was carried out by the Deputy to the Special Representative of the Secretary General, Behrooz Sadry. In a report published on February 25, 1994, in Maputo, he declared, 'In certain cases it seems that ONUMOZ staff have sought the sexual services of minors'; it is known that this accusation has since been made again about peacekeepers and humanitarian workers, especially in Sierra Leone, Ethiopia/Eritrea and RDC. In Haiti, the attitude of the leaders of the mission, at the highest level, immediately appeared very firm on these questions. From the time UNMIH was deployed, the Special Representative of the Secretary General gave very precise instructions, and ensured they were made known.[35] There were in fact sanctions in all cases of abuse reported in the course of my field investigations. This line of conduct had, to some extent, been started by the Multinational Force itself, which recorded cases of misbehaviour by its troops and tried to make some adjustments. Involvement of United Nations soldiers in illicit business is mentioned less often, or at least is often based on rumours hard to verify. The case of UNPROFOR in Bosnia is the only one where investigations were carried out into these matters. A Dutch commission of inquiry joined a team of UN civpols in the spring of 1993 to investigate accusations of Ukrainian and French Blue Helmets' involvement in various illicit trades and prostitution networks in Sarajevo. The affair was none the less settled very discreetly.

Real changes can be seen in the way that the UN Secretariat and most member states supplying troops manage this aspect of their presence in various countries. The UN Secretary General issued a circular on that subject dated August 6, 1999.[36] In all the missions where problems of UN personnel's behaviour were noted, commissions of inquiry were set up by the Secretary General or his Representative. The UN Human Rights Commission has also been following this matter for several years, especially on the issue of violence against women.

So we have here a generalised and wide-ranging problem. Local political entrepreneurs are more careful than one might expect in exploiting this issue; they generally consider that these questions are a matter of anecdotes and isolated incidents. In my inquiries among the people, problems of driving on the roads and accidents caused by international staff generally came at the top of the list. People were shocked by some

---

[35] In a public speech, during a training seminar for mision staff. Lakhdar Brahimi called on UNMIH members to 'respect the dignity of the Haitian people', explaining further that he would be giving 'very strict' instructions on respect for that dignity (words widely reported in the local press, in March 1995).

[36] ST/SGB/1999/13.

accidents, and still more so by the scant attention paid to them and the lack of respect too often displayed by international staff. The accounts given after the event often appeal to a wide range of phantasmagoria and are usually fuelled by a dose of exaggeration. At the end, they reveal a great deal of accumulated frustration. In the rural areas of El Salvador, peasants readily showed visitors the speed ramps (*tumolos*), which they had to lay down in their communities to force the United Nations vehicles to slow down. This became a necessity after several accidents had happened and all discussions with senior United Nations officials had produced no change. However, the same people rejected the press campaign against 'child-killers' launched by the far right after an accident leading to a child's death.

Accidents involving members of the UN mission were relatively few in Haiti. However, each one was described in ways that revealed the resentment that had built up over time. Two examples illustrate this. In August 1995, at Port de Paix in the north of the country, some UNMIH soldiers ran into a funeral procession, apparently without causing damage. The newspaper *Libète* published an article in which 'the inhabitants of the North-West call on the head of UNMIH to make sure that those soldiers restrain themselves.'[37] Still more revealing, on Saturday January 27, 1996, at Grésier (at the southern exit of Port-au-Prince), a collision between an UNMIH vehicle and a public transport lorry left one dead and twelve injured. Many rumours flew around about the accident. In its account of the event *Libète* said, 'After the accident, the UNMIH soldiers burned the lorry with a grenade and fired shots into the air. The population was very angry…'[38] Apart from incidents that more or less influenced *imaginaires* strongly, people I interviewed pointed to a same lack of respect. During my field investigations, the sight of UNMIH vehicles driving at breakneck speeds induced similar reactions. Such recklessness, even in heavily populated areas, driving with all their lights on and right in the middle of the road—forcing any other vehicles to pull up quickly to the side—invariably aroused the same reactions of mixed fear and anger. Very similar images emerged from interviews in Cambodia where, relatively, road accidents in which UNTAC vehicles or staff[39] were implicated were much more numerous. In interviews in urban districts and in the provinces, 'problems caused by a vehicle accident' were the only ones spontaneously mentioned. From one country to another, the same accusations were made

[37] See *Libète*, August 23 to 29, 1995.
[38] *Libète* 125, January 31 to February 6, 1996.
[39] In cases where vehicles hired for private use were involved—which seems to have been the case in most of the accidents.

against 'those who place themselves above the law'; besides the road accidents, it was a 'lack of respect' that was emphasised most often; besides speeding, there was the recurring image of cars splashing mud as they went by or forcing their way through the road.

Problems of prostitution are almost never raised spontaneously in the interviews, still less when there was also sexual abuse of minors. Regardless of the society, this sort of subject is not among those that people talk about openly. Those are questions that have to be 'kept to oneself or else settled within the community', as the head of a Cambodian women's association put it.[40] In addition, in most of the countries nobody would think of directly confronting someone who is considered as a figure of authority. Problems are generally settled partly through the agency of mediums and healers who are often women, and who traditionally play that kind of role within the community. In Cambodia and Haiti, in interviews, several allusions were made to what had been settled 'inside the community', 'away from the foreigners'. This is the 'hidden' face—'what happened at night and escaped the mission's attention'.[41]

In its outward appearance this problem can also be treated according to other modes, such as derision and phantasmagoria. There are many plays on words, jokes, comic songs to describe, with great or less indulgence but always with plenty of humour, the curious habits of the peacekeepers. 'In the morning we do exercise; in the afternoon, we go out in the car; in the evening, we go back to the bar'...The 'oddness' of the 'foreigners' can also be made into a theatre by local people, when watching United Nations soldiers jogging, an apparent universal 'classic' of comedy. When what is not understood also disturbs the order of things, it must be given a figure that can be mastered, or else moved into the spaces of the *imaginary*. Myths and dreams are then called on to do that.[42] The case of Haiti is very typical of the way these things are managed, with resort to large scale registers close to sorcery, which is probably not unconnected from the fact that the 'Whites' are perceived in terms very close to those used to represent the state and power. During the presence of the Multinational Force, but also during the very first phase of the United Nations mission in Haiti, the craziest rumours spread about the fate of women who had consorted with foreign soldiers. They were said to be infected with strange diseases

[40] Interview with Kien Serey Phal, Chair of the Cambodia Women's Development Association (Phnom Penh, December 20, 1995).

[41] Extracts from interviews with community actors in Cambodia and Haiti.

[42] See Franz Fanon on the stabilisation and exorcism function of mythical and dream structures among colonised people: F. Fanon, *The Wretched of the Earth*, Grove Press, 1986; see also Gérard Althabe, *Oppression et libération dans l'imaginaire*, Paris: La Découverte, 1982.

and victims of 'sexual savagery', along with the recurring images of 'Whites with big penises' or using *kapot blende* (hard condoms tearing women's vaginas). The images were explicit: the 'White man' wants to penetrate us by force, or else he too wants to poison us... At the beginning of 1996 new rumours took over. I was persistently told about scenes of panic in several towns of the country. Afterwards I witnessed them first hand. Parents would rush to collect their children from school because the 'White men' (*Blan yo*), which meant foreign soldiers—there was no doubt in the minds of the people who spoke to me—were going to schools supposedly for a vaccination campaign, and the children were dying immediately afterwards. In other words, what I was being told, in hardly disguised terms, was that UNMIH soldiers were poisoning Haitian children, nothing more and nothing less! The affair lasted only a few weeks and was never fully explained, but radio stations and the written press echoed it widely, and *zen* (rumour) did the rest. All those whom I questioned on this subject were certain that this was indeed *zen* of which Haitians had the secret. But it was not without reason that they commented, like some heads of district committees in Port-au-Prince, 'Anyway, that proves that people know well that with the Whites, it's always like that; you have to protect yourself, or else...'[43]

For that reason the rumours surrounding peacekeepers' habits should receive proper attention from senior United Nations officials and should be understood for what they are. In the fantastic images they invoke some frightening stories can help discern quite quickly that something is going on in a local society, even that the people's perception of the mission is shifting. But in the various countries where I made investigations, those various manifestations seem to have entirely escaped the UN's notice, so that one would think UN people were not living in the country at all. At best, they were considered negligible, because they were not 'rational' and did not lead to hostile demonstrations. But in understanding what is going on for local actors, especially in contexts of great insecurity, there is usually only a very thin line between 'facts' and 'paranoia', 'evidence' and 'rumour'. All those registers of knowledge and imagination are related to dreaming. What is known is understood in vast zones of what is unknown or even imagined. Rumours can teach us a good deal, not through the direct information that they provide, but because they reveal what is going on in a given social group.[44] To a great extent rumours, like the legends

[43] Words recorded in Port-au-Prince, March 1, 1996.

[44] It is known, especially through the work of Turner and Killian, how important the role of rumour can be, especially in collective definitions of a situation, through what they call 'symbolic interaction': R. T. Turner and L. M. Killian, *Collective Behavior*, Englewood Cliffs, NY: Prentice Hall, 1972 (1st ed. 1957), p. 41.

studied by Marie-Louise von Franz, constitute the dreams of peoples and tell the people what is going on in the collective unconscious.[45] These analytical tools are not commonly used by peacekeepers, but they can help them get a bit closer to changes going on in social groups. However, this depends on whether peacekeepers want to take seriously the experiences these groups have with the UN mission—going beyond what they say about it, going beyond appearances. The rumours that built up around the Blue Helmets in Haiti should be understood as stories of distancing and understanding. Most often they expressed a feeling of being dispossessed of one's self. In the most moderate versions, those signs expressed what people I met often stated: 'We do not take them [the foreigners] seriously because they do not take us seriously', or, as a man in one of the lower-class districts of San Salvador put it, 'they do not [take] us for anything at all.'[46] Those signs can also make it possible to anticipate more serious problems that arise, especially when there are repeated oppressive acts by international staff, as happened in Somalia, and more recently in Afghanistan and of course in Iraq.

FACTORS OF MOBILISATION AGAINST THE UN

On January 3, 1993, a few weeks after the start of Operation Restore Hope, conducted by a US-led Multinational Force, the UN Secretary General was greeted in Mogadishu by an angry crowd. Banners written in English for the benefit of the foreign press proclaimed, 'Down with the UN Protectorate! Somalia for the Somalis.' Five months later, in the middle of the confrontation between the movement headed by Mohamed Aydid (who had a price on his head) and American troops, leaflets were distributed in the streets of southern Mogadishu telling the United Nations 'neo-colonialists', in very violent language, to leave the country immediately. There were successive demonstrations in the Somali capital to denounce the military operations conducted by UNOSOM and the American troops, whom Aydid threatened with 'total war' if they did not change their attitude towards it. At a press conference on the morning of June 11, he warned that 'any violent action can lead to a general uprising of the civilian population.'

Anyone who has been at the head of a peace operation will tell you that this type of scenario is among those dreaded most. The same fear is found

---

[45] Marie-Louise von Franz, *L'Interprétation des contes de fées*, Paris: La Fontaine de Pierre, 1980, pp. 51–61; Marie-Louise von Franz and Emma Jung, *La Légende du Graal*, Paris: Albin Michel, 1988.

[46] Translated from Spanish.

among many Western, especially American military leaders since the occupation of Iraq. So it is not at all surprising that local political and military entrepreneurs play on those fears. In Haiti, in the weeks preceding the Multinational Force's intervention in 1994, discourse and images (especially religious images) were brought up that related specifically to all the 'White man's' supposed fears. Western journalists were invited to attend training sessions for civilians 'in anticipation of military intervention'. On September 9 the Commander in Chief of the army, General Raoul Cedras, and other senior military officers joined auxiliaries (militia members)—who were offering their services to 'defend the territory in case of foreign invasion'—in an 'anti-invasion march' through several streets of the capital. During this time a portrait of the Virgin Mary was hung up in the general headquarters of the armed forces. Banners were strung up in the big avenues of the capital with the words '*Seyè, peyi a nan men w*' ('Lord, the country is in your hands'). The provisional government called on the people to pray; Voodoo ceremonies were also organised. On September 8, a demonstration against American intervention was led by a Protestant pastor and a priest (*pé savann*) wearing a long black robe and making Cabbalistic signs all along the route to 'call on the power of the Most High to drive out evil spirits'. The next day, a short ceremony was organised close to the outside enclosure of the American embassy. The worst fate was promised to anyone who dared trifle with the soil of Haiti. Demonstrators shouted, '*Nou pral manje grèn blan*' ('We are going to eat the Whites'), a refrain taken up by a rara band during the Carnival period at the beginning of 1995. In fact, those various demonstrations probably had something to do with the precautions taken by the American administration to prevent the risk of clashes. With real fears of 'resistance' existing in the Pentagon, instructions were given to the soldiers to avoid all physical contact with Haitians and to refuse all food and drink for fear of poisoning.[47]

However, hostile demonstrations against UN missions themselves are fairly rare. In general gatherings are only local, *ad hoc* demonstrations targeting specific demands. To understand this, three elements that can constitute potential mobilisation must be studied: the collective aims for which they are organised; the registers brought to the forefront on that occasion; and the structures of opportunities or conditions that go along with the effective formation of a movement.

---

[47] Instructions that, by no coincidence, reproduced those issued earlier in Somalia: consume no food or drink offered, do not let anyone touch you, etc.

The aims of anti-UN movements

To embark on a collective adventure, social actors need to at least share certain aims. But when a country is emerging from a conflict, more than in any other context, the interests of the main political entrepreneurs coincide very little with the concerns of the majority of the people. This goes far in explaining why it is rare for them to try to mobilise social and community actors to achieve their purposes. On their side, when trying to force the UN to take account of their interests, social and community actors tend to mobilise over very localised problems. They may do so even if these issues are raised simultaneously in different parts of the country, like landed property problems. The march organised in December 1994 in El Salvador, between Chalatenango and San Salvador, could have marked the beginning of wider mobilisation, but it did not go beyond the bounds of the communities directly concerned. In Haiti, in various regions of the country, some groups tried, with very similar tactics, to involve American and then United Nations military personnel in local land disputes, but those incidents did not lead to wider mobilisation. In El Salvador as in Haiti, community actors quickly understood that the United Nations mission was not able, and above all did not want, to come to their aid. While it was still possible to 'try one's luck', the UN was not seen as an authority on which one could rely on to settle the country's problems seriously. There was no more mobilisation against 'the UN' than there had traditionally been against the state, for in both cases people knew nothing could be expected from either.

In Haiti, however, there was a short-lived but massive mobilisation to try to force the United Nations mission to deal with the problems of disarmament. On November 11 1995, at the funeral of a deputy murdered a few days earlier, President Aristide launched an appeal for disarmament. The aim was clearly expressed, and echoed a central preoccupation of the various components of society, even if they were to experience the consequences in different ways.[48] Throughout the year, various organisations had published statements on the subject. Written and especially broadcast media had widely echoed a concern expressed daily by community organisations. Aristide had his back against the wall. Cornered by the 'international community' and 'frustrated', he wanted to 'make the White people

---

[48] From March 17 to 24, 1995, the Arias Foundation for Peace conducted a 'national public opinion poll' among a sample of 1,200 people in Haiti. Its results corresponded fairly broadly with the impression gleaned from interviews I carried out at the same time across the country. The problems of insecurity and the disarmament of paramilitary groups were the major preoccupation of the people questioned; 66 per cent still expected the Multinational Force to 'disarm the Tontons Macoutes auxiliaries'.

pay', in response to the pressure they were putting on him, and to show that he could 'make trouble'.[49] For that he knew that he should choose a clear, explicit theme. 'The foreigners should help pacify the country, and that has not been done since my return,' he said. He lashed out at 'the Whites' who had heavy weapons but refused to use them to disarm the criminals. 'I order Haitians and the international community to march together for the disarmament of all criminals, terrorists and extremists to be total, legal, fundamental.'[50] For three days, demonstrations and rampaging abounded in the main towns of the country. For the first time, UNMIH was at the centre of street slogans. Under outside pressure the government had to issue a countermanding order. Even though it left traces, notably a dozen deaths, tension subsided after a few days. Community groups remained 'mobilised', as they were bound to be since they were the first to experience the consequences of insecurity in rural areas and the poorer districts of the towns. However, as they had the impression of having been manipulated by Aristide, without getting any result or any commitment from him, they reoriented their action towards safeguarding their vital space in their daily lives. In particular, this involved the re-establishment of watch brigades, but also once again recourse to trickery of the 'Whites', who could not be expected to establish security.

Apart from these incidents, youth organisations (FEDKA, KILE, AMAK, etc.) and student organisations, which joined to form a 'Collective against the IMF', tried to mobilise 'against the foreign occupation'. On July 18, 1995, during celebration of the national day they organised a public meeting on the theme of the 'struggle against the occupation'. In October 1996 a petition was launched while one of the numerous extensions of the mission's mandate was under discussion. Anti-UN slogans marked demonstrations 'against imperialism and occupation', organised essentially in Port-au-Prince, in the spring and then the autumn of 1995, and consecutively at the beginning of 1997 and 1998. But they did not succeed in mobilising beyond the limited—and often nebulous—circles of those groups.

Demonstrations calling for the departure of a UN mission have been rare and their promoters have generally other objectives in mind. In El Salvador minority groups on the far right of the political spectrum tried, at an early stage in ONUSAL's deployment, to obtain the early departure of the mission. But essentially, their objective was rather to force the mission to adopt a low profile. In addition, the leaflets which they used as their

[49] Interviews with members of the government and UNMIH (Port-au-Prince, February–March 1995).
[50] As reported in Haïti-Hebdo 89, November 21, 1995.

favoured means of communication were aimed not so much at mobilising possible supporters but at intimidating members of the UN mission and those associated with it. In the first months following the establishment of the mission, leaflets attributed to the Frente Anticomunista Salvadoreño (FAS) were distributed in shops and restaurants in the *Zona Rosa* (the district close to the hotel where the mission was installed). They declared: 'From today, you must avoid giving any services to the foreigners or to the nationals belonging to organisations such as: the United Nations, ONUCA, Médecins du Monde, Médecins sans Frontières, the ICRC, the UNHCR. If not, you will be collaborating with the internationalists who are conspiring with Communism to take our national territory, and you will deserve the sanctions that the Front has in store for your business, your person and your family.'[51] It was similar with the press campaigns orchestrated by several groups between the summer of 1991 and the end of 1992.[52] On October 22, 1992, radio and television stations and the written press publicised a statement by the Brigada Maximiliano Hernández demanding, on pain of having to 'face the consequences of national justice', the departure of the UN force from the country, describing it as a 'white plague' (*pesta blanca*).

The 'anti-Western' and 'anti-UNTAC' discourse broadcast in Cambodia by the Khmers Rouges' radio during the UN mission's presence followed a similar logic. It sought to put pressure on the mission and to strengthen the movement's identity as an opposition force, but not to mobilise (which the Khmers Rouges had no means of doing anyway). In fact, the departure of the mission was never actually called for.[53] The only demonstrations aimed directly at UNTAC took place at Kompong Cham, Svay Rieng and Prey Veng, from June 10 to 12, 1993, following the attempted secession of Chakrapong; this was in a highly specific context, and the demonstrations remained very limited.

When peacekeepers become oppressors

In most countries the presence of a UN mission seems never to have been resented as a real 'occupation', and there is no feeling of being under any

---

[51] Translation from Spanish. In July 1991 the FAS had threatened to 'launch a bloody civil war if the internationalists returned to El Salvador in force'. Subsequently other leaflets were distributed and advertising inserts put in the press; they were signed by another far-right organisation, the Cruzada Pro Paz y Trabajo.

[52] Besides the Frente Anticomunista Salvadoreño, these were the Brigada Maximiliano Hernández and the Movimiento Cívico para El Salvador Libre.

[53] Sources: documents of the UNTAC analysis unit; transcription of PKD radio broadcasts during this period.

form of 'oppression'. This appears to be decisive in the perceptions people have of the UN, as the contrary example of Somalia seems to prove. While the main political leaders mobilised against the UN very early on, especially on the theme of imposition of trusteeship over the Somali people, that mobilisation became clearly more intense from the moment UNOSOM appeared to be 'making war on the Somalis'. The theme of resistance to occupation was omnipresent in statements and public declarations by Aydid and his movement. It was aimed notably, and conspicuously, at the 'democratic' references in the United Nations' own discourse.[54] That theme was echoed among other actors, especially those considered to represent 'civil society' and able to present an 'alternative'. The broadening of UNOSOM II's mandate by Resolution 514, just after the Addis Ababa agreements, was interpreted as 'placing under trusteeship' and 'total assumption of responsibility by UNOSOM instead of accompanying the Somali process.'[55] Ali Mahdi himself, Aydid's main rival, and some of those close to him also regularly made statements in this sense. Ali Mahdi's position was however more delicate, because he was the one who had called for the dispatch of the first mission at the beginning of 1992.

Apart from the coherence of the various registers it invoked, the 'anti-occupation' register was able to mobilise people in Somalia because it could exploit the growing frustration caused by problems of the troops' behaviour. In this mission, they clearly crossed a threshold, heading increasingly towards massive violations of human rights, notably with cases of torture and homicide, documented later by some commissions of inquiry. In 1993 the military operation launched against General Aydid also affected the civilian population, especially the bombings. All analyses of this turning point in the Somalia operation consider that it greatly contributed to the increasing hostility to the UN, extending even to those Somalis who had shown themselves most favourable to the UN presence. When, on the 9 and 10 of September 1993, helicopters of the US Army

---

[54] In a press statement dated December 1, 1993, the SNA accused UNOSOM of wanting to 'confiscate' the representation of the Somali people, particularly by wanting to place its own men (in the district and region committees, for example), and to deny their right to settle their country's political problems (Office of the Vice-Chairman, Somali National Alliance).

[55] See especially M. A. Mohamed Salih and Lennart Wohlgemuth (eds), *Crisis Management and the Politics of Reconciliation in Somalia*, Statements from the Uppsala Forum, January 17 to 19, 1994, Uppsala: Nordiska Afrikainstitutet, 1994, pp. 62–3. There are also illustrations of this in the work by a leader of the Somali Women for Peace organisation: Mariam Arif Gassem, *Hostages: The People who Kidnapped Themselves*, Nairobi: Central Graphics Services Ltd, 1994, especially p. 128, and in Marcel Djama's film *Somalie, le prix du sang versé*, La Sept/Arte and Point du Jour, France, 1995.

fired on a crowd of civilians, including women and children, Major David
Stockwell, Chief UN military spokesman in Somalia, described the action
as consistent with the UN rules of engagement, and decried the use of
'human shields': "There are no sidelines or spectators seats. The people
on the ground are considered combatants." But for most Somalis, the UN
and the Americans had gone to war against them. They had turned into
guneysi (foreign oppressors). 'First they brought us food. Now, they bring
arms. We fear they have in fact come to kill us.' At once the other 'foreigners' present in Somali were associated with this perception, including
journalists whose role was called into question. On July 12, 1993, four
journalists were lynched.[56] The act happened on the day of the attack on
Aydid's headquarters, which itself caused numerous civilian casualties.
On that occasion, Admiral Howe, head of UNOSOM, called the operation
a 'surgical strike', saying that those who were killed during the attack
formed part of a group of hard-liners wanting to attack the international'
community and the Somalis.[57] Some days later, UNOSOM printed a leaf-
let saying, 'The SNA officials who were killed were responsible for the
deaths of six innocent Somalis. The SNA said women and children were
killed, but that was pure propaganda.' Meanwhile, video images taken
immediately after the attack had been distributed, showing that civilians
and elders known for being moderates were actually among the victims.[58]
It was in that precise context that Aydid was able to mobilise against the
'oppressor' and demand that it should fulfil its promises. On June 15,
1993, in the heart of Mogadishu, he harangued several thousands of followers: 'We want humanitarian aid, not bombs!' The same day leaflets
were distributed condemning 'the UN, killing peace' and 'suppressing the
poor'. When the United Nations fired on crowds, the SNA called the
operation 'cowardly and barbarous' and swore to fight 'until the last
colonial soldier of the UN leaves.' Two years later, the last UN soldiers did
leave. During a visit to the Qoryoley district (70 km south of Mogadishu),
Aydid asked the crowd, 'Where are the helicopters of the United Nations
and the United States?' 'We have destroyed the foreign aggressors!' The
crowd roared back.[59]

[56] The African Rights organisation considers that those murders were not ordered by Aydid,
as has been sometimes stated, but were rather the expression of collective fury. Journalists were guided to the place of the attack by members of the SNA who were then
unable to protect them from the angry mob: African Rights, *Somalia: Human Rights
Abuses by the United Nations Force*, London, July 1993, p. 3.
[57] BBC World Service, July 12, 1993.
[58] AFP, 17 July 1993; Human Rights Watch Africa, *Somalia Faces the Future: Human
Rights in Fragmented Society*, Washington, April 1996, p. 60.
[59] Agence France Presse, July 28, 1995.

Exceptional as it seems, this situation could very well be repeated itself. The possibility is especially great in areas where peace has not yet been established, as has been shown by the recent examples of Sierra Leone and Afghanistan and, of course, Iraq.[60] Despite the imperative for every peace-keeper to adhere to the principles of human rights and the laws governing war,[61] he has to be aware that his behaviour in a foreign setting is assessed in exactly the same way as if he was in his own village or district: as a 'foreigner' not speaking a word of the local language, arriving in a big car driving at all sorts of speed, splashing and running over those who had the misfortune to be in its way, breaking all the laws of politeness and normal propriety, and beginning to flirt with his daughter and, in the worst case, rape her... No contingent is immune from misbehaviour; and experience shows that those best behaved are not necessarily the ones you would imagine.

Conditions for effective development of mobilisation

If certain politicians can mobilise like Mohamed Aydid, it is because they can activate ties of solidarity already present within a society. In Somalia, mass mobilisation directed against the United Nations mission was organised around one man, but it was also supported by the very extensive resources of a very fluid and malleable system of loyalties and solidarities. The informal 'social contract' represented by the *xeer* in Somali society (based on the payment of *diya*, the 'blood price'), means that the idea of individual culpability does not much exist. In those conditions, any individual accused of a misdeed by an element outside the group is 'covered' by his clan. To make war against a member of a clan, whoever he is, means to some extent embarking on war against the whole clan. In confronting Aydid, that dimension was never seriously taken into account, either by the American administration or by the UN, especially in the man-hunt launched in June 1993. On June 5, 24 Pakistani Blue Helmets were killed in an armed clash between UNOSOM and militias of the Aydid group. Aydid was declared guilty by the UN. Air attacks were launched to destroy his positions and a price was put on his head ($ 25,000). Many observers have emphasised how much that decision was 'incomprehensible', 'ridiculous and humiliating' in the context of how Somali society functions.[62]

---

[60] In Afghanistan, repeated 'mistakes' in bombing by American forces causing civilian victims provoked the first 'anti-American' demonstrations in Kabul, in July 2002.

[61] This obligation was reaffirmed in a circular from the Secretary General on 'Observance by United Nations forces of international humanitarian law', ST/SGB/1999/13, August 6, 1999.

[62] Cf. especially Hussein Mohamed Adam's criticism: 'Somalia: A Terrible Beauty Being

Three additional errors of judgment were made by the top United Nations officials. They sought first of all to disconnect Aydid from his clan, the Habir Gedir. In radio broadcasts and leaflets dropped by helicopter over Mogadishu, UNOSOM proclaimed that it was not the enemy of the Habir Gedir, but only wanted to capture Aydid. The leaders of the clan decided to make a gesture, with Aydid's apparent agreement, by forming a supreme council of the Habir Gedir. The council did not include Aydid himself, and each of the five sub-clans was represented on an equal footing. On July 12, 1993 in a house in Mogadishu, which UNOSOM suspected of being Aydid's headquarters, a meeting was held to establish that same council. Under false pretences, American Cobra helicopters fired missiles at the house. In total, according to the International Committee of the Red Cross, fifty-four people were killed, including several respected religious leaders. Some of them—including Sheikh Mohamed Iman, religious leader of Aydid's sub-clan—were then considered by UNOSOM as a possible 'alternative' to Aydid. In fact Howe, then head of UNOSOM, had met the Sheikh three days earlier. The episode strengthened the solidarity of Aydid's clan around him, and beyond. In fact, the legitimacy of the resort to force to defend the group is beyond dispute in a system where 'reason belongs to the strongest'.[63] In other words, UNOSOM had no chance in counting on the support of other politico-military groups, even those opposed to Aydid's. Moreover, some have accused the United Nations of helping to build up the myth of Aydid by presenting him as the only person capable of defying the foreign military presence. Lastly—and this point is crucial—Aydid was all the better able to count on the 'neutrality' or even the support of groups that were not favourable to him because, at least in Mogadishu, the war crossed too many lines, particularly with machine-gun fire from American helicopters hitting many inhabitants of the city. Even opponents of Aydid could not approve this. UNOSOM and the American rapid intervention forces that were lumped together in people's minds, had become forces of 'oppression'. The personalised vendetta against a 'spoiler' rapidly became a notorious fiasco, particularly in human terms. It ended in the autumn of 1993 with the political victory of the one who, having succeeded in evading all the searches for him, and strengthened by the violent episode of July 12, became once again a negotiating partner who could not be bypassed.

In their pilot study of the United Nations force in the Gaza Strip, Johan Galtung and Ingrid Eide had earlier emphasised the risk that 'maintenance

---

Born?', p. 85 in Ira William Zartman, *Collapsed States: the Disintegration and Restoration of Legitimate Authority*, Boulder, CO: Lynne Rienner Publishers, 1995.

[63] I. M. Lewis, *A Pastoral Democracy*, London, New York and Toronto: OUP, 1961, p. 25.

of law and order' could involve actions against people enjoying support among the local population, and that martyrs and heroes would be manufactured as a result.[64] It is in this context that the numerous successive hostile demonstrations against the UN, setting off a sequence of violence against the Somali population, should be understood. The fact that they were the object of various forms of manipulation (including the use of women and children as 'human shields') does not remove the need to understand the bases on which Mohamed Aydid was able to activate existing ties of solidarity in the conflict between him and the multinational forces. In Kosovo the proliferation of anti-UNMIK demonstrations and slogans in the summer of 2002, while former leaders of the UCK were arrested for oppressive acts committed during the war, was another illustration of that type of scenario. In this case they were fortunately checked in time. However, it seems that the lesson has not been learned by the American army operation in Iraq.

IDEAS OF 'LEGITIMACY' AND 'IMPARTIALITY' REDEFINED BY LOCAL CONDITIONS

Understanding the idea of intervention in local terms in this way is essential. It reminds us that the legitimacy of any intervention, whatever it may be, whatever very generous motives it may have, is never always secure. Unlike events in Iraq, in Somalia the Western military forces originally landed as part of a multinational operation aimed at creating security for the delivery of humanitarian aid. Similarly, a Security Council resolution, even with a strong consensus, is not sufficient. The power relations among its members and with other international bodies play a decisive role in the conditions surrounding the decision to send in a UN mission, and explain why international law is subjected to very variable interpretations—an aspect that local actors are aware of. In addition, the whole weight of this intergovernmental and institutional game is not enough for a peace operation to be perceived as legitimate locally. This remains to be established in the country of intervention—an aspect too often ignored.

Investigations on the ground throw an interesting light in this respect. First, the legitimacy given by the Security Council is rarely assigned much value. While they refer to it for instrumental purposes, local actors—even those who are supposed to have a limited level of information, such as

[64] Johan Galtung and Ingrid Eide, 'Some Factors Affecting Local Acceptance of a UN Force: a Pilot Project Report from Gaza', pp. 240–63 in Johan Galtung, *Peace, War and Defense*, Copenhagen: Ejlers, 1976 (Essays in Peace Research, vol. 2).

community actors—seem to have no illusions about references to the 'international community'. The contradictions running through the diplomacy of the main UN member states, reflected increasingly in the multiplicity of institutions involved in a peace operation (as illustrated by the mounting of the mission in Kosovo: UN-NATO-OSCE-European Union) reduce the credibility of the intervening forces, of their discourse and of their actions. In the last resort, a decision taken one day in one institution may well be called into question not long afterwards, at another level. In the countries of intervention those diplomatic subtleties are often followed and analysed by the average citizen with attention and understanding unequalled in Western countries.

Above all, peacekeepers' legitimacy is built up during the mission. The intervening forces are judged by results: on what they say they intend to do, on what they actually do, and on how they behave and face up to their responsibilities. The 'good intentions' declared at the beginning of an intervention are rapidly called into question by deeds. From that viewpoint, invoking universal values is not enough to guarantee legitimacy, which is never definitely established. A major difficulty in building legitimacy for a peace operation arises from the fact that it is most of all dependent on perception. A number of analysts have stressed the importance of impartiality as a key ingredient of legitimacy. However, they have forgotten the inherent difficulty of such a position: no intervention is perceived as 'neutral', or even 'impartial', by local political and social actors. To be understood correctly, the ideas of 'neutrality' and 'impartiality' must be considered in their *interactive* and *inter-subjective* dimensions. In that matter as in many others, there is no 'objective' neutrality or impartiality. This fact must be considered together with another: intervening in another country, whatever form the intervention may take, means influencing the social, political and economic foundations of local society. Indeed applying the idea of impartiality, never a simple matter, is complicated further when it has to do with highly varied activities involving a noticeably increased number of actors.[65] Among the local actors as well as the members of missions, there are in fact many varied subjectivities that will give their own interpretations of what it is to be 'impartial'. As can also be observed among humanitarians, the military doctrines of countries providing troops vary considerably on this point. Sometimes it is quite difficult to grasp the concrete field implications of fancy concepts such as the 'active impartiality' (which some translate as 'impartial but not neutral') favoured by French doctrine, for instance. In particular, it has

---

[65] This is a long way from the difficulties, very real themselves, in giving 'impartial' information on violations of a cease-fire or crossing of a front line, as was the case in classic peacekeeping operations.

182   'Intervention' and 'sovereignty': the View from Below

direct implications on the type of training given to personnel sent to the
area, and can lead to divergent attitudes in the face of concrete situations.[66] Local actors, for their part, will play not only on what they see as
the 'preferences' of the mission as a whole, but also on those that they
identify on an individual level among the people they deal with, complicating matters considerably.

Concerning that diversity, the elements to which local actors refer,
when they are questioned about UN missions' 'impartiality', are revealing. Among social and, still more, community actors, the company kept
by members of the missions is seen as an important sign of their preferences. In practice, the owners of the restaurants where mission members
go, the houses and hotels where they stay, and the shops they regularly
visit, generally belong to the local oligarchy and are clearly situated politically. The United Nations staff members also live in the same districts as
the oligarchy. Some even marry people belonging to those same groups.
Of course, it is easier for UN staff to make spontaneous contact with people who have a certain level of education and with whom communication
is easier, especially when questions of language are concerned. In Haiti,
the political adviser to the head of the mission admitted that 'the bourgeoisie [paid] court to them and [came] to [them] more easily than the
other sectors. Sectors whom the mission [had] to make the first move to,
which it [did] not do often, because they were made up of people more difficult to identify and time [was] short.'[67] The missions have similar difficulties when they recruit local staff, and still more when they appeal to
qualified people from the Diaspora, who may already be politically
placed. This practice is observed closely by social and community actors.

It is very rare for those criticisms to be adopted by political actors.
Nonetheless, their assessments bring out other aspects of the complexity
of a search for a 'balance'. Among the parties themselves, the poise of
forces is most often unstable, and it varies according to the issues under
consideration. In these conditions a mission's intervention cannot fail to
be seen, in practice, as more favourable to one party or another. This is
particularly marked in cases where, as in El Salvador and Mozambique,
one of the parties is an established government and the other a guerrilla
movement. The former generally considers that the obligations falling on
it are more restrictive. The UN mission is permanently accused of interference: every action on its part is in practice seen as an encroachment on

[66] See Stephen John Stedman, 'Consent, Neutrality and Impartiality in the Tower of Babel
and on the Frontlines: United Nations Peacekeeping in the 1990's', pp. 51 ff. in UNIDIR
(ed.), *Managing Arms in Peace Processes: The Issues*, Disarmament and Conflict Resolution Project, Geneva, 1996.
[67] Words quoted from Nicole Lannegrace (Port-au-Prince, April 22, 1995).

the government's prerogatives. '[ONUMOZ] behaves as if it had a mission to watch over the government and demand everything from it, and not to see the implementation of the General Peace Agreement among the parties', complained Mozambique's Permanent Representative to the UN, in one of his many protest messages sent to the Secretary General.[68] On their side, guerrilla movements will readily accuse the United Nations mission of not 'interfering' enough, of being over-scrupulous and too afraid of denouncing the government's failures sufficiently.

The missions in Cambodia and Haiti had to face dilemmas that were fairly similar in the last analysis, though expressed in different forms. In Cambodia a government was also in place. As the only party with a complete administration all over the country, the State of Cambodia could only consider that it was more controlled by UNTAC than the other parties. Several times its representatives drew a parallel between the pressure to which they were subjected by UNTAC and the weakness shown by the mission towards the Khmers Rouges. At a press conference on August 29, 1992, Prime Minister Hun Sen denounced this 'partiality'; he emphasised the pressure put on the PPC while 'a bamboo barrier and a simple soldier on the Khmers Rouges side can make Akashi withdraw.' As for the other parties, of course they considered that the mission was showing too much indulgence towards the State of Cambodia. At the same time, leaders of FUNCINPEC and the PBLD who were questioned agreed with their PPC counterparts. From the beginning, the issue was biased among the parties because of the obvious existing imbalance.[69] Conversely UNTAC, anxious to make up for the *de facto* advantages enjoyed by the PPC in the election campaign, gave more substantial assistance—notably through its radio station—to the other political parties, especially FUNCINPEC. In return, even within the mission 'Radio UNTAC' was perceived as having campaigned openly for FUNCINPEC, which led to continual protests by PPC representatives.[70] Similarly, material support was provided for FUNCINPEC to carry out its campaign; Prince Ranariddh, for example, travelled in a United Nations helicopter. Naturally this too was interpreted as a sign of UNTAC's partiality.[71] The case of the Khmers Rouges was also a challenge. Their obstruction of the process made UNTAC their *de facto*

---

[68] Letter of July 7, 1994.

[69] Interviews in Phnom Penh (November–December 1995).

[70] Source: UNTAC memoranda and internal notes recording the results of interviews with leaders of the party. That partiality was also regularly denounced in the media controlled by the party (the daily *Pracheachon* and the State of Cambodia radio) (source: interviews in Phnom Penh, November–December 1995).

[71] See, notably, the official protest by the State of Cambodia on that subject at the April 29, 1993 meeting of the Supreme National Council.

enemy; whatever the mission did, it could only be seen as a participant in a battle against their movement.

In Haiti the fact that the restoration of democracy went together, at least initially, with the return of President Aristide to his country could only be interpreted by his opponents, and more broadly by the other political actors, as the mission taking sides. Conversely, the maintenance of an imposing military force while the army had been dissolved was interpreted by most social and community actors as aimed at 'protecting the former putschists, the *macoutes*'—a phrase that covered, in bulk, former soldiers and members of paramilitary groups as well as members of the oligarchy.[72] In practice, interventions by members of the Multinational Force and later by UNMIH appeared to be giving protection to former 'auxiliaries', to representatives of a judicial system perceived as sympathetic to the putschists, or to big landowners. In several communes in the provinces of Artibonite (especially at Petite Rivière de l'Artibonite) and Nord (especially at Pwilbowo and Pilate), judges, challenged by the people, fled at the time of Aristide's return for fear of reprisals. Meetings were then organised to choose replacements among the population, meanwhile the gates of the courts remained closed. Later, the judges returned to their posts, but under the protection of the Multinational Force. When incidents occurred later on, UNMIH also 'intervened.' Generally, it was content to send a military patrol to ensure incidents did not get any worse, but the soldiers sometimes also took part in the removal of barricades. In the province of Bas Artibonite, where land disputes are frequent, soldiers of the MNF, and after of UNMIH, were involved in situations where, faced with groups of angry peasants, they appeared to be protecting the 'big lords' and their henchmen.[73] While the presence of the Blue Helmets (most often symbolic under UNMIH) was aimed at avoiding the possibility of matters getting out of control, in the eyes of the people concerned the soldiers were protecting their oppressors.

In my field investigations, it was clear that the vast majority of local actors, whoever they were, did not want a neutral intervener but rather an ally. According to a well known adage, if the UN mission is not on your side it is against you. Testimony from various parties is often very explicit from this point of view. 'Pseudo-neutrality' is interpreted as a sign of favouring the other party. Refusal to adopt a position, or mere inaction, is seen as 'taking a *de facto* position'. Public declarations made during the process by the main political actors are very revealing. According to the

[72] Interviews in Port-au-Prince and in the provinces (April–May 1995).

[73] Interviews in the region in May 1995, and a video report on land disputes in the Bocozelle rural section, 5th rural section of Saint March, co-production by PERISCOP/CEPEDAV, Port-au-Prince, 1995.

circumstances, they may suggest that top UN officials have—even privately—expressed agreement with their position, or on the contrary denounce the UN officials as 'useless' because they did not target the other party. Indeed, one of the objectives for local actors is precisely to compromise the mission by forcing it to adopt their position on specific points.

The challenge appears even more insurmountable when missions intervene without a cease-fire—still less peace—coming first. In those cases, for each of the parties in conflict, being 'impartial' can only mean being the enemy of one's enemies. The misfortunes of the UNOSOM Belgian contingent based at Kismayo in Somalia are a good example. In March 1993, the town—until that time controlled by the followers of Colonel Jess, then an ally of Aydid—was surprise attacked by the forces of Morgan, an ally of Ali Mahdi, who infiltrated the town disguised as herdsmen. The Belgian Blue Helmets could do nothing to interpose themselves in the street fighting that followed, in which many civilians were involved. Jess' forces, with their heavy weapons taken away from them by the UNITAF disarmament programme, were forced to take flight. When they launched a counter-attack, the United Nations troops reacted and the US rapid reaction forces interposed themselves. Subsequently, the UNOSOM troops regularly stopped Jess retaking control of the town. For Aydid, such an attitude on the part of the UN troops amounted to a declaration of hostility to him and *de facto* support for Morgan. He withdrew from the peace talks then in progress.

The position of UN missions is also more complicated when they are entrusted with a mandate to protect the distribution of humanitarian assistance in contexts where such assistance is a weapon of war. In Bosnia-Herzegovina, the Blue Helmets were also increasingly becoming involved in evacuation of Muslim populations, which made them appear to be *de facto* accomplices in the Serb policy of 'ethnic cleansing'. The Bosnian case illustrates the extreme situation in which mission members can find themselves when member states hesitate between, on the one hand, treating the parties to a conflict on an equal footing and, on the other, applying specific coercive measures against one of them.[74] In this context, any action or statement can only be considered a hostile act by one party or another: if the first course is taken, by those who consider that the guilty are not being targeted; if the second, by those who are described as guilty and treated as such. From this viewpoint, the difficulties in managing threats of coercive measures against the Serbs in the Bosnian conflict echo the numerous procrastinations of United Nations missions in dealing with the Khmers Rouges in Cambodia and General Aydid in Somalia.

[74] That contradiction runs through all Security Council resolutions made after May 20, 1992.

Thus, missions are caught in multiple contradictions. It is understandable that in order to limit the risks of manipulation and, worse, breakdown if the 'balance' that is sought cannot be achieved, the UN readily tries to set limits to its appearance as an actor in internal politics. But in so doing, it tends to forget that its very presence in a country involves it in the local political arena. Whatever temptations the international staff may have to withdraw, in the last resort the only option is to manage the interaction frankly, as well as the uncertainties that characterise it. This attitude of abdication generally appears as the 'lowest common denominator'; but it only weakens the missions' position. The idea—very widespread among both decision makers and analysts—that the mere presence of a United Nations mission is psychologically, if not symbolically, what matters the most, can only lead to deadlock, often felt as such by the staff on the ground.

In fact, past experience reminds us that such attitudes of withdrawal have definite consequences on the attitude of local actors. First, they reveal to those actors the increasingly narrow limits of UN intervention, clearing the field further for the main politico-military entrepreneurs. As in Somalia and Bosnia, when armed confrontation among the parties continues, any significant withdrawal acts as a blank cheque for the continuation of war. In Somalia, from July 1993, night patrols were stopped because they were considered too dangerous. In the last two years of its presence in Somalia, UNOSOM withdrew into truly entrenched positions. Preoccupied above all by their own security, the Blue Helmets—and the Rapid Intervention Force—practically disappeared overnight from the streets that they had once occupied in massive strength. From then on the troops rarely left their bases, they moved around by helicopter or in convoy. During this time the various Somali politico-military groups rearmed, waiting for the mission to leave the country for good,[75] and retook full possession of the different districts of Mogadishu. In other situations, the fact that United Nations soldiers and civpols do not venture into certain districts of cities, or even into some entire regions, quickly makes those areas 'no-go'. Areas where, at the very least, the 'order' that the UN claims to be restoring does not reign, and where those bearing arms can apply the law of force without interference. In most cases the local political actors seek to make use of these deficiencies to limit the impact of the UN mission's action, especially in presenting the desired appearances to outsiders. The testimony of former members of the UNTAC Civil Administration Component, along with documents of that

---

[75] When the evacuation of the mission took place, the two main politico-military groups cooperated well in its organisation.

mission, shows that officials of the State of Cambodia readily exploited the failures of their UN interlocutors in this way. Also, on electoral issues the failure of UNTAC—forced to use intermediaries and local staff for most operations—to achieve control over the process explains why many things largely escaped the international staff's notice. This was all to the advantage of various Cambodian political networks. The more a mission wants to be grand and ambitious, the more the observer gets the impression of a gap between 'Planet UN' (which can be taken to include all international assistance) and the 'true country'; this was particularly the case in Kosovo, during the first 18 months of the peace force's presence.

Secondly, failures in understanding situations in cases of conflict also make for much greater exposure to the indoctrination of operations, as was seen in Bosnia-Herzegovina where UNPROFOR was regularly the victim of such propaganda. In Somalia, the main politico-military actors did not fail to take advantage of the confusion among outsiders by practicing disinformation. This was costly to the American military intelligence services, in particular during the clash with Aydid.

Thirdly, an attitude of withdrawal among missions strengthens the perception of them as 'something far off' among the majority of inhabitants in the countries where they are deployed: they are 'not interested in the people'. In this respect it should be noted that lack of knowledge of the language is not in itself considered an insurmountable obstacle. The visitors are not expected to speak one's language perfectly; but they are expected to 'try', to 'make efforts', to 'try at least to communicate'. Failing that, the distance maintained from the local people is often seen as a form of 'contempt' or even 'arrogance'—words which recurred frequently in my investigations. When one seeks to know what those terms denote more exactly, the feeling emerges of having been treated 'as if we had no history', 'as if the UN mission was year zero', as if 'nothing happened before them'; they 'did not care about what happened apart from them'. That contempt is doubly resented: there is frustration at never having been able to simply talk about past sufferings, to put one's history into words (that activity which Hannah Arendt has described as being specifically human).[76] 'They never tried to get even a bit close, to understand what we have suffered.'[77] To take time to meet people and listen is to bring the 'Other' back into one's humanity, into what is unique in everyone. This

[76] Hannah Arendt, *The Human Condition*, University of Chicago Press, 1998 (2nd edition), p. 110.

[77] Words recorded in a district of Phnom Penh, November 18, 1995 (translated from Khmer).

also means recognising them, and their modes of organisation and reference. However, ideas that people are 'not organised', that the modalities of their organisation are an obstacle to reconstruction of a country, or else that the people 'lack political maturity' or are quite simply 'violent', are among the most common ideas around. It is possible that local people answer the questions they ask themselves with systems of belief that foreigners may consider 'odd' (or even 'archaic', 'primitive'—what words have not been used!), but that system is no less valid for those who follow it. With their own words, people I met in the course of my investigations recalled that very concrete and quite simple dimension of the notion of 'impartiality', so dear to the United Nations: to place oneself at a good distance from something or someone, you have to have already been near to it. To maintain an equal distance from different actors involved in a conflict, and continue in that way to be credible in the eyes of all, one has to have some minimum involvement in the reality of the country concerned. And never to stop questioning the understanding one has of it.

5

STRATEGIES OF LOCAL ACTORS

While trying to identify the people he has to deal with on the ground, a civilian or military member of a peace mission must at the same time ask himself the question, 'What are they doing, and why?' Indeed, recognising the importance of local practices in the course of a peace operation also requires an ability to understand the logics peculiar to various groups of actors. Human behaviour is analysed here for what it is: assertion and updating of a choice among a range of possibilities. It cannot be denied that there are constraints weighing on local actors, or that some of their acts remain difficult to grasp. Saying that an individual's action is 'rational' means, quite simply, recognising that it is possible to understand the motives behind it, that his acts can have sense in a given context. Obviously, the analytical presentation that can be suggested for it cannot make one forget the permanent adjustments that the people concerned have to make, and the characteristic element of chance in these changes. Similarly, the rationality of actors and the meaning of their action (whether individual or collective) develop and change in the very process. In other words, embarking on comprehensive sociology does not mean explaining everything, still less categorising everything. This venture simply means trying, as Ricoeur put it, to think of the subject as *historical consciousness* and, for that purpose, to look for some reference points.[1] When they interact with UN missions, local political, social and community actors pursue a certain number of objectives. These are not always explicit; the people concerned are themselves not always fully aware of them. Even so, their actions have a significance that analysis can help reconstitute *a posteriori*, from one situation to another.

---

[1] Jean Greisch, *Paul Ricoeur: L'itinéraire du sens*, Grenoble: J. Million, 2001.

WHAT LOCAL ACTORS EXPECT FROM THE UN

UN legitimation

The quest for legitimacy is a classic aim for all political actors. It is often at the heart of negotiations aimed at ending a conflict,[2] but it is also pursued throughout the duration of missions, whether they follow a peace agreement or not. At the end of a conflict that has created many victims among the civilian population, the leaders of the main political groups can, in this way, try to give the impression of being 'men of peace'. Men such as Joaquim Chissano in Mozambique and Alfredo Cristiani in El Salvador devoted plenty of energy to that end. Cristiani even set up a Foundation for Peace (Fundapaz) whose main aim was to keep up that image and make it a platform to regain control over the ARENA party, which he did not succeed in doing. The public backing that senior United Nations officials gave him in that venture was fundamental. In practice there can be intertwined legitimating processes involving local political actors and senior international officials. In the case of the United Nations operation in El Salvador, the concern to present the mission as a success, even as a 'model', should be seen in the light of a convergence of interests between certain Salvadorian politicians and senior UN officials who devoted much of their time to the Salvadorian case and considered it as one of the high points of their careers.

The case of Haiti too is a most revealing example of a situation where the quest for legitimacy on the international side is supposed to compensate for a shortage of internal legitimacy. During the three years following the September 1991 coup d'état, being admitted to negotiating tables or simply being received by this or that visiting delegation in Haiti became the main activity of politicians in Port-au-Prince. Throughout that period it was beyond any doubt that President Aristide benefited most from that factor, making up for the *de facto* weakness of his enforced exile by, among other things, international recognition in which the UN played a major part. His reception at an extraordinary session of the Security Council on 3 October 1991 was crucial in this respect. The various international awards he received were also part of the process.[3] With the United Nations missions that succeeded Operation Restore Democracy, Aristide retained that comparative advantage. Other politicians were

---

[2] See especially Ira William Zartman and J. Lewis Rasmussen (eds), *Peacemaking in International Conflict: Methods and Techniques*, Washington, DC: US Institute of Peace Press, 1997.

[3] An example was the UNESCO Human Rights Education Prize awarded to him on January 8, 1997, in Paris, for his 'exceptional commitment to human rights and democracy...'

openly inspired by that model: 'Since that's how it's done, everyone plays the game'; 'We look at Aristide and we understand that it's from outside that you can get power.'[4] Boasting of having met the Special Representative of the Secretary General, or of being his quasi-'adviser' or unofficial informer on this or that subject, quickly became the favourite activity of some elite people in Port-au-Prince. The Representative's political adviser testified: 'Being received by the Special Representative is proof that you exist politically. So they pass messages hinting that they would not be averse to a meeting. And when a meeting is suggested to them, they are literally enchanted...'[5] Local election candidates also tried to play that card. Being able to boast the presence of members of the UN mission at the celebration of a patron saint's feast day, for example, was not something to be disregarded a few weeks before polling day. The exact status of these UN people did not matter; they were unfailingly raised to the rank of 'UN representatives in Haiti'.

The legitimacy that the UN is able to provide can be related to issues that are still more vital for some political movements. In Cambodia, quite apart from the power sharing issue—not an insignificant one, of course—the peace process represented, for all sides, 'a question of life or death'.[6] What was at stake, even more than the construction of immediate legitimacy, was the defence of historical legitimacy and that of their struggle, as well as the struggle for political survival. That was particularly blatant in the case of the members of the resistance who were making their political comeback in the country. For example, the FANLPK, the former armed wing of the FNLPK from which it had split in 1984–5, had to receive recognition from UNTAC to succeed with its transformation into a political party. 'UNTAC recognised us; on the military plane, it is with us that they held discussions, and we had a representative in the mixed group. If they had decided to hold discussions only with Son Sann, we would have ceased to count for anything. At that time we no longer had any means to create problems, and above all, we wanted to get a place for ourselves in Cambodian political life.'[7] Interviews with former members of the UNTAC Military Component and Civil Administration Component (Defence department), and examination of internal mission reports,

---

[4] Words uttered by Haitian political leaders (interviews in Port-au-Prince, April-May 1995).

[5] Remarks by the political adviser to the Special Representative of the Secretary General in Haiti (Port-au-Prince, April 22, 1995).

[6] An expression used, significantly, among several Cambodian politicians (investigations in Cambodia, November–December 1995).

[7] Remarks by General Chhim Om Yon, Chairman of the PDL, the party emerging from the FANLPK (Phnom Penh, December 13, 1995).

confirm the impression of the group as a 'good boy' only too happy to be given such consideration, even on the margins.

In El Salvador the FMLN found itself in a very similar situation. In addition, like the government, it pressed for the continual extension of the UN mission's mandate in the country. In fact the mission guaranteed the maintenance of a special position for a movement that had been weakened and was struggling to structure itself as a political party. RENAMO was in a comparable position in Mozambique. In securing recognition as a nego-tiating partner, and then as a 'party' to the agreements on the same footing as the government,[8] RENAMO in a certain sense 'won the war', even though it did not win the elections later.[9] On the day of signing of the Rome agreement, Dhlakama declared, 'Today, we have won international recognition...The government is a party in power and RENAMO the opposition. The agreement gives RENAMO the status of a political party.'[10] The leaders of the movement, headed by Dhlakama, saw this legitimacy continually reaffirmed.

A specific aspect relates to the RENAMO case here: the aim of trans-forming it into a political party involved material means that were not provided in any other case. This contributed greatly to a permanent ming-ling of material aspects with the symbolic significance of a continual demand for help. Dhlakama pushed this point to the limit. He knew that he was probably going to lose the elections, and did not himself expect any personal legitimacy through the ballot box.[11] On the first day of voting, he threatened to withdraw from the process, on the pretext that fraud had been committed. During the night a procession of leading international figures appealed to him. The international Supervision and Control Com-mission (SCC), of which the Special Representative of the Secretary General was chairman, adopted a statement reaffirming the importance of the RENAMO leader. When he announced that his party's boycott was over, Dhlakama did not conceal his satisfaction, although he had not gained any serious concessions in response to his apparent claims.

This question is even more decisively important in situations where there is no constituted government, as in Somalia. There it is even more

---

[8] Each party's challenging of the other's legitimacy was a particularly central point in the Mozambican negotiations. For a long time RENAMO was described as 'armed bandits' by FRELIMO, which wanted, in that way, to deny the movement any political reality.

[9] On this point see the analysis by Christine Messiant, 'La paix au Mozambique. Un succès de l'ONU', p. 59 in Roland Marchal and Christine Messiant (eds), *Les chemins de la guerre et de la paix. Fins de conflit en Afrique orientale et australe*, Paris: Karthala, 1997.

[10] See *Le Courrier* 140, July–August 1993.

[11] The forecasts (confirmed by the election results) were quite favourable for the parlia-mentary elections but suggested a heavy defeat for Dhlakama in the presidential election.

vital to appear as a negotiating partner of the UN. Every meeting then constitutes a public photo opportunity. Mohamed Aydid had a camera-man with him permanently, ready to film his distinguished visitors. The attention paid to him and Ali Mahdi by international representatives and the media was an essential trump card to show their supporters that the man they backed had an assured worth, and to establish their international status. It reached a point where many observers wondered whether the publicity accorded to those two leaders had not served to exaggerate their role and their representation. Dissident groups within each clan also played the game. These opportunists, unable to secure a mandate from their fellow citizens, could hope to get seats at the conference table—and maybe a post in a future government—by winning the favours of UNO-SOM. Reconciliation conferences thus served not to open a way to peace, but to reinforce one group's status at the expense of others.[12] In the self-proclaimed Somaliland Republic, relations with UNOSOM were even more specifically seen as a hope of obtaining international recognition. It was with that idea that talks were started with UNOSOM on deployment of troops at Berbera and at Hargeisa airport, the two main arrival points for aid for Somaliland. However, for the Somaliland authorities, giving in too quickly meant losing one of the few means of applying pressure that they had, while nobody seemed ready to recognise them.[13]

In Bosnia-Herzegovina, throughout the conflict, negotiations became 'a propaganda platform' upon which Bosnian leaders, despite their limited popular constituency, blatantly presented their cases to a wider interna-tional audience, making ever more demands and criticising each other.[14]. The aim then was to present one's case as 'just', deserving of support, and to deny such credit to one's adversaries. The 'media war' then became an essential component of the conflict, political negotiations becoming merely an instrument as a result. There too, the process of legitimacy was turned back to front: legitimacy was acquired on the international side before being built up locally or won through the ballot box. The leaders of the three nationalist parties had won the highest numbers of votes in the first elections in 1990, but they based their support on precarious coalitions of governance. They were promoted, by European Community,

[12] See especially the analysis by Ken Menkhaus, 'International Peacebuilding and the Dynamics of Local and National Reconciliation in Somalia', pp. 45–58 in Walter Clarke and Jeffrey Herbst (eds), *Learning from Somalia: The Lessons of Armed Humanitarian Intervention*, Boulder, CO: Westview, 1997.
[13] P. S. Gilkes, *Two Wasted Years: The Republic of Somaliland (1991–1993)*, Save the Children Fund (UK), August 1993, p. 51.
[14] Edgar O'Ballance, *Civil War in Bosnia, 1992–1994*, Basingstoke: Macmillan/New York: St Martin's Press, 1995, p. 246.

CSCE and UN negotiators, to the status of statesmen, leaders of nations struggling for independence, and legitimate negotiating partners. All of them used the negotiations to increase their own visibility, their stature and their authority in internal power struggles. Opponents favouring a democratic solution did not get the same treatment and were weakened accordingly.

In this process, the officials at the head of UN missions have little margin for manoeuvre; ensuring the cooperation of the main politico-military leaders is essential before the deployment of troops. Similarly, on the ground, United Nations staff must, on a daily basis, ensure some minimal collaboration on the part of local entrepreneurs, to whom they can give legitimacy through the mere fact of speaking to them. The risks of manipulation and loss of credibility are always there, and the situation is worsened by the general weakness of analysis of the contexts of intervention. In fact, as has been seen very regularly in Afghanistan and Iraq, there is a big risk of entering immediately into contact with partners whose status and representation has not been clearly assessed, but who are, in that way, given instant legitimacy. That strategy is not limited to political actors alone; it is also followed, though in varying ways, by economic and social actors, for whom the search for contact with United Nations missions corresponds to the need for recognition or simply for an improved image. In El Salvador and Haiti, the business bourgeoisie was among the main elements 'courting' senior UN officials. For economic actors traditionally allied with the army it was a way of breaking away, including symbolically, from an alliance that had become too awkward, without having to pay too high a price. The 'international community' was supposed to become, after the army, the guarantor of their economic interests.

When, as in Cambodia, certain social actors—especially local NGOs—owe their very existence, or at least the possibility of emerging onto the country's socio-political scene, to the United Nations mission, the legitimacy process is obvious. An examination of the profiles of founders and leaders of these organisations, which are after all highly personalised, is very revealing. In at least two of the cases concerned, they came from leading families and formed part of political power networks. In all cases their links with those networks were obvious.[15] In Cambodia, the creation of an NGO was directly related to political considerations: either it took place in an extension of classic power networks, with no possibility of seeing anything fundamentally new in it; or, on the contrary, it occurred as

[15] Interviews in Paris and investigations in Cambodia (November–December 1995 and August 2003).

an alternative way of occupying the political sphere, by trying to form an opposition force—a function which is not traditionally assumed by parties in Cambodia. Besides financial aid, UNTAC provided legitimacy that was indispensable for the individuals concerned and their organisations. Representatives of the mission introduced meetings that they organised, facilitated contacts with Western embassies in Phnom Penh, organised and financed their journeys to Geneva for the Human Rights Commission and to Vienna for the World Conference on Human Rights in June 1993. In Phnom Penh heads of NGOs attended all the cocktail parties. Other associations, while less directly aided by the mission, tried to take advantage of its presence in order to give themselves a new image. In that country, a similar strategy was followed by some Buddhist leaders, both to pursue their own political agendas and to re-create a space that, in recent history, had largely been taken away from them. The revival of their role coincided, for them, with that period, making it possible to impose an image of Buddhism synonymous with peace, trying to efface the memory of their past political alignments.[16]

In most other missions, this effect is limited by the fact that contacts with local social actors are rarely considered important by United Nations missions. In Cambodia, attention was focused on a certain organisational profile, but the objective of helping the creation of Cambodian 'civil society' explains why more was done in that direction. In Somalia, for the purpose of broadening negotiations and avoiding blockages at the level of a small political elite, UNOSOM's political division decided to invite about 250 intellectuals and traditional and religious leaders, women, artists and NGO heads, all supposed to represent 'civil society', to Addis Ababa. They did so with the help of international NGOs that paid for the travel arrangements of the people concerned and for the holding of some preparatory meetings[17]. Before the actual proceedings, they met with political leaders. Afterwards, UNOSOM tried to ensure a 50 per cent participation of 'civil society' in the preparatory committees set up by the Addis Ababa agreements. Many of those who were brought to the front of the stage in this way would otherwise not have managed it.[18] The UN representatives were then the target of attention from former officials and

---

[16] Interviews in Phnom Penh and Battambang (November–December 1995 and August 2003).

[17] Especially the Life and Peace Institute (LPI) based in Sweden, which collaborated closely with UNOSOM, with funding from the Swedish government.

[18] See especially the analysis by Sture Normark of the LPI in M. A. Mohamed Salih and Lennart Wohlgemuth (eds), *Crisis Management and the Politics of Reconciliation in Somalia*, Statements from the Uppsala Forum, January 17 to 19, 1994, Uppsala: Nordiska Afrikainstitutet, 1994.

individuals of all kinds who saw an opportunity to emerge or, alternatively, to return to the front of the stage even though they had been closely
linked with the Siyad Barre regime.[19]

Elsewhere, people and organisations 'coming from nowhere' have
courted UN missions assiduously, hoping to gain an image or even a specific status. In addition, it has been quite common for political actors to try
wearing the 'civil society' hat. Some suddenly discover that they have a humanitarian commitment, the human rights cause seeming an effective
means of getting into the political space (and, as an accessory, to raise funds).

When, as in El Salvador and Haiti, local NGOs (especially those involved in defending human rights) do not owe their existence to the UN, the
relationship with UN missions is much more ambivalent. According to an
expression often heard, the missions come 'to overshadow'. 'Local associations are suspicious because they have the feeling that the United Nations
mission is going to take their place and do their work.'[20] This 'unfair competition' is all the more difficult to endure because, in the human rights
arena, those organisations 'have worked on very difficult questions in
very dangerous circumstances for years; some of their colleagues have
even been killed for their convictions. And here comes the UN with all its
resources, helicopters and everything that follows, despising them, not
even taking them into consideration, not asking their opinion; hence their
resentment', explained the head of an international NGO.[21] During
interviews, indeed, there recurred this thirst for recognition and this
feeling that 'NGOs have in fact been eclipsed' by the United Nations
mission, as the head of a Salvadorian organisation declared: 'And yet,' she
added, 'there are many cases where the UN would not have been able to
work without the basic information provided by Salvadorian human rights
organisations.'[22]

The UN grants access to additional material resources

The search for advantage is not confined to the symbolic domain. Local
actors also seek, in some cases, to extract material advantage from their

---

[19] See the analysis by Mohamed Sahnoun, former Special Representative of the Secretary
General, who was nonetheless a strong defender of that approach: Mohamed Sahnoun,
Somalia: The Missed Opportunities, Washington: US Institute for Peace Press, September 1994, pp. 25–6. I refer also to an interview with John L. Hirsch, former political
adviser to UNITAF (New York, January 11, 1995).

[20] Interview with Philippe Texier, former head of the ONUSAL Human Rights Division
(Paris, March 7, 1995).

[21] Comment by Martha Doggett of the Lawyers Committee for Human Rights (New York,
January 13, 1995).

[22] Interview with Celia Medrano, spokesperson for the Comisión de Derechos Humanos de
El Salvador (CDHES) (San Salvador, August 24, 1995).

interaction with United Nations missions. Missions can be no more than mere intermediaries for access to additional political resources. In fact the most substantial resources liable to be diverted—those included in the emergency relief or reconstruction aid category—come through traditional bilateral and multilateral aid channels and do not appear in peace operations' budgets. Hence the presence of a United Nations mission is often perceived, by the established authorities, as a factor able to facilitate access to international aid, by giving greater visibility to their country's situation, or even additional legitimacy for themselves. This dimension also operates for other protagonists, and is an essential channel through which local political and social actors seek, with the help of UN missions, to get access to additional material resources.

When the UN acts as a transitional authority, as in Kosovo and East Timor, and to a large extent in Cambodia, the peace mission appears as a key economic actor. In Cambodia, UNTAC was supposed to ensure that the country's macro-economic situation did not deteriorate too fast, and, above all, that state property was not misappropriated. Steps were taken to regulate the process of selling off of state property, to avoid excessive price increases for essential goods, and to halt the depreciation of the riel, the national currency.[23] While some of these actions directly affected the established state structures and the PPC, those relating to the distribution of basic foodstuffs such as rice, or even the currency, affected more directly those who controlled the essential portion of trade in Cambodia— members of the Chinese Diaspora. Although they never appeared formally in talks with UNTAC, they manoeuvred behind the scenes.[24]

Even when a peace mission has no specific mandate to bring its weight to bear on a country's economic structures, it can easily seem like a spoiler to those for whom the war-peace transition can mean a loss of substantial material advantages. In Mozambique, Alberto Chipando, minister of Defence since 1975, was among those individuals. While other generals of the FRELIMO old guard had their retirement assured by already heading various enterprises, he personally had much to lose in the transition to peace. His aim was therefore to ensure on the one hand the appropriation of a supplementary defence budget for one year, and on the other the continuation of a number of illicit trade operations that he controlled, especially with South Africa. For that, he needed time. Whereas his colleagues in the Mozambican government, once the critical phase of demobili-

---

[23] In February and March 1993, UNTAC put rice on the market with the help of the World Food Programme (WFP) so as to discourage hoarding and bring prices down.

[24] Interviews, and UNTAC archives and Phnom Penh Chamber of Commerce documents consulted (November–December 1995).

sation had passed, did everything to hasten that process—in view of the
growing difficulty they had in funding military forces that had become
too bulky—Alberto Chipando sought, by all means, to hold up the implementation of the peace agreements. For this purpose he occasionally used
the grievances of demobilised soldiers as part of his scheme. For some of
those soldiers participation in Chipando's rackets (especially the petrol
rackets) was merely a matter of survival.

In Mozambique the UN was in an unprecedented situation, since the
peace agreement provided that the RENAMO party, as one of the parties
to the peace process, could claim financial aid to ensure its transformation
from a military organisation into a political party. The former special
adviser to the Special Representative of the UN Secretary General in
Mozambique has spoken openly of 'corrupting a guerrilla movement to
entice it into civilian life, making it get a taste for city life'.[25] Aldo Ajello
himself never made any mystery of his idea of this sort of 'corruption'.[26]
Another member of ONUMOZ was equally explicit at the time: 'Peace is
bought. We have succeeded in getting the tiger to leave the forest, now
what is needed is to install him comfortably in a democratic process...
Since then, Dhlakama [leader of the movement] goes around in a Mer-
cedes. The UN has set him up in Maputo in a fine white villa overlooking
the ocean. He wears Italian suits and ties. Some dozens of his acolytes are
lodged in one of the best hotels in the city...'[27] Such an operation required
the creation, in May 1993, of a Trust Fund to which Italy made an initial
contribution of $ 5.7 million, increased later to meet further arising needs.
A sum of $ 300,000 was supposed to be paid each month until the elec-
tions. This innovation did not fail to cause problems both for the UN
administration and for donors. That 'modest subsidy', as Aldo Ajello portrayed it, wetted Dhlakama's appetite. Initially, he and the essential portion
of this staff refused to settle in the capital until they had sufficient means
provided. Some months later, RENAMO withdrew its delegation from
Maputo, arguing that its members had not received the appropriate allocation of housing, transport and means of communication. This meant
that the work of the mixed commissions for supervision of the peace
agreement was blocked. In a parallel move Dhlakama—who was still
refusing to move to Maputo—announced that his forces would only begin
to proceed to the cantonment points when RENAMO would have received
$ 15 million to support its activities. Meanwhile, the special fund had

---

[25] Words quoted from Eric Lubin in Paris, February 2, 1995.
[26] He declared, 'Afonso Dhlakama is considered as an African chief, and he must be able to
act as such. He needs money to retire his generals and distribute largesse.' Quoted in
Courrier International, February 24, 1994.
[27] Quoted in *Le Nouvel Observateur*, August 11, 1994.

been established, but Dhlakama persisted in his demands. When the UN Secretary General, worried about the delay in the peace process, went to Mozambique in October 1993, the RENAMO chief repeated: 'We need money'. Again, in December 1993, during a meeting of the Supervision and Control Commission, Afonso Dhlakama launched an urgent appeal for his organisation to be provided with financial resources, without which RENAMO would be forced to abstain from participating in the elections. The threat was continually brandished through the following months. In July 1994 the $11-million fund placed at RENAMO's disposal had run out, without, by then, any spending on the election campaign being made.[28] In October 1994, RENAMO asked for an extra $5 million, threatening to withdraw from the electoral process. The threat was again taken seriously. Finally, the total bill amounted to $15 million, for highly individualised returns that only reached a small group of men, who had not wanted to enlarge the number of beneficiaries. The mass of RE-NAMO troops saw nothing of that manna. It is not impossible that the repeated incidents involving demobilised soldiers were exacerbated by the reports that they had heard of the lifestyle of their former leaders in the capital. But they were not the only ones to have their appetite wetted in this way. The leaders of other political parties also sought to obtain financial resources from the UN. On April 27, 1993 twelve of them, forming what was called the 'unarmed opposition', left a multi-party consultative meeting on the draft electoral law, demanding material and financial support to establish their own headquarters. A second Trust Fund was set up, in April 1994, to help all the registered parties that had not signed the Peace Agreement to prepare for the elections. In August 1994, when a Security Council mission went to Mozambique to examine the persistent hold-ups in the process, the 16 smaller political parties also stressed the need to receive adequate financial support in order to enable them to engage fully in the election process.[29] They knew that the UN needed multi-party elections. Their threat to withdraw from the elections, although carrying less weight than the RENAMO threat, could at least enable them to draw some dividends from their position. In fact an initial sum of $ 50,000 was paid to each of them in August 1994; an additional payment was provided for, on the basis of proof that these funds would have been exclusively devoted to the organisation of the elections. Most of the groups never received the second payment. The attraction of that

[28] Many observers highlighted the extravagant lifestyle of the RENAMO leaders in Maputo at that time. See especially Richard Haines and Geoffrey T. Wood, 'The 1994 Election and the Mozambique Democratic Transition', *Democratization* 2/3, Fall 1995, p. 365.

[29] Report of the Security Council Mission to Mozambique, August 7 to 12, 1994 (S/1994/1009, August 29, 1994, para. 38).

aid probably led some entrepreneurs to found political parties with the sole objective of getting financial aid.

Also, in Somalia, though to a much smaller extent, the United Nations mission distributed direct material benefits to political actors. In particular, the organisation of numerous so-called reconciliation conferences, at the national, regional or local level, was the occasion for payment of *per diem* to those taking part and the supply of food. For former members of UNOSOM, such generosity could have been a reason for the talks dragging on.[30] Many commentators have wondered whether the conferences organised in Nairobi or Addis Ababa were related to anything other than the participants' hope of living very comfortably off the United nations for a few weeks. When the time approached for the mission to leave, some also realized that UNOSOM needed to show that 'national reconciliation' was in progress and things had been at least attempted. They literally sold their participation in peace conferences for a high price, and raised the bidding for the regional meetings that UNOSOM organised in 1994. The mission received numerous proposals from leading local personalities for organisation of 'reconciliation meetings' and other 'discussion forums'. To give one example, the Lower Juba (Kismayo zone) conference was said to have cost between $ 500,000 and $ 600,000. Some Imams (considered by UNOSOM as possible counterweights to the 'warlords') negotiated a high price for the organisation of conferences to encourage peace in their regions.[31] Similarly, members of the councils that UNOSOM had begun to set up in districts applied continual pressure to obtain more material assistance from the mission. Such aid, that was supposed to help establish a minimal local administration, above all made personal enrichment possible for some.[32]

What happens more often is that United Nations missions provide funding not for political parties but for the creation of NGOs. Here political and material interests coincide, and there are financial stakes that may, as in Cambodia, not be insignificant. At that time in Cambodia, the UN provided the only resources available to the organisations concerned. As for the sums, they were quite considerable in relation to the normal budgets of local human rights organisations. The first three associations

---

[30] Meetings with former members of UNOSOM and the Somalia Desk Officer at the Political Affairs Division of the UN Secretariat (New York, January 10, 1995).

[31] One of the most famous was the Imam of the Hiraab, who received $ 300,000 in August 1994 for having organised talks to bring about a reconciliation process in his region, but claimed more for mediation among Hawiye clans.

[32] A fund (financed by the Nordic countries) was established to support each district or regional council, together with administrative 'kits'. It included a sum allocated to repair of council buildings and basic office equipment.

received $500,000 from UNTAC 'to launch their first activities'. UNTAC also provided aid for staff training and helped organise international seminars, etc. Some heads of Cambodian organisations admitted that UNTAC was, in this way, 'a bit of a milk cow'.[33] One of the individuals concerned admitted that the creation of an NGO was first of all a means of providing oneself with a job. She recalled: 'I was working in a bank, but I was interested in working with UNTAC because I could get better pay there. Through a friend I was able to meet Mr McNamara [director of the Human Rights Component]. I told him I was looking for a job. He replied, "Why don't you set up a human rights organisation instead, an NGO which will last? I will give you everything you need for that." So I approached some friends and we set up Outreach, then I went back to see Mr McNamara and told him, "Here you are, I've set up an NGO". Then he gave us a room in the UNTAC offices, to start with, as well as financial aid. We stayed there for four months... Before, none of the founder members had ever done anything related to human rights questions. But the problems of Cambodia are above all material problems, problems of means. Now, we have the means and more than thirty people are working for us.'[34] Other heads of NGOs have recalled how the news that UNTAC was giving out plenty of money spread fast. But the mission could not go on creating NGOs indefinitely. So the people concerned were left with finding a 'well paid job' in one of the existing NGOs—and the director of the UNTAC Human Rights Component was said to have worked on this as well, with the help of additional aid provided. This sort of patron-client relationship, however, considerably complicated relations among NGOs. Several Cambodian organisations have spoken of being victims of the pressure exerted by some NGOs seeking to retain exclusive benefits from the United Nations rent.

Even when a mission is not immediately in the position of a distributor of aid, its decisions can have sufficiently important implications for aid to make it the object of special attention on the part of some actors, seeking additional material advantages for themselves or their followers, to strengthen their political bases. This concerns, in particular, aid for the return of refugees and the reintegration of former combatants. The UNTAC Rehabilitation and Economic Affairs Component in Cambodia essentially provided short-term assistance for people returning from the frontier refugee camps. The choice of resettlement zones was carefully

[33] Interview with Pung Chhiv Kek Galabru, Chairperson of the Ligue Cambodienne pour la Défense des Droits de l'Homme (Phnom Penh, November 25, 1995).
[34] Recollections by Srey Chanphallara, Chairperson of Outreach, Phnom Penh, 28 November 1995 (translation from Khmer).

negotiated by representatives of former resistance members. Their aims were above all vote-related: to ensure a favourable distribution of voters for elections that would be held under proportional representation by each region. But for the Khmers Rouges, what mattered most was maintaining control over the resettled people and the aid that would be distributed to them. The movement's collaboration with the UNTAC Repatriation Component did not in any regard create problems. The PKD was ready to receive many refugees in the zones under its control. Similarly, the intervention of aid agencies was well received. On the other hand, the Khmers Rouges generally made their agreement, to the Electoral Component's intervention in the zones under their control, conditional on material assistance being provided, especially food aid. They did not hesitate to raise the bidding in cases where UNTAC members arrived unexpectedly with sacks of rice, hoping, in that way, to cut short protests and show their good will.[35] Meanwhile rackets in distribution cards, and various arrangements for getting more aid, abounded.[36]

In El Salvador, a similar strategy was adopted by leaders of the FMLN. In that country, when most of the population had been resettled before the beginning of the United Nations operation, the major remaining issue was the land transfer programme that concerned demobilised soldiers and about 50,000 civilians. On the left of the political scene, political leaders pushed for an extensive interpretation of the agreements so as to increase the number of potential beneficiaries, generally located in zones formerly controlled by the guerrillas. Some also negotiated an acceleration of transfers of land and agro-industrial enterprises to former commanders, which made it possible to redistribute a number of dividends associated with the return to civilian life.[37] Where, as in Mozambique, the interests of former commanders and those of the troops diverged greatly, former combatants took charge themselves of recovering the material benefits to which they considered they had a right. In this way 'spontaneous cantonment zones' emerged. Even when they did not regroup together, people left out of the peace process, not fitting into any of the categories for which the agreements made provision, sought to draw the United Nations'

[35] Interviews with former UNTAC members and local employees of the mission.

[36] As the aid was distributed in a lump sum, by family unit, it seemed that families were often split up at the time of repatriation, so as to receive a proportionately greater amount of aid. See especially Vence Geiger, 'The Return of the Border Khmer: Repatriation and Reintegration of Refugees from the Thai-Cambodian Border', p. 198 in Peter Utting (ed.), *Between Hope and Insecurity. The Social Consequences of the Cambodian Peace Process*, Geneva: UNRISD, 1994.

[37] This strategy, followed particularly by Joaquín Villalobos, was denounced by the FPL: cf. ONUSAL internal documents and interview with the Special Representative of the United Nations Secretary General in El Salvador (San Salvador, September 6, 1995).

attention to their fate.[38] They erected roadblocks and took humanitarian workers and United Nations staff hostage, most often outside the provincial capitals.[39] In the 'official' cantonment camps too, soldiers often staged demonstrations. Their demands varied—demands to be demobilised faster, to receive their lump sum pay-off immediately (economic assistance was paid to 95,000 demobilised soldiers over a period of 18 months), or simply to be better fed in the meantime. There too, hostage taking and threats to UN staff multiplied.

Elsewhere, peacekeepers can be in positions where they are perceived as ensuring, or else as blocking, access to aid supplied by others. This typically happened in cases where the Blue Helmets did not manage humanitarian aid directly, but were expected to ensure the security of its delivery, as in Somalia and Bosnia-Herzegovina. In Somalia, the leaders of the armed groups controlled the essential portion of the illicit trade activity, at least in the country's nerve centres, but they were not alone. Locally, new economic-mafioso actors emerged, and sought to control aid that represented an important stake in the conflict. From the end of 1992 onwards, that struggle was superimposed over the dual battle for the control of commerce and land. In Bosnia-Herzegovina, the protection of humanitarian aid was the central axis of the whole first phase of UN intervention, but also the object of the most lucrative rackets. Levying of transit dues on United Nations convoys, and pure and simple misappropriation, notably enabled the various armed forces to finance the war effort.[40] Supplies of food, clothing and even arms for the troops also depended partly on the humanitarian convoys into which other transport was infiltrated. Similarly, each camp had its own humanitarian organisation that essentially controlled the distribution of aid to the people, over which the High Commission for Refugees often found it very difficult to exercise the smallest degree of control.[41] The mafioso networks organised on that occasion could transcend the parties to the conflict, dragging in individuals following logics of survival, even though the military leaders of the various armed factions were holding the key positions in them—which made it

[38] This situation was due, in particular, to the proliferation, in the last years of the conflict, of militias operating on the margins of the two armed groups, especially of RENAMO.

[39] Fabricio Soares, a UNHCR member working in the Mutara district in Tete province, had his vehicle stopped by one of the roadblocks. The soldiers wanted the same food and the same help that they had heard others had received.

[40] Between 1992 and 1994, 30 to 50 percent of the humanitarian aid was believed to have been misappropriated by the various armed forces.

[41] For example, at the beginning of 1993 there was a fierce contest between the HCR and the Sarajevo city authorities, who were themselves in conflict with the Bosnian government for control over distribution and hence over the population.

possible for those leaders to accumulate some capital and get access to new business opportunities in the post-war period. The blockades and sieges of towns and villages became, for some, sources of big profits. In Tuzla illicit operators of all sorts, who were profiting from the siege of the town, took a very poor view of the idea of starting a UN air bridge from the town's airport. In such situations the Blue Helmets can be seen as those who either help or hinder access to aid. So even when UN missions do not behave as economic operators themselves, they can be regarded by certain local actors as if they were economic actors. Generally, those practices pre-date the arrival of the United Nations people, in countries where the aid and extortion culture has a long history. War conditions, in this sense, do not constitute a complete break, even though they may be the occasion for redeployment of former practices and changes—often profound changes—in the country's social and economic organisation.

Some sectors also try to divert to themselves the indirect economic benefits linked to a UN mission's presence in a country. Locally, missions make a certain amount of expenditures—on services, repairs, local purchases of supplies, renting of buildings and offices, hire of vehicles and payment of local salaries. At the same time they give their international personnel (civilians, police and military) a daily subsistence allowance, variable from one country to another, and part of this is spent on housing, food, and leisure activity. A systematic effort to pinpoint the various budget items that may have led to local spending has produced estimates varying, according to period, from 5 to a maximum of 10 per cent of the missions' total budget. Considering the way in which missions are deployed, and also the type of products and the needs of mission members compared with what the countries concerned can offer, the economic impact of their presence has essentially been concentrated on capital cities and, possibly, some provincial towns. The people able to profit by this demand organise quickly. There are many landlords who suddenly terminate leasing contracts to re-let their houses on much better terms, often with payment in U.S. dollars, to individual mission members or else to the Organisation itself for use as offices. Those who run small businesses, or are able to set one up, also look for customers among United Nations mission members, if only to sell them drinks, cigarettes, or small handcrafts. The efforts to secure a share of the economic benefits linked to a UN mission's presence are partly a matter of individual tactics, which can include begging. This category may include some initiatives taken to get a 'little job' with the UN or with mission members, for example as domestic staff. The missions are often very sought-after employers. However, what can be observed of the recruitment channels suggests that in many cases it is possible to go beyond the stage of resourceful personal initiative.

Securing as many jobs as possible for one's supporters makes it possible to create or reinforce a patronage network (not forgetting, of course, the advantages of being able to count on possible informers or intermediaries). This became even more important in a case like Somalia where local jobs offered by UNOSOM were heavily concentrated in Mogadishu itself. The capital being controlled by the two major politico-military groups in conflict, each controlling half the city.[42] In such situations, renting houses or vehicles can also become sources of income sought for reasons that are no longer simply individual. Similarly exchange control, in the absence of central authority, becomes a substantial stake in itself, since the United Nations missions have considerable needs in this area. The line dividing such things from mafia-like practices is often thin. In Somalia, the twofold American-UN operation made it possible, for example, for former ministers of President Siyad Barre to benefit from certain advantages acquired at that time, while setting up their own militia for protection.[43] In Zagreb, where the headquarters of UNPROFOR was transferred at the beginning of the Bosnian war, the Croatian authorities in particular leased the offices where the mission was established for an enormous rent (most of the humanitarian organisations were subjected to the same regime). In Bosnia-Herzegovina illicit dealings in petrol—a major item of expenditure in the mission's budget—were essentially shared among the armed forces of the three camps.[44] Even if they represented more modest economic interests than humanitarian aid itself, these earnings were not insignificant for the actors concerned.

Misappropriation of the economic manna can also go as far as plunder and robbery, a phenomenon present in all UN missions, but often only marginal and the work of isolated individuals. But it can take more serious proportions, as in Cambodia where robberies multiplied in the weeks before the withdrawal of UNTAC, with thefts of vehicles, computers and communications equipment.[45] Those thefts were committed, in particular, by local employees of UNTAC. It is obviously difficult to tell whether

---

[42] According to the organisation Africa Watch, those groups also levied sums from the pay of locally employed staff of UNOSOM.

[43] An example was Mohamed Sheikh Osman, minister of Finance for fifteen years under the former regime. Owner of about fifty villas in Mogadishu, he was said to have leased them for high rents to aid organisations and foreign representative offices.

[44] See especially Xavier Bougarel, 'L'économie du conflit bosniaque: entre prédation et production', pp. 233–68 in François Jean and Jean-Christophe Rufin (eds), *Economie des guerres civiles*, Paris: Hachette, 1996.

[45] As an indication, an audit report estimated the cost of 'missing and stolen' vehicles at $757,300. Besides, the auditors recommended cancellation of the stock-lists and writing off of 347 items of property valued between $ 1,500 and $ 6,000 and 183 items of value exceeding $6,000 (including gifts). Source: Audit Report A/49/943 of August 2, 1995.

some of the robberies were organised, or at least encouraged, by political actors who, when questioned on the subject, vied with each other in evasive answers. The answer I received from an important figure in FUNCINPEC is fairly representative: 'We regretted that property was leaving to be used by other missions. It was a problem because that property had been allocated under the UNTAC budget to Cambodia, and so it would have been logical for all the heavy items to stay in Cambodia. What we finally recovered, without UNTAC really giving it, was not much...You understand, we could not stop people helping themselves...'[46] In Somalia, UN property regularly 'disappeared', in quite considerable quantities. The theft of cash from the headquarters of UNOSOM II in Mogadishu, amounting to $3.9 million, was the most famous case, and never fully explained.[47] The final financial report on the mission showed that property amounting to a total of $ 3 million had been written off, of which a not so insignificant portion was probably lost through theft.[48] At the end of 1994 there was fighting between militiamen who were trying to take up positions close to the United Nations camps, near the airport and Mogadishu harbour, and so were in a good position to take over control there when the moment arrived. On the evacuation of the United Nations headquarters by the last Pakistani Blue Helmets guarding it, on February 1, 1995, militiamen loyal to Mohamed Farah Aydid invaded the premises, looting what was left. Whether the people carrying out robbery and looting are directly obeying orders or not is no longer so crucial in situations where the economic effects brought about by the presence of UN missions fuels a 'war economy'.

What remains behind after missions' departure does not come from theft alone. There are other ways of trying to secure such material gains. When they move out, missions leave some equipment in the country, a part of which is sold to local entrepreneurs while the rest is transferred, in the form of gifts, either to the government or to local communities and associations. With some exceptions, the total amounts concerned are fairly modest,[49] but at the individual level, for a local organisation, they can represent an essential part of its property capital. It is important, then, to position

[46] Recollection by Pok Marina, spokesman for Prince Ranariddh since 1989 and throughout the peace process, then Under-Secretary at the Foreign Affairs and International Cooperation ministry (Phnom Penh, December 15, 1995).

[47] See the report of an investigation supervised by the Office of Internal Oversight Services of the United Nations (A/49/843 of February 2, 1995).

[48] Final Financial Report on the mission (A/50/741 of November 9, 1995).

[49] In the Cambodian case, the material left behind as gifts amounted to $41,048,041 (see Audit report reference A/49/943 of August 2, 1995). In Somalia, transfers of material (water and petrol supply equipment, generators, prefabricated buildings, etc.) amounted to a total of $1,160,000 (see Final Financial Report on the mission).

oneself well in the months preceding the end of a mission. In practice property transfers rarely follow transparent procedures. So the interested parties need to identify as best they can the person able to guarantee them the greatest access to material, and ensure that person's goodwill. Local personnel can be well placed to act as intermediaries, if only for identifying material that can be given away. Where associations are concerned, it is not uncommon for organisations that are already the best provided for to emerge as the main beneficiaries of these transfers of property.[50]

Lastly, UN peace missions are perceived as being just like any other international aid agency. People seek to obtain from their members material gains that in theory they cannot provide. That has to do with ill-considered expectations, sometimes encouraged—as we have seen—by the missions themselves. There may also be cases of going to the wrong office. Because of the rivalry and confusion often prevailing in relations between peace missions and the various aid structures in a country, local actors tend to approach members of UN peace missions 'for anything and everything', as those members sometimes put it. Confusion may also be encouraged by small Quick Impact Projects, as they are called, started with bilateral funding by military contingents. Those contingents readily make plenty of publicity about such projects, and this does not fail to sharpen jealousies and rivalries. In Cambodia, Haiti, Somalia and Mozambique, community groups and leaders have competed in this way to acquire such aid, with hopes often far removed from what, in reality, could be offered to them. There can be a broad interpretation of a mission's mandate, based on a voluntary initiative strategy: the interested parties know for a fact that their requests, in theory, do not fall within the mission's mandate, but they 'try their luck' and 'keep on trying', adapting their language according to the person they are speaking to and understanding well that if they can get nothing from the mission as such, they can always hope for something from its members as individuals. As reported by members of a community of returned refugees in the Santa Clara region in El Salvador, 'It's simply a matter of choosing the right people ...'[51]

Compromising the UN: making the mission an ally

Local political and social actors' strategies are also directed, in part, at the UN peace missions in their regulatory function. Different categories of

---

[50] In Cambodia, it was human rights organisations set up with direct assistance from UNTAC that benefited most from this transfer of material, while they were yet unable to spend all their own budgets.

[51] Interviews with communities of *repoblaciones* organised in an association (returnees from Costa Rica and Honduras), Santa Clara region, north of San Vicente, September 11, 1995.

actors try to deflect the course of United Nations interventions in their favour. When a mission intervenes after the signing of a peace agreement, political actors will try to win what they could not win in negotiations, forcing the interpretation of some aspects, trying to limit that of others. In El Salvador, 'after the signing of the agreements, a good deal had to be renegotiated or reinterpreted. In reality the follow-up of the implementation of the agreements resulted in continuous negotiation.'[52] This was aggravated by the decision made to continuously re-schedule the matters left in suspense (a *recalendarización* operation). Originally arising from concern for adaptation to reality on the ground, this option—also chosen, in different terms, in Mozambique—in fact led to reopening of discussions every time. Each time this gave protagonists a new opportunity to obtain what they could not get during the negotiations for the peace agreements. While the former guerrilla movements in those two countries tried to secure a more favourable interpretation of certain points, sometimes with material considerations in mind, the governments and armed forces conducted a 'war of interpretation' with the contrary aim of minimising what had been conceded in the negotiations. In Mozambique, the government also pushed for the most restrictive possible interpretation and application of the agreements, trying to retain maximum control over the police, the administration and the media. In Cambodia, the government in place did the same vis-à-vis the UNTAC Civil Administration Component, supposed to exercise control over it.

This sort of obstruction strategy is common, even when actors state the opposite in public. In Haiti President Aristide never stopped condemning the absence of effective UN action in the area of security, but he was the first to put up obstacles to any idea of organising and structuring the police, so as to retain control of it. The former chief of staff of UNMIH has charged: 'Sometimes he wanted us to do the job for him because it suited him at the time, but he certainly did not want us to do any in-depth work.'[53] Even when political actors opt for an obstruction strategy as a priority, especially because they think they have more to lose than to gain in the peace process, they also try to draw some symbolic benefit from it. In Cambodia, the leaders of the Khmers Rouges movement 'would have preferred not to have UNTAC in the picture, but because those people were there and it was not possible to shove them aside completely, they decided to work with them, until their departure.' If they never intended to implement the peace agreements, they tried to get some advantage from

[52] Recollection by Salvador Samayoa, FMLN representative in the Dialogue Commission: San Salvador, September 5, 1995 (translation from Spanish).
[53] Interview with Colonel William Fulton, Chief of Staff of the UNMIH Military Component (Port-au-Prince, February 24, 1996).

their presence, especially so as to maintain their access to the resources of certain regions of the country and weaken the State of Cambodia's control.[54] The various rival tendencies within the movement probably shared, until the end, that same hope of guaranteeing, by other means than through the ballot box, the survival of the movement, and obtaining *de facto* alterations in the Agreements.[55]

This process goes further in cases where a mission intervenes without a peace agreement being completed beforehand, even more where a conflict is still ongoing. The mission is then a possible ally in the war, if necessary even by forcing its hand. For instance, a group will provoke armed incidents and then pin the blame on other parties. In Bosnia-Herzegovina, throughout the presence of UNPROFOR, President Izetbegovic followed '*la politique du pire*' (the strategy of making things worse). In negotiations, while his forces were losing the battle on the ground, Izetbegovic used his veto against all formulas put forward and resisted all demands in the hope that a military option would be put into operation and Western troops would intervene in the conflict on his side.[56] On the ground, the Bosnian Muslims regularly obstructed the smooth performance of UNPROFOR's work, and, in the words of General Morillon, then commanding the UN troops in Bosnia-Herzegovina, 'continued fighting which did not—and they knew it did not—have any chance of success, but had the merit of attracting the world's attention'.[57] This did not stop them trying, in the meantime, to use some aspects of the mission's mandate to their advantage. For example, while the Bosnian government constantly criticised the 'safe areas' established from May 1993 onwards, it used those zones as bases for rest and replenishment of supplies for its troops within enemy territory that it hoped to retake, and as bases from which it could attack Serbian enclaves. In addition, the various parties employed tactics aimed at forcing the UN to take sides. Thus the United Nations troops and

---

[54] That priority was declared by the movement at the time of signing of the Paris Agreements (statement of October 22, 1991). It was restated several times in messages sent to UNTAC (including the letter Khieu Samphan sent to Yasushi Akashi on July 14, 1992). Some observers consider that the emphasis on that point was proportional to the movement's leaders' growing awareness that they would not emerge unharmed from the process themselves.

[55] Here I refer mainly to interviews with specialists in study of the movement (Christophe Peschoux, Steve Heder and Suzann Downie), and with former allies, especially in the former FNLPK; and to analysis notes prepared for UNTAC that I have consulted. See also the manuscript by Lao Mong Hay, *The UNfinished Settlement of the Cambodia Conflict*, Phnom Penh: Khmer Institute of Democracy, 1994, p. 45.

[56] It was in the same spirit that he pleaded at a very early date for a policy called 'lift and strike': lifting the embargo on arms for Bosnia and launching air strikes.

[57] Quoted in the daily *Le Monde*, February 4, 1993.

the food convoys were regularly the target of firing aimed at pushing the Blue Helmets into striking back at the enemy. In November 1992, at Bosanska-Krupa, Bosnian artillery targeted food convoys to provoke the Blue Helmets into firing back towards the Serb lines. In November 1993 it was, at that time, three Croat liaison officers who tried to use UN-PROFOR against the Bosnian authorities.[58] In this the fighters were helped by the fact that the front line was changing daily, which facilitated infiltration to fire on United Nations forces from enemy territory, giving the impression that the firing came from the adversary's side. Sniper fire and terrorist acts were also used for this purpose.

This kind of tactic may also be employed by social actors, in areas that do not always come under the missions' mandate. A typical example is the occupation of land or houses when war has caused major population displacements. In some countries, peasant organisations blatantly created incidents, hoping to force the United Nations soldiers to go to their village and then deal with a local problem that had been left hanging for a long time. In El Salvador, the land transfer programme included in the peace agreements provided legalisation of occupations in former conflict zones. At the beginning of 1992, every week, several land occupation operations were carried out. Regularly, the army intervened to remove the occupiers, watched by ONUSAL observers, whom the occupiers did not fail to call to witness. Several times, community groups tried to create incidents during those military operations, with the hope of forcing ONUSAL to take their side.[59] Subsequently, protest marches were regularly organised. In December 1994 a big march was organised from Chalatenango to San Salvador. The mayor of the capital refused to let the demonstrators enter the city, but they confronted ONUSAL with a *fait accompli*: the mission had in fact to act as an intermediary, and the demonstrators took advantage of this to get their demands more widely heard.[60] Throughout the mission, demonstrations were organised in various places. 'The government and the army always wanted to stop the demonstrations. We told the ONUSAL people: whether you like it or not, we are going to demonstrate, and you will be responsible if there are any problems; so, you have to

---

[58] Private interviews with former French Blue Helmets; see also Commandant Franchet (pseudonym) and Sébastien Fontenelle, *Casque bleu pour rien: Ce que j'ai vraiment vu en Bosnie*, Paris: Lattès, 1995.

[59] Interviews in San Salvador and in various ex-conflict regions; see also *Proceso* no. 593, February 12, 1992.

[60] Interviews with heads of *repoblaciones* committees in the Chalatenango region (September 1995) and with Colonel Henry Morris, principal ONUSAL/MINUSAL coordinator (San Salvador, August 24, 1995); translations from Spanish.

protect us. They were fed up!' some peasants of the Santa Clara region testified.[61] It was the same scenario in the Chalatenango region: 'We wanted them to be there. That way, if there were any problems they could not say they did not know or could not do anything.'[62]

In Cambodia, 'Most of the complaints received [by members of the UNTAC Human Rights Component] in fact related to neighbourhood and land conflicts'.[63] A former local interpreter of the mission testified: 'Many people came to ask for help of all sorts, but especially to settle land problems. UNTAC could not help, it was much too complicated. But people tried all the same. When you arrived in a village, people said, "Oh, there's a big problem, you absolutely have to deal with it, peace is in danger"...In reality the *nez pointus* (literally 'pointed noses') did not understand much, and I think they rather complicated matters.'[64] That, in fact, was an accusation often made by local authorities, in sub-districts and districts. 'It was most difficult for us because UNTAC did not bring direct solutions, but simply added more problems.'[65] Situations of this sort multiplied fairly regularly around the country, including urban areas, as the deputy governor of the Phnom Penh municipality explained: 'The government of the State of Cambodia had organised a Council for resolution of land disputes, from the district to the village level, with right of appeal to the provincial level. If there were problems again, it was the Council of Ministers that decided. But on many occasions, UNTAC received requests from people who had lost in this process. UNTAC tried to resolve things in its own fashion, whereas a decision had already been made by the Council of Ministers. A compromise had to be found; if a decision was made by the Council of Ministers, UNTAC could not examine the case; if none had been made, UNTAC could intervene. So people went to see UNTAC before a case reached the Council. The UNTAC people were overrun by requests and became involved with numerous problems, which they could not manage because they could not know all that had gone on before. During the time of UNTAC's presence, people took advantage of it

---

[61] Interview with members of a *repoblación* of the Santa Clara region, north of San Vicente (September 11, 1995).

[62] Interview with José Isabel Membreño Amaya, member of the Executive Council of the Coordinadora de Comunidades y Repoblaciones of Chalatenango (Chalatenango, September 13, 1995).

[63] Recollection by a former UNV based in Svay Rieng province (Siem Reap, December 5, 1995).

[64] Recollection by Rous Nol, French-language interpreter for UNTAC with the election supervisor for the district, a retired teacher (Kompong Thom, December 16, 1995).

[65] Recollection by Huy Chiet, district chief of Maung Russey, December 7, 1995 (translation from Khmer).

by squating on public and private land because, in Phnom Penh at least, some had understood that the Human Rights people would protect them.'[66]

In these conflicts, generally longstanding, the return of refugees added more discord: there were conflicts over property and houses between people returning from the camps and Cambodians who had remained in their country. United Nations civpols often had a ringside seat for these quarrels. A former UNV has recalled: 'The instructions were that these matters should be dealt with by the normal justice system, but often problems were not settled and the civpols were just forced to handle them. People gave them no choice; if necessary they created an incident to force UNTAC to intervene, because it was feared that things would get out of hand.'[67] Immediately after the elections even more problems arose due to occupation of land following ill-considered election promises by some candidates.[68] There was a very similar scenario in Haiti, where groups of peasants sought to implicate the UN in settlement of land disputes. The most numerous cases occurred in the Bas-Artibonite region, where the question was particularly thorny.[69] In some cases peasant organisations created incidents in the hope of forcing the United Nations military to deal with this vital question that had gone unanswered for so long. In addition, they sometimes hoped to see the United Nations mission take up a position on their side (which would have considerably strengthened their position in the balance of forces between them and the big landowners). Similar problems confronted the UN in Somalia, when people were resettled in certain zones. Not having any directive for handling this type of dispute, UNOSOM members were often subjected to manipulation.

Besides land disputes, security problems are a subject on which social and community actors have vigorously pursued UN missions for favours. In Haiti, in the months following UNMIH's assumption of responsibility, incidents broke out in various regions. Their motive was 'to force them to do their work and make them understand that they must alter their

---

[66] Recollection by Kry Beng Hong, deputy governor of the Phnom Penh municipality (Phnom Penh, December 12, 1995).

[67] Interview with Béatrice Trouville, former UNV, based in Batheay district, Kampong Cham district (Phnom Penh, November 18, 1995).

[68] For example, at Svay Rieng FUNCINPEC candidates had promised land to people who voted for them; after the elections, some of them took possession of land by force and asked for help from UNTAC. Even if it adopted the pose of a passive observer, the mission was cornered: doing nothing amounted to taking the side of the occupiers.

[69] In the Bas-Artibonite region land property is extremely fragmented, property titles very uncertain and demographic pressure particularly strong. Between 1986 and 1991 land disputes led to numerous acts of violence and massacres, causing the death of hundreds of peasants whose homes and various property (cultivated fields and livestock) were destroyed.

methods in dealing with thieves and bandits.'[70] The method varied very little from one area to another: the population staged a noisy demonstration, cut national roads, closed or even burned public buildings, until a detachment of UN soldiers arrived on the spot. The soldiers were then received by a committee which explained all the problems. Similar cases were reported in El Salvador where, especially during the first months of its presence, ONUSAL saw people in many regions bringing to its offices criminals that they had caught. In other places there was a stream of denunciations to force the UN to deal with cases of crime that were proliferating while the new national police force was not yet trained. In some cases town halls were occupied to force the mission's teams in the regions to deal with most immediate disputes.[71] On November 19, 2003, in Chalatenango, the heads of local community organisations started a hunger strike. The group's objective on that occasion was broader: to force the establishment of a commission of inquiry into the death squads. 'On the 23rd day of the strike, ONUSAL called a meeting with European countries, the "friends of the Secretary General", the government and the FMLN. And they were well and truly forced to appoint the commission. For the UN, a hunger strike did not improve the landscape.'[72]

On various occasions, during the last phase of the UN mission in El Salvador, trade unions also insistently approached the mission for it to intervene for mediation of social conflicts. In February-March 1994, ONUSAL was implicated in this way in a conflict at the Rosales hospital in San Salvador. Here too the trade unions knew how to appear persuasive by threatening to incite disorder at the approach of elections. They obtained, through the mission's mediation, interviews with the government and some commitments in principle.[73] In November 1994, among the major social conflicts in which ONUSAL was implicated at that time, there was one affecting the Instituto del Seguro Social (ISS). In that case ONUSAL became the guarantor of observance of the agreements.[74] Similar requests were made to ONUSAL by demobilised soldiers who had formed associations. In September 1994 they occupied the parliament building for three days, taking 27 deputies hostage. They demanded the

---

[70] As recalled during a meeting with members of the committee of the Akolad Pwilbowo organisation, affiliated to the Tèt Kole movement: Pwilbowo, Nord department, May 3, 1995 (translation from Haitian Creole).

[71] Interviews with former members of ONUSAL who had been in the regions (Paris and San Salvador).

[72] Interview at Guarjila (north of Chalatenango), September 16, 1995 (translated from Spanish).

[73] 'Conflictos gremiales mediatizados', *Proceso* 603, March 16, 1994, pp. 7–8.

[74] Private interviews in San Salvador with senior ONUSAL officials, and *Proceso* 642, December 28, 1994, p. 23.

payment of allowances and grants of cultivable land, in accordance with the peace agreements. The affair was resolved peacefully after the demonstrators received an assurance from the government that talks would be held with ONUSAL mediation. In the first days of 1995 they occupied public buildings again; talks continued throughout January 1995, under the direction of the ONUSAL chief. They were concluded at the mission's headquarters in San Salvador on January 25.[75]

The most harsh and dangerous situations of this sort have involved taking of international personnel as hostages, as happened with Blue Helmets in Bosnia-Herzegovina and Sierra Leone. But such events can be preceded by more isolated acts which, even if they go no further, are no less sensitive for a United Nations mission. In fact, whether they wish it or not, members of operations often find themselves drawn far beyond the limits laid down by their mandates and their superiors. To a great extent the situations in which they are implicated, including occasions when politico-military actors are involved, are part of daily life, of 'ordinary' activity. However, that daily life shapes the profile that an operation gradually assumes in the eyes of the population. The fact that, in every case, local actors try to turn mission members into allies rather than neutral parties is not the least of the consequences of that process. In practice, winning an argument often means having the UN on one's side.

The UN as an alibi and a scapegoat

The United Nations and the broader 'international community', including the most hazy and contradictory elements covered by that term, are also an ideal scapegoat for political leaders in transitional situations that carry some risk to their power. The most usual tactic seeks to assign to the missions responsibility for the limitations of the peace process. In El Salvador, for example, the problems of insecurity, and a rising crime rate experienced in the wake of the peace process, were invariably attributed to the UN, which 'did not want to include a portion of the demobilised people in the agreements, hence the multiplying problems of violence. Many promises were also made for the demobilised but not fufilled.'[76] This language was used on many occasions in 1993 and 1994 by representatives of the armed forces and by the government, while there were

---

[75] 'Los desmovilidados son movilidados', *Proceso* 647, February 1, 1995, and local press articles.

[76] Interview with General Mauricio Ernesto Vargas, member of the Dialogue Commission, representative of the Salvadorian army in the negotiations, and Presidential Commissioner for the Implementation of the Peace Agreements. San Salvador, September 14, 1995 (translation from Spanish).

numerous demonstrations by ex-soldiers excluded from the reconversion programmes. The Salvadorian government tried to drag ONUSAL into involvement in dealing with a question that it had completely neglected itself. In doing so it passed on the message that it was not responsible for the rise in crime. The argument was also used in connection with another failure of the peace process: that of the Foro de Concertación Económico y Social. As an adviser to President Cristiani acknowledged, 'It is clear that for those who did not agree, it was easier to target the UN, to say it was the foreigner's fault.'[77]

During the period of a mission's presence and after its departure, for governments in place, this argument is a convenient one to use. The UN is useful both as a scapegoat and for washing one's hands of one's own responsibilities. In Haiti, President Aristide typified the politician who 'played all the time on the fact that, so he said, he was stymied by foreigners. He was very active in using that theme and sent people into the poorer districts to pass on a message', which he did not fail to use at meetings he held at the National Palace.[78] Demonstrations were also held at that time, targeted loosely at the UN, the IMF, the Americans, foreigners in general and the Prime Minister, Smarck Michel, whose relations with the President had gone very sour. There were many who saw the hand of the President behind this, like one head of a youth organisation: 'People were given transport to those demonstrations, and slogans were launched by certain individuals. Many people think Aristide himself was behind all that.'[79] In November 1995, the spectacular mobilisation that Aristide attempted on the disarmament question was aimed both at forcing UNMIH's hand and at side-tracking public opinion. 'It was a way of putting people on his side to show that if disarmament did not occur, it was not his fault but the fault of the international community.'[80] In that country the argument was also used by agents of the political system holding front-line positions regarding delicate subjects like elections and investigations into past human rights violations. The chairman of the Electoral Council at the time, Anselme Rémy, strongly criticised for the way he was preparing for the elections, said over a local radio on April 24, 1995: 'The United Nations is not releasing the money, and wants to give out contracts itself; it buys material from abroad although it could be

---

[77] Interview with David Escobar Galindo, member of the Dialogue Commission, San Salvador, September 14, 1995 (translation from Spanish).

[78] Private interview in Port-au-Prince, April 28, 1995, and interviews in the provinces (1995–6).

[79] Comment by Toto, member of the management committee of Chandèl, a youth organisation, Port-au-Prince, April 25, 1995 (translation from Haitian Creole).

[80] Private interview (Port-au-Prince, February 25, 1996).

found straight away, and cheaper, in the country. If there are delays, it is their fault.'

Indeed, one part of such a strategy is to condemn the inadequacy of funds provided or delay in making those funds available. It is true that this argument echoes real difficulties of linkage between the peace process and economic and social reconstruction. But the argument is aimed, above all, at covering up the failures of local political actors themselves. In El Salvador, President Cristiani regularly protested that 'the funds that Pérez de Cuellar promised to accompany the peace process did not arrive. For him, that explained why he could not honour all his commitments, for lack of means.'[81] Delays in establishment of the new national police force, in particular, were often explained in this way. The argument on that occasion was all the more practical because those delays made it possible for the army to justify its continued control of some key services. This same argument was advanced by the Chairman of the Banco de Tierras, one of the individuals who did the most possible to hold up the land transfer programme.[82] In Somalia, the political leaders on all sides complained that it was UNOSOM that had repudiated the Addis Ababa agreements by not implementing them. Condemning United Nations bias in the organisation of regional conferences, General Aydid accused UNOSOM over Radio Mogadishu of opposing the implementation of the Addis Ababa agreement instead of applying it. Several times he accused UNOSOM of sabotaging the peace process: why was UNOSOM not backing a peaceful solution? he asked over his radio station.[83]

Whatever the context, United Nations missions thus appear as a convenient scapegoat for political actors, but not only for them. When everything goes wrong, peacekeepers are also those who will be blamed for the rise in living costs or traffic jams in the capital—an accusation thrown at peace missions everywhere. Where, as in Somalia, tragic aspects are more important than anecdotal occurrences, the Blue Helmets appear as 'those who worsened disorder and destruction...Instead of calming all that down, the UN provoked another war. It is the UN that is behind the civil war. The Blue Helmets are partly responsible for the war.'[84]

[81] Recollection by Oscar Bonilla, former member of COPAZ, San Salvador, August 22, 1995.
[82] Interview with Raul García Prieto, San Salvador, September 1, 1995 (translation from Spanish).
[83] BBC Summary of World Broadcasts, April 5, 1993.
[84] Woman's interview in a movie made during ONUSOM II by Marcel Djama, anthropologist from Somalia: "Somalie, le prix du sang versé", *Arte et Point du Jour, France*, 1995.

HIGHLY VOLATILE BALANCE OF POWER

Even where the UN is readily accused of every evil, actors will emphasise the contrary—the UN's superficiality. This apparent contradiction relates to the ambivalence of feelings aroused by the presence of international forces, but also to the fact that not all actors base their assessments on exactly the same criteria. Above all, they do not draw the same lessons from them. This may be related to differences in the aims they pursue, but also to inequality of their positions in a given balance of forces, and difficulties in self-evaluation. While some political and social actors are aware of their relative power and the possibility they have of 'winning' in interaction with outsiders, others tend, on the contrary, to minimise their capacity for action. That assessment varies according to situations and over time. The same actor who feels sure of being in a position of strength at one given moment may feel constrained later on. This stems from the fact that power relations have been reshaped in the intervening time, or because the actor is involved in dealings relating to another domain without the same resources. These variations are all the more frequent because interaction does not take place in face to face contact between a mission and each actor in isolation; it rather fits into networks of often complex and shifting inter-relations. It is often necessary to reconstitute the acts and deeds of each actor in order to grasp the small but sometimes decisive changes, to understand the choices—sometimes surprising— made. Indeed, every actor is 'by turns and simultaneously creator and reducer of uncertainty, the one who creates problems and the one who solves them.'[85] One adapts as one can, on a daily basis, like most of the politicians and senior UN officials themselves. To manage these situations with less improvisation and amateurism than there has been until now on the part of outsiders, the need for at least a minimum of microsociology has to be accepted.

Why references to figures of 'spoilers' do not add up

The UN mission is not the only concern a local political actor has in mind. At the same time, he is most often engaged in an effort to maintain or alter his position in a locally defined configuration of forces; that is what matters most for him. Therefore, in a dual situation, such as those that occurred in El Salvador and Mozambique, everyone tends to react to the behaviour of the other side, including in the relationship with the United Nations mission. In general, when one side plays the game of confron-

---

[85] As Erhard Friedberg put it: see 'Strategic reasoning as a method of analysis and as a tool of intervention' in Francis Pavé (ed.), *L'analyse stratégique. Sa genèse, ses applications et ses problèmes actuels*, Colloque de Cerizy, Paris: Seuil, 1994, pp. 135–42.

tation with the mission, the other shows willingness to cooperate, and vice versa. Another example can be found in Somalia. In most instances, the position of the two main politico-military entrepreneurs with regard to the intervening external forces (whether the Multinational Force or UNO-SOM) varied according to the assessment each side made of its own forces in comparison with those of its main adversary. When UNOSOM was created in April 1992, Aydid was in a relative position of strength; this explains why he was against this deployment, which risked blocking his forward march. On his side, Mahdi hoped that it would at least facilitate a return to the status quo. In contrast, when the Multinational Force arrived (beginning of Operation Restore Hope) in December of the same year, Aydid's forces were in a bad situation on the fronts in the south and north-east of the country; hence openly welcoming of US troops.

In practice the choice of a more or less cooperative strategy depends a good deal on actors' assessment of their relative strengths. This perception is a moving one; the many parameters that fashion it can lead actors to change their attitude towards intervening forces, sometimes very rapidly. Similarly, those who choose not to cooperate can do so with extremely varied ultimate aims, rather than those suggested by most analyses with regard to 'spoilers' and other 'bad guys'. Here we reach the limits of analyses and doctrines of intervention inspired by game theory.[86] The large number of actors and parameters to take into consideration, and the often very rapid changes that characterise them, are ill suited for mathematical matrices. Moreover, they are overly simplistic schemes that end up complicating the peacekeepers' task rather than helping them on the ground. In Somalia the main politico-military leaders adapted as best they could to what they perceived of the strategy—and what a variable strategy that was!—followed by their interlocutors. They resisted when they could the control that the United Nations mission wanted to impose on them in one form or another and only cooperated, when resistance appeared to be counter-productive, continually testing the limits to which they could go. Perhaps more than in any other mission, those adjustments were often made from one day to the next. Aydid, who was personally opposed to the then UN Secretary General, organised a demonstration against him on his visit to Mogadishu, on January 3, 1993; but that did not stop him going the next day to the Addis Ababa conference and playing there, to a great extent, the card of collaboration with the UN.[87] This skilful mix of

---

[86] See Stephen John Stedman, 'Spoiler Problems in Peace Processes', *International Security* 22/2, Fall 1997, pp. 5–53.

[87] See especially, on this point, John L. Hirsch and Robert B. Oakley, *Somalia and Operation Restore Hope: Reflections on Peacemaking and Peacekeeping*, Washington: United States Institute of Peace Press, 1995, pp. 101–2.

cooperation and opposition to the United Nations was a constant in Mohamed Aydid's strategy, even during the most violent phase of his clash with United Nations and American troops. To give some examples, among others: in a press note dated June 6, 1993, the day after the attack on his movement's radio station, Aydid condemned the negative attitude of the United States and UNOSOM towards the Addis Ababa agreements and all the peace initiatives taken by his movement and others that had joined his side. He accused them of wanting to establish a 'puppet' government in their place. The tone was resolutely confrontational.[88] On the morning of June 9, 1993, leaflets were distributed in the streets of southern Mogadishu, calling on the United Nations 'neocolonialists', in very violent terms, to leave the country immediately. And yet, in the evening of that same day, Aydid signed a communiqué in which he said he was ready to cooperate again with the UN, in a very moderate tone that contrasted with the violence of his leaflets.[89] In the morning of June 11, at a press conference, Aydid tried to calm feelings and proposed a 'new alliance' between his movement and the United Nations. Even so, he warned that 'any violent action can lead to a general uprising of the population'. On June 19, 1993 a major demonstration was organised in Mogadishu to denounce the military operations by UNOSOM and the American troops. While threatening them with total war if they did not change their attitude towards him, Aydid declared to the crowd, 'We are gathered here today to show the international community that we are ready for peace as we have always been.' He made an appeal for a return to humanitarian operations and the application of the Addis Ababa agreements, on the matter of disarmament among others.[90] Aydid, an emblematic figure of the 'spoiler' if ever there was one, thus played continuously on the twofold register of cooperation and confrontation, which should be considered in a *continuum* along which attitudes can vary rapidly, in often highly volatile contexts.

The case of the Khmer Rouges movement's leaders in Cambodia provides another example of how actors behave in ways that are often considered contradictory, illogical or even 'irrational' because they played precisely on the twofold register of cooperation and confrontation. They sometimes do so simultaneously, often within a very short period of time.

---

[88] See press note of June 6, 1993.

[89] Extract from the communiqué: 'We want peace in Somalia so as to be able to bring the country back to normal conditions…For that, we need the United Nations troops to help us to check the bandits, maintain the cease-fire and complete the disarmament process. These are reasons for which we have truly welcomed and cooperated with UNITAF and now with UNOSOM II.'

[90] Source: text of M. F. Aydid's speech during the demonstration of June 19, 1993.

An actor who, like President Aristide in Haiti, is immediately put in the position of a privileged negotiating partner has a wider margin of manoeuvre. Awareness of this may have led him to occasionally overestimate his strength, especially on the question of a three-year extension to his term of office to 'compensate' for the years of exile, along with his successive manipulations of the elections. But over time Aristide undoubtedly won a great deal, as his dominant position led the rest of the political class to feel in a position of inferiority. '[Aristide] is the only one who can apply pressure. As for us, whatever we say and do, the UN, like the Americans, don't give a damn about us.'[91] The other Haitian politicians, limited to the position of 'spectators', also had to handle their ambiguous position vis-à-vis a military intervention that they did not want, that some had denounced until the very end, and that sealed their failure to find a way out of the crisis by themselves. They considered that they were 'in a strategy of withdrawal, of wait and see', while 'everyone [was] counting his forces'.[92] They thought they had 'no means of real intervention in the eyes of UNMIH...which did not give a damn about what they were able to think and do', and that the American administration cared even less for their opinion. Evans Paul, of the KID/FNCD, recalled: 'I remember that at the time of the crisis following the municipal and parliamentary elections, Mr Talbott came with a seven-point plan and, at a meeting with all the most important parties, said to us: "Good, the President has accepted this seven-point plan; so I think you will accept it also." In other words, there was no room for discussion. All of us were not in agreement with at least one of those points, but he made us clearly understand that he did not care one bit.'[93] Those who then constituted the main opposition to Aristide in fact committed strategic errors, especially on electoral questions where they had the most to gain, but whose importance they underestimated.[94] First, they failed to press their views on UNMIH, at a sufficiently early stage, on an electoral process that had in fact started badly. And even though they contested the composition of the

---

[91] Interview with Evans Paul, leader of the KID/FNCD, for long Aristide's main rival (Port-au-Prince, February 21, 1996) and other political leaders (Port-au-Prince, April–May 1995 and February–March 1996).

[92] Interview with Micha Gaillard of KONAKOM, candidate for the mayoralty of Port-au-Prince (Port-au-Prince, April 25, 1995). Some political parties, having also adopted an ambiguous attitude during the period of the coup d'état, considered that they 'had a bad part and had to keep a low profile' (that was notably the view of Serge Gilles, leader of the PANAPRA; interview in Port-au-Prince, March 1, 1996).

[93] Interview in Port-au-Prince, February 21, 1996.

[94] The official who was head of the electoral mission at one time testified that he had received very few requests or complaints at the time. (Interview with Colin Granderson, head of MICIVIH, Port-au-Prince, February 18, 1996).

Electoral Council, they failed to play the 'blackmail' card by threatening to withdraw from the elections. That was their first mistake, as Evans Paul recognised in retrospect: 'The mistake was to go to the elections with the Electoral Council and all the deficiencies we had been able to observe. For if the elections had been boycotted, there would have been no turnout and it would have been necessary to negotiate from that very moment.'[95] Serge Gilles, leader of the PANPRA, also testified: 'I have no problem in saying that we blundered. It is true that we should have threatened immediately to withdraw, but the Americans are very strong; they took us for a ride. I was at the head of negotiations for PANPRA, with KONAKOM and Evans Paul. They sent us high-level delegations each week and we were had, because it flattered us that, suddenly, people were taking an interest in us, and we took ourselves seriously.'[96] They pulled themselves together too late, after the first round of voting, when proof had been shown of their very weak following among an electorate that voted massively for the *Bo tab la* coalition. At that juncture, not only had their denunciation of the whole electoral process seriously lost credibility, but their withdrawal from the second round had limited impact. The elections could be declared 'free and fair' whether the small parties were there or not, satisfied or not.[97]

This impression of weakness explains, in particular, why the majority of Haitian politicians sought, even unconsciously, to limit the impact of the United Nations operation: 'Haitian affairs must be settled among Haitians'. While political actors interviewed in 1995 and 1996 generally considered that the United Nations mission 'was doing nothing', they actually wanted it to do no more than give out 'material compensations'. In 1997, the situation had hardly changed, while the United Nations mission had been much reduced and problems of insecurity were becoming more pressing. Yet a Haitian deputy declared, 'UNSMIH, we don't see it any more than we did UNMIH. They don't bother us because they do not meddle in our affairs; it's as if they were not there, since they do nothing. The most important things for the country, today, go on without them. It's better that way.'[98] For three years Haitian parliamentarians, who refused a public debate on the subject, constantly repeated that view: 'They do not care about us; we do not care about them'. This attitude echoed, on the

---

[95] Interview with Evans Paul of KID/FNCD and Victor Benoît, Secretary General of KONAKOM (Port-au-Prince, February 21 and 26, 1996).

[96] Interview in Port-au-Prince, March 1, 1996.

[97] I refer here also to interviews with political advisers of UNMIH (Port-au-Prince, February 25, 1996).

[98] Comment by Jasmin Joseph, deputy elected on the OPL ticket, but later joining the 'anti-neo-liberal bloc' (Paris, February 23, 1997).

other side, an attitude of withdrawal on the part of the United States and the United Nations. The formal nature of the objective initially laid down by the intervening forces—to install a new president on February 7, 1996—did not fundamentally solve anything, but it was convenient for everyone. Problems of power sharing could be settled among Haitians later. That attitude led the Haitian political class as a whole to resist, from the summer of 1997 onwards, all international pressure to find a solution to the crisis that has deprived the country of a constitutional government until President Aristide's forced exile at the end of February 2004.

Political actors most often pursue several ultimate ends at the same time, and adapt their behaviour to the responses to their expectations. If they find they cannot attain all their objectives at the same time, they have to make choices, and this too can explain the adoption of widely different behaviour from one situation to another. The fact of not being able to 'win on all fronts', as they put it sometimes, may, in particular, lead them to put themselves in a *de facto* position of weakness on points that they may not have considered as priorities. In El Salvador the FMLN, having given priority to the success of its transformation into a political force—which was indispensable to its very survival—sacrificed some aspects of the process, including the economic and social aspects, though these were essential for its militants and its affiliated organisations.

The assessment of each actor's relative position relates to more complex equations when the number of parties to peace agreements is multiplied. In Cambodia the PPC and FUNCINPEC shared, among other points in common, the view that the Khmers Rouges' withdrawal from the peace process was to their advantage: UNTAC could not risk turning another party against it. They used that argument to avoid respecting provisions of the agreements that were unfavourable to them, thinking that UNTAC had to handle them with care, especially if the mission wanted to organise elections at the scheduled date. At a meeting between the State of Cambodia and UNTAC on March 22, 1993, when the Civil Administration control team had begun its spot checks operation, Prime Minister Hun Sen directly threatened Yasushi Akashi with 'serious problems' and put this question to him (two months away from the elections): 'You are in the process of trying to persuade the other parties to take part in the elections, what will happen if you exceed your powers and I decide not to take part in the elections?'[99] The FUNCINPEC leaders, for their part, took a more cautious view of their relative strength. On the one hand they thought they could win the elections, pinning their hopes on the image of Sihanouk, still very powerful among the population. But Sihanouk re-

[99] Report of the meeting dated March 25, 1993, p. 4; source: UNTAC internal documents.

mained unpredictable and regularly gave signs of support for the Communist Prime Minister Hun Sen, his son's main rival. On the other hand, the entire leadership of the party consisted of people from the Diaspora, arriving in a country that was to a great extent unknown to them, where they would have to rebuild everything. The FUNCINPEC leaders clearly saw, from this point of view, that they were in a weak position vis-à-vis the PPC, in power for the past fourteen years. Consequently, they needed UNTAC to compensate both for their material deficiencies and for their poor knowledge of some aspects of their own country's reality. Pok Marina, Prince Ranariddh's spokesman throughout the peace process, has testified: 'You need to put yourself back in the state of mind of the core group of people who came back from abroad, who found themselves confined to Phnom Penh and to two or three places: the FUNCINPEC office, the house where all the FUNCINPEC people lived, Ranariddh's house and all there was around, a television and radio station, and the broadcasting antenna. At the end, we were very much withdrawn into ourselves. That is why logistics were so important at that time; without UNTAC's help, we would not have come through.'[100] The former FNLPK/PBLD, for its part, was all the weaker because it could not entirely count on the help of FUNCIPEC, though it had previously been its ally in the resistance. One of its members testified: 'When we held discussions with the FUNCINPEC people, outside the CNS, they backed us, but when we were at a CNS meeting, it was very different. They thought they would win and did not need us. Our representative on the CNS made requests, but nobody paid attention to them and UNTAC did not agree with them.'[101] Even for the PPC, the PBLD's positions hardly counted for anything, because it did not have the nuisance capacity that the Khmers Rouges still had. Besides, the PBLD knew that it could not win many seats in the elections. The strategy of its leader, Son Sann, was therefore to search for any possible route to arrive at power sharing without going to the polls. For that purpose it placed its hopes essentially on Prince Sihanouk and on many occasions suggested making the CNS a true government. Sihanouk regularly kept his former ally's illusions alive, but did not follow him.[102]

---

[100] Interview at Phnom Penh, December 15, 1995.

[101] Interview with Kem Sokha, PBLD deputy (Phnom Penh, December 2, 1995).

[102] At a special meeting of the CNS in Beijing on May 14, 1993, just before the elections, the FNLPK, through the intermediary of Say Bory, proposed the suspension of the electoral process, amendment of the CNS statute to confer all powers of a head of state on Prince Sihanouk, and alteration of the UNTAC mandate for it to be turned into Prince Sihanouk's executive. The Prince himself rejected the proposal, although he had pushed

How local actors pressure the UN

Son Sann no longer had the means to pressure as far as the UN was concerned. Despite his verbal gesticulations, he knew for a fact that his threats to resort to force were not credible and that he could not make the choice of pursuing armed confrontation, unlike the Khmers Rouges. The essential portion of his armed wing was autonomous and had already agreed to abide by the peace agreements; so non-participation by the PBLD could not fundamentally challenge their implementation. The party could brandish the armed threat, but it held no weight. On March 15, 1993 Ieng Mouly, one of its representatives on the CNS, thundered, 'The election will happen with blood. Some of our people want to go back to the jungle to fight, to join the Khmer Rouges.'[103] Two years later, the same man admitted, 'It was not possible to envisage taking up arms again. No country was going to continue to give us military aid. In addition, among our fighters nobody wanted to return to fight on the border. We had no other choice than to take part in the elections. Yes, we were bluffing. But you know, in that little game nobody was fooled.'[104] Son Sann's son, who succeeded his father as head of the PBLD, regretted this: 'UNTAC did not give a damn about what we said or requested. They only gave way on questions of detail, which did not commit them too much, like making sure that there was land for resettling repatriated people. But they fundamentally only gave way to people who had kept arms in their hands. We should have kept our armed forces and police forces.'[105] That situation in fact explained the split between Ieng Mouly, who was convinced of the party's weakness, and Son Sann, who supported a hard line even though his immediate entourage felt, at least in retrospect, that 'withdrawing would have signed the party's death warrant'.[106] Two weeks before the elections, the PBLD leadership seized on the pretext of the murder of two of its members to threaten again to withdraw. 'Vague assurances from the international community' were enough for it to agree to 'play the game'.[107] Actually the potential of politico-military actors to do harm depended in

his former allies into putting it forward. See minutes of the meeting and interviews with Ieng Mouly and Say Bory, two former PBLD representatives on the Conseil National Suprême (Phnom Penh, November 28 and 30, 1995).

[103] Statement by Ieng Mouly, reported in Far Eastern Economic Review, March 15, 1993.

[104] Interview with Ieng Mouly, Phnom Penh, November 28, 1995.

[105] Interview with Son Soubert, Secretary General of the PBLD (Phnom Penh, December 2, 1995).

[106] Interviews with Kem Sokha, PBLD deputy, and Say Bory and Ieng Mouly, the two FNLPK/PBLED representatives on the CNS (Phnom Penh, November–December 1995).

[107] Interview with Son Soubert (Phnom Penh, December 2, 1995).

part on the possibilities they had of refusing to play the cooperation game. Loss of the capacity to resort to war was generally a major turning point in that respect, something that was understood very early on by the PPC and FUNCINPEC, which only demobilised about 30 percent of their troops.

In Mozambique the two parties at first delayed handing over to ONUMOZ the full list of their forces and their arms, ammunition, mines and other explosives.[108] The rate of movement of troops into the cantonment and demobilisation zones was thereby greatly slowed down. RENAMO linked the cantonment of its men to the deployment of all, then of at least 65 percent, of the ONUMOZ troops.[109] For RENAMO, the threat of reopening the conflict was for long the only significant lever at its disposal. This strategy made it possible, among other things, for its leader, Afonso Dhlakama, to maintain pressure so as to obtain more generous financial compensation. However, he was not fully in control of that lever. Indeed, RENAMO saw its military apparatus disbanding: fighters wanted to put it all behind them, to return home after receiving a small hand-out which, thanks to foreign aid, was not completely insulting. Paradoxically, Dhlakama's strength was above all related to FRELIMO's suspicion that he had aggressive aims. Yet the war option no longer had any prospects from the moment when the UN, taking note of what had happened in Angola, decided at the outset that elections would not take place as long as the military aspects of the agreement were not completely settled.[110] That decision was regularly invoked by the Special Representative of the Secretary General. On the government side, while senior officers, anxious to retain their prerogatives (especially in economic matters), tried on many occasions to play on tension, they were not followed by their troops. In August 1994 garrisons revolted and demobilised on their own initiative, forcing the government and the army to stop delaying the demobilisation.[111]

It is thus a real turning point in a peace process when local military actors lose the possibility of using, with a minimum level of credibility, this threat of resort to force. It can be difficult to manage for those who

[108] See Report of the Secretary-General on Mozambique (S/25518, April 2, 1993), para. 12.

[109] That occasioned successive delays in the demobilisation timetable, while the UN Secretariat struggled to obtain contributing states' troops quickly. Thus the location of the 49 cantonment points for demobilised fighters was not decided until the end of February 1993.

[110] See Report of the Secretary-General on the United Nations Operation in Mozambique (S/23892 of December 3, 1992), on the basis of which the Security Council decided on the creation of ONUMOZ, para. 30.

[111] In different bases, between 80 and 98 per cent of government soldiers, to whom the question was put systematically during their registration by ONUMOZ, replied, despite the pressure of their officers present, that they wanted to be demobilised.

have not succeeded, in the meantime, in making up entirely for that foreseeable loss of power. In El Salvador the FMLN leaders, who used military pressure until the negotiations were actually in progress, practiced delaying tactics for several months. The government tried to maintain the level of application of the agreements to a minimum, indispensable for the process not to be blocked, but avoided starting any fundamental reform while waiting for the FMLN to demobilise a substantial portion of its troops. The FMLN responded by slowing down considerably the demobilisation of its fighters and the handing over of its weapons. The tactics were classic ones: stretching out the time scale for demobilisation, making stock lists minimising the amount of weapons at one's disposal, handing over the most antiquated weapons, etc. When, at the end of September 1992, the army refused to provide the list of military officers who were supposed to leave the forces under the purge provisions, the FMLN threatened to attack strategic sites in the capital. The FMLN still had considerable stocks of explosives and one of its branches, the ERP, still had a certain number of missiles. The surrender of those weapons was negotiated against the purge of the army and plans for reconversion of FMLN commanders. This crisis was one of the most serious that the peace process went through. However, the process of turning the FMLN into a political party, even with delays, made progress. The leaders of the Front knew that they were gradually losing their principal means of applying pressure: 'We had not foreseen that once the agreements were signed, such a long period of negotiation would start…And that second phase was more difficult for us because, while we were tackling such delicate subjects as the training of the new police force and the maintenance of control by the armed forces over some key services, we had already laid down our arms. We no longer had anything to apply pressure with. ONUSAL was alone facing the government to demand that it should abide by the agreements.'[112] For the former fighters, entering the cantonment zones was also a turning point: 'We no longer really had the means to create problems, and it was wrong to counter on the Front's leadership. The FMLN had less and less power.'[113] The moment when a group loses its armed nuisance capacity is particularly critical; indeed, it brings a substantial change in the balance of forces and can upset the balance with dramatic implications for the future of the peace process. It is important in such cases that war is no longer a credible option. What

---

[112] Interviews with Shafick Jorge Handal, General Coordinator, head of the FMLN delegation to the negotiations (San Salvador, September 15, 1989), as well as heads of various branches of the FMLN (August–September 1995).

[113] Recollections recorded in the Santa Clara region, north of San Vicente, September 11, 1995.

counts—more than the incapacity of one party or the other to win is the estimated cost of continuing the conflict, the physical capacity of the main armed groups to choose that option, and the scale of outside backing.

Conversely, as long as actors have an armed force at their disposal and think they can use it to their advantage, they have few reasons to abandon the violent way for negotiations. They are all the less inclined to collaborate with a UN mission which, by its presence, obstructs their movements. In such situations all politico-military actors may, at one moment or another, feel able to refuse to cooperate with the United Nations troops. As long as actors are still in a preliminary phase of negotiation aimed at possible peace agreements, keeping the military card in their hands is indispensable to acquiring a position of strength. In Somalia the Addis Ababa agreement provided for the 'total disarmament' of the country; the UN mission was supposed to control its smooth implementation. But the main politico-military leaders did everything to ensure that in practice it was made impossible; they sometimes opposed it violently. They had at least one thing in common—waiting for UNOSOM to reduce its presence or even to leave the country before re-emerging. While some, like Aydid, tried to precipitate the outcome because the mission was becoming too much of a threat to their power, others waited more patiently. In fact, when in the spring of 1993 Aydid chose the route of confrontation with the UN, he found himself at an impasse. At this point in March 1993 the Addis Ababa conference had given UNOSOM a mandate to proceed to disarmament of the factions and facilitate political reconstruction. Aydid had certain indications that the Americans were determined to establish effective control over heavy weapons. In addition to this, his ally, Jess, had been held in check at Kismayo and UNOSOM was beginning to establish a new police force that he suspected would short-circuit him. His shift to the offensive seemed to him the only way to try to influence events in his favour. Conversely, a year and a half later, aware of the need for the United Nations troops to withdraw in the best possible conditions, he negotiated that withdrawal in the way best suited to his interests. As he had been at the centre of the conflict with UNOSOM and the American troops, Aydid was the best able to play that other game.[114]

In this sort of context, keeping the military tool in hand is also indispensable for some groups that think they will not survive (economically, among other senses) in a context of restored peace. The Khmers Rouges

---

[114] To negotiate the withdrawal as best it could, the US administration sent back to Somalia Ambassador Oakley, who had dealt with the political side of UNITAF. See especially the report of the mission sent by the Security Council to Somalia in October 1994, to pass the message to the Somali factions concerning UNOSOM's probable withdrawal (S/1004/1245, November 3, 1994).

movement in Cambodia is a good illustration of such a situation, which is common in contemporary wars. The movement's survival in fact required control over people. Opening occupied zones up to control by UNTAC was therefore unthinkable. In the view of an expert on the movement, Steve Heder, the problem for PDK was clearly 'will we survive the peace process?' They cruelly lacked of human resources (the leadership was getting older, the younger members lacked of competency), but also material and political ones. Indeed, at the time the movement was experiencing many defections, and former members have testified to the weariness and bad conditions prevailing in the zones under its control.[115] Ta Mok, a supporter of the hard line, was said to have led offensives of which the two Khmers Rouges representatives on the CNS, Khieu Samphan and Son Senn, disapproved, considering them to be diplomatically counterproductive. At a meeting at Pailin on February 6, 1992, Pol Pot explained that the movement only existed to the extent that it could continue to apply pressure, to have an offensive policy. On the eve of the elections, a section of the movement's leadership changed strategy; not only did it make no obstruction to the holding of the elections, it made at least some of the population under its control take part in the voting.

This example underlines one of the difficulties posed by situations of 'no war, no peace' in which UN peace missions are, in practice, called upon to intervene more and more. In such contexts a major element in the assessments in how local actors view their strength relates to their understanding of the intentions of member states that have most influence on the crisis, as well as the backing and pressure that they can expect. They test their international interlocutors, calculate the distance (often considerable) between public discourse and real commitments and decisions taken behind the scenes. Even actors that are in a dominant position locally may lose some of their relative advantages when they are subjected to very strong foreign pressure—especially economic pressure—providing, of course, the pressure is credible. In contrast, others who may appear, in certain situations, in a militarily weak position, like Ali Mahdi in Somalia, can for a moment hope to regain at the conference table what they have lost on the ground. In Bosnia-Herzegovina, the three main parties to the conflict had to take into consideration the pressures applied to them—economic sanctions for the Serbs, threats of sanctions for the Croats, the need to preserve their image abroad for the Bosnian Muslims—and their backing, which was also inconsistent, among the foreign states most

---

[115] Interview in Phnom Penh, November 30, 1995, and analysis documents prepared by Heder under UNTAC auspices, which I consulted.

directly involved in the crisis. All found themselves under constraint at one time or another in the process.

Even if they think they have much to lose in a peace process, not all actors have the means to oppose it openly. For those who find themselves in that position, the only possible way ahead is often in delaying, which in itself can be a means of pressure not to be ignored. This situation is often characteristic of local employees of the state, like judges and policemen. It is rare that they refuse cooperation openly; but they will play tricks as much as they can and cause obstruction whenever they are able, taking advantage, in particular, of their better knowledge of the local situation than that of their United Nations counterparts. In Cambodia, at meetings with UNTAC control teams, ministers and directors of the ministry departments regularly brandished the threat of suspending their cooperation or ceasing to ensure a certain number of functions vital for the smooth running of the country, knowing that the UN would be incapable of taking over from them.[116] The former deputy governor of Battambang, frequently mentioned in UNTAC internal documents for having given trouble to the control teams, recalled what he called his 'work method': 'As I was deputy governor responsible for the Plan, for the first months the UNTAC people came to see me constantly to ask me for things directly, and they gave me no time to make inquiries, to see what the problem was. That never stopped. At one moment, I said to myself, "You're letting yourself be had, old chap." So I asked the Director of Civil Administration for Battambang for everything to be channelled through him. I told him, "From now on, I will no longer answer questions from anyone." Finally, we agreed that there would be monthly meetings to settle problems. At these meetings, they told me what was not going well for them, and then I conducted my own inquiries. Apart from the meetings, I refused to answer any request of any sort. They tried hard but they did not succeed. After that, they did not bother us anymore, and they did not enter into our affairs anymore.'[117] Study of UNTAC archives gives evidence of that effective capacity for bypassing. The account of the deputy governor of the Phnom Penh municipality is equally instructive: 'We held meetings twice a week at the municipal offices, or more if there were urgent problems. With the [UNTAC] personnel who were permanently based at the municipal offices, there were some misunderstandings. Often they did not believe what Cambodian officials told them. So we said to our colleagues, "Don't get annoyed, leave them to it, you'll see". And indeed, invariably, the

[116] See report of control visits and meetings held with the various ministries concerned (UNTAC confidential memoranda).
[117] Interview with Teas Heanh (Battambang, December 7, 1995).

UNTAC people quickly came up against an obstacle somewhere and were obliged to come back to us because they needed our help. They needed us because they knew practically nothing about the country; they could not themselves find answers to their questions. So they were obliged to compromise.'[118] The nuisance capacity of actors of that sort, though far from being unlimited, can none the less be a serious curb on UN teams' actions.

Lastly, local political actors are aware that it is difficult for UN peace missions to admit failure. If they do not succeed, they must at least continue to search for peace, to keep negotiations open. To do that they need a minimum of cooperation from the main local political actors, at least as much as those actors need them. In Cambodia, just before the elections, Yasushi Akashi declared to the international media, 'I cannot allow myself not to succeed'—a warning that he repeated on many occasions at meetings of the Conseil National Suprême. From the moment when the Khmers Rouges withdrew, the cooperation of the other parties, especially the State of Cambodia and FUNCINPEC, was crucial. Those two parties did not fail to seize the opening, especially by exercising blackmail about withdrawal, with varying success. In addition, the fact that the date of the elections was fixed at a very early stage by the United Nations Security Council, and was clearly indicated as a criterion for success for the operation, provided an additional lever for the politicians concerned. 'The UNTAC people were haunted by the thought that another faction would withdraw from the elections; that all their work would have been reduced to nothing. At all costs there had to be elections, and the results had to be accepted. Then, they could leave. That was very clear, and there was no reason why we should not play on that. So, yes, we regularly threatened to withdraw from the electoral process, as a tactic, in particular to get additional help in logistical terms.'[119] 'FUNCINPEC acted out a comedy to obtain some facilities from the United Nations. I personally went several times to see Akashi and some of his collaborators, telling them, "We are thinking of withdrawing if you do not give us satisfaction", or indeed, "if you do not give us means for travelling around". That was how Akashi lent us helicopters…Everyone applied blackmail about non-participation, because it was undoubtedly the thing that made the United Nations most afraid. It put them in a blue funk.'[120] Once the elections had passed, the results had to be accepted by the various parties. It was at that stage that

[118] Interview with Kry Beng Hong (Phnom Penh, December 12, 1995).
[119] Interview with Pok Marina, spokesman for Prince Ranariddh throughout the peace process (Phnom Penh, December 15, 1995).
[120] Interview with Sam Rainsy, second FUNCINPEC representative on the Conseil National Suprême under UNTAC (Phnom Penh, November 27, 1995).

the PPC mainly applied its own blackmail.[121] As denunciation of rigging and explicit challenging of the elections were not enough, the threat of secession by Prince Chakrapong, after the elections in June 1993, forced UNTAC to change its view. Though the elections had 'gone off well', everything risked being put in doubt again. Prime Minister Hun Sen exploited this to seize back the advantage. On a visit that the Special Representative of the Secretary General paid to him, he spoke to him of the possibility of a 'bloodstained revolt by the PPC'.[122]

But, in that country, Sihanouk was the uncontested master of blackmail about withdrawal. The issue was most immaterial for him, since he had no specific obligation under the Agreements and had neither an administration nor an army, nor even really a political party at his disposal. His resources were essentially symbolic in nature, but they were far from being negligible. Sihanouk knew that among the foreign governments involved in the process, several considered that his withdrawal would put peace in peril. When he frequently ran off to sulk in Beijing, he was playing on that register. Were ambassadors and the Special Representative of the Secretary General not pressing him to change his position? However, Sihanouk also knew that he was in a delicate position. Even regarding the possible holding of presidential elections he changed his opinion several times, trying to decide what would ensure his regaining of status in the best conditions; if there was no such election, he feared that he would lose any role on the political stage, yet to submit himself to universal suffrage risked bringing him down from his pedestal.[123] As for the parliamentary elections, he feared that they would not allow the restoration of the monarchy; he was not sparing in criticisms on that point. When he understood that the polls would take place anyway, he rejoined the process at the last moment. After the first challenge to the elections, he set himself up, with the help of Hun Sen, as an indispensable mediator.

---

[121] Interview with Om Yien Tieng, political adviser to Hun Sen, with special responsibility for the follow-up to the electoral process (Phnom Penh, December 19, 1995); UNTAC internal documents; personal archives of former PPS representatives on the CNS (including correspondence addressed to UNTAC).

[122] See Yasushi Akashi, 'The Challenge of Peacekeeping in Cambodia', *International Peacekeeping* 1/2, Summer 1994, p. 207.

[123] In Cambodia kingship is in fact of divine essence. And Sihanouk never concealed his ambition to regain his title of King, which he did in 1993. In a message dated February 17, 1993 he said: 'I consider that in refusing to "lower myself" into a presidential election…I will keep my moral authority intact as "the Father of the Nation, a neutral father above political factions and parties", the Conciliator, the "Bridge" between those factions and parties, the Reconciler, the rebuilder (when the time comes) of national unity and the territorial integrity of Kampuchea.' See also 'Message of Norodom Sihanouk of Cambodia to the People of Cambodia' (Beijing, January 26, 1993) and his letter to the Australian foreign minister on January 28, 1993.

Missions are also dependant on political actors who control *de jure* or *de facto* a portion of the territory, especially when the UN has to take on the tasks of administration, as in Cambodia, East Timor and Kosovo. In these cases, but also where vestiges of the state administration are still in place, local employees of the state, policemen, and sometimes members of the armed forces or militias often use the register of circumvention, or obstruction, in dealings with UN staff: they delay granting an interview, they cancel meetings at the last moment, they deliver information in driblets, etc. Generally, members of United Nations missions acknowledge that it is difficult to prove that there has been a will for obstruction pure and simple. With some exceptions the individuals concerned have, in the meantime, shown great courtesy, making many declarations of good intentions, declaring themselves ready to 'cooperate'. In reality, however, most often 'nothing happens'. Considering, notably, the difficulties encountered by personnel in understanding an unknown environment in a very short period of time, it is generally very difficult for them to decide on the right reaction to face that sort of behaviour. This kind of obstacle will never be entirely removed. It will always be relatively easy to get round the actions of a mission or any other 'outsider', by various routes. In these conditions the issue for members of missions, who embark on interaction with people acting this way, is to induce them to choose to cooperate rather than finding a way round. For that the people concerned must see an interest in doing so, if only for their own future. In fact, to involve them more directly in reconstruction issues can help gain better cooperation, as proved, though too rarely, in certain cases. Former members of missions have noted changes in the behaviour of people they had to deal with (policemen, judges or local representatives of the administration, for example) when they had the feeling that reform of the system of government was truly underway. Then employees of the state showed themselves more inclined to cooperate, if only to guarantee their future and their possible reconversion. To put things in the reverse, they knew that they might lose much if they would not agree to take part in the reform of the state. Contacts that I had in various countries with actors corresponding to this description tend to confirm this hypothesis. In dealing with actors of this type, the reconstruction gamble must be taken more openly. Unfortunately, this supposes the 'international community' is serious about the reforms, which is far from always being the case.

In other instances the ruling governments can cause crises to arise, which are always difficult for the United Nations' image. In El Salvador the senior UN officials 'knew very well that a crisis was never very good for their image. Repeated visits by De Soto (the UN negotiator of the peace agreements) and Goulding (then the head of UNDPKOs) caused confusion, and worried the embassies. They had to reassure them...If ONUSAL wanted things to continue to go well for it, it had to adapt to save the process as a whole...When there was a problem or when they told us: "This or that part of your commitments has not been carried out", we said, "You should make a move in our direction, the most important thing is to save the process".'[124] The problems surrounding the purge of the armed forces, the retention of death squads, and the creation of the new police force are explained partly by the concessions made by the United Nations to maintain the 'success' of the operation. That concern was, almost as much as in Cambodia, especially strong at the moment when elections approached. The former coordinator of the Salvadorian institution responsible for supervision of elections has commented: 'The electoral process just had to take place; it was like a novel by García Márquez, "Chronicle of a Success Announced". We knew that whatever deficiencies could already be seen, the process could not be placed in doubt again, it had to be a success and it would be. ARENA, which essentially controlled the structures organising the elections, was swallowed up in the big breach opened.'[125]

In Haiti President Aristide was clearly aware that neither the United Nations nor, even more, President Clinton—who had committed himself personally to the problem—could allow the process to fail. When he launched his appeal for disarmament by the population in November 1995, he made quite explicit threats for President Clinton's ears. And when Aristide declared, 'The month of November 1995 should be a month of peace, of success, so that the month of November 1996 can be a success in the United States,' he alluded to the US President's desire to be able to boast of a success in Haiti that would contribute to his own re-election. To 'foreigners in general' he proclaimed, 'You need me, as I need you. Count on me and show me that I can count on you.'[126]

The international calendar, which so often weighs on local logics, can, in some circumstances, also be converted into an instrument of pressure on foreign intervention forces.[127] That type of argument was also used in

---

[124] Interview with Rodolfo Parker, adviser to President Cristiani during the negotiations and former head of the Coordination Unit for Application of the Peace Agreements (San Salvador, August 29, 1995).

[125] Interview with Felix Ulloa hijo, former Coordinator of the Junta de Vigilencia and then magistrate at the Supreme Electoral Tribunal (San Salvador, September 1, 1995).

[126] As quoted in the *Haïti-Hebdo* bulletin, 89, November 21, 1995.

[127] There are some similarities with, in the case of Bosnia-Herzegovina, the negotiation and then the beginning of implementation of the Dayton Accords, in the midst of the election period in the United States. There too, while the calendar probably did not coincide with that of local actors in the conflict, the latter had in this way an obvious

Mozambique by Afonso Dhlakama when, on the first day of voting, he announced his withdrawal from the elections; the United Nations had to make concessions if it did not want to repeat the failure in Angola. Dhlakama's calculation then was simple: the UN could not allow itself to have elections with only FRELIMO and a few scattered small parties. Four months earlier, on a visit to the United Nations Secretariat in New York, he had declared publicly, 'Regarding the Secretary General, Mozambique could well be his only success during his term as head of the UN; if he misses that opportunity, he could also lose his second term.'[128]

NEITHER 'INDIFFERENT' NOR 'APATHETIC': WHY LOCAL COMMUNITIES PROTECT THEMSELVES FROM THE PEACEKEEPERS

In order to act, local actors need the UN missions to give them, in one way or another, a minimum of space, and a minimum amount of attention. Social and community actors often lack both. In individual cases, they may try to force the members of missions to take their problems into account, but most often they rapidly come up against the limits of that strategy. In El Salvador ONUSAL was widely perceived to be giving almost exclusive attention to the two parties to the agreements. Even the Human Rights NGOs—though at least one of the mission's divisions had to keep up regular contact with them according to its mandate—were conscious of carrying little weight. Their requests were not acted upon. They could slam the door during discussions, but that would have no result. Contacts with them were not vital for the mission. The scenario was absolutely identical in Haiti where the 'utilitarian' idea that the United Nations had of NGOs was denounced by the latter: 'When they come to look for us it's because they need information, or need to justify work they have already done, but they are not going to take any account of our opinion, and that is not going to change one iota of their policy direction.'[129] The organisation responsible for supervising the elections in El Salvador (the Junta de Vigilencia) had the same experience. Despite a considerable labour of follow-up and proposals throughout the process (especially for the creation of an electoral register, a key to many problems, in view of the non-participation of the left in elections throughout the war years), it did

---

means to apply pressure on the Democrat administration, which had mounted the battlements on the Bosnia problem.

[128] As reported in *Le Monde*, June 19, 1994.

[129] Interview with Jean-Claude Jean, Secretary General of the Platform of Haitian Human Rights Organisations (Port-au-Prince, April 20, 1995).

not succeed in getting its analyses adopted. It had no way of imposing its ideas.[130]

In order to alter the balance of forces, and change the rules of the game, social and community actors must draw on their own strength or find allies, especially among political actors. Most often they find both lacking. In El Salvador social actors were, for the most part, in a weak position at the end of the conflict. That was particularly true of the trade union movement, which was, in addition, highly dependent on the FMLN. On land disputes and on the electoral frauds the FMLN dropped the social actors, instead of drawing support from their base to put pressure on the UN.[131] In Haiti social actors, like most of the political ones, as a whole found themselves in a delicate position with regard to the foreign forces' mere presence. The leaders of the two main platforms regrouping indigenous NGOs have testified to this, each in his own manner: 'Even at the psychological level, we are not at ease with our conscience, even regarding those people's presence. It's something we are obliged to accept, that's all. So the position is this: "Get through the time you have to spend here, and then go".'[132] 'Members of the Inter-OPD grouping were puzzled, because we were helpless in the face of the putschists' power... There is a lot of resentment, fear; everyone refuses even to start discussing it. One should not forget, either, that many organisations have serious problems within their ranks. In those conditions, they are unable to react.'[133] So essentially, they remained in the background. Those social actors were still less capable of giving backing to the community movement, itself much weakened by three years of repression and forced to 'go underground'. Constant moving around by its members, for self-protection and survival, also considerably disorganised contacts that had served as a basis for past mobilisation movements. The organisations in that sector did not generally consider themselves capable of deploying a 'concerted strategy', limiting themselves to ad hoc initiatives.[134] Essentially, they considered that they 'did not have sufficient strength to face the intervening forces in a concerted manner.'[135] That position of inferiority in

---

[130] Interview with the former coordinator of the Junta de Vigilencia (San Salvador, September 1, 1995).

[131] Interviews with various leaders of the FMLN as well as representatives of trade unions, organisations participating in the Forum, and community organisations (San Salvador, August–September 1995).

[132] Interview with Emile Eyama Jr, READA/KAP, platform of popular education organisations (Port-au-Prince, February 23, 1996).

[133] Interview with Gérald Mathurin, member of the coordinating committee of Inter-OPD (Inter-Organisations Privées de Développement) (Port-au-Prince, April 27, 1995).

[134] Investigations in various regions of the country in 1995 and 1996.

[135] Those words are from Moïse Jean-Charles, spokesman for the Mouvman Peyizan Milo

which social and community actors were very often placed tends, as we have seen, to be reinforced by the way in which UN staff generally approach local societies. That has consequences for possibilities of reconstruction in the contexts under consideration.

Among social and community actors, attitudes of avoidance, in various forms, often appears as the ultimate resort of the weak when other registers of action seem to have been exhausted or have not given the expected results. That is a strategy that has been tried out for a long time, in many contexts, in the face of anyone representing the power of the state; it leads to adoption of attitudes often described from the outside as 'indifference' or 'apathy'. Nevertheless, it is a true strategy of action, which takes the form of what actors themselves call 'passive resistance': refusing to answer questions from peacekeepers—sometimes on the pretext of not understanding the questions, in the knowledge that interpreters can play a part in that strategy—or providing false information, as happened, for example, in the poorer districts of San Salvador, some Haitian cities including Port-au-Prince, and more recently in Pristina, Freetown and Bunia. According to a well-tested scenario, people play tricks, they may sometimes play on derision or hold the UN up to ridicule,[136] and they deal with serious matters 'away from outsiders'. That behaviour is equally active when it includes decisions to settle, at the popular level, problems left aside by the 'foreigners' or actually caused by their presence.

However, even if a general trend towards a bypassing strategy can be observed among the population, that strategy never exhausts the possibilities of action by the actors concerned. Sudden transition to a movement of anger is generally not neutral, especially if it occurs among people who until then seem to have ignored the peacekeepers. It can also mean a call for help, as when, in districts thought to be calm or even 'apathetic', stones are thrown at a patrol, or a local office of a mission. The last thing to do then is to withdraw; on the contrary, efforts should be made to understand why such an incident has occurred.

It should never be forgotten that the vast majority of community actors with which United Nations missions interact have also to live, to a large extent, in a setting of day-to-day survival, which obliges them to be inventive and adaptable. In fact community actors generally show a capacity for very rapid adaptation to the attitudes of those they have to deal with. Probably their skills in this respect are much greater than those of the

---

(Milot, Nord department, May 1, 1995) and Auguste Claudel, leader of MUPAK (Mouvman Inite Pèp Okay) (Les Cayes, May 13, 1995).

[136] Even in Ituri in the eastern Congo, foreign soldiers could be surprised that Congolese seemed to be taken so many things 'as a joke'.

missions themselves, whose adjustments require more time. The testimony of former mission members is there to recall that community actors can pay court to them one day because they need their help and ignore them the next day, or even insult them if they are displeased with the attitude of the person they have to deal with. As inhabitants of poorer districts in cities where UN operations were in progress, often repeated to me, 'You need to adapt yourself'. 'When we see there are things that may be worth taking, we take them; when we see there is a risk of it not being to our advantage, we don't take them.' In Cambodia the account of a former UNTAC member, present at Svay Rieng in June 1993 at the time of the attempted secession by Chakrapong after the elections, provides another illustration of that capacity to pass rapidly from one attitude to another: 'That evening, it was striking: everyone was turning his back on us, literally. Some landlords of houses where UNTAC members were living threw their tenants out because authority had changed hands. When the attempt failed, people turned round again, as if nothing had happened.'[137]

---

[137] Recollection by Fabienne Luco, former UNV working within UNTAC (Siem Reap, November 5, 1995.

6

FORGOTTEN PROMISES
HOW THE UN PRETENDS TO ACHIEVE PEACE

UN staff always bring in their luggage, if not a fully coherent project, at least an idea of the engineering supposed to contribute to the establishment of 'peace and stability' in the country concerned. In that sense they generally fall prey to the classical reflex, well known in the field of development aid, of proposing a new framework from outside, believing the local society is incapable of proposing one of its own, and has thus been plunged into war. Such a framework is twofold. It consists, on the one hand, of new rules based on different rationalities, especially technical. These essentially govern the peace engineering promoted by the UN missions, engineering which varies fairly little from one mission to another despite differences of context: formal democratic grammar, rules aimed at establishing a state based on the rule of law, procedures for disarmament and reintegration of former combatants, economic and institutional reforms, etc.. On the other hand, new institutions are to be built, destined both to become 'representative' interlocutors and to enforce the new rules. Peace missions deployed in the last decade had more or less ambitious mandates in this regard, but they were based on the same models and encountered the same difficulties when applied on the ground. The democracy component, for example, poses problems linked not only to an underestimation of the stakes attached to founding elections, but also to a failure to articulate them with the various transformations affecting a society just emerging from conflict. Such a society is supposed to carry out a triple 'transition': political, socio-economic, and in the realm of security. Indeed, beyond the transition from war to peace the issue at stake is the (re)construction of the state and consequent (re)definition of the social contract. That relates to such crucial subjects as the reconfiguration of politico-economic networks and ways of rent sharing (which includes, in most countries, land tenure questions); the redefinition of the state functions, especially in matters of security and justice (what aid programmes would call 'the rule of law'); and relations among the various territories of the state (issues of 'decentralisation' which take various forms according to their context). To a great extent these processes underline the intrinsic connection between the respect for procedures aimed at reducing the peculiar uncertainties of periods of transition and the substance of the democratic project itself.

THE LIMITS OF IMPOSED 'PROCEDURAL DEMOCRACY' IN POST-WAR SOCIETIES

Long queues of voters, often looking wretched, waiting patiently for hours, sometimes days, for their turn to vote under the more or less vigilant gaze of people wearing UN jackets and caps, sometimes even civpols and Blue Helmets. This scene is one of the rare images that the public gets of a peace operation. The holding of elections in a calm atmosphere, in a country that is just emerging from a war, has for long been considered a sign that the UN peace operation had succeeded. Indeed, the process of 'democratisation' is aimed at providing a country with a stable and legitimate framework facilitating post-conflict reconstruction. Apart from the case of Haiti, where the 'defence of democracy' objective was given the most obvious publicity, this approach is found in most peace operations carried out in the past fifteen years, whether under UN auspices or not. This trend is framed within an international context where the liberal democracy model seems to be triumphing, for lack of an alternative. However, it also highlights the resurgence of an old theme, that of democratic peace, dear to Kant[1] and that informed Wilsonian idealism at the core of the League of Nations: democracy is the best guarantee of worldwide peace, ushering in the birth of a new order.

But to what type of democratisation do we refer? Paradoxically that idea, which probably suffers from having too many meanings, a source of many ambiguities, lacks any real definition in United Nations discourse and practice.[2] Therefore, it tends to be taken as an intangible 'thing' comprising a variety of formal procedures which, it is hoped, will be used by the principal local political actors in order to accommodate their disputes and reduce the risks associated with situations of uncertainty. For this reason, external interventions tend, in practice, to focus upon a formal 'democratic grammar' of which the organization of elections is a central

[1] Immanuel Kant, *Perpetual Peace, and Other Essays on Politics, History and Moral Practice*, transl. with intro. by Ted Humphrey, Indianapolis: Hackett, 1983.
[2] One may think that this situation is partly intended to accommodate the numerous debates concerning the values attached to that political regime and their universality.

component. In emergence from conflict, elections are supposed to serve a dual purpose. On the one hand, they make it possible to install a legitimate and democratic government; this element is particularly critical in situations where, as in Kosovo, East Timor and Iraq, there is a political vacuum at the state level, partially and temporarily filled by the UN (and *a fortiori* by an occupying force) through officials who have no democratic legitimacy and next to no accountability but hold effective power—hence locals' description of them as 'tsars' or 'masters of independence'. The Special Representatives of the Secretary General often alternate between *de facto* delegation to political forces that in fact occupy the terrain (even when their representation and legitimacy is questionable) and sometimes nagging interventionism. That alternation may, as in Bosnia-Herzegovina, be all the more ill received by the population because it seems not to respond to any visible strategy and is based on highly volatile criteria. On the other hand, elections encourage the consolidation of peace structured by a durable democratic system. Ultimately, the definition given, 'by default', to the political regime that the 'international community' pretends to promote may be seen in terms of Adam Przeworski's 'procedural democracy'.[3] It also shares its limits in that it may tend to empty the very project of democratization. The United Nations personnel responsible on the ground for observing, supervising or organising elections—as the case may be—most often adopt a highly technical approach to the task. From one case to another similar models and methods are applied (electoral laws, models of voting cards and ballot papers, etc.); overall, the UN 'knows how' to organise elections. It does know how, technically—but is that enough? Such a questioning echoes the traditional debate on democracy as an institutional arrangement or as a project for a society—an argument that political analysis has carefully avoided settling. Without questioning the merits of the electoral way in the search for solutions to a conflict, it is worth highlighting the problems posed by the modes it has been promoted in a number of recent cases.

A number of analysts have already pointed out the risks inherent in electoral processes organised in the immediate aftermath of a war. Premature political competition may, in some cases, revive the logics of confrontation and lead to the destabilisation of the socio-political situation. In this perspective, the UN's strong focus on elections—at least in some instances—may reflect the inaccurate view that they are a quick-fix solution. This 'exit strategy' may put too much pressure on the electoral process, since it is only one step on the road to democracy and sometimes

---

[3] Adam Przeworski, *Democracy and the Market*, Cambridge University Press, 1991.

not even the most important one. In many cases it leads to interpretations of the electoral model on authoritarian rather than democratic lines. By definition, when a society is just emerging from a serious crisis (*a fortiori* from a war), it has not yet had the time to rebuild habitual ways of settling conflicts. During that interval the prize generally goes to the main parties in the armed conflict who can most easily establish control over the political landscape, and even more to their most extreme wings. This remained very much the situation in Bosnia-Herzegovina until the municipal elections of 1997 and the general elections of November 2000. Angola offers an extreme example of imposition of control to exploit a situation, caused by premature elections in post-conflict situations, with all the harmful side-effects of legitimist and legalistic discourse.

From this point of view the ambiguous attitude adopted, in many recent cases by the 'international community' faced with the presence of significant flaws in the organization of initial elections, should not be seen as neutral. Several UN peace operations have been put into question either for defaults in the organization of the elections themselves (as in the case of UNTAC in Cambodia),[4] or for their reactions to the flaws emerging at different stages of the process (El Salvador, Haiti, Mozambique; similar criticisms were addressed to the Organization for Security and Cooperation in Europe (OSCE) regarding municipal elections in Bosnia and Herzegovina). Caught between divergent local pressures, outsiders (whether United Nations missions or other multilateral organisations) tend to save face and can be led into *de facto* cover-ups of serious problems encountered in the first stages of the organisation of polls. On the lines of what happened in El Salvador and also in Haiti, there is a tendency to consider that if rigging does not fundamentally alter the results of the vote (that is, if those who are supposed to win in fact come first), it is preferable to turn a blind eye.

This is also due to the emphasis generally placed on security criteria in election monitoring in post-conflict situations. The holding of polls in the absence of excessive violence can be considered as a legitimate criterion. But it should never be confused with the criteria supposed to be satisfied for describing elections as 'free and democratic', as the costs of such a claim may rise considerably in the mid-term.[5] In some cases, even the

---

[4] In Cambodia, UNTAC dismissed, without any real explanation, the accusations of fraud and irregularities, though they were numerous (ballot boxes badly sealed, non-existent or poor quality indelible ink, ballot papers destroyed, defects in the computerised system for creation of registers and counting of votes, etc.).

[5] Not to mention the usual relativism that inevitably comes in: the number of deaths considered tolerable varies according to the part of the world concerned.

mere fact that the election was able to proceed is considered in itself as a victory. Cambodia, in 1993, was a caricature of such a scenario, as the 'smooth running' of the elections contrasted so strongly with a mission that was, in other respects, up against the worst difficulties, especially regarding the security components of its mandate. The agendas of Western leaders also carry plenty of weight. The Clinton administration's need to ensure 'success' for Operation Restore Democracy in Haiti had something to do with the fact that eyes were closed to the many problems encountered in the 1995 elections in that country. Similarly, in Bosnia-Herzegovina in 1996, the American administration applied pressure for elections to be organised when, according to the opinion of all observers, all the necessary conditions were not present. The OSCE mission was then commonly called in Sarajevo 'the Office to Secure Clinton's Election'.

This can be particularly problematic when pressure to hold elections comes mainly from the outside, and still more when there is rivalry between national and international processes for legitimising the political elites. In Bosnia-Herzegovina the efforts of the 'international community' and the work of the OSCE on the ground aimed at favouring (and financing) 'moderate' parties, which were, for a long time, challenged by the voters' choice. Moreover, the decisions made on several occasions by the High Representative responsible for securing compliance with the Dayton Accord, or his assistants, to dismiss democratically elected political leaders (not only at municipal government level but also at the level of the presidency of the Republika Srpska) contributed to strengthening the irresponsibility of local political actors and discouraging voters. In Kosovo, at the communal level, UNMIK civil administrators had a discretionary capacity to declare invalid decisions adopted by municipal councils democratically elected in 2001. On what side are 'legitimacy' and 'democracy' in such a case? This question relates to another often asked in post-conflict situations: according to what criteria is a local political actor considered by the 'international community' as 'legitimate', 'democratic' or 'representative'?

Problems encountered in the first so-called 'democratic' elections can arise partly from defects in organisation or technical competence, but also from fraudulent practices on a grand scale. The dividing line between the two is often very thin: problems that appear to be highly technical are almost always related to the major political issues at stake, whether they concern demarcation of constituencies, counting of votes or compilation of electoral registers. Elections can also be a means of continuing to pursue the aims of war by other means, including separation of communities, as in Bosnia-Herzegovina (deciding the place for casting votes for a largely displaced population being a crucial issue there), or the continued exclusion of a large section of the citizens. From that point of view the compilation of voting lists represents a crucial issue at stake: recognition of the equal identity of citizens. This is fundamental in situations where ethnicity is a repertoire of political disputes and is highly manipulated by local political entrepreneurs (as in Bosnia, Kosovo, the Democratic Republic of Congo, Ivory Coast and Afghanistan), but in other places too (El Salvador and Haiti, for example), in view of the strong demand that can exist among citizens for recognition and participation. The very fact of having a voting card and being able to vote has often emerged, during my investigations, as even more important than the idea of being able to choose one's representatives. Sometimes some of the voters obtain their first official identification documents in that way. And in cases where, as in El Salvador, problems of electoral registers were not settled at the time of the first elections, they can remain unresolved for a long time.

In this way it is possible to establish enough control over an election, before polling, for it to be no longer necessary to rig the vote on polling day, when international observers will be deployed on a wide scale. From that point of view the extreme concentration of election observer activities on polling day itself is highly questionable. From analysis of past experience it can be seen that the most fundamental and most serious failings do not necessarily occur on polling day, but rather before or after it. Operations of counting and tabulation of votes and transmission of the results from local to national level are just as crucial as what goes before. But the withdrawal of international observers generally starts in the evening of polling day, or the next day. Sometimes, as in Mozambique where voting was extended for one day, most of the observers had left even before the closing of the polls, *a fortiori* before the start of counting. In that instance the decision plunged Mozambicans into the greatest complexity, often mingled with anger, shared by some observers commissioned by the UN, of whom I was one. Strict surveillance of this phase assumes the retention of observers to be present at the counting, calculation and transmission of results, as well as at the offices of the central electoral body to check on the way the total vote is tabulated. It may be preferable to send fewer observers for a longer period, and to reinforce their action by careful follow-up of what happens before and after polling.

In addition, international election monitoring is most often conducted in a very technically oriented way. Very little political background is provided to the observers, yet fraud or an electoral irregularity may have very different consequences, and require various interpretations according to the local context. Similar patterns can be found in the technical assistance given by the United Nations system (for instance in programmes designed to contribute to judicial reforms or 'good governance' promotion). But the will to stick to a strictly technical approach may, *de facto*, favour certain political options, and often rewards sham democracies.

The fact that flaws in founding elections are 'covered', for varying reasons, by outsiders has short- and medium-term consequences on both the electoral system itself and on the popular representation of the democratic regime. Electoral institutions are the first to suffer from the effects of this situation. In several countries where elections have been held in the wake of peace processes, the weaknesses observed in the first post-conflict polls have not only remained unresolved, but have often grown worse. In January 1993, in El Salvador, the Junta de Vigilencia, the body responsible for supervision of the elections, spoke out against the risk of massive exclusion of citizens from voting: at least one Salvadorean out of three did not have a voting card, while the registers remained full of deceased. Once international pressure had fallen off after the end of the peace mission, the traditional parties which continued to control the electoral institutions had no more reason to bring order to the registers. After the parliamentary and municipal elections of March 1997, the presidential election of March 7, 1999 was considered as equally lacking in transparency. The problems concerning the tidying up of electoral registers, in particular, had still not been resolved. How could one forget that the outbreak of the Salvadorian conflict in January 1981 had been preceded, four years earlier, by guerrilla actions launched in the wake of demonstrations against massive rigging that had stained the elections of February 1977? The United Nations peace operation did not solve this core issue. The difficulties encountered in Cambodia when the 1998 elections were held, and above all the way in which they were managed, underlined, after the event, the danger of letting it be thought that the technical failings recorded in 1993—failings that in several cases opened the way to real frauds—were inherent in the organisation of 'free, democratic elections'. How could anyone demand that future authorities should prevent what the UN itself had not only been unable to guarantee against, but had 'covered'? How could anyone take offence at practices to which a blind eye had been turned five years earlier? There was a similar scenario in Mozambique, Haiti and Bosnia-Herzegovina. The irresponsibility of the 'international community', which wanted elections at any price, has often opened the way to institutionalised election fraud.

Professional politicians may draw a number of lessons from the electoral experience—often their first—especially regarding the way in which the electoral system can be manipulated (including the results of the vote) and the façade that needs to be presented to appear democratic in the world's eyes. It is possible to appeal to the democratic creed and display certain appearances required by the 'international community' without excessively challenging certain traditional methods of management and power sharing, including those resorting to violence. The experiences of Cambodia, El Salvador and Haiti are evidence of those perverse effects and of the constant use of political violence (murders, outrages, vendettas, etc.), especially during election periods. The electoral system, which excludes a portion of the population not registered or not mobilised by a dubious electoral contest, has trouble taking hold and is often subjected to massive boycotts. A number of countries (including El Salvador, Haiti, Mozambique, Bosnia, etc.) thus seem to have been drawn into a series of 'elections without voters', sometimes more than one in a year, that are fraudulent and change nothing. The standard arguments (lack of democratic maturity among the people, their disappointment, the impact of dire poverty, etc.) are not enough to explain the very low turnouts, sometimes contrasting with very impressive mobilisation in the past. Besides word being passed from community organisations telling people not to lend plausibility to 'rigged' or 'fake' elections, investigations on the ground reveal repudiation of a system that remains corrupt and violent, that seeks to impose democracy 'without the people'. When, as in Haiti, repeated elections lead to more and more fraud and smaller and smaller turnouts, the perversion of the system reaches its apogee.

In all cases, stronger structuring of electoral institutions, from the first post-conflict poll on, is indispensable. In the short term, the outsiders need to take on the political cost of this. Indeed, the considerable attention that the UN has usually given to elections in the past has had the tendency to encourage the idea that elections were an expedient and the clearest indicator of 'success' for a peace operation. The impact of this impression alone is often favoured over minimal consistency between words and deeds. This often caused excessive pressure on the electoral process, whereas it represents only a step on the road to democracy and peace, and not necessarily the most important one. The message has begun to be heard at the UN, as was demonstrated by the report published on the subject by the Secretary General in October 2000,[6] and the repeated

---

[6] 'Support by the United Nations system of the efforts of Governments to promote and consolidate new or restored democracies' (A/55/489). This report adopted, notably, a certain number of recommendations made in a report drawn up for the International Institute for Democracy and Electoral Assistance, 'Democracy and Global Cooperation at the United

warning to member states that there can be 'no exit without strategy'. But outside the Balkans—for reasons easy to understand in view of the 'proximity' to Europe—the 'international community' largely persists in its irresponsible attitude.

In doing so, people forget that voting is not useful only for designing representatives of the local people. Besides its explicit functions, voting also fulfils a certain number of latent functions—legitimising governments, social liturgy reactivating the feeling of belonging to a group (the act of voting attests to the individual's socialization as a citizen), and testing the political system's capacity for constructing a frame of reference. Flaws in the organisation of the first founding elections can thus prove to have damaging consequences for the process of post-conflict reconstruction.

THE POLITICAL NON-SENSE OF MOST ECONOMIC RECONSTRUCTION PROGRAMS

The rebuilding of post-conflict societies is played out at the overlap of the political, social and also economic spheres. It is within this triangle that local political and economic actors negotiate the readjustments that, in part, mirror the sites and repertoires imposed by the donors, such as democracy and the free market (supposed to ensure better allocation of resources).[7] For the political elites, the essential point is retention of power or access to it, and possible power sharing, with the rent that goes with it. This linkage explains, in particular, why the democratic/undemocratic dichotomy cannot reflect the whole range of concrete strategies of political actors. To give one example among others, in Cambodia the FUN-CINPEC/PPC rivalry never sufficed for understanding of the way political, economic and religious power was being reorganised among family networks, or why alliances, which appeared surprising at first sight, were established, or how allegiances were being redefined in Cambodian society. Similarly, the redefinition of balances among leading families possessing economic power, and the issues at stake in state-building, cannot be understood if, in El Salvador for example, attention is focused only on the ARENA/FMLN rivalry, or in Haiti, on the Lavalas/non-Lavalas rivalry. In other words, the explanation of alliances and pacts described by analysts

Nations', 2000 (report drawn up in collaboration with Izumi Nakamitsy Lennartsson and Martin Wikfalk).

[7] Structural adjustment programmes are supposed to attack some economic arrangements based on plunder and redistribution through patronage, especially through the administration.

of democratic transitions lies also in those other issues, which need to be understood and deciphered as such.

Despite the omnipresence of discourses on 'free market democracy', the economic dimensions of the political transformations that these countries are going through have for long remained forgotten. Certainly the economic role of peace operations is often limited, except for attempts to coordinate aid donors who have themselves demonstrated no intention of accepting coordination. Even so, peace operations have a local economic impact, which is not a neutral factor in the way 'reconstruction' is carried out. In my investigations the effects of the influx of 'United Nations dollars' on growth, inflation and exchange rates seemed much less obvious than expected, and more staggered over time; above all, those effects can be explained to a great extent by the arrival, on mass, of other public and private actors alongside the peacekeepers. The countries' capital cities, indeed, experience what local actors invariably describe as a real 'invasion' by hundreds of intergovernmental and non-governmental organisations, as there is strong competition on the peace and 'reconstruction' market—a dimension of UN member states' rivalry that has found very concrete expression in the Balkans, for instance. Moreover, in their wake come investors, eager to make short-term profits. The economic and social consequences of this international presence, generally very short-term and concentrated in the capital, are often badly felt by the local middle classes. Dollarisation of the economy and increases in rents and prices of imported products, as well as in salaries of key local staff, are among the consequences. Beyond the immediate effects, it is generally difficult to find reliable empirical data making it possible to distinguish the economic impact of UN missions' presence from development that would have occurred without them. However, it is less the macroeconomic results—often worthy of the IMF's best pupils—than the forms and structures of economic growth, that raise most questions in relation to the objectives of peace in those countries.

From the first years on, growth is often accompanied by increased extraversion of the economy and a boom in very specific sectors (building, trading, banking, other service activity, etc.), stimulated by the presence of foreigners and ensuring ways to get rich quickly. During this time traditional productive sectors (like agriculture) experience a noticeably steeper decline, which contributes to hastening of the drift to the towns and dependence on the outside world for satisfaction of basic food needs. In crisis situations, politico-economic entrepreneurs' calculations are, more than ever, short-term in nature. Post-conflict international aid adopts and strengthens this short-term mind-frame, especially where no promising market can be envisaged quickly and no geographical proximity encourages industrialised countries to invest in the long-term for harmonious development of a market economy (as in the Balkans). In most post-conflict situations the preoccupations of aid donors are limited to humanitarian emergencies and relative 'stabilisation' of the situation, as well as access to natural resources when they exist. They care very little for the way in which power structures traditionally based on plunder and patronage are reorganised and adapted—most often very well—to external constraints imposed on them. When the peace plan calls for demobilisation and reintegration of former combatants, when the IMF imposes reduction in the civil service payroll, the elites develop a range of circumvention strategies and partly undergo reconversion into new entrepreneurs or NGO leaders, roles more in accordance with the new international creed. But what is left of the others? Among the heritage of wars and sanctions regimes is the informalization, and sometimes criminalization, of the local economy, as closer linkages are developed with the illegal spheres of the world market. In many cases, there is a very noticeable increase in the share of wealth derived from drug trafficking or laundering of drug money (in El Salvador, and still more in Haiti), or involving precious natural resources (including precious stones and timber, as in Cambodia and Sierra Leone). In other places, like Bosnia-Herzegovina and Kosovo, war money is recycled, providing for the financial reconversion of nationalist elites and former officers now heading private enterprises and, in certain cases, real monopolies. These dimensions remain widely underestimated by macro-economic stabilisation programmes that quite simply care nothing about this context. These changes are not unconnected with changes in the forms assumed by violence in these same environments, and raise questions, notably, about the possibility of democratisation in economic systems that remain based on predation.

For the majority of the people concerned, so-called 'informal' practices also encompass strategies of mere survival—most often reduced to its simplest form, the quest for food. The peace process is nearly always accompanied by a noticeable worsening of living conditions, sharpening the divisions created by the conflicts. At the end of a war, more people are still poorer while a small minority has become richer, some of those privileged few—but only some of them—being *nouveaux riches*. For the vast majority the economic spin-off from the international presence is almost nil, apart from small-scale trading and ad hoc assistance, which is often based on inter-personal relations. Those who have the 'good luck' of having been refugees, displaced people or war wounded can hope to have access to international aid which, in helping them, creates questionable hierarchies among the population, as the Cambodians and Bosnians can testify. In this context the continuation, at the local level, of 'illegal' activities imposed by belligerents during the war is often indispensable for survival, even if it keeps the people at the mercy of politico-mafioso groups who are usually more successful in their reconversion than the average people.

These dimensions are largely forgotten by the aid programmes. This is partly due to the traditional lack of coordination among international agencies. Within the UN system, coordinating efforts at the highest level, especially under the aegis of Kofi Annan,[8] have only slightly altered the behaviour on the ground. There, agencies remain very jealous of their prerogatives. Personality clashes and preoccupations of career explain this poor record. It does not even work better when peace missions themselves include socio-economic components—particularly for the repatriation and reintegration of refugees and displaced persons (as happened in Cambodia and Mozambique where, in addition, a system of coordination under the authority of the Special Representative of the Secretary General was established). Even when, as in Haiti, the resident Coordinator and UNDP Representative is appointed Deputy to the Special Representative of the Secretary General who heads the peace mission. More serious is the disconnection with the agenda of the Bretton Woods institutions. Not only do they control a large proportion of the financial resources needed for reconstruction; in addition they play, in practice, the role of leaders of the aid donors and promote neo-liberal austerity programmes often in contradiction with the objective of rebuilding state authority. In El Salvador, Cambodia, Mozambique and Haiti, and again in Bosnia-Herzegovina, the obstacles placed in the rebuilding of infrastructure and services essential for peace-building and also for socio-economic reintegration of former combatants, have made a political non-sense of those programmes. Those effects go together with harmful commitments by aid donors: massive on emergency measures, and sometimes very short-lived. Donors are more reserved when it comes to making longer-term commitments and investing in actual peace building. It is also well known that between the promises announced at donors' meetings and the reality of sums eventually invested, there can be a gulf never bridged. It is a long way from the 'Marshall Plans' sometimes announced. The two major differences from the programme of American aid to Europe following the Second World War are, first, that the countries receiving aid today generally receive much less money, but secondly, that they have reform plans and investment programmes more firmly imposed on them.

---

[8] The major exception remains, within the UN Secretariat itself, the division of labour between the Department of Peace Keeping Operations and the Department of Political Affairs, based, in particular, on an abstract and largely obsolete distinction between 'restoration', 'maintenance' and 'consolidation' of peace.

AMBIGUITIES OF PEACEKEEPERS' ROLE IN MAINTAINING 'LAW AND ORDER'

United Nations missions deployed over the past ten years have, with one exception,[9] no longer had the mandate of interposition between two armies and supervising cease-fires, but to restore, or contribute to the restoration and maintenance of 'law and order'. In fact they have often been presented as 'international police' operations. But it is not certain that the consequences of this big semantic change have been clearly understood. The etymological origin of the word 'police' itself (*polis*, 'city'), in its modern accepted meaning, recalls that it functions as the intrinsic link between the safeguarding of the state and the protection of the individuals who compose society.[10] In other words, conducting a police operation in another country amounts to intervening in the social contract, in relations between society, the individuals composing it, and the state[11]. The tasks assigned, in practice, to intervening forces are for the most part—and very soon after the start of an intervention—civil and police tasks, even if, in most cases, the operations continue to be largely military in their composition. Several factors explain this: the instability of contexts of intervention (neither war nor peace), the fears of troop contributors for their safety on the ground (which explains that a high proportion of contingents are assigned to the security of international personnel rather than that of the local people), and lastly the cost and difficulties of recruiting civpols who, by definition, are trained to act within the borders of their own state. Indeed, UN missions have recurring problems in recruiting police personnel, as was illustrated by UNMIK's shortage, for several months, of civpols in Kosovo. This explains in part why the police have remained, by far, the weakest component in most peace operations. In addition, police teams are generally established on a multinational basis, which means that they include individuals who have very diverse and sometimes antagonistic conceptions and practices of their profession—for example, with differing references to Latin or Anglo-Saxon codes of procedure regarding proof and guilt. Lastly, the mandate of a mission's police component is generally the least well defined. Apart from the cases of Kosovo and East Timor where the UN was acting as a provisional authority and its police

---

[9] This exception was the mission of interposition between Ethiopia and Eritrea (UNMEE), although the socio-political (a preferable term to 'internal') dimensions of that conflict seem to have been widely underestimated, following an excessively classical approach.

[10] In the modern acceptance of the idea, which dates from the seventeenth century and is closely linked to the idea of public order.

[11] It should be recalled that in the theories of Hobbes and Rousseau both society and the state are based on contract.

force was therefore clearly in charge of public security during the interim period, the mandates of UN civpols oscillate between monitoring of the local police forces, technical assistance and continuous training, sometimes *de facto* substitution. This is often complicated by the fact that initial training for local police officers is not under UN missions' control. It is in the hands of bilateral programs or other agencies such as ICITAP (the International Criminal Investigative Training Program), which comes under the US Department of Justice and is financed by the US administration. This includes, obviously, the selection of future police officers, generally recruited on a basis of parity among the former belligerent groups or in new recruiting grounds. This gap between training and monitoring tasks, allied to uncertainty about the responsibility of UN civpols in all the cases where the UN is not the transitional authority, explains the hesitation during the first months—if not years—of intervention. During that period, the control exerted over local police is often greatly lacked, with more or less serious blunders covered under the pretext of 'youthful mistakes'. The UN and the 'international community' are often reluctant to criticize a new institution, the creation of which they are contributing to. The effects of such an approach were particularly damaging in the development of police forces in El Salvador and Haiti.

All these handicaps relate, basically, to two more fundamental questions that the changes in doctrine proposed so far continue to disregard: the possibility of doing police work in a society other than one's own, and dividing the line between law and order and military functions. There is indeed a contradiction that is difficult for external forces to overcome: to be effective, police work requires proximity to local communities, which UN civpols, by definition, do not have. Contrary to what the top UN officials seem to continue to believe (especially when advocating the establishment of penal codes or international systems of rules), the social and political 'order' relates to variable histories and systems of reference, which need to be understood at least minimally. The fact that peacekeepers are generally seen by the local population as 'very distant', 'outsiders', 'not interested in the people' is a heavy handicap on the day when they have to intervene in a village or district and count on some minimal cooperation and local trust. As people repeatedly told me in very similar terms, despite differences in language, the UN is 'like the state', 'it does not give a damn about us', 'it does not protect us', 'we can't have any confidence in it'… It is no surprise then, that people resort to dodging UN personnel as the last resort of the weak against the strong, symbolised by the state or those considered the same as the state: refusing to answer questions from United Nations police officers, supplying false information, passive resistance, even sabotage and theft of light weapons, etc.—incidents that the missions try to cover up and then to minimise, so as not to become an object of ridicule. In practice, United Nations civpols very quickly come to avoid penetrating some areas considered as 'outlawed' zones, where criminal networks can thus carry out activities at their leisure, as long as they let the UN civpols and military deploy their appearances of order. On the ground, it is common for the real world—real 'order'—to escape the peacekeepers, as in Pristina, Kosovo, despite the massive presence of UNMIK.

Here we get to the heart of police work. Much is played out in day-to-day life, in a work of proximity and small gestures, seemingly insignificant, which will none the less make it possible or not to build relations of confidence. From that point of view, apparently insignificant details like getting out of your car, walking in the side streets of poorer districts, not being content with just 'passing by', all have a symbolic value. As police officers often pointed out to me during training sessions before their departure for a peace operation, all this is not so different from the work they are called upon to do in their own countries, in any difficult district. However, the foreign nature of systems of reference to which local actors refer, leads to the incapacity to think seriously about the function of maintaining order when it has to be carried out overseas. This stems from the growing impression that, outside the West, wars are no longer rational and the societies concerned are prey to anarchy. Indeed, civpols must adapt to contexts different from those in which they have operated hitherto. But they need to go through a learning process very similar to the one they must follow for a new posting at home, and basically do very similar work.

Because there are not enough civpols, while the local police force generally has to be entirely (re)constituted, quite commonly order has to be maintained by United Nations soldiers or those of a multinational coalition. But they have neither the means nor the training to carry out police tasks properly—doing community policing on the model of neighbourhood police, keeping order during demonstrations, dismantling terrorist networks and groups linked to organised crime, etc. This also assumes that they can go beyond their usual capacity for military intelligence and carry out police investigations like units specialised in crime and terrorism. What is involved goes beyond the category to which personnel belong (the local people themselves do not always distinguish civilians and soldiers, all of who wear uniforms, but rather observe how they behave and the arms they carry); it is their conduct, their capacity to adapt to highly volatile environments, the tasks assigned to them and the means to carry out those tasks. Several recent situations (Bosnia, Kosovo, Sierra Leone, Iraq) have brought reminders of the impotence of heavily-armed forces in the face of groups continuing war by other means including organised crime and terrorism. Similarly, the deployment of weaponry for deterrent purposes may, in some contexts, prove highly counter-productive. The image of tanks being deployed may have a definite psychological impact, as the military chiefs say, but is quite irrelevant to snipers or militiamen who may not display their arms in daylight but none the less continue to occupy the terrain. Among the population concerned, the gap between the deployment of heavy weaponry and the insecurity that they experience every day (small-scale and large-scale crime, extortion, domestic violence, murder, etc) has consequences that are not minor. Not only does this situation not reassure them, it makes them wonder: if these strangers are not here to protect us, what hidden reason is there behind their presence…? In contexts as varied as those of Haiti, El Salvador, Bosnia and Kosovo, and Ituri in eastern Congo, this perception has been shown to be very prevalent. And in many cases this arises from precise historical experiences, more exactly the experience of an oppressive state that never protected its citizens. The usual lack of communication between United Nations troops and local people (shortage of interpreters, lack of interest in how the ordinary people live) explains why the arrival of some armoured vehicles in a village or district, in the absence of any explanation or dialogue with the inhabitants, can cause panic and spread fear. Conversely, the ritual of daily passing of military 'parades' (as the inhabitants sometimes call them), sometimes at a fixed time, in districts where insecurity remains high, especially at night, is only funny the first time. Yet in UN jargon all these 'showing the flag' patrols are aimed at ensuring a visible presence, a deterrent to possible troublemakers, a reassurance for the people.

Of course there are cases where the restoration of order requires resort to armed force, in situations that are very often of a 'neither war nor peace' sort. The crises experienced by the peace mission in Sierra Leone, in the spring of 2000, showed the limits of Blue Helmets' capacity in such situations. They were literally taken hostage by rebel troops, and only owed their salvation to the targeted intervention of the British army to support the local government (Operation Pallister). The alarm signal launched at the time by the UN Secretary General underlined, once more, the contrast between decisions by the Security Council to reinforce certain peace operations and the refusal of the same member states to provide the resources, especially human resources. The increasingly wide gulf between those who decide on interventions and those who are in fact ready to deploy military personnel on the ground,[12] or even to provide funds for

[12] The now regular meetings with the representatives of countries providing troops has only partially reduced the tension, as those countries do not conceal their frustration at

operations, confirms a division of labour between the West and the rest of the world that is already being carried out on a wide scale, to judge by the trends in the list of contributors of military contingents and the allocation of tasks on the ground. However, the realities on the ground call into question not so much a lack of training and equipment for Blue Helmets, the majority of whom come from poor countries, as the actual conditions of recourse to armed force. The large variety of actors and logics, their volatile behaviour (permanently passing from the confrontation register to that of cooperation or else that of dodging), the possibility that Blue Helmets may be in a position of having to protect human lives—all this makes it necessary to look at the possible use of force in a different way. While it cannot be always ruled out, it must be envisaged carefully. It is particularly risky in highly volatile contexts, where capacities for collective mobilisation are poorly known to the intervening forces. Somalia has shown that muscular action against a spoiler, if it does not take due account of variable interaction networks of which he is part, and *a fortiori* of his capacity to mobilise, may prove not only ineffective but risky because it will be felt as a declaration of hostility towards a whole social group. In Somalia the peace mission was gradually turned into a war operation, causing, in four months of clashes, between 6,000 and 10,000 deaths on the Somali side, the number of wounded being estimated at twice that.[13] The United Nations forces, on their side, lost 83 soldiers killed and 302 wounded.[14] The testimony of soldiers who took part in the operation reveals the fears they endured regarding Somalis who, as a whole, very quickly came to be seen as 'enemies', the 'danger' being everywhere and nowhere.[15]

That scenario, extreme as it is, is revealing of the particularly delicate equation that any peace operation may be confronted with. On the one hand, it is a reminder of the risks of slipping out of control that are almost inevitable when making war and making peace are confused. From this

---

receiving only partial information, while in practice important decisions continue to be taken without them.

[13] These are the estimates of Mohamed Sahnoun, former Special Representative of the Secretary General in the country; the UN did not provide official figures on this subject and maintained the division between 'militiamen' and 'civilians', which, in most of the clashes under consideration, was practically impossible to make.

[14] Total losses for the whole operation were 136 men.

[15] The published testimony of American soldiers is particularly evocative. See S. L. Arnold, 'Somalia: An Operation Other Than War', *Military Review*, December 1993, pp. 26–35; Kent Delong and Steven Tuckey, *Mogadishu/Heroism and Tragedy*, Westport, CT: Praeger, 1994. This atmosphere is found also in many recent cinema productions, especially the film *We Were Soldiers*, which deals with precisely that episode in Somalia.

point of view, the distinction proposed in the Brahimi report between use of force against an aggressor and to defend a population is no more convincing than the various doctrinal quibbles of states tending to support the idea of 'active impartiality', implying resort to force to defend peace (the British concept of a 'peace support operation' is typical). Any resort to force exposes a peace mission to being perceived locally, and in the future, as a *de facto* oppressive operation. To think one can 'clinically' target an individual or a group independently of any environment and without any impact on the local balance of forces is, at best, disconcerting naivety. In addition, on the ground the relative importance of security for international civilian personnel and soldiers, compared with that of the people they are supposed to have come to help, remains a major stumbling block. This discrepancy was shown in a particularly glaring way in Somalia, but also in Rwanda, Bosnia-Herzegovina and Kosovo and more recently in eastern Congo, considering the violence suffered at the same time by the local people. In Somalia, notably, Operation 'Unified Shield' launched on February 28, 1995, to protect the evacuation of the remaining 2,500 Blue Helmets in the country and the reloading for shipment of heavy equipment loaned to UNOSOM by the United States, mobilised 18 ships and nearly 10,000 men. In Rwanda, after the start of the massacres in April 1994, the Security Council took the extraordinary decision to reduce the strength of United Nations forces on the ground, already very limited. In Bosnia, in the enclave of Srebrenica in July 1995, the security of 300 Dutch soldiers had priority over the security of the 27,000 Bosnian Muslims that they were supposed to protect. Indeed, one of the declared objectives of UNPROFOR was its own protection; those who had to exercise responsibility at its head have spoken of the time and energy devoted to that purpose and the elaboration of hypothetical evacuation plans, constantly updated.[16] In Kosovo, the NATO 'extraction force' was stationed on the borders of the country to protect the OSCE observers in the province of Serbia, in case the security of those observers was threatened. They were evacuated immediately after the failure of the Rambouillet agreements, although it was known that the ethnic cleansing operation had already started on the ground. As for the NATO air raids of the spring of 1999, they showed for many weeks the gulf between an air intervention—sophisticated but of questionable effectiveness—and fighting on the ground from which a careful distance was kept, and which bore the character of ethnic cleansing. At Bunia in Ituri, in east Congo, in May 2003, MONUC was unable even to protect civilians who had taken refuge

[16] Private interviews in Paris and New York.

within the perimeter of its base to escape the massacres. Yet Security Council Resolution 1417 gave it a mandate to protect civilians immediately threatened with physical violence. In all cases the result was similar: in the minds of the killers, as of the victims, the local people were literally abandoned by those who were supposed, locally, to represent the 'international community'. The need to protect the civilian population, and to give United Nations troops firmer rules of engagement for that purpose, was the object of a specific report by Kofi Annan in the autumn of 1999, and was reaffirmed by the report of the panel of experts on peace operations, made public shortly before the Millennium Summit. But in reality no government is ready, today, to take on these human and political costs.

Back in Bunia, August 7, 2003: France is heading a multinational force (Artemis) responsible for providing security in the city pending relief by a force of MONUC, now given more muscle. On that day, early in the morning, there was a quarrel (not serious) between the MONUC Blue Helmets and armed men of the Union of Congolese Patriots (UPC) guarding the home of Thomas Lubanga, their leader. Immediately French soldiers were deployed alongside the UN forces and sealed off the whole sector, systematically searching all passers-by, including women and children. The inhabitants at once pointed out the contrast with the absence of any international presence whenever their people's lives were in real danger. When, by chance, a military patrol went to a place where an air patrol had spotted smoke, the charred remains of a village, it was too late, and they did not go after the attackers, the killers, or the cattle thieves. Similarly, at night, when militias were firing in districts of the town, the international soldiers were invisible. For the local people, the message was clear: the French were like 'Mademoiselle la MONUC' (or 'Monique'), they only budged when their own security was in danger, not that of the population. Over all operations there extends a true hierarchy of values assigned to the lives of different categories of individuals. Another proof of this is the instructions given to international election monitors as in Mozambique, with absolute priority given to 'the safety of UN Staff and property'.[17] At the slightest incident or sign of violence or insecurity, members of missions are supposed to leave the scene, abandoning any possible victims to their fate. Such instructions may, whatever the Bush administration or any other government may say, effectively lead Blue Helmets into covering crimes against humanity and contravening interna-

---

[17] ONUMOZ, *Guidelines on Emergencies* (Annex 23), page 2, para. (b): 'In case of any sign of violence…move well away from the scene. The safety of UN Staff and property comes first'; an oral briefing in Johannesburg (October 1994) said the same thing.

tional law, exposing them by such acts alone to prosecution, International Criminal Court or not. In French domestic law 'failure to assist a person in danger' can be a matter for criminal prosecution.

For the citizens of the countries concerned, the end of a conflict rarely means the end of security problems. They are usually 'reframed', in the sense that an issue is transferred or displaced without being solved at the core. Such situations are generally related to two aspects of peace processes which, until now, have not been satisfactorily managed: the conditions in which disarmament and the reintegration of former combatants are carried out, on the one hand, and the difficulties in creating or reforming police structures on the other. Everywhere, there is a considerable increase in the number of light weapons in circulation, and especially a wider distribution among all layers of society, while disarmament programmes (quite simply absent in certain cases, such as Haiti) have rapidly proved their limits. Similarly, from one country to another, the way in which the programmes of reintegration for former combatants is carried out neglects a considerable number of individuals who do not belong to 'regular' groups and for whom possessing a weapon has for years, perhaps for a whole lifetime, been the principal means of earning a living, whether in wartime or in the setting of a predatory repressive system. In practice, some of them undergo reconversion to banditry. That sort of life and 'integration' into collective existence also includes an increasingly young population to whom no prospect is offered for survival—economically, but also for existence vis-à-vis the state. Seen in this way, the gangs that rampage around the poorer districts of capital cities are strangely similar from one country to another. Disillusioned by the lack of results of the political struggle or the wars waged by their elders, envying modes of rapid self-enrichment and looking to areas of identification and socialisation, jobless young people, in very large numbers, are an ideal recruiting ground. The degree of control over them is very difficult to estimate, and seeing the incidents in which they are implicated, it is probable that they sell their services alternately to different sectors and sometimes act on their own initiative, on the borderline between politico-mafioso logics and ordinary delinquency. Known as gangs of armed motor-cyclists in Cambodia, self-styled 'people's organisations' and '*chimè*' in Haiti, fake 'law enforcers' and real 'death commandos' in El Salvador or Guatemala, former child soldiers in Sierra Leone and the Democratic Republic of Congo, etc., they are also entrusted, by some political entrepreneurs, with underhand tasks.

For a diplomat, peace is probably the absence of war, or more exactly that 'secure and stable environment' which is defined much more by the international balance of forces at a particular moment than by the situation prevailing on the ground. For his part Hobbes defined peace according to the absence of violent death; many of the inhabitants of Cambodia, Rwanda, Bosnia, Kosovo, Guatemala, El Salvador and other places would probably be glad if it did mean that in their countries. In El Salvador the number of civilians killed by firearms each year is higher than the number of civilian and military deaths during the whole civil war. With more than 150 homicides per 100,000 inhabitants (more than 10,000 murders per year), the country has one of the highest homicide rates in the world. Beyond the statistics, and the 'objective' image of increased insecurity and its changed forms in the societies concerned, it is its perceptions that matter most. For example, there has been a grave underestimation of the consequences of the irruption at the heart of the popular neighbourhoods, of a violence which threatens a number of the rules of coexistence, indispensable for survival in over-populated areas with inconceivable levels of deprivation, where clashes between rival gangs (in San Salvador, Port-au-Prince, Freetown or Pristina) and a large proportion of 'ordinary' crime occurs. Moreover, these threats and the increase in the level of delinquency and violence may serve to help disguise political crimes, as the current situations in Haiti, El Salvador, Cambodia or Kosovo show, albeit in different contexts. When violence starts to impregnate daily life again, fear sets in and people change their lifestyle; for example, they avoid going out after nightfall. Some forms of solidarity practiced beforehand are dropped, people are barricaded in their hovels... When, in the morning, faces with drawn features and haggard eyes continue to show sleepless nights, when that time which should have been one for the body and mind to let go is interrupted by automatic arms fire, when dogs howl at death...peace remains just a pious hope.

Such a situation means especially, for the majority, that the state has not changed and is still not going to protect them. The population rapidly loses confidence in a local police force that is at best overwhelmed by the size of its task, often rapidly gangrened within by mafioso activity partly inherited from networks set up in wartime. In countries that have been 'at peace' for a short time, 'everyone has weapons', according to common expression. In fact the main political entrepreneurs have their own armed guards, while private security firms proliferate. In the poorer districts of cities, but also in some rural areas, the population sets up vigilante groups to ensure security, which the new police force, monitored to a greater or lesser extent by the UN, does not provide. Those groups, exasperated by the inaction of the police force and the justice system, may administer justice themselves. This is often considered by outsiders, as a 'normal development' in post-conflict societies;[18] whereas it poses serious political challenges.

THE FORGOTTEN DIMENSIONS OF 'JUSTICE' AND 'RECONCILIATION' PROGRAMS

The 'rule of law' promised by the UN remains a long way from being established. Although the expression conveys a certain degree of polysemy and a fairly abstract meaning in international practice, it generally refers to the guaranteeing of the rights and freedoms of citizens or, in other words, of their security and integrity. This includes their equal protection and non-discrimination, due process, police accountability, judicial independence, crucial elements in any peaceful and democratic society. The reforms needed to achieve that goal take time; peace processes must none the less start them, to ensure that in the future the citizen is effectively protected by the state and can expect to receive justice.

The involvement of United Nations missions in reforms of the judicial system varies from one case to another, but is often fairly weak. At best it often amounts, as in El Salvador and Haiti, to production of more or less complete and relevant diagnoses describing the main impediments in the existing system. Those documents end up joining the many expert reports that are unfailingly produced about the countries concerned. The missions themselves often have few resources for entering directly into reforms of structures (including the prison system) and training of judges, for which there are programmes funded by bilateral aid, with more or less extensive and coordinated involvement of the United Nations Development Programme and the UN High Commissioner for Human Rights. Justice is not always seen as a priority for peace, whereas efforts should be started rapidly. In addition, the UN's approach in places where it acts as a transitional authority, like Cambodia, Kosovo and East Timor, remains very technical and formal. This is shown by the establishment of new legal codes, brought in practically ready-made by experts, and the highly legalistic approach that involves pushing for a country's adoption of all international instruments in one domain, without concern for the way in which they can really be included in the country's legislation and, above all, in actual practice there. The challenge for peace operations is, however, not limited to reform of local legislation that does not comply with international norms. In many countries law is not much more than a piece of paper which has very

---

[18] Sometimes with disastrous errors of communication on that theme, as happened with the UNMIH spokesman in Haiti.

little to do with reality and less still with the informal rules that apply in practice. In addition, international programmes almost completely put aside the question of internal production of legal rules and the role of national parliaments in producing them. Cambodia is a very good example. After the peace operations, reforms in this field often give rise to battles between heirs of two legal traditions (one Latin, the other Anglo-Saxon) through different aid programmes. Among other things, this competition makes it possible for established interests without inducing actual reforms despite high expectations among the population.

In post-conflict situations the 'retrospective' and 'prospective' dimensions of the demand for justice are closely tied together. Signals that make it possible to ensure that certain acts and crimes cannot be covered up by society, are as important as work on memories of violence. Now, such work relates to varied, partial, contradictory and intrinsically subjective processes. Beyond the necessity to 'think about the past', what matters is being able to live in the present and imagine the future. At the individual level, memory refers to a range of mental functions that enable the past to be represented precisely as something belonging to the past. When political and armed violence is involved, the past may continue to be present, because of a number of 'objective' factors (maintenance of a system of repression and social control reactivated and reinforced by fear) and 'subjective' ones (insomnia, nightmares, stress, and other more or less serious pathological effects of a traumatic experience). The work to be done must make it possible to 'let go'. A certain amount of 'forgetting' is needed to achieve healing and be able to build on a chosen, rather than an imposed, basis. At the collective level, society was not only the victim of violence that profoundly affected it, it has often been just as much the author of the violence, even in a partial and involuntary way; it allowed what happened or did not prevent it. That explains why, in a 'post-violence' phase, the ways of collective living must be rethought and rebuilt. Questions as basic as 'Who are we as a people?' 'Who are the state?', 'What will happen to us as a people?', require new answers. In very concrete terms, representations of the individual self and the collective self need to be rethought through the daily practices of citizens.

Apart from the very real advances in international law in recent years (especially with the creation of an International Criminal Court), this dimension remains the most neglected in peace processes. Until today, individual traumas and their collective implications continue to be insufficiently taken into account in the long process often wrongly described as 'reconciliation'. That explains to a great extent the snags encountered up till now by politico-judicial responses to crimes in wartime. One snag relates to the continuing contradiction between building peace and applying justice. In every case, either the demand for justice is sacrificed for the demand for peace, or else justice ends up by being seen as 'victors' justice',[19] as the Nuremberg trial was and the justice of the special courts for former Yugoslavia and (a joint UN-Sierra Leonean court) in Sierra Leone continue to be. The tension between the two original conceptions of international criminal tribunals and 'truth and reconciliation' commissions is no easier to settle. In fact 'truth' is generally accompanied by *de facto* impunity accorded to those responsible for crimes, or even a declared amnesty as in El Salvador and South Africa. The example of that country, where confession made it possible to get amnesty, needs to be closely observed from that point of view, not in the appearances of the image of success exported widely to other countries by new law entrepreneurs, but in the many frustrations that the process has aroused within South Africa. In El Salvador as in Haiti, Truth Commissions have carried out their work far from society, and their reports, centred on symbolic cases, have almost not been distributed. A record of events reduced to some 'symbolic cases', and to a narrative that is not restored to the victims and their families, can be the contrary of a real labour of memory and mourning. One woman met in a poor district of San Salvador expressed what many others repeated to me in that country: 'Not only did the war serve no purpose, because we cannot see what it has changed in the functioning of society; people also want to make us believe it never took place, that nothing happened during all those years, that our people are not dead, that our children were not kidnapped...'[20]

The decision to establish international criminal courts in the cases of Rwanda and the former Yugoslavia arose from that need expressed by victims, as well as from refusal to accept impunity when mass crimes have been committed. Those courts have, notably, helped ensure that the facts and the responsibilities are established, and that victims and survivors stop feeling guilty. In fact, besides the various psychological mechanisms explaining that feelings of guilt are an important aspect of the relationship between a torturer or executioner and his victims,[21] guilt often forms part of repressive strategy. In Guatemala, part of the army and those backing it still assert that the majority of the 200,000 killed in the civil war were

---

[19] See H.-P. Brodeur, 'Justice des droits de l'homme ou justice des vainqueurs?' *Le Monde des Débats*, July–August 1999.

[20] Words uttered in San Salvador in September 1995; translation from Spanish. During the Salvadorian conflict, the army kidnapped a still unknown number of children.

[21] Françoise Sironi, *Bourreaux et victimes. Psychologie de la torture*, Paris: Odile Jacob, 1999.

guerrillas or individuals supporting them, or even that Maya *indígenos* massacred each other. Establishing the facts (which involves, in that case, a long and painful work of exhuming mass graves) and acknowledging them publicly should also permit the dignity of the deceased to be restored and survivors and families to engage in a mourning process. If such a process does not occur, that which official discourse intends to eradicate, as if nothing had ever happened, finds no space to lodge itself in order to be reflected upon and retold, remaining absent from the individual stories as well as from the collective history.[22] The process of transmission to the next generation is then handicapped. In Cambodia, particularly among those younger than thirty years of age, who compose the majority of the Cambodian population, the memory of the genocide seems to be completely devoid of points of reference, as if swallowed up in a collective amnesia, which has caused a number of analysts to say that Cambodians 'want to forget'. Yet if a visitor takes time to listen to the people he meets, to meet them several times over a sufficiently long period such that a relationship of mutual trust is built up, if he takes an interest in written material and in the various forms of expression—going beyond words— that the young use to relate to each other, he will discover the extent to which this history is omnipresent for them. It happens precisely this way because the young cannot relate to each other through a history which has been passed on to them in things left unsaid, in silence and other strategies used by their parents to try to survive with that past.

Public narrations of the past, official or authorised accounts (celebrations, commemorations, places of remembrance, etc.) can in that way either give meaning to individual memories or, on the contrary, mutilate them.[23] This linkage does not come in to itself, especially because it entails real efforts to ascertain that each individual can be heard as such, not only as a 'victim' but also as a person capable of reflecting on his situation and commenting upon it.[24] The requirements of an investigative process or legal proceedings do not always encounter the tortuous path and the unconquerable suffering of the individual narrative. The testimony of a young woman before the International Criminal Tribunal for Rwanda in Arusha tragically highlighted this rift between the individual's story and bureaucratic procedures. During the genocide she was raped several times by Hutu militiamen. At the court hearing, counsel for the

---

[22] Renée Kaës, *Violence d'Etat et psychanalyse*, Paris: Dunod, 1989, pp. xv.

[23] See Maurice Halbwachs, *La mémoire collective*, Paris: Albin Michel, 1997, amended new edition.

[24] See the analysis that I propose in 'An ethic of responsibility in practice', *International Social Science Journal*, no. 174, December 2002, pp. 529–38.

defence asked her, 'There was no water during the genocide, so you must have smelt quite unpleasant; explain to me how, in spite of that, these men could desire to rape you several times?' The young woman's reply was crushing: 'Sir, I understand that you are not very different from the Hutus.' When I was working for human rights defence organisations, I often heard investigators complaining of divergent and changing testimony reaching them: 'Why do we never have the same version of what happened?' or—to stay with the example of Rwanda—Why did that woman, who first said her mother had been killed in the church, later say that the murder had been committed in the swamps? Had she 'lied'? Or rather was it less painful to her first to make herself think of her mother murdered in a respectable place and not in the middle of nowhere, hunted down like an animal?

Several registers of truth coexist but do not always find a meeting point. Accounts reproduced in a judicial setting, national or international, or by 'truth and reconciliation' commissions suggest themselves a certain representation of what happened; in that sense, they shape collective memories but may also create contradictions that have to be considered as such—going beyond right-thinking discourse sanctifying consensual visions, which can be no more than the imposition of a version of history by one group over others.[25] One should be able to maintain the tension between individual and collective experiences and memories of violence. In the spring of 2003, in Bosnia-Herzegovina, officers of the Prosecutor's office of the International Criminal Tribunal for former Yugoslavia stated that most of the complaints and testimony gathered over the years was not passed on to The Hague because the massacres they referred to were not 'important' enough (according to criteria based on statistics or the identity of the people responsible—standards that do not interest the victims). Even among the voluminous files passed on to The Hague, only some led to prosecutions. As for the lists of witnesses proposed, for material reasons and reasons of time, the judges often had to reduce them considerably. All these considerations can be understood rationally, but the pain of the victims and their families? In addition, the efforts to publicise the International Criminal Tribunal hearings have not been sufficient to compensate for the foreignness of the proceedings continuing far from the society affected, even more in Rwanda than in Bosnia. The precedent of post-war Germany, where, in the country itself, the Frankfurt trial (in which Germans tried Germans) had much more echo than the Nuremberg trial, gives cause for reflection.

[25] Mark Osiel, *Mass Atrocity, Collective Memory and the Law*, New Brunswick, NJ: Transaction, 1977.

Several reasons can be given to explain the importance of including these subjective dimensions in the work of memory on both the individual and the collective levels. Experiences of traumatic events may have been very different from one region to another, from one person or group of people to another; the dates and places that are to be considered especially important or even representative of the violence, can vary greatly. Reconstruction of local histories of the violence is therefore essential. In addition, the religious, cultural and symbolic dimensions of the trauma can be as important as the more physical and immediate ones: the disappearance or death of someone close, being tortured, etc. In Guatemala, as in Cambodia and Rwanda alike, the genocide project also asserted its determination to destroy a culture, a history. In fact it is culture itself, the possibility of social life that was assailed by the violence. In the narratives of victims and survivors, these dimensions form an integral part of the violation of their rights and their emotional experience. These wounds are of a sort that are treated with difficulty and slowly, but they are also at the heart of what ought to be the process of building a 'rule of law'. They should, in addition, encourage more caution about exporting supposed 'models', borrowed from post-dictatorship situations, especially in South America, to countries that have experienced large-scale massacres. The issue in post-war situations is 'thinking' of oneself together, that is, rebuilding a representation of the collective 'self', hitherto organised on the basis of a denial. In this sense, being 'reconciled' may mean 'no longer being opponents', to have the possibility of sharing a present that it is not a repetition of the past. This process is all the more crucial because the killers and torturers may come from the same places of survival as those they murdered or mutilated, they may have lived in, or may still live in, the same districts. They are rarely from 'elsewhere', even when they have given themselves an identity as 'Other' (especially an ethnic 'Other'). The proportion of violence committed in a neighbourhood, even within the same family, is often higher than we imagine. That drama, affecting the heart of each person's identity and of the group as a whole, formed part of the mass crimes committed in Cambodia, Burundi, Rwanda, the former Yugoslavia (Bosnia and Kosovo), Liberia, Sierra Leone and the Democratic Republic of Congo. This explains, notably, how in Bosnia-Herzegovina, in the spring of 2003, a number of Bosnians, while expressing satisfaction at the trial of Milosevic, recalled, like one young woman of Mostar, 'The one who raped me is not Milosevic, he is the man I see passing every morning under my window. As long as nothing is done about that, there can be no peace.'

Whether justice is done within the national territory or outside, it must always be accompanied by reactivation of channels of communication within and among communities, overcoming suspicions aroused by years of war or oppression. This work needs to involve, notably, symbolising efforts to allow each person or group in society to start approaching the experience of others and relating it to their own.[26] This implies understanding of what has been irrevocably destroyed or transformed, which excludes a simple return to pre-war conditions, but requires consideration of the ways taken by the societies in question to survive horror and, again, trying to make sense of what has no sense. Even societies that are, for various reasons, most often presented as especially warlike and capable of hiding within themselves self-destructive forces that drove them to unparalleled violence, have modes of regulation and resources capable of serving as a basis for reconstruction. To go out to meet those modes and resources, of course, means—as a Haitian colleague put it—considering the people concerned as 'subjects of law' and not simply 'objects of legal or humanitarian assistance'.[27] That implies taking account of different 'meaning systems'[28], in the light of which values and codes of conduct are being redefined, or traumas are being treated in ways that go beyond words (for instance, the value of silence as a mark of respect for another's pain can be substituted for the therapeutic value associated with talking in Western societies). Traditional rituals can then make it possible to start a process of re-reading the past without having to confront the trauma directly.

In Mozambique, through purification rituals involving the whole community, mediums and healers (*kimbanda*) particularly helped peaceful reintegration of child soldiers within communities. Referring to concepts of pollution and purification, they made it possible to designate and describe the period of violence as 'abnormal', 'unacceptable', but also to redefine the rules indispensable for the group's coexistence and survival.[29] In Cambodia, mediums and healers (*kruu* and *ruup*) played a decisive role in the reintegration of displaced people and refugees. In particular, they made it possible to rebuild symbolic links among members of a reference

[26] This approach is suggested by the Greek origin of the word (*sumballein*=bridge).

[27] Preface to Béatrice Pouligny, *L'intervention en faveur des droits de l'Homme. Manuel-guide*, Port-au-Prince: Ed. de l'ICKL, 1997.

[28] See Clifford Geertz, *The Interpretation of Culture*, New York: Basic Books, 1973, p. 89.

[29] See Alcinda Honwana, 'Children of War: Understandings of War and War Cleansing in Mozambique and Angola' in Simon Chesterman (ed.), *Civilians in War*, New York: Lynne Rienner, 2001, pp. 123–42; Harry G. West, 'Creative Destruction and Sorcery of Construction: Power, Hope and Suspicion in Post-war Mozambique', *Cahiers d'Etudes Africaines* (37) 147, 1997, pp. 657–98; Sara Gibbs, 'Postwar Social Reconstruction in Mozambique: Reframing Children's Experiences of Trauma and Healing', pp. 227–38, in Krishna Kumar (ed.), *Rebuilding Societies after Civil War*, Boulder, CO: Lynne Rienner, 1997.

community and reinterpret the various violent ruptures suffered by the society.[30] Here, it is not a matter of wanting at any cost to recover 'traditions' which sometimes no longer exist, but rather of listening to the resources that ordinary people may mobilise so as to pick up the threads of disrupted history. In Guatemala, Maya rituals expressed in ceremonies commemorating the dead, especially when there are exhumations, are no longer a bygone tradition; they reflect a will both to recover one's roots and to re-interpret them in a world that has gone through a profound upheaval. Mediums and healers thus appear to complement transformations taking place in transitional societies, especially endowing them with meaning. It is important to take them into account to understand how, in a concrete situation, alternative modes of participation and inclusion of the majority can be ensured. The will to 'build peace' assumes, indeed, giving back their proper places to the *imaginary* and representations. From this point of view the transition from a world of war to a world of peace also needs to be marked by rituals. People sign peace treaties (often outside the country concerned) but do not accompany the sharp break felt in the mind, although these wars are nearly always 'lost' wars, at least for the majority of the people. Popular rejoicing has been rather rare in the 'peace processes' of the past decade. Monuments, commemorations and other rituals should be considered in that sense. They should signify, notably, a change in the nature of the state, a breach with the past that only trials carried out, at least partly by national institutions, can ritualise.[31]

Understanding the conditions on which peace can be built in a given society means trying to make the numerous changes going through it, in its structures and its rules, intelligible, so as to assess the bases on which reconstruction is possible. In fact, far from being the intangible foundation to which the 'international community' readily refers, 'the rule of law' is the product of concrete histories, the expression of worldviews and of social relations.[32] It is a project built up through successive compromises and processes. As the anthropologist Georges Balandier reminds us, this enterprise involves renunciation: to a way of thinking that rejects the irra-

---

[30] See Maurice Eisenbruch, 'Mental Health and the Cambodian Traditional Healer for Refugees who Resettled, were Repatriated or Internally Displaced, and for those who Stayed at Home', *Collegium Anthropologicum* 18/2, December 1994, pp. 219–30. See also Joop de Jong (ed.), *Trauma, War and Violence: Public Mental Health in Socio-Cultural Context*, New York: Kluwer Academic/Plenum Publishers, 2002.

[31] See Humphrey Michael, 'From Victim to Victimhood: Truth Commissions and Trials as Rituals of Political Transition and Individual Healing', *Australian Journal of Anthropology*, vol. 14 no. 2, 2003, pp. 171–87.

[32] Norbert Rouland, *Aux confins du droit. Anthropologie de la modernité*, Paris: Odile Jacob, 1991, and *Anthropologie juridique*, Paris: PUF, 1998.

tional and the imaginary in the aim of achieving, at all costs, a society of reason.[33] Local resources for peace are not necessarily found where they are usually looked for. They may even be hidden and belong in part to the networks of 'the invisible', as for healing rituals.

But, as Maurice Merleau-Ponty has recalled, the domain of the invisible sphere 'is neither above or below the appearances, but at the juncture'; it is like 'the fastening that secretly ties an experience to its variants'.[34] By that definition, it is, in the fullest sense, a space for healing, for opening to the world beyond death and agony. One needs to agree to go beyond appearances and understand the war-peace transition in its different collective and individual dimensions, including those that, until now, have been widely underestimated and relate to psychoanalysis.

It is equally important to take account of what happens in the 'interstices' of societies, in that this contributes to greater 'density' for social ties, which participate with greater confidence in oneself and others. From that point of view, exchange is like the sense of civic responsibility: as it is used, so it grows and imposes its usefulness. This is essential in view of one of the main challenges to any peace process: ensuring that individual and collective choices now give priority to peaceful means of resolving conflicts. Finding out how 'bridges' between communities and groups are built, encouraging the creation and support of such bridges, should be among the priorities of peace missions. That assumes a true revolution in understanding local contexts, in the peace missions' intelligence and communication capacity, in order, particularly, to identify the local actors likely to be the major motors for change. The highly formal and—it must be said—'elitist' approach, generally favoured by UN programmes, ignores a large portion of the changes occurring within the societies concerned, especially at the community level.

However, the timid forms of reconstruction that can be identified in community settings need to accommodate intermediary spaces if a larger political project is to develop. These are often saturated with many different interveners that rush into the 'peace building' and democracy market-place. Not only do they occupy many spaces themselves, they often encourage a veritable explosion of the local NGO sector, encouraged both by the ideology of promoting 'civil society' and the arrival of substantial funds. Those local NGOs, oriented first towards the outside world, often have difficulty finding their place as intermediaries with what takes place at the community level; they are also often diverted by local political networks (which sometimes create them) into patronage channels. There

[33] See Georges Balandier, *Le désordre. Eloge du mouvement*, Paris: Fayard, 1988, p. 247.
[34] Maurice Merleau-Pontry, *Le visible et l'invisible*, Paris: Gallimard, 1964, p. 155.

is a major issue at stake here: avoiding withdrawal into the community, where in actual fact forms of exercising citizenship, and also ways of enhancing economic and physical security, are reinvented in many countries. In fact returning to a partly reinvented community space may—because this space has been so disturbed by years of war, repression and forced displacement—be like a retreat into oneself, indeed an identity intensified by ill-treatment. In this case what is needed is to ensure mediation towards the political sphere of what happens at the community level. That is the price to pay, in particular, so that identity-based particularities can effectively appear as a mode of participation and redistribution. While Bosnia and Kosovo present, for differing reasons, an enhanced image of the risks of such a process, those risks are present elsewhere in other forms.

In this respect peace engineering promoted by the UN is based on another contradiction, a major one. While it claims to be (re)building the state, it continually reduces the process to highly technical dimensions, depriving it of all political substance. This attitude is partially dictated by the need to bypass (if one cannot come to terms with) the ambushes of ideological debates at the international level—a precaution that the liberal messianism of the Bush administration certainly does not burden itself with. 'Depoliticisation' or 'technicisation' is supposed to accommodate those differences. It has to do with the recurring flaws in United Nations missions: lack of preparation and improvisation explain why action is based essentially on 'kits' that may indeed be useful in emergencies for building of makeshift hospitals, nutrition centres or refugee camps, but are absurdly over-systematised when it comes to institutional rebuilding. In Bosnia, and often in Kosovo, the 'international community' has been navigating by sight. In this connection 'technicisation' affects both democratisation programmes and those devoted to judicial reforms, police training and, still more, promotion of 'good governance'. That option may amount in practice to making certain political choices, notably, encouraging fake peace and fake democracy.

This is reinforced by the exaggerated importance given to exit strategies by Western governments, concerned, above all, with the security of their personnel and the risks of mission creep. In consideration of this, the capitals of the countries concerned experience in a few months—as in Phnom Penh in 1992–3[35]—an 'invasion', and an equally rapid withdrawal, of organisations and aid of all sorts, without serious impact on the life of the majority of the inhabitants. Meanwhile, the declared ambitions of the mission have been noticeably revised downwards. The interests of the

[35] Cambodia was a textbook case in this respect: eighteen months for one of the most costly and ambitious operations in the history of the United Nations.

intervening forces may find common ground with those of the local elite: 'consolidating' the status quo or redistributing cards without stimulating any major change, which obviously contradicts the ambition to 'build peace'. It is true that it may be much easier to overthrow a regime, or indeed win a war, than to rebuild a country on a durable basis. This project certainly does not relate to linear processes, and may find it difficult to come to terms with the immediacy of international politics. The roads to peace are much less like the motorways one could have hoped for than broken and bumpy roads, sometimes barely laid out, that are the norm in the countries concerned. It is these 'non-roads'[36] that the UN must also agree to take, both physically and symbolically.

[36] 'Non-roads' was the term adopted by Blue Berets, with whom I worked under ONUVEH in Haiti in 1990, to describe the roads (fairly unfit for traffic, it is true) that I invited them to use in the Artibonite valley.

CONCLUSION

May 11, 2002, at UN headquarters in New York. At the request of the Secretary General, the members of the Security Council have just spent two days debating the report of the International Commission on Intervention and State Sovereignty, set up on the initiative of the Canadian government with Gareth Evans and Mohamed Sahnoun as co-chairmen.[1] Published five months earlier, the report sought to define a 'responsibility to protect' the population, which would make it possible to overcome opposition aroused by the idea of a 'right to interfere'. Where some observers saw 'unhoped-for' progress or even a real 'arousing of awareness' on the part of some states, I for my part heard only very vague and cautious words, going together with self-satisfaction and cynicism which are common in multilateral diplomacy but no less depressing to me.

A few minutes after the conclusion of the session, a diplomat I met in September 1999 at a meeting organised by the International Peace Academy on the theme of protection of civilians in war, approached me and, giving me a friendly tap on the shoulder, said laughing, "we did not speak so much of your people, did we?". Indeed, these comments propelled me to think of someone whom I had met a little earlier in Paris, in the hostel where he was staying at that time. I shall refer to him as Johnny. Johnny was one of the innumerable children sacrificed in war. At the end of a journey, all the more fantastic because he reinvented it for every new listener, he landed in France. While starting therapy with a psychiatrist, he was going to school, and his behaviour problems did not totally prevent the beginnings of socialization in his new surroundings. Like many of his mates, he learned French very quickly. But the traumas and nightmares of his past remained with him. As we all know, miracle cures exist only in fairy stories. At some point in our conversation, Johnny recalled the Blue Helmets who went to his country, Sierra Leone, and concluded, 'Those people are not serious!' The same words uttered by others before him, in San Salvador, Port-au-Prince, Phnom Penh, Sarajevo or Beira, and in several other places since. The same words also used to describe the post-

---

[1] *The Responsibility to Protect*, report of the International Commission on Intervention and State Sovereignty, Ottawa: IDRC, 2001.

war 'vacuum' that replaced the hope that people had been able to retain, that peace resemble something real. These words are difficult to 'hear'. Who can believe that the end of war might have changed nothing? Far away from there, in New York, in the antiquated and cold corridors of the UN, thinking also about the way in which the most decisive recommendations of the report of the Panel of Experts on Peace Operations (the 'Brahimi Report') have been buried by UN member states, I turn to the diplomat and say, 'Do you think what is going on here is serious? Do you think that all of us are serious when we deal with these questions?' After a short silence, another laugh and another tap on the shoulder: he advised me to rest, before leaving.

Too many of our academic, diplomatic or bureaucratic discussions take place as though we were working on 'objects' outside our own world (where human life has a price), as though the people in question are not women and men like us. Reflections by diplomats as well as analysts on war and peace tend too often to raise 'a barrier between [our] intelligence and [our] humanity', to paraphrase Raymond Aron. Analysis can, even if it is involuntary, dehumanise the Other and reduce him to a digit—a digit, not a history. In the fall of 1996, the refugees in North Kivu (East Congo) were no more than dots on satellite pictures for the diplomats in New York discussing whether it was opportune to undertake a humanitarian operation. The discrepancy is all the more stark when discourse calling for 'global', 'human' or 'common' security is compared with inaction that made possible the tragedies of Rwanda, Srebrenica, Kosovo and many others, more anonymous because they have received less media attention or have been deliberately 'forgotten' (Sri Lanka, Chechnya, Democratic Republic of Congo, Angola, Guatemala etc.).

The retreat of the prospect of war into distance from Western societies, together with the end of the Cold War, has influenced both studies of international security over the past decade and the image of international insecurity conveyed to the political class as well as to public opinion. No longer capable of interpretation through the prism of the East–West confrontation, or the rigid framework of economic rationalism which in fact does not explain our own behaviour either, conflicts have all too often tended to be characterised as irrational, on the basis of that regrettable habit whereby anything that our frameworks of analysis cannot (or can no longer) explain is said to be non-existent or inexplicable. Against that background, the theme of 'barbarity', linked to that of 'chaos' has re-emerged with force. Outside home territory, war waged by Western contingents is supposed to be not only 'professional' but more 'scientific', and supposedly 'clean' because it is largely conducted at a distance, through air strikes and launching of missiles. Other countries' wars, however, give rise to outpourings of violence, which surpass understanding and revolt the conscience. They belong to a world of barbarism and madness. The 'dialectic of the bourgeois and the barbarian', to use Pierre Hassner's terribly apt expression, has rarely been so well illustrated.[2] Besides often leading to strange sweeping overviews of history (those wars, it is said, are more numerous and violent than in the past), the label of 'barbarous' generally serves once more to denote not that specific part of the human nature which is present in everyone, but rather the behaviour of the Other. It corresponds, albeit unconsciously, to a desire to distance ourselves, as if for reassurance that "we are not like that".

In many respects, those who take part in UN peace operations have the formidable task of intervening at the very heart of this contradiction. 'Intervening' means getting involved, in one way or another, in the tangle of actions and reactions described in these pages. The documentary fiction film *Warriors*, produced by a BBC team in 1999, through describing the progress of a small group of British Blue Helmets in Bosnia during the war, presents an extreme, but none the less effective vision of plunging into a reality that can be, in the fullest sense, unendurable. Those who survived the bombing against the UN headquarters in Bagdad, on August 19, 2003, can also testify to that, as can the colleagues who have been on the edge of the abyss in Rwanda or elsewhere. In most cases, members of peace missions are not confronted with such tragic situations. It is probably more difficult for them to grasp the different effects of their presence. That is the fate of any outsider. In this sense, the action of the 'international community' can never be analysed in itself; it forms part of a local reality that grasps it partially, and that must be grasped. Even an ideal international scenario, far from being achieved today (unfailing political support, clear mandate, good organization and provision of sufficient material and financial means), would not change this basic reality. Intervention cannot be limited to a mere military presence, however imposing it might be.

The parameters that any member of a peace operation, whether civilian, police or military, needs to take into account are numerous. The situations that these individuals will be called upon to cope with, will often owe a lot to chance. Nothing is entirely predetermined. Much of what is being rebuilt—or else, unfortunately, continuing to be destroyed—in societies just emerging from war, escapes the notice of outsiders, whoever they are. This is often the commonplace, if not 'ordinary' daily life, which must be absolutely penetrated again if one wishes to understand what is happening

---

[2] Pierre Hassner, 'Par-delà de la guerre et la paix. Violence et intervention après la guerre froide', *Etudes* 385/3, September 1996, pp. 149–58.

during a peace operation. It can contribute to clarifying interests, strategies, events, places, actors and institutions that are usually neglected. What occurs in this 'detail' of missions can prove as important as developments in what is identified as the 'centre' of political negotiations or even in the UN Security Council or before an International Criminal Court.

This implies a mental revolution in which the UN Secretariat must play its part. It must overcome the constraints, especially material ones, imposed by states and involve itself more clearly in the battle for a better knowledge and understanding of local contexts by members of missions. Everyone—not only members of the mission's analysis unit or the military intelligence cells—must have at their disposal, at all stages of their work, relevant tools of analysis to understand and monitor what is changing in the societies in which they are working. This information must be at the continuous disposal of field teams. It does not assume years of study and expertise, but simply taking account of what various social science disciplines have to say about the situations under consideration, and using that knowledge in an operational and analytical approach, constantly updated. Political science, economics, geography, sociology, history, anthropology, psychoanalysis and other disciplines have much to say about war and peace, in the intersection of the light that each discipline provides. Resort to a true trans-disciplinary approach (until now more readily invoked than put into practice) would also have the advantage of helping to re-link the individual and collective dimensions of concrete situations, especially when it is a question of traumas caused by conflicts.

Furthermore, this approach assumes that those involved in such operations cease to consider the local people either as passive recipients of their largesse or as potential obstacles to the smooth progress of their work. Members of UN missions are no more modest, flexible or open than the average human. Among civilians such qualities have not been encouraged by the creation, in a little over a decade, of fairly limited networks of individuals located at the meeting point of militancy and expertise, state and non-state. They move among national administrations, NGOs, international organizations and other bodies with doubtful status,[3] which now share the new market of state building, democracy and transitional justice. The individuals who are part of those networks are for ever between contracts, forced constantly to anticipate their next post. Albeit with a few exceptions, they have little inclination to question their work, as most of the conferences organised on the subject, and as many publications, have testified. That 'community'—of which academics engaged in the area of

---

[3] For instance, the National Endowment for Democracy, a private foundation, but set up and funded by the US Congress.

expertise are also a part—also shows a fairly low effective ability to learn. Because its members work under a succession of short-term contracts, without any real follow-up of performance from one mission to another, and operate in a closed circle often far removed from the ground reality with which relations are strongly asymmetrical, they are, in the last resort, not responsible either to their employers or, above all, to the supposed 'beneficiaries' of their action. Reforms are desperately needed to change a system rightly qualified by the Brahimi Report as 'diametrically opposed to meritocracy'. Such reforms need to be vigorous, to include an effective performance assessment and sanction system. The preparation, pre-brief-ings, continuous training, monitoring and debriefing of missions' staff should be a priority. This should include specific psychological support, particularly when the staff has to be deployed in violent contexts. This is the first front that we must fight on if we want to start 'being serious' in our desire to contribute to peacebuilding in other countries.

On a second front, the objective should be to reduce the gap between what happens in the corridors of diplomacy and the reality on the ground. It is most certainly not the easiest task to accomplish, if only because gov-ernments of member states refuse to give themselves or, still more, the UN Secretariat the necessary means. The debates on the Brahimi Report in the General Assembly in the autumn of 2000 were a clear illustration of this. The policy of double standards in decisions to deploy peace oper-ations, their increasing interference in domestic affairs, the fear that any strengthening of the capacity of peace operations will be to the detriment of resources for development aid already in sharp decline, and other factors explain the hostile attitude of most representatives of member states to strengthen the UN's capacity for analysis. In addition, the Secur-ity Council is sometimes perceived as fulfilling a legislative role formerly allotted to the General Assembly and assigning itself an increasingly wider agenda, whereas all plans to broaden its membership have reached a dead end. This partly explains why budgetary decisions in the General Assembly remain the main point of leverage for the majority of member states, with concrete consequences for the means at the disposal of UN peace operations. In the absence of a generous, voluntarist and coherent policy on the part of the Council's permanent members (most notably France and Britain) there can be scarcely any hope for decisive progress in the near future.

All that remains is to count on the good will of diplomats. They are often much more influenced by their experience of a previous crisis than by their knowledge of the precise case they are examining. Furthermore, the practice has shown that even when they are aware of the lessons of the past, they are still far from actual application. There is a large gap between knowing those lessons and taking the consequences on board in the decision-making process. Here individual qualities are often jeopardised by group effects, the fairly high rate of rotation of diplomatic staff, and even more the pressures of political leaders whose personal agendas coincide only exceptionally with the defence of peace in the world. Besides, the concern of a Western diplomat representing his country on the Security Council is, with some exceptions, not the actual application of a resolution, but first of all the fact that it has been adopted in better or less good conditions. Shortly afterwards, his superiors will remind him of the urgency of defining an 'exit strategy' (more of an 'exit' than a 'strategy' in fact, despite fine-sounding declarations of intent), especially when some of the troops are from his country. Outside Europe, this imperative remains a weighty one in practice. The objective sought in dispatching a peace operation may be, as much as 'containing' a conflict, taking a situation off the international agenda—as was the case in Cambodia and El Salvador. That is the criterion of its 'success' in the eyes of the 'international community'.

Progress in resolving these major political contradictions will only be made if citizens of the world 'at peace' begin to mobilize and call their political leaders to account for these questions. Unless they have visited a country at war or 'in crisis'—spending more than 48 hours there, and on condition of going to places other than international hotel and conference rooms 'out of the world'—a European or North American citizen cannot, at any time, convey to himself the daily preoccupations of an inhabitant of a country in the world of 'chaos'. Contrary to what one might think, that distance was not fundamentally challenged by the outrageous terrorist attacks of 11 September 2001. Even the streets of Manhattan, outside the very limited territory of 'Ground Zero', very quickly confirmed that they still belonged to the world of security, a world where terror can strike, and strike spectacularly, but where it is still understood that this is exceptional, that our life is not threatened at every moment. The way in which 'the' phenomenon of terrorism has been analysed since then—far from the local and international political, social and economic logics that have formed it through histories that have themselves been diverse—tends also to confirm that division into two 'camps', notwithstanding all the conflicts where, as in Africa, 'terrorism' does not explain much. In the West, the main image that we receive of the other world is still that so very selective one appearing on our television screens. Apart from that, everything is done to maintain the appearance of separation, including concealment of the numerous links and connected interests between those 'madmen' who exterminate their fellows and the political and economic actors of our supposedly rational, peaceful and regulated world.

Fortunately, neither compassion nor the growing, if fleeting conscious-ness of common humanity is stopped by the real disarray of many of our fellow citizens faced with difficulties in obtaining reliable, varied inform-ation and finding their bearings within it. However, beyond that, we seem intuitively to fear that if we get closer to those situations, understand them, and realize that we are not so far removed from the misfortune of the people concerned, we will be forced into revolutionary action in our own life. We obsessively fear that the world at war and the human beings inhabiting it will catch up with us and, that by appearing so close to us and so human, they will question us about what needs to change in our lives now. The fear is that we will lose our 'peace and quiet', an idea directly opposed to that of 'responsibility'. The 'responsibility to protect' does not belong to states only; it is also a responsibility for us, the citizens.

Our societies have always been preoccupied with winning wars. It is time that we reflect on ways of winning peace. These questions cannot be left to national and international officials alone. This strictly ethical exercise, beyond a necessary deeper reflection on 'the moral reality of war',[4] should lead us to question ourselves about the value everyone assigns, as a decision-maker, as an analyst, as a citizen, to our own humanity and hence to that of others. If the idea of 'human security' is one day to have a concrete meaning, it must incorporate such reflection. This essay has aimed to be a modest contribution to that project, proposing a different image of peace operations conducted by the UN across the world: the image conveyed by the people themselves.

---

[4] See, for instance, Michael Walzer, *Just and Unjust Wars: A Moral Argument with His-torical Illustrations*, New York: Basic Books, 3rd edn, 2000.

SELECT BIBLIOGRAPHY

For a detailed bibliography and a full list of sources, see the book website at: http://www.ceri-sciences-po.org/cherlist/pouligny/indexen.htm. Exclusive data, graphics, documents of reference and chronologies are also available.

INTERNATIONAL CONFLICT AND SECURITY

Books

ADEBAJO Adekeye and Elizabeth COUSENS. *Managing Armed Conflicts in the Twenty-First Century*. New York: International Peace Academy, 2000.

AVRUCH K., P. BLACK and J. A. SCIMECCA. *Conflict Resolution: Cross-Cultural Perspectives*. London: Greenwood Press, 1991.

BADIE Bertrand. *Un monde sans souveraineté. Les états entre ruse et responsabilité*. Paris: Fayard, 1999.

BOULDING Elise (ed.). *New Agendas for Peace Research: Conflict and Security Reexamined*. Boulder, CO: Lynne Rienner, 1992.

BRADFORD James C. *The Military and Conflict Between Cultures. Soldiers at the Interface*. College Station, TX: Texas A and M University Press, 1997.

BROWN Michael Edward (ed.). *The International Dimensions of Internal Conflict*. Cambridge, MA: MIT Press, 1996.

—————— and Richard N. ROSENCRANCE (eds). *The Costs of Conflict: Prevention and Cure in the Global Arena*, coll. Carnegie Commission on Preventing Deadly Conflicts Series, New York: Carnegie Corporation of New York; Lanham, MD: Rowman and Littlefield, 1999.

BUZAN Barry. *People, States and Fear: An Agenda for International Security Studies in the Post-Cold War Era*, 2nd ed. New York: Harvester Wheatsheaf, 1991.

——————, WAEVER Ole and Jaap DE WILDE. *Security: A New Framework for Analysis*. Boulder, CO: Lynne Rienner, 1998.

CHESTERMAN Simon. *Just War or Just Peace? Humanitarian Intervention and International Law*. Oxford University Press, 2001.

—————— (ed.). *Civilians in War*, Project of the International Peace Academy. Boulder, CO: Lynne Rienner, 2001.

CILLIERS Jackie and Peggy MASON (eds). *Peace, Profit, or Plunder: The Privatization of Security in War-Torn African Societies*. Halfway House: Institute for Security Studies, 1999.

CROCKER Chester A., Fen Osler HAMPSON and Pamela AALL (eds). *Managing Global Chaos. Sources and Responses to International Conflict*. Washington, DC: US Institute of Peace Press, 1996.

277

DAMROSCH Lori Fisler (ed.). *Enforcing Restraint. Collective Intervention in Internal Conflicts*. New York: Council on Foreign Relations Press, 1993.

DANIEL Donald C. F. and Bradd C. HAYES. *Coercive Inducement and the Containment of International Crises*. Washington, DC: US Institute of Peace Press, 1999.

DAVIS Jane (ed.). *Security Issues in the Post-Cold War World*. Brookfield: Edward Elgar, 1996.

DEUTSCH Morton. "Subjective Features of Conflict Resolution: Psychological, Social and Cultural Influences." in Raimo VÄYRYNEN, Dieter SENGHAAS and Christian SCHMIDT (eds). *The Quest for Peace: Transcending Collective Violence and War among Societies, Cultures and States*, London: Sage, 1987.

DONINI Antonio, NILAND Norah, and Karin WERMESTER (eds). *Nation-Building Unraveled? Aid, Peace and Justice*. Bloomfield, CT: Kumarian Press, 2004.

DOYLE Michael W. *Ways of War and Peace: Realism, Liberalism and Socialism*, New York/ London: W. W. Norton, 1997.

FISHER Ronald J. (ed.). *Interactive Conflict Resolution*. New York: Syracuse University Press, 1997.

FORBES Ian and Mark HOFFMAN (eds). *Political Theory, International Relations and the Ethics of Intervention*. Basingstoke: Macmillan / New York: St Martin's Press, 1993.

GALTUNG Johan and Carl G. JACOBSEN. *Searching for Peace: The Road to Transcend*, London: Pluto, 2000.

HANNOYER Jean, *Guerres civiles. Economies de la violence, dimensions de la civilité*. Paris: Karthala, 1999.

HASSNER Pierre. *La violence et la paix. De la bombe atomique au nettoyage ethnique*. Paris: Le Seuil, 2000.

———. *La terreur et l'empire. La violence et la paix* II. Paris: Le Seuil, 2003.

HASSNER Pierre and Roland MARCHAL (dir.). *Guerre et Sociétés. Etats et violence après la guerre froide*. Paris: Karthala, 2003.

HOLBROOKE, Richard. *To End a War*. New York: Random House, 1998.

HOLSTI Kalevi J. *The State, War, and the State of War*. Cambridge University Press, 1996.

JENTLESON Bruce W. *Opportunities Missed, Opportunities Seized: Preventive Diplomacy in the Post-Cold War World*. The Carnegie Commission on Preventing Deadly Conflict. Lanham, MD: Rowman & Littlefield, 1999.

KRASNER Stephen. *Sovereignty: Organized Hypocrisy*. Princeton University Press, 1999.

KRAUSE Keith R. *Culture and Security: Multilateralism, Arms Control and Security Building*. London: Frank Cass, 1999.

KRIESBERG Louis, NORTHRUP Terrell A. and Stewart J. THORSON (eds). *Intractable Conflicts and Their Transformation*. New York: Syracuse University Press, 1989.

LITTLE Richard. *Intervention: External Involvement in Civil Wars*. London: Martin Robertson, 1975.

LYONS Gene M. and Michael MASTANDUNO. *Beyond Westphalia: State Sovereignty and International Intervention*. Baltimore, MD: Johns Hopkins University Press, 1995.

MACCRAE Joanne and Anthony B. ZWI. (eds). *War and Hunger: Rethinking International Responses to Complex Emergencies*. London: Atlantic Highlands (NJ): Zed Books in association with Save the Children Fund, 1994.

MAYNARD Kimberley A. *Healing Communities in Conflict*. New York: Columbia University Press, 1999.

MCADAM Doug, Sidney TARROW and Charles TILLY. *Dynamics of Contention*. New York: Cambridge University Press, 2001.

MIALL Hugh, Oliver RAMSBOTHAM and Tom WOODHOUSE. *Contemporary Conflict Resolution: The Prevention, Management and Transformation of Deadly Conflicts*. Oxford: Polity Press, 1999.

MOREAU DEFARGES Phillipe. *Un monde d'ingérences*, 2nd edn. Paris: Presse de Sciences Po, 2000.

MOSKOS Charles C. *The Post Modern Military: Armed Forces after the Cold War.* Oxford University Press, 1999.

RAMSBOTHAM Olivier and Tom WOODHOUSE. *Humanitarian Intervention in Contemporary Conflict: A Reconceptualization*, Cambridge: Polity Press, 1996.

REGAN Patrick. *Civil Wars and Foreign Powers: Outside Intervention in Intrastate Conflict.* Ann Arbor: University of Michigan Press, 2000.

ROBINSON Piers. *The CNN Effect. The Myth of News, Foreign Policy and Intervention.* London: Routledge, 2002.

RUBINSTEIN Robert A. and M. L. FOSTER. "Revitalizing International Security Analysis: Contributions from Culture and Symbolism" in R. A. RUBINSTEIN and M. L. FOSTER (eds). *The Social Dynamics of Peace and Conflict: Culture in International Security.* Boulder, CO: Westview Press, 1988: (1–14).

RUPESINGHE Kumar. "The Disappearing Boundaries Between Internal and External Conflicts" in Elise BOULDING (ed.). *New Agendas for Peace Research: Conflict and Security Reexamined.* Boulder, CO: Lynne Rienner, 1992: (43–64).

——— (ed.). *Conflict Transformation.* New York: Saint Martin's Press / Basingstoke: Macmillan, 1995.

———. *Civil Wars, Civil Peace. An Introduction to Conflict Resolution.* London: Pluto Press, 1998.

SALAMÉ Ghassan. *Appels d'empire. Ingérences et résistances à l'âge de la mondialisation .* Paris: Fayard, 1996.

SCHIRCH Lisa. *Keeping the Peace: Exploring Civilian Alternatives in Conflict Prevention.* Uppsala: Life and Peace Institute, 1995.

SCHRAEDER Peter (ed.). *Intervention into the 90s: US Foreign Policy in the Third World*, 2nd edn.. Boulder, CO: Lynne Rienner, 1992.

SHAW Martin. *The Global State and the Politics of Intervention.* London: LES / The Centre for the Study of Global Governance, 1994.

SHAWCROSS William. *Deliver Us from Evil: Warlords and peacekeepers in a world of endless Conflict.* London: Bloomsbury, 2000.

SNOW Donald M. (ed.). *UnCivil Wars: International Security and the New Internal Conflicts.* Boulder, CO: Lynne Rienner, 1996.

THUAL François. *Les conflits identitaires.* Paris: Ellipses, 1995.

VON HIPPEL Karin. *Democracy by Force: US military intervention in the post-Cold War world.* Cambridge University Press, 2000.

WALLENSTEEN Peter (ed.). *International Intervention. New Norms in the Post-Cold War Era?* Uppsala University, Sweden, 1997.

———. *Preventing Violent Conflicts. Past Records and Future Challenges.* Uppsala University, Sweden, 1998.

WALTER Barbara F. and Jack SNYDER. *Civil Wars, Insecurity, and Intervention.* New York: Columbia University Press, 1999.

WALZER Michael. *Guerres justes et injustes.* Paris: Belin, 1999.

WEISS Thomas G. (ed.). *Collective Security in a Changing World.* Boulder, CO: Lynne Rienner, 1993.

WHEELER Nicholas. *Saving Strangers: Humanitarian Intervention in International Society.* Oxford University Press, 2000.

WHITTAKER David J. *Conflict and Reconciliation in the Contemporary World.* London/New York: Routledge, 1999.

ZARTMAN Ira William (ed.). *Collapsed States: The Disintegration and Restoration of Legitimate Authority.* Boulder, CO: Lynne Rienner, 1995.

———(ed.). *Elusive peace: Negotiating an End to Civil Wars.* Washington, DC: Brookings Institution Press, 1995.
———and Lewis J. RASMUSSEN. *Peacemaking in International Conflict: Methods and Techniques.* Washington, DC: United States Institute of Peace Press, 1997.
ZARTMAN Ira William. *Traditional Cures for Modern Conflicts: African Conflict "Medicine."* Boulder, CO: Lynne Rienner, 1999.

Articles

AGGESTAM Karin and Christer JÖNSON. "(Un)Ending Conflict: Challenges in Post-War Bargaining". *Millennium,* vol. 26, no. 3 (1997).
APPADURAÏ Arjun. "Dead Certainty: Ethnic Violence in the Era of Globalization". *Public Culture,* vol. 10, no. 2, (winter 1998): 225–47
FIERKE K. M. "Multiples Identities, Interfacing Games: The Social Construction of Western Action in Bosnia." *European Journal of International Relations,* vol. 2, no. 4 (1996): 467–97
HASSNER Pierre. "Par-delà la guerre et la paix: violence et intervention après la guerre Froide." *Études,* vol. 385, no. 3 (Septembre 1996): 149–58
HOLSTI Kal. "The Coming Chaos? Armed Conflicts in the World Periphery." *International Order and the Future of World Politics.* Cambridge University Press (1999): 283–310
KALYVAS Stathis. "'New' and 'Old' Civil Wars: A Valid Distinction?" *World Politics.* vol. 54, no. 1 (2001): 99–118
KING Charles. "Ending Civil Wars." *Adelphi Paper 308.* Oxford University Press for the International Institute for Strategic Studies (1997).
KRAUSE Keith and Michael Charles WILLIAMS. "Broadening the Agenda of Security Studies: Politics and Methods." *Mershon International Studies Review,* vol. 40, sup. 2 (October 1996): 229–54
LAUE James H. "Ethical Considerations in Choosing Intervention Roles". *Peace and Change,* vol. 8, no. 2/3 (summer 1982): 29–41
MARTIN Denis-Constant. "Identity, culture, pride and conflict" in S. BEKKER and R. PRINSLOO (eds). *Identity, Theory, Politics, History.* Pretoria: Human Sciences Research Council (1999), p. 197.
RATNER Steven R. and Gerald B. HELMAN. "Saving Failed States". *Foreign Policy,* no. 89 (winter 1992–3): 3–20
VENNESSON Pascal. "Renaissante ou obsolète? La guerre aujourd'hui". *Revue Française de Science Politique,* vol. 48, no. 3–4 (July–August 1998): 515–34

UN PEACE OPERATIONS (GENERAL)

Books

AALL Pamela, Daniel MILTENBERGER and Thomas George WEISS. *Guide to IGOs, NGOs, and the Military in Peace and Relief Operations.* Washington, DC: United States Institute of Peace Press, 2000.
BERMAN Eric G. and E. Katie SAMS. *Peacekeeping in Africa: Capabilities and Culpabilities.* United Nations Institute for Disarmament Research: Institute for Security Studies. Geneva, 2000.
CAPLAN Richard. *International Governance of War-torn Territories.* London: Adelphi Paper no. 341, 2002.

CHESTERMAN Simon. *You, the People: Transitional Administration, State-Building, and the United Nations.* Oxford University Press, 2004.

CHESTERMAN, Simon, IGNATIEFF, Michael and Ramesh TAKHUR, (eds) *Making States Work: State Failure and the Crisis of Governance.* Tokyo: United Nations University Press, 2004.

CHOPRA Jarat. *Peace-Maintenance. The Evolution of International Political Authority.* London/New York: Routledge, 1998.

COUSENS Elisabeth and Chetan KUMAR (eds). *Peacebuilding as Politics: Cultivating Peace in Fragile Societies.* Boulder, CO: Lynne Rienner, 2001.

CROCKER Chester A., HAMPSON Fen Osler and Pamela AALL (eds), *Turbulent Peace: The Challenges of Managing International Conflict,* Herndon (VA): USIP St. Albans, 2001.

DOYLE Michael, JOHNSTONE Ian, and Robert C. ORR (ed.). *Keeping the peace. Multidimensional UN operations in Cambodia and El Salvador.* Cambridge University Press, 1997.

FETHERSTON Ann Betts. *Towards a Theory of United Nations Peacekeeping.* Basingstoke: Macmillan / New York: St Martin's Press, 1994.

FINDLAY Trevor. *Fighting For Peace: The Use of Force in Peace Operations.* Oxford University Press, 1999.

HAMPSON Fen Osler. *Nurturing Peace: Why Peace Settlements Succeed or Fail.* Washington, DC: US Institute of Peace, 1996.

HOLM Tor Tanke and Espen Barth EIDE. *Peacebuilding and Police Reform.* NUPI. London: Frank Cass, 2000.

IGNATIEFF, Michael. *Empire Lite: Nation Building in Bosnia, Kosovo, Afghanistan.* London: Minerva, 2003.

LEDERACH John Paul. *Building Peace: Sustainable Reconciliation in Divided Societies.* Washington, DC: United States Institute of Peace Press, 1997.

LEHMANN Ingrid A. *Peacekeeping and Public Information.* United Nations Information Centre. London: Frank Cass, March 1999.

LOUISE Christopher. *The Social Impacts of Light Weapons Availability and Proliferation.* Geneva: UNRISD (Discussion Paper no. 59). March 1995.

MACKINNON Michael G. *The Evolution of U.S. Peacekeeping under Clinton: A Fairweather Friend?* London: Frank Cass, 2000.

MALONE David M. *The UN Security Council, from the cold War to the 21st Century.* Boulder, CO: London: Lynne Rienner, 2004.

MONTGOMERY Tommie Sue. *Peacemaking and Democratization in the Western Hemisphere: Multilateral Missions.* Boulder, CO: Lynne Rienner, 1999.

NEWMAN Edward and Albrecht SCHNABEL (eds). *Recovering from Civil Conflict: Reconciliation, Peace, and Development.* London: Frank Cass, 2002.

PUGH Michael (ed). *Regeneration of War-torn Societies.* New York: St. Martin's Press, 2000.

RIKHYE Indar Jit (ed.). *The United Nations and Peacekeeping: Results, Limitations and Prospects.* Basingstoke: Macmillan, 1990, pp. 147–69.

SHAWCROSS William. *Deliver us from Evil: Peacekeepers and Warlords in a World of Endless Conflict.* London: Bloomsbury, 2000.

SMOUTS Marie-Claude (dir.). *L'ONU et la guerre, La diplomatie en kaki.* Bruxelles: Eds Complexe, 1994 (Collection du CERI "Espace international").

STEDMAN Stephen J. ROTHCHILD Donald and Elizabeth M. COUSENS. *Ending Civil Wars: The Implementation of Peace Agreements.* Boulder, CO: Lynne Rienner, 2002.

STERN Brigitte (dir.). *La vision française des opérations de maintien de la paix.* UNU/CEDIN-Paris I, Paris: Montchrestien, 1997.

282   *Select Bibliography*

WOODHOUSE Tom and Oliver RAMSBOTHAM. *Peacekeeping and Conflict Resolution.*
London: Frank Cass, 2000.

Articles

ADEKANYE J. "Arms and Reconstruction in Post-conflict Societies." *Journal of Research*, vol. 34, no. 3 (1997): 359–66.

BERDAL Mats R. "Lessons Not Learned: The Use of Force in 'Peace Operations' in the 1990s." *International Peacekeeping*, vol. 7, no. 4 (winter 2000–1): 55–74.

BERDAL Mats and Richard CAPLAN. (eds). "The Politics of International Administration." *Global Governance*, vol. 10, no. 1 (2004): 1–137.

CHOPRA Jarat (ed.). Special issue on Peace-Maintenance Operations, *Global Governance*, vol. 4, no. 1 (January–March 1998).

DIEHL Paul F., DRUCKMAN D. and J. WALL. "International Peacekeeping and Conflict Resolution." *Journal of Conflict Resolution*, vol. 42, no. 1 (1998): 33–55.

DOYLE Michael and Nicholas SAMBANIS. "International Peacebuilding: A Theoretical and Quantitative Analysis". *American Political Science Review*, vol. 94, no. 4 (December 200): 779–812

FETHERSTON Ann Betts. "Peacekeeping, Conflict Resolution and Peacebuilding: A Reconsideration of Theoretical Frameworks." *International Peacekeeping*, vol. 7, no. 1 (2000): 1–7.

———. "Peacekeeping for a New Era: Why Theory Matters". *Global Dialogue*, vol. 2, no. 2 (Spring 2000): 109–19.

HELMAN Gerald B. and Steven R. RATNER. "Saving Failed States." *Foreign Policy*, no. 89, (Winter 1992–3): 3–20.

LEHMANN Ingrid A. "Public perceptions of UN peacekeeping: a factor in the resolution of the international conflicts." *Fletcher Forum of World Affairs*, vol. 19, no. 1 (Winter–Spring 1995): 109–19.

LICKLIDER Roy. 'The American Way of State Building: Germany, Japan, Somalia and Panama', *Small Wars and Insurgencies* vol. 10 no. 3 (Winter 1999): 82–115.

LUTTWAK Edward N., "Kofi's rule: Humanitarian Intervention and Neocolonialism." *National Interest*, no. 58 (Winter 1999/2000): 57–62

MALONE David M. "Le conseil de sécurité dans les années 90: essor et récession." *Politique étrangère* (February 2000): 403–21.

MALONE David and Ramesh THAKUR. "UN Peacekeeping: Lessons Learned?" *Global Governance*, vol. 7, no. 1 (January–March 2001): 11–17.

MILLIKEN Jennifer (ed.), "State Failure, Collapse and Reconstruction", special issue, *Development and Change*, vol. 33, no. 5 (November 1992): 753–1072

NEDERVEEN PIETERSE Jan. "Sociology of Humanitarian Intervention: Bosnia, Rwanda and Somalia Compared". *International Political Science Review*, vol. 18, no. 1 (January 1997): 71–93.

OTTAWAY Marina. "Nations Building." *Foreign Policy* (September–October 2002): 16–24.

RUBINSTEIN Robert A. "Cultural Aspects of Peacekeeping: Notes on the Substance of Symbols." *Millennium*, vol. 22, no. 3 (winter 1993): 547–62.

——— and M. L. FOSTER (eds). *The Social Dynamics of Peace and Conflict: Culture in International Security.* Boulder, CO: Westview Press, 1988.

RUPNIK Jacques. "L'avenir des protectorats internationaux dans les Balkans." *Critique internationale* no. 16. (July 2002).

STEDMAN Stephen John. "Spoilers problems in peace process." *International Security*, vol. 22, no. 2 (Fall 1997): 5–53

TALENTINO Andrea Kathryn. "Intervention as Nation-Building: Illusion or Possibility?" *Security Dialogue* vol. 33 no. 1 (March 2002): 27–43.

Publications of governments and international organizations

BOUTROS-GHALI, Boutros. *An Agenda for Peace*. New York: United Nations, 1995.
Supplement to *An Agenda for Peace: Position Paper of the Secretary-General on the Occasion of the Fiftieth Anniversary of the United Nations*, UN Doc. A/50/60-S/1995/1 (3 January 1995).
Carnegie Commission on Preventing Deadly Conflict. Final report, *Preventing Deadly Conflict*. New York: Carnegie Corporation of New York, 1997.
International Commission on Intervention and State Sovereignty. *The Responsibility to Protect*. Ottawa: International Development Research Center, December 2001.
OECD. Helping Prevent Violent Conflict. The DAC Guidelines. Paris: OECD, 2001.
Report of the Panel on United Nations Peace Operations (Brahimi Report), UN Doc. A/55/305-S/2000/809 (21 August 2000).
Report of the Secretary General. Support by the United Nations system of the efforts of Governments to promote and consolidate new or restored democracies, UN Doc. A/55/489 (13 October 2000).

General publications of NGOs and international conferences

AMNESTY INTERNATIONAL. *Peacekeeping and Human Rights*, IOR 40/01/94. London, January 1994.
ASPEN INSTITUTE. *Honoring Human Rights and Keeping the Peace: Lessons from El Salvador, Cambodia and Haiti. Recommendations for the United Nations*. New York: Aspen Institute / Justice and Society Program, 1995 (Rapport partiel d'un séminaire).
HUMAN RIGHTS WATCH. *The Lost Agenda. Human Rights and UN Field Operations*. New York: Human Rights Watch, June 1993.
International Peace Academy, UNHCR. *Healing the Wound: Refugees, Reconstruction and Reconciliation*. New York/Geneva, 1996.
OXFAM. *Improving the UN's Response to Conflict Related Emergencies*. Oxfam Briefing no. 6, November 1993.

THE POLITICS OF DEMOCRATISATION AND POST-CONFLICT RECONSTRUCTION

Books

BAYART, Jean-François (ed.). *La greffe de l'État*. Paris: Karthala, 1996.
BROWN Michael Edward, Sean M. LYNN-JONES and Steven E. MILLER *Debating the Democratic Peace*. Cambridge, MA: MIT Press, 1996.
CASTORIADIS Cornelius. *L'institution imaginaire de la société*. Paris: Seuil, 1975.
CHANDLER David. *Bosnia: Faking Democracy After Dayton*. London: Pluto Press, 2000.
DEUTSCH Karl. "Nation-building and national development: some issues for political research" in K. Deutsch and W. J. Foltz (eds). *Nation-building*. New York: Atherton Press, 1963.

284 *Select Bibliography*

DOBBINS, James *et al. America's Role in Nation-Building: From Germany to Iraq*. Santa Monica (CA): RAND, 2003.

ELMAN Miriam Fendius. *Paths to Peace: is Democracy the Answer?* Cambridge (MA): MIT Press, 1997.

GRIFFITHS Ann L. (ed.). *Building Peace and Democracy in Post-Conflict Societies*. Halifax (NS): Dalhousie University, 1998.

HANN Chris and Elizabeth DUNN. European Association of Social Anthropologists (eds). *Civil Society: Challenging Western Models*. London/New York: Routledge, 1996.

International Institute for Democracy and Electoral Assistance. *Democracy and Global Cooperation at the United Nations*. 2000. (policy brief written by Izumi Nakamitsy Lennartsson, Béatrice Pouligny and Martin Wikfalk).

KANT Immanuel et Françoise PROUST (ed.). *Vers la paix perpétuelle. Que signifie s'orienter dans la pensée? Qu'est-ce que les lumières?* Paris: Flammarion, 1991.

KUMAR Krishna (ed.). *Postconflict Elections, Democratization and International Assistance*. Boulder (CO): Lynne Rienner, 1998.

MILBRATH Lester W. *Political Participation: How and Why People Get Involved in Politics*, 2nd edn. Chicago (IL): Rand McNaly, 1977.

O'DONNELL Guillermo A., Philippe C. SCHMITTER and Laurence WHITEHEAD (eds). *Transitions from Authoritarian Rule: Prospects for Democracy*. Baltimore, MD: Johns Hopkins University Press, 1986.

PRZEWORSKI Adam. *Democracy and the Market*. Cambridge University Press, 1991.

RUSSETT Bruce. *Grasping the Democratic Peace, Principles for a Post-Cold War World*. Princeton University Press, 1993.

TILLY Charles. *Coercion, capital and European States, A.D. 900–1990*. Oxford: Basil Blackwell, 1990.

Articles

CALL Charles T. and Susan E. COOK (eds). Special Issue on Governance after War: Rethinking Democratization and Peacebuilding. *Global Governance*, vol. 9, no. 2 (April–June 2003).

CHAN Steve. "In Search of Democratic Peace: Problems and Promise". *Mershon International Studies Review*, vol. 41, no. 1 (May 1997): 59–92.

FRANCK Thomas M. "The Emerging Right to Democratic Governance." *American Journal of International Law*, vol. 86, no. 1 (January 1992): 46–91.

GUILHOT Nicolas. "Les professionnels de la démocratie: logiques militantes et logiques savantes dans le nouvel internationalisme américain." *Actes de la recherche en sciences sociales*, no. 139 (Sept. 2001): 53–65.

HAYNES Jeff. "Democratic Consolidation in the Third World: Many Questions, Any Answers?" *Contemporary Politics*, vol. 6, no. 2, (June 2000): 123–41.

HOFFMANN Stanley. "The Crisis of Liberal Internationalism." *Foreign Policy*, no. 98, (Spring 1995): 159–77.

LAYNE Christopher. "Kant or Cant: The Myth of the Democratic Peace." *International Security*, vol. 19, no. 2 (Fall 1994): 5–49.

LE ROY Etienne. "L'odyssée de l'État". *Politique africaine*, no. 61 (March 1996): 5–17.

LEMARCHAND René. "Uncivil states and civil societies: how illusion became reality." *Journal of Modern African Studies*, vol. 30, no. 3 (June 1992): 177–92.

MORPHET Sally. "UN Peacekeeping and Election-Monitoring." In ROBERTS A. and B. KINGSBURY (eds). *United Nations, Divided World*, 2nd edn. Oxford: Clarendon Press, (1993), 183–239.

PEARCE Jenny. "Building civil society from the outside: The problematic democratisation of Central America". *Global Society*, vol. 12, no. 2 (May 1998): 177–96.

POULIGNY Béatrice. "Promoting Democratic Institutions in Post-Conflict Societies: Giving Diversity a Chance". *International Peacekeeping*, vol. 7, no. 3 (autumn 2000): 17–35.

SCOTT M. and Kelly J. WALTERS. "Supporting the Wave: Western Political Foundations and the Promotion of a global Democratic Society", *Global Society. Journal of Interdisciplinary International Relations*, vol. 15, 2001.

VAISSE Justin. "Les Etats-Unis sans Wilson. L'internationalisme américain après la guerre froide". *Critique Internationale*, no. 3 (spring 1999) p. 101.

JUSTICE AND HUMAN RIGHTS LAW IN POST-CONFLICT RECONSTRUCTION

Books

ABU-NIMETR Mohammed (ed.). *Reconciliation, Justice and Coexistence: Theory and Practice*. Lanham (MD): Lexington Books, 2001.

ANTZE P. and M. LAMBEK. *Tense Past: Cultural Essays in Trauma and Memory*. London: Routledge, 1996.

ARENDT Hannah. *The Human Condition*. University of Chicago Press, 1998.

BENEDUCE Roberto. "Peacebuilding Strategies and Community Rehabilitation after Mass Crime: A Medico-anthropological Critical Approach" in Beatrice Pouligny *et al.* (eds). *After Mass Crime: The Challenges of Rebuilding States and Communities Following Mass Violence*. Tokyo/New York: United Nations University Press, 2004.

CRAGG Wesley. *The Practice of Punishment: Towards a Theory of Restorative Justice*. London: Routledge, 1992.

EISENBRUCH Maurice. "The uses and abuses of culture—mass crime and cultural competence in post-conflict peacebuilding in Cambodia." In Beatrice POULIGNY *et al.* (eds). *After Mass Crime: The Challenges of Rebuilding States and Communities Following Mass Violence*. Tokyo/New York: United Nations University Press, 2004.

HUMPHREY Michael. *The Politics of Atrocity and Reconciliation: From Terror to Trauma*. London: Routledge, 2002.

KLEBER, R., FIGLEY, C. and B. GERSONS. *Beyond Trauma: Cultural and Societal Dynamics*. New York: Plenum Press, 1995.

MANI Rama. *Beyond Retribution: Seeking Justice in the Shadows of War*. Cambridge: Polity, 2002.

NORDSTROM Carolyn. *A Different Kind of War Story*. Philadelphia: University of Pennsylvania Press, 1997.

OSIEL Mark. *Mass Atrocity, Collective Memory and the Law*. New Brunswick, NJ: Transaction, 1997.

ROTHSTEIN Robert L. (ed.). *After the Peace, Resistance and Reconciliation*. Boulder, CO: Lynne Rienner, 1999.

TAVUCHIS, N. *Mea Culpa. A Sociology of Apology and Reconciliation*. Stanford University Press, 1991.

THAKUR Ramesh and Peter MACONTENT (eds). *From Sovereign Impunity to International Accountability: The Search for Justice in a World of States*. Tokyo/New York: UNUP, 2002.

WESSELS Michael. "Culture, Power, and Community: Intercultural Approaches to Psychosocial Assistance and Healing." In K. NADER, N. DUBROW and B. STAMS (eds). *Honoring Differences: Culture Issues in the Treatment of Trauma and Loss.* Philadelphia: Taylor & Francis, 1999. pp. 267–82.

Articles

BODEI R. "Farewell to the Past: Historical Memory, Oblivion and Collective Identity". *Philosophy and Social Criticism.* vol. 18, no. 3/4 (1993): 251–65.

BORNEMAN J. "Reconciliation after Ethnic Cleansing: Listening, Retribution, Affiliation." *Public Culture*, vol. 14, no. 2 (spring 2000): 281–304.

COMAROFF J. "Healing and Cultural Transformation: The Tswana of Southern Africa." *Social Science and Medicine*, vol. 3, no. 15b (July 1981): 367–78.

DARBON Dominique. "La Truth and Reconciliation Commission. Le miracle sud-africain en Question." *Revue française de science politique*, vol. 48, no. 6 (Décembre 1998): 707–24.

HUMPHREY Michael. "From Victim to Victimhood: Truth Commissions and Trials as Rituals of Political Transition and Individual Healing". *Australian Journal of Anthropology*, vol. 14, no. 2 (2003): 171–87.

KRIESBERG Louis. "Reconciliation: Conceptual and Empirical Issues." Paper presented to the ISA annual conference, Minneapolis, March 1998 (mimeo.).

MANI Rama. "Conflict resolution, justice and the law: rebuilding the rule of law in the aftermath of complex political emergencies." *International Peacekeeping*, vol. 5, no. 3 (Fall 1998): 1–25.

POULIGNY Béatrice. "UN Peace Operations and Promoting the Rule of Law: Exploring The Intersection of International and Local Norms in Different Post-War Contexts." *Journal of Human Rights*, vol. 2, no. 3 (September 2003): 359–77.

SEWEL James P. "Justice and Truth in Transition". *Global Governance*, vol. 8, no. 1 (2002): 119–34.

POLITICAL ECONOMY OF THE PEACE PROCESS

Books

ANDERSON Mary B. *Do No Harm: How aid can support peace or war.* Boulder, CO: Lynne Rienner, 1999.

BERDAL Mats and David MALONE (eds). *Greed and Grievance: Economic Agendas in Civil Wars.* Boulder, CO: Lynne Rienner, 2000.

CHARBONNIER Gilles. *Conflict, Postwar Rebuilding and the Economy: A Critical Review of the Literature.* Geneva: UNRISD, March 1998 (War-torn Societies Project Occasional Paper no. 2).

COLLIER Paul & al. *Breaking the Conflict Trap: Civil War and Development Policy.* World Bank Policy Report. Washington, DC: World Bank and Oxford University Press, 2003.

COLLIER Paul. "The Economics of Civil Wars." Mimeo, Development Research Group, Washington, DC: World Bank, 1998.

DIETRICH Jung (ed.). *The Political Economy of Intrastate Wars.* London: Routledge, 2002.

DOXEY Margaret. *United Sanctions: Current Policy Issues.* Halifax (NS): Centre for foreign Policies Studies, Dalhousie University, June 1999.

FORMAN Shepard and Stewart PATRICK. *Pledges of Aid for Postconflict Recovery.* Boulder, CO: Lynne Rienner, 2000.

GINIFER Jeremy (ed.). *Beyond the Emergency, Development within UN Peace Missions.* London: Frank Cass, 1997.

International Committee of the Red Cross. *War, Money, and Survival.* Geneva: ICRC, 2000.

JEAN François and Jean-Christophe RUFIN (eds). *Economie des guerres civiles.* Paris: Hachette, 1996.

WORLD BANK. *Post-Conflict Reconstruction: The Role of the World Bank.* Washington, DC: World Bank, 1988.

BERDAL Mats and David KEEN. "Violence and Economic Agendas in Civil Wars: Some Policy Implications." *Millenium*, vol. 26, no. 3 (1997): 795–818.

COLLIER Paul. "Understanding Civil Wars." *Journal of Conflict Resolution*, vol. 46, no. 1 (February 2002): 3–170.

COLLIER Paul. "Demobilization and Insecurity: A Study in the Economics of the Transition from War to Peace." *Journal of International Development*, vol. 6, no. 3 (1994): 343–51.

DUFFIELD Mark. "Post-modern Conflict: Warlords, Post-Adjustment States and Private Protection." *Civil Wars*, vol. 1, no. 1 (Spring 1998): 65–102.

GORDON Joy. "A peaceful, Silent, Deadly Remedy: The Ethics of Economic Sanctions." *Ethics and international affairs*, vol. 13 (1999): 123–50.

HIBOU Béatrice. "Économie politique du discours de la Banque mondiale en Afrique subsaharienne. Du catéchisme économique au fait (et méfait) missionnaire." *Les Études du CERI*, no. 39 (March 1998): 1–44.

MOHAMMED N. "Economic Implications of Civil Wars in SSA and Economic Policies for Successful Transition from War to Peace." Paper presented at the AERC Bi-Annual Research Workshop, Harare, Zimbabwe, December 6–11, 1997.

PARIS Roland. "Peacebuilding and the limits of Liberal Internationalism." *International Security*, vol. 22, no. 2 (fall 1997): 54–89.

PUGH Michael. "Postwar Political Economy in Bosnia and Herzegovina: The Spoils of Peace." *Global Governance*, vol. 8, no. 4 (October–December 2002): 467–82.

ANALYSIS OF PEACE OPERATIONS FROM THE POINT OF VIEW OF LOCAL POPULATIONS

GALTUNG Johan and Ingrid EIDE. "Some factors affecting local acceptance of a UN force: a pilot project report from Gaza." In GALTUNG Johan (ed.), *Peace, War and Defense*, Copenhagen: Ejlers, 1976, pp. 240–63 (Essays in Peace Research, vol. 2).

HEIBERG Marianne. "Peacekeepers and Local Populations: Some Comments on UNIFIL." In RIKHYE Indar Jit (ed.). *The United Nations and Peacekeeping: Results, Limitations and Prospects.* Basingstoke: Macmillan, 1990, pp. 147–69.

JAMES Alan. "International Peacekeeping: The Disputants' View." *Political Studies*, vol. 38, no. 2 (1990): 215–30.

POULIGNY Béatrice. "Peacekeepers and Local Social Actors: The Need for Dynamic, Cross-cultural Analysis." *Global Governance*, vol. 5, no. 4 (October–December 1999): 403–24.

RICHMOND Oliver P. *Mediating in Cyprus: The Cypriot communities and the United Nations.* London: Frank Cass, 1998.

ANALYSIS OF PEACE OPERATIONS FROM THE POINT OF VIEW
OF 'PEACEKEEPERS'

Books

CALLAGHAN, Jean M. and Mathias SCHÖNBORN (Dir): *Warriors in Peacekeeping: Points of tension in complex cultural encounters*, George C. Marshall ECSS, 2003.

COULON Jocelyn. *Les casques bleus*. Montréal: Ed. FIDES, 1994.

COULON Jocelyn. *Soldiers of Diplomacy: The United Nations, Peacekeeping and the New World Order*. University of Toronto Press, 1998.

FINDLAY Trevor. *Challenges for the New Peacekeepers*. Oxford University Press, 1996 (SIPRI Research Report no. 12).

GALTUNG Johan and Helge HVEEM. "Participants in Peacekeeping Forces." In GALTUNG Johan (ed.). *Peace, War and Defense*. Copenhagen: Ejlers, 1976, pp. 264–81 (Essays in Peace Research, vol. 2).

MOSKOS Charles C. *Peace Soldiers: The Sociology of a United Nations Military Force*. Chicago University Press, 1976.

WINSLOW Donna. *The Canadian Airborne in Somalia: A SocioCultural Inquiry*, étude préparée par la Commission d'enquête sur le déploiement des Forces canadiennes en Somalie. Ottawa: Travaux publics et Services gouvernementaux, 1997.

Article

MOSKOS Charles C. and Laura L. MILLER "Humanitarians or Warriors?: Race, Gender, and Combat Status in Operation 'Restore Hope'." *Armed Forces and Society*. vol. 21, no. 4, summer 1995, pp. 615–37.

INDEX

Advisory Committee on Administrative and Budgetary Questions ACABQ 10, 150; *see also* UN General Assembly
Afghanistan 33, 47, 56, 101, 129, 130, 146, 171, 178, 194, 243
Agenda for Peace and *addendum* 3, 13
Ajello, Aldo 162, 198
Akashi, Yasushi 55, 125, 133, 183, 209, 222, 230, 231
Angola 2, 3, 62, 225, 234, 241, 271
Annan, Kofi 137, 138, 249, 256; *see also* Secretary General, UN
Aristide, Jean Bertrand 5, 8, 20, 42, 43, 49, 50, 51, 63, 64, 84, 153, 158, 164, 173, 174, 184, 190, 191, 208, 215, 220, 222, 233
armed forces 3, 4, 5, 8, 17, 45; regular armies 57–64, 66–67, 132, 136, 152, 157, 172, 202–205, 208, 214, 224, 226, 232, 233, 251; para-military groups and militias 60–62, 173, 178, 202–203, 232, 256, 252–253
Australia 8, 12, 15, 126, 129
Aydid, Mohamed Farah Hassan 45, 46, 60, 99, 100, 105, 118, 130, 137, 138, 153, 171, 176, 177, 178, 179, 180, 185, 187, 193, 206, 216, 218, 219, 227

Barré, Siyad 17, 23, 45, 46, 99, 100, 160, 196, 205
bipolarity/post-bipolarity 13, 14, 18, 21
Bosnia-Herzegovina ix, xii, 2, 6, 8, 9, 11, 17, 18, 19, 21, 22, 24, 25, 26, 28, 31, 33–34, 44, 53, 60, 61, 62, 66, 67, 81, 86, 90, 91, 92, 93, 105–106, 121, 123, 126–127, 128–129,

138, 139–140, 144, 146, 153, 157, 160, 167, 185, 186, 187, 193, 203, 205, 209–210, 214, 228, 240, 241, 242, 243, 244, 245, 248, 249, 252, 253, 255, 258, 263, 264, 268, 272; HDZ Croatian Democratic Union 53; HVO Croatian Defence Council 53; Implementation Force, IFOR 6; SDA Party of Democratic Action 53, 153 ; SDS, Serbian Democratic Party 53; Stabilization Force, SFOR 6; United Nations Protection Force, UNPROFO 6, 9, 17, 18, 33, 34, 53, 91, 106, 122, 126–127, 128, 129, 139, 140, 146, 153, 167, 187, 205, 209–210, 255
Boutros-Ghali, Boutros 3, 13, 129, 136, 163; *see also* Secretary General UN
Brahimi, Lakhdar 84, 111, 114, 116, 167
Brahimi Report; high-level panel on peace operations 138, 143, 255, 271, 274
Briquemont, Lieut.-General Francis 126, 127, 129, 139, 140
budget 10, 32, 89, 150, 197, 204, 205, 206, 207, 274
Bush, George 14, 118

Cambodia ix, xii, xiii, 2, 4, 5, 6, 10, 11, 12, 15–16, 21, 22, 25, 28, 30, 31, 44, 51–52, 55–56, 60, 64–65, 66, 69, 70, 79–80, 84–86, 87, 88, 89, 90, 91, 93, 94, 97–98, 104, 109–110, 112, 113, 116, 120, 121, 123, 124–125, 129, 131, 132, 133, 134, 135, 139, 140, 142, 143, 144, 146,